GENSHIKEN

8

KIO SHIMOKU

TRANSLATED AND ADAPTED BY
David Ury

LETTERED BY
Michaelis/Carpelis Design

DEL REY

BALLANTINE BOOKS • NEW YORK

Genshiken volume 8 is a work of fiction. Names, characters, places, and incidents are the products of the author's imagination or are used fictitiously. Any resemblance to actual events, locales, or persons, living or dead, is entirely coincidental.

A Del Rey Trade Paperback Original

Published in the United States by
Del Rey Books, an imprint of
The Random House Publishing Group, a
division of Random House, Inc., New York.

Publication rights arranged through Kodansha Ltd.

First published in Japan in 2005 by
Kodansha Ltd., Tokyo

ISBN 978-0-345-49156-5

Printed in the United States of America

www.delreymanga.com

9 8 7 6 5 4 3 2 1

Translator/Adaptor—David Ury
Lettering—Michaelis/Carpelis Design Associates Inc.

Honorifics Explained

Throughout the Del Rey Manga books, you will find Japanese honorifics left intact in the translations. For those not familiar with how the Japanese use honorifics and, more important, how they differ from American honorifics, we present this brief overview.

Politeness has always been a critical facet of Japanese culture. Ever since the feudal era, when Japan was a highly stratified society, use of honorifics—which can be defined as polite speech that indicates relationship or status—has played an essential role in the Japanese language. When addressing someone in Japanese, an honorific usually takes the form of a suffix attached to one's name (example: "Asuna-san"), or as a title at the end of one's name, or in place of the name itself (example: "Negi-sensei," or simply "Sensei!").

Honorifics can be expressions of respect or endearment. In the context of manga and anime, honorifics give insight into the nature of the relationship between characters. Many English translations leave out these important honorifics, and therefore distort the feel of the original Japanese. Because Japanese honorifics contain nuances that English honorifics lack, it is our policy at Del Rey not to translate them. Here, instead, is a guide to some of the honorifics you may encounter in Del Rey Manga.

-san: This is the most common honorific, and is equivalent to Mr., Miss, Ms., or Mrs. It is the all-purpose honorific and can be used in any situation where politeness is required.

-sama: This is one level higher than "-san" and is used to confer great respect.

-dono: This comes from the word "tono," which means "lord." It is even a higher level than "-sama" and confers utmost respect.

-kun: This suffix is used at the end of boys' names to express familiarity or endearment. It is also sometimes used by men among friends, or when addressing someone younger or of a lower station.

-chan: This is used to express endearment, mostly toward girls. It is also used for little boys, pets, and even between lovers. It gives a sense of childish cuteness.

Bozu: This is an informal way to refer to a boy, similar to the English terms "kid" or "squirt."

Sempai/Senpai: This title suggests that the addressee is one's senior in a group or organization. It is most often used in a school setting, where underclassmen refer to their upperclassmen as "sempai." It can also be used in the workplace, such as when a newer employee addresses an employee who has seniority in the company.

Kohai: This is the opposite of "—sempai" and is used toward underclassmen in school or newcomers in the workplace. It connotes that the addressee is of a lower station.

Sensei: Literally meaning "one who has come before," this title is used for teachers, doctors, or masters of any profession or art.

-[blank]: This is usually forgotten in these lists, but it is perhaps the most significant difference between Japanese and English. The lack of honorific means that the speaker has permission to address the person in a very intimate way. Usually, only family, spouses, or very close friends have this kind of permission. Known as *yobisute*, it can be gratifying when someone who has earned the intimacy starts to call one by one's name without an honorific. But when that intimacy hasn't been earned, it can be very insulting.

げんしけん

THE SOCIETY FOR ~~~~ ODERN VISUAL CULTURE

KIO SHIMOKU

Contents

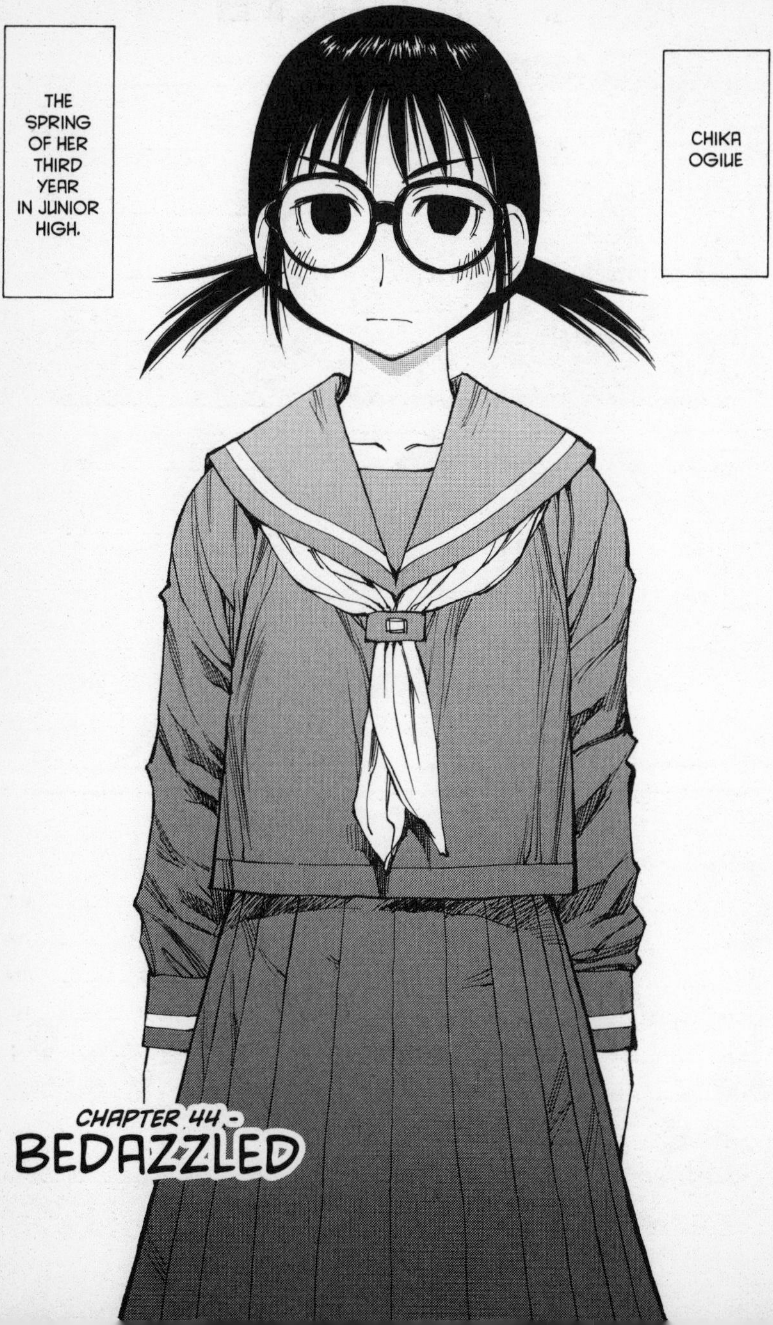
CHIKA OGIUE
THE SPRING OF HER THIRD YEAR IN JUNIOR HIGH.
CHAPTER 44 -
BEDAZZLED

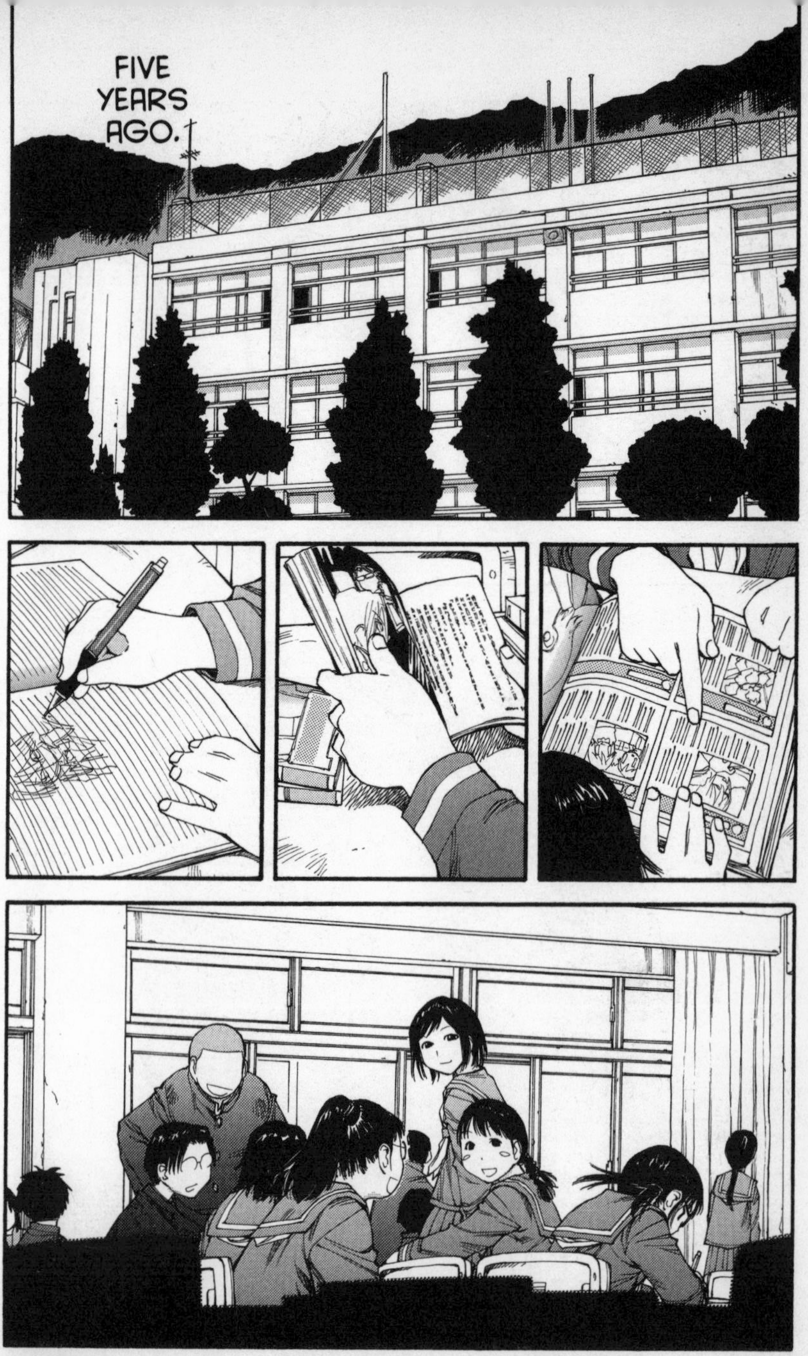
FIVE YEARS AGO.

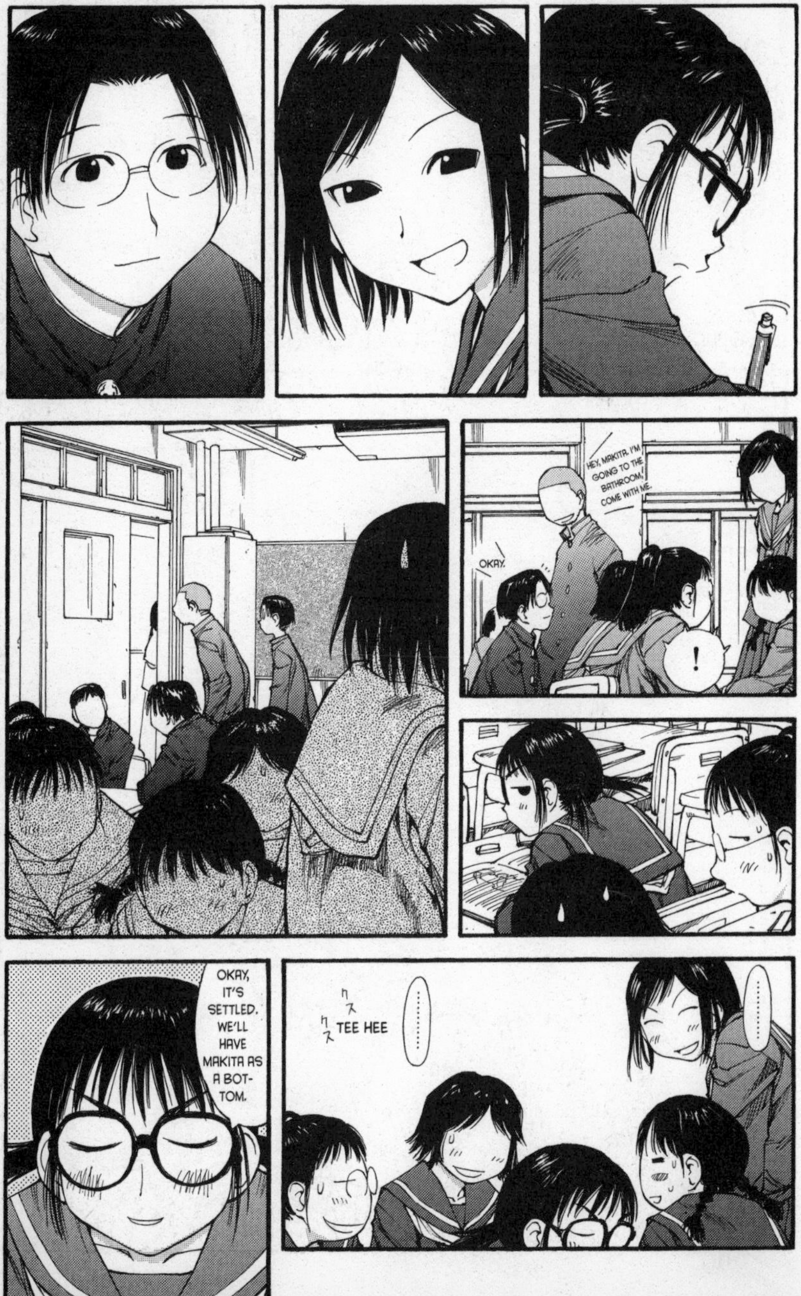
HEY, MAKITA. I'M GOING TO THE BATHROOM. COME WITH ME.
OKAY.
!
....
....
クス クス TEE HEE
OKAY, IT'S SETTLED. WE'LL HAVE MAKITA AS A BOT-TOM.

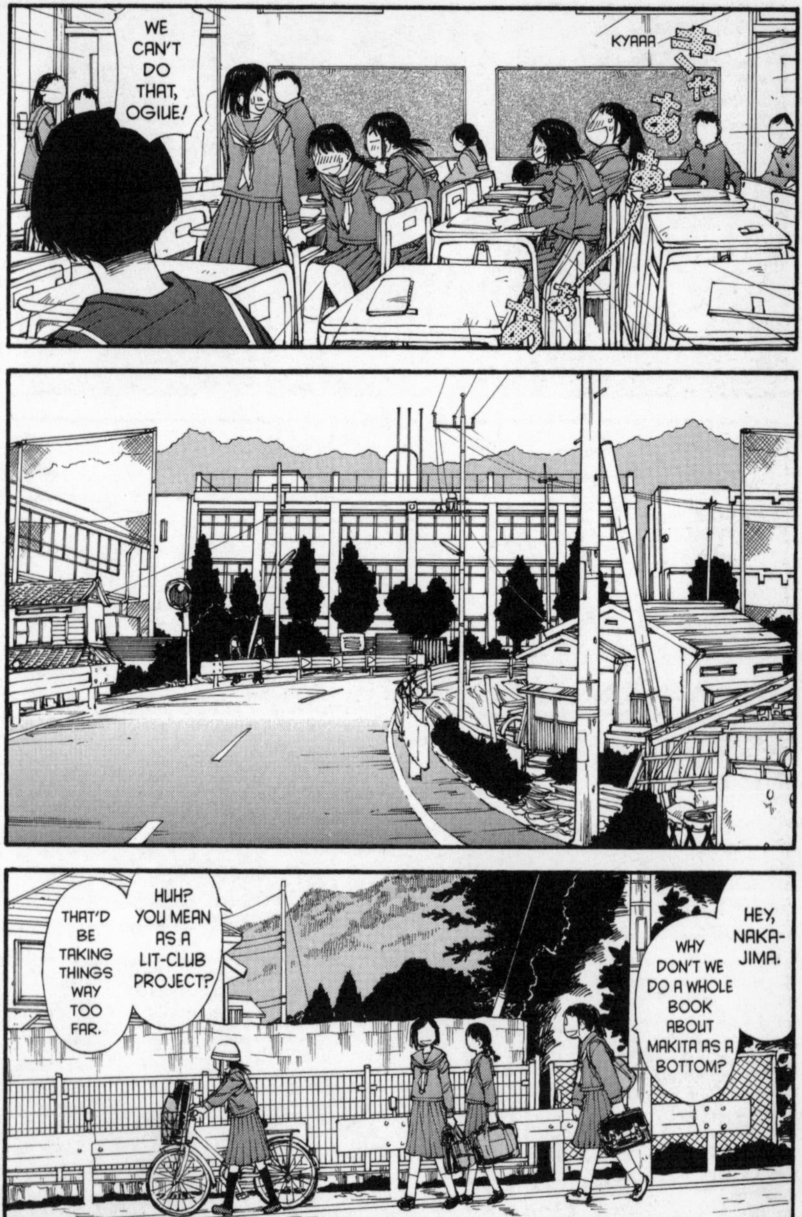
KYAAA
WE CAN'T DO THAT, OGIUE!
HEY, NAKAJIMA.
WHY DON'T WE DO A WHOLE BOOK ABOUT MAKITA AS A BOTTOM?
HUH? YOU MEAN AS A LIT-CLUB PROJECT?
THAT'D BE TAKING THINGS WAY TOO FAR.

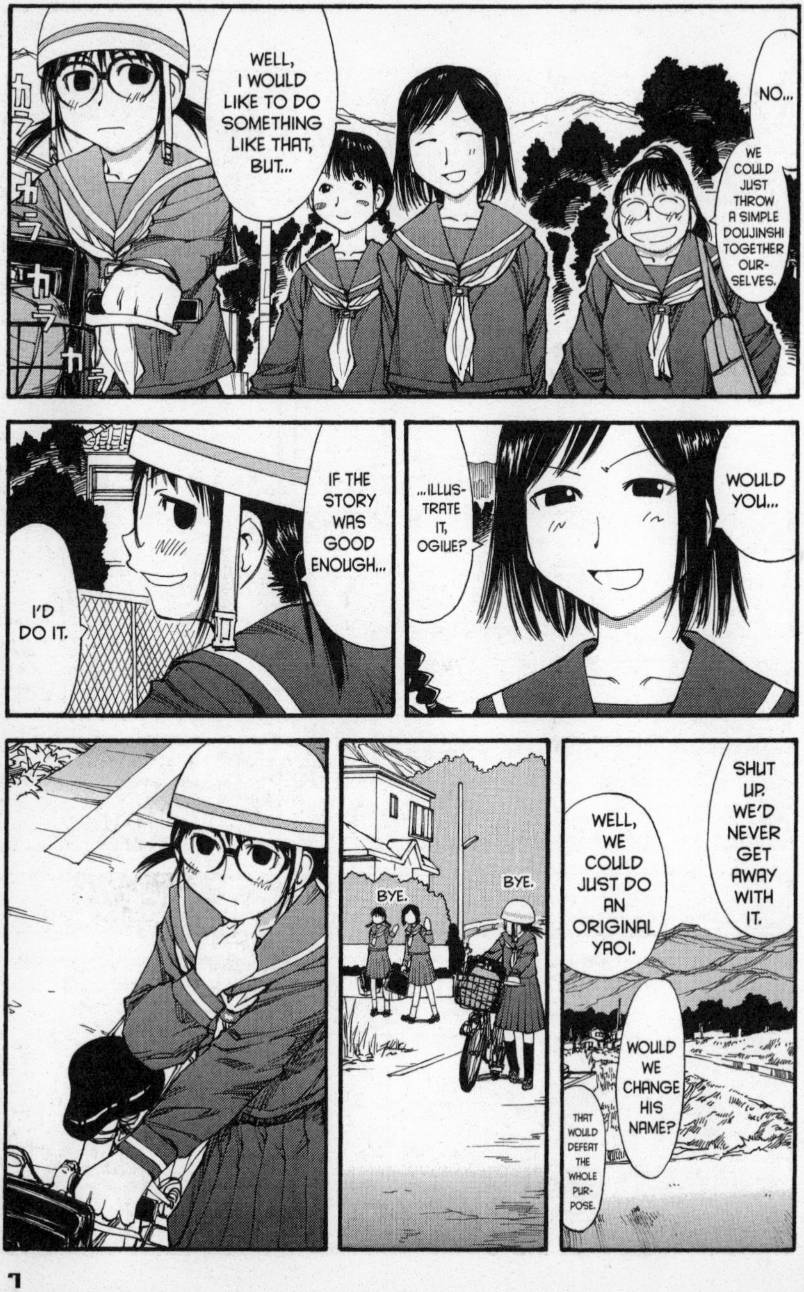
NO...
WE COULD JUST THROW A SIMPLE DOUJINSHI TOGETHER OURSELVES.
WELL, I WOULD LIKE TO DO SOMETHING LIKE THAT, BUT...
カラ カラ カラ カラ
WOULD YOU...
...ILLUSTRATE IT, OGIUE?
IF THE STORY WAS GOOD ENOUGH...
I'D DO IT.
SHUT UP. WE'D NEVER GET AWAY WITH IT.
WELL, WE COULD JUST DO AN ORIGINAL YAOI.
WOULD WE CHANGE HIS NAME?
THAT WOULD DEFEAT THE WHOLE PURPOSE.
...
BYE.
BYE.

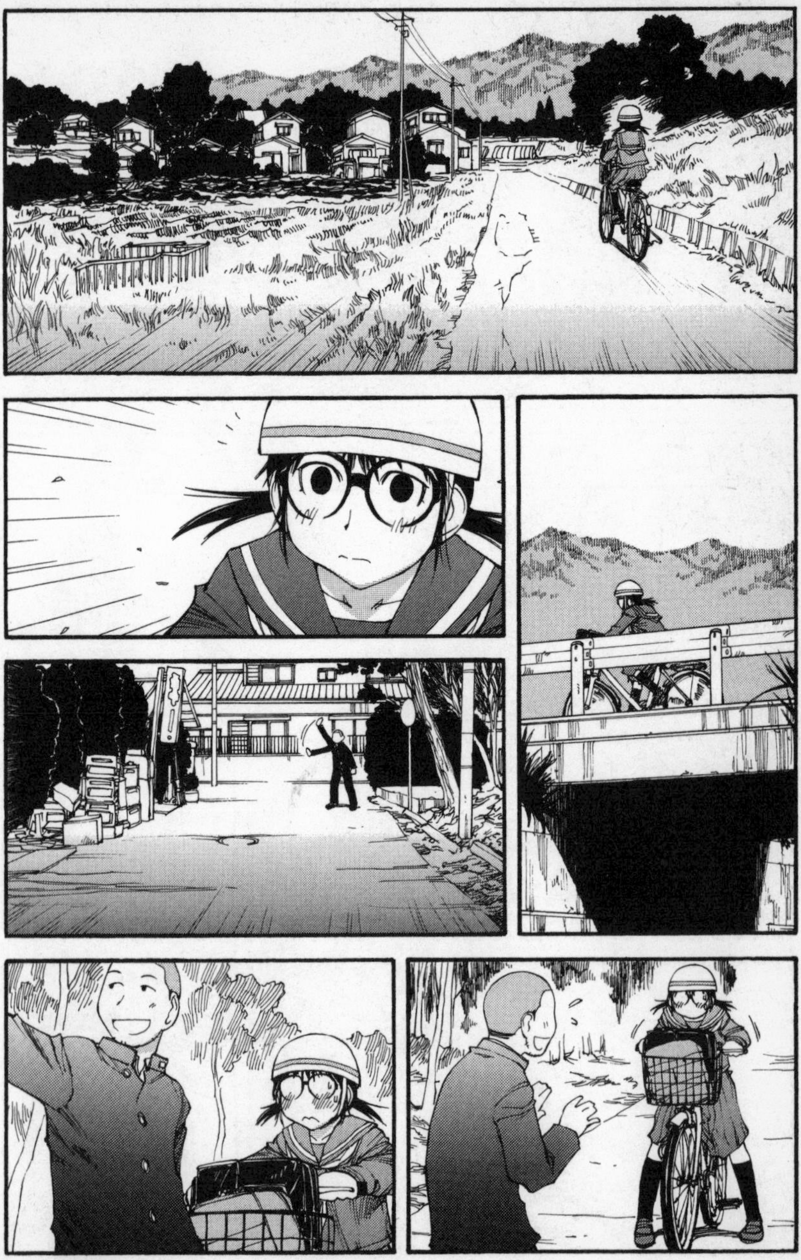

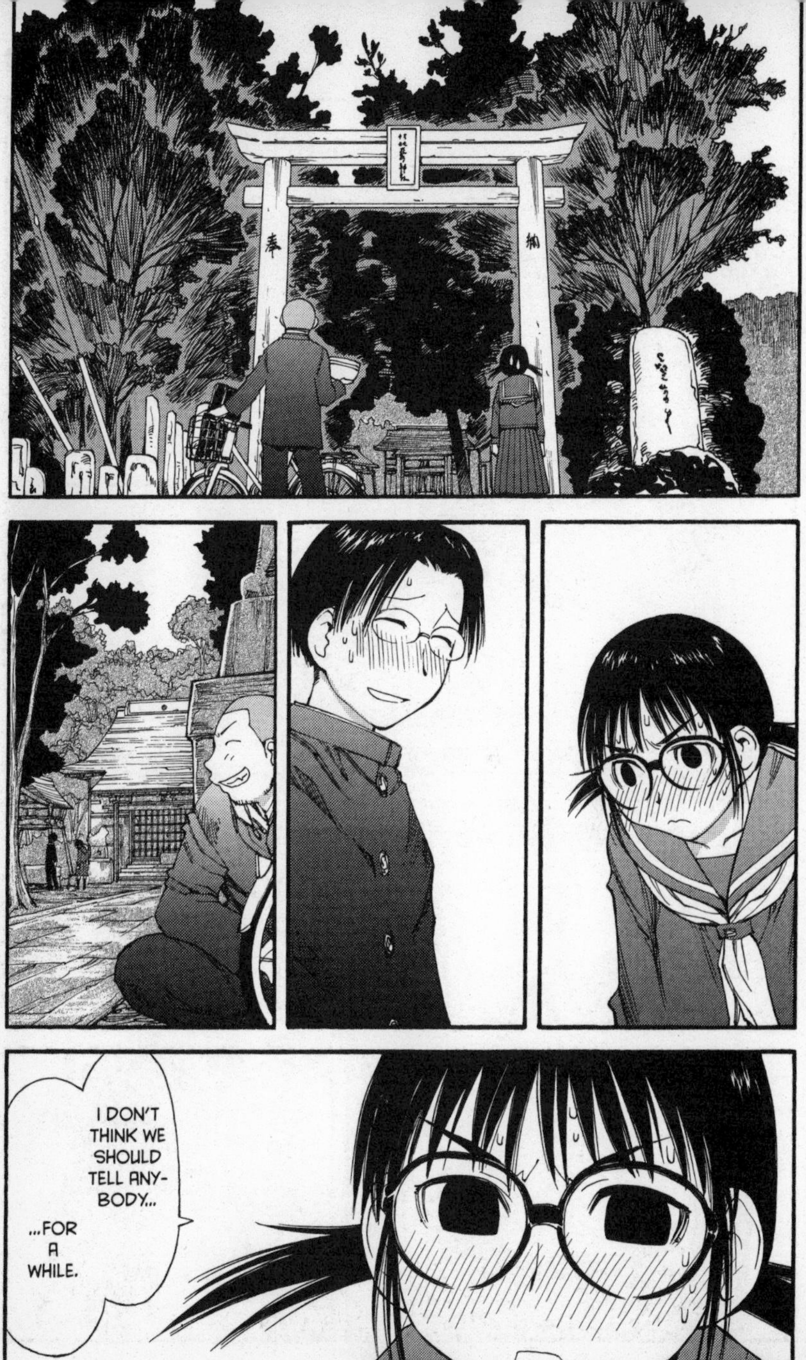
I DON'T THINK WE SHOULD TELL ANY-BODY...
...FOR A WHILE.

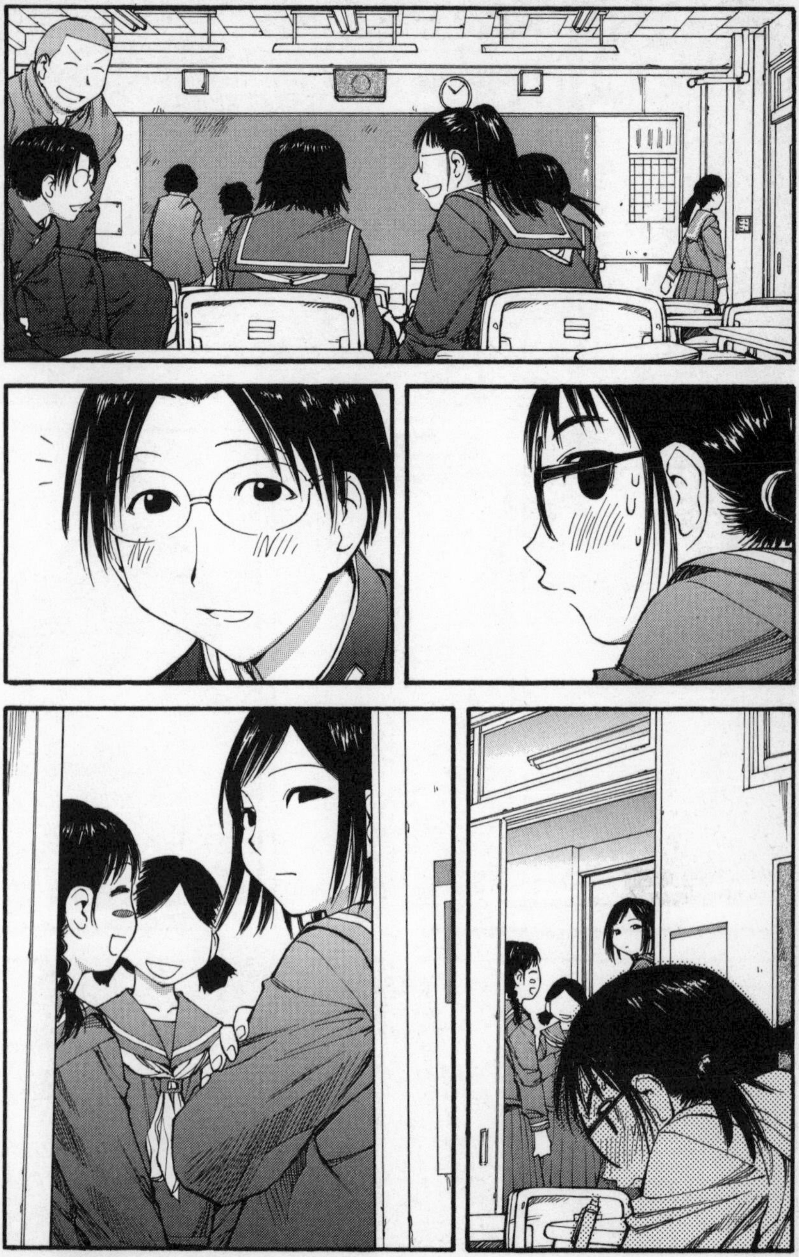

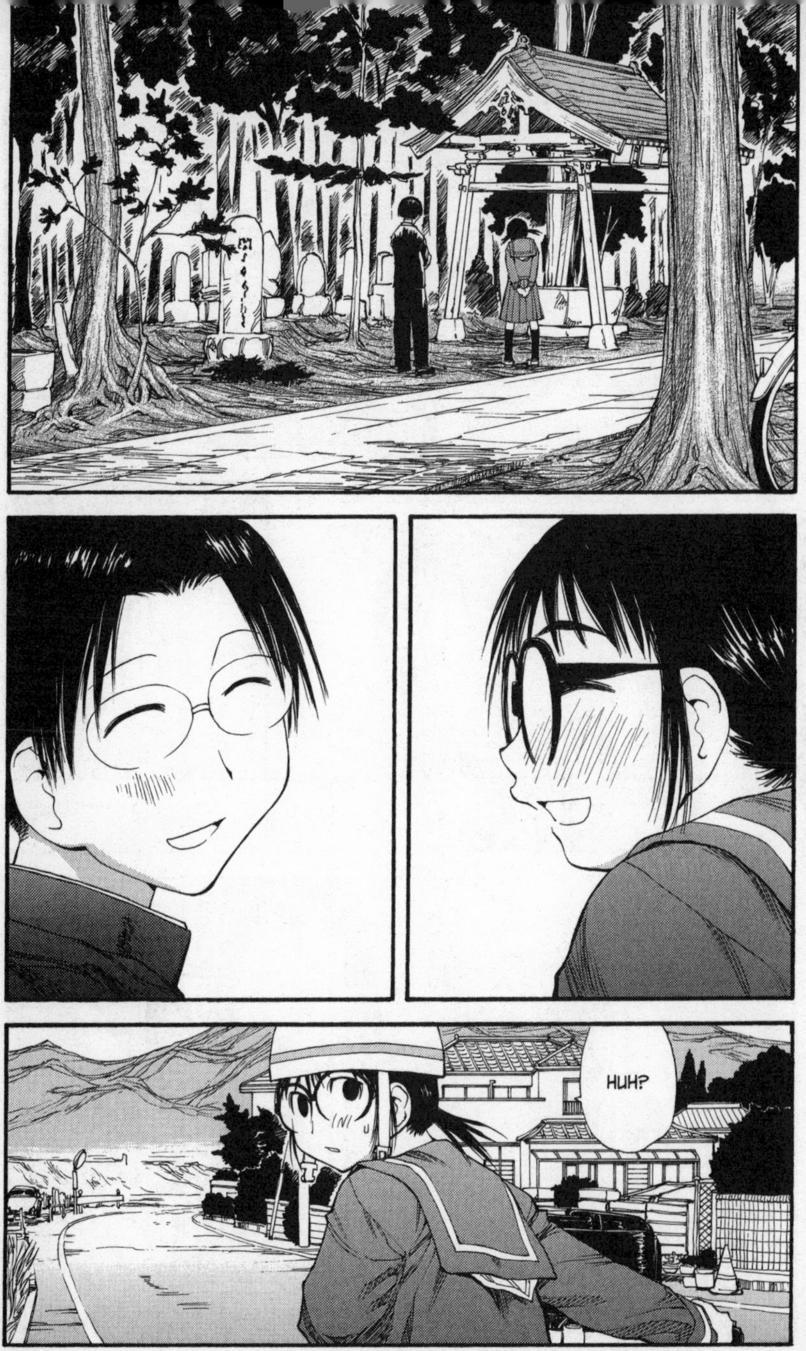
HUH?

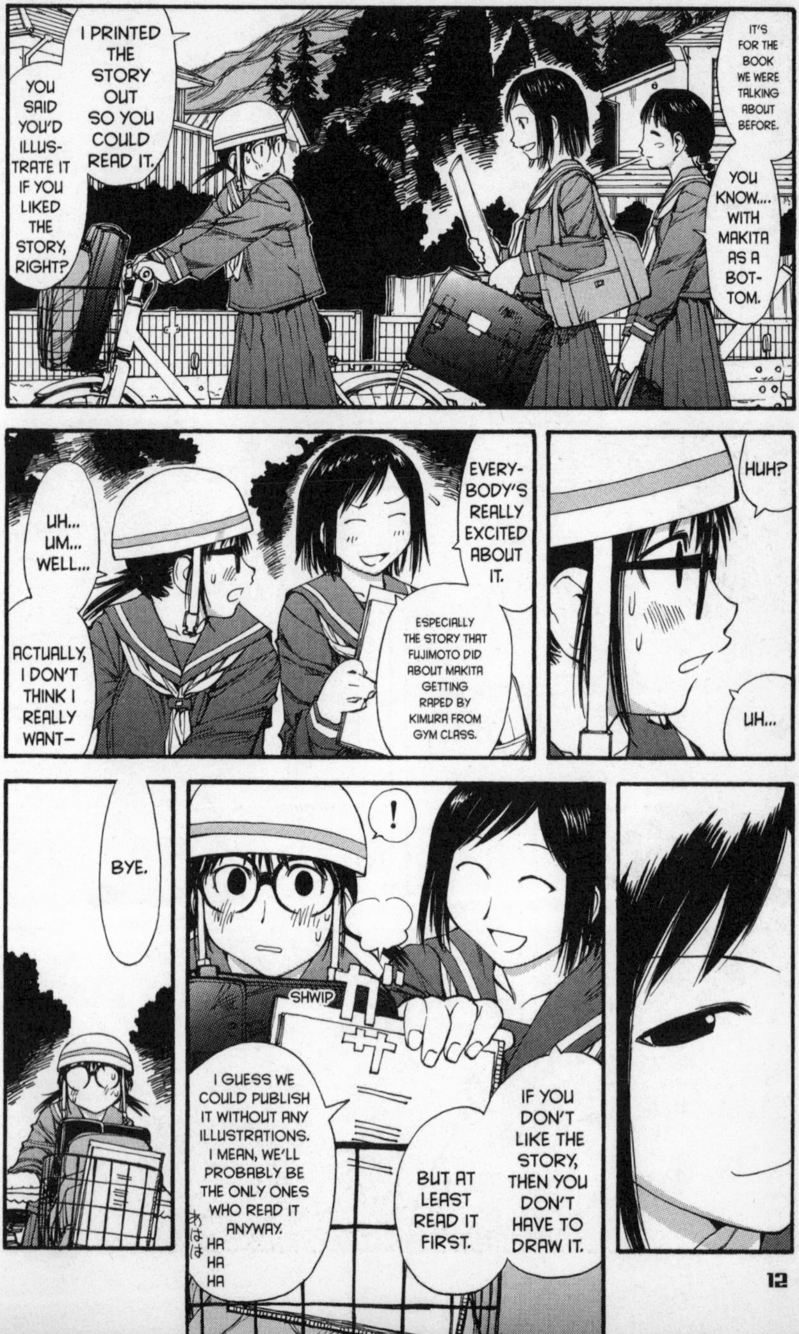
IT'S FOR THE BOOK WE WERE TALKING ABOUT BEFORE.
YOU KNOW.... WITH MAKITA AS A BOT-TOM.
I PRINTED THE STORY OUT SO YOU COULD READ IT.
YOU SAID YOU'D ILLUS-TRATE IT IF YOU LIKED THE STORY, RIGHT?
HUH?
UH...
EVERY-BODY'S REALLY EXCITED ABOUT IT.
ESPECIALLY THE STORY THAT FUJIMOTO DID ABOUT MAKITA GETTING RAPED BY KIMURA FROM GYM CLASS.
UH... UM... WELL...
ACTUALLY, I DON'T THINK I REALLY WANT—
IF YOU DON'T LIKE THE STORY, THEN YOU DON'T HAVE TO DRAW IT.
BUT AT LEAST READ IT FIRST.
!
SHWIP
I GUESS WE COULD PUBLISH IT WITHOUT ANY ILLUSTRATIONS. I MEAN, WE'LL PROBABLY BE THE ONLY ONES WHO READ IT ANYWAY.
あはは
HA HA HA
BYE.

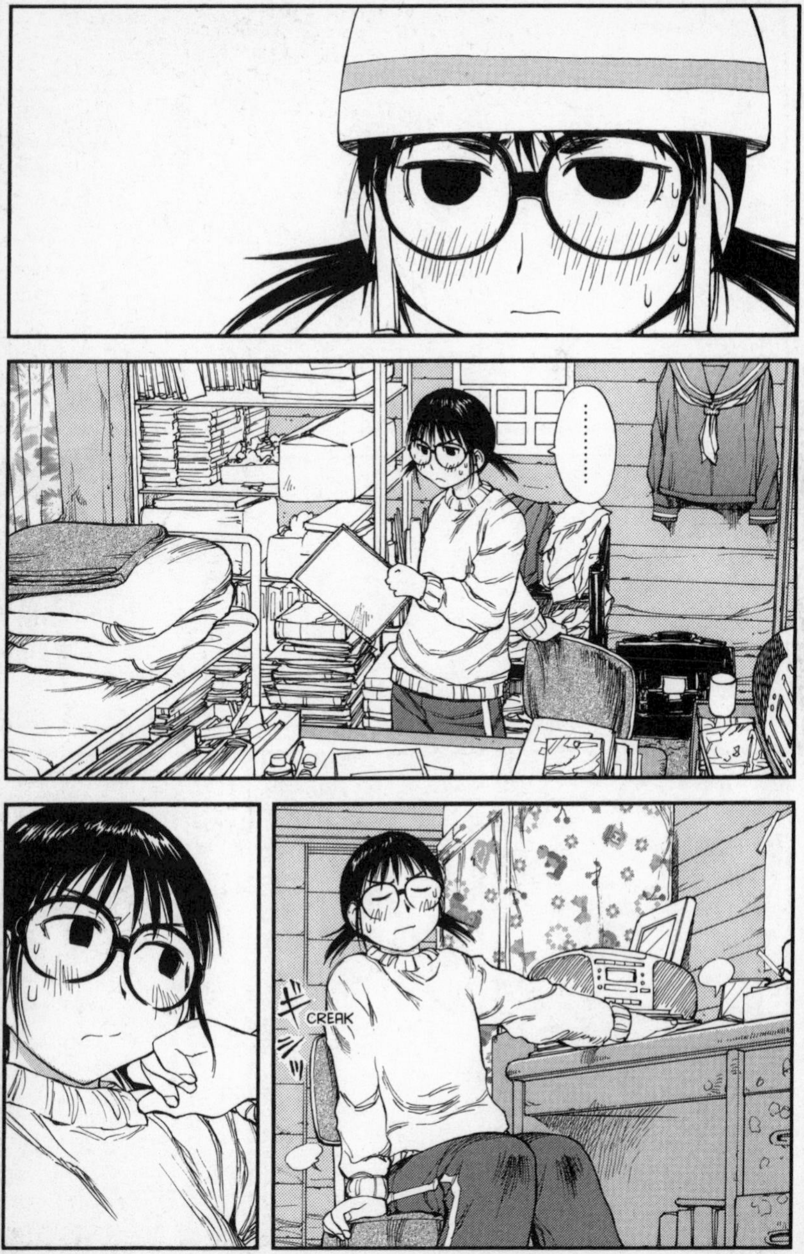
……
CREAK

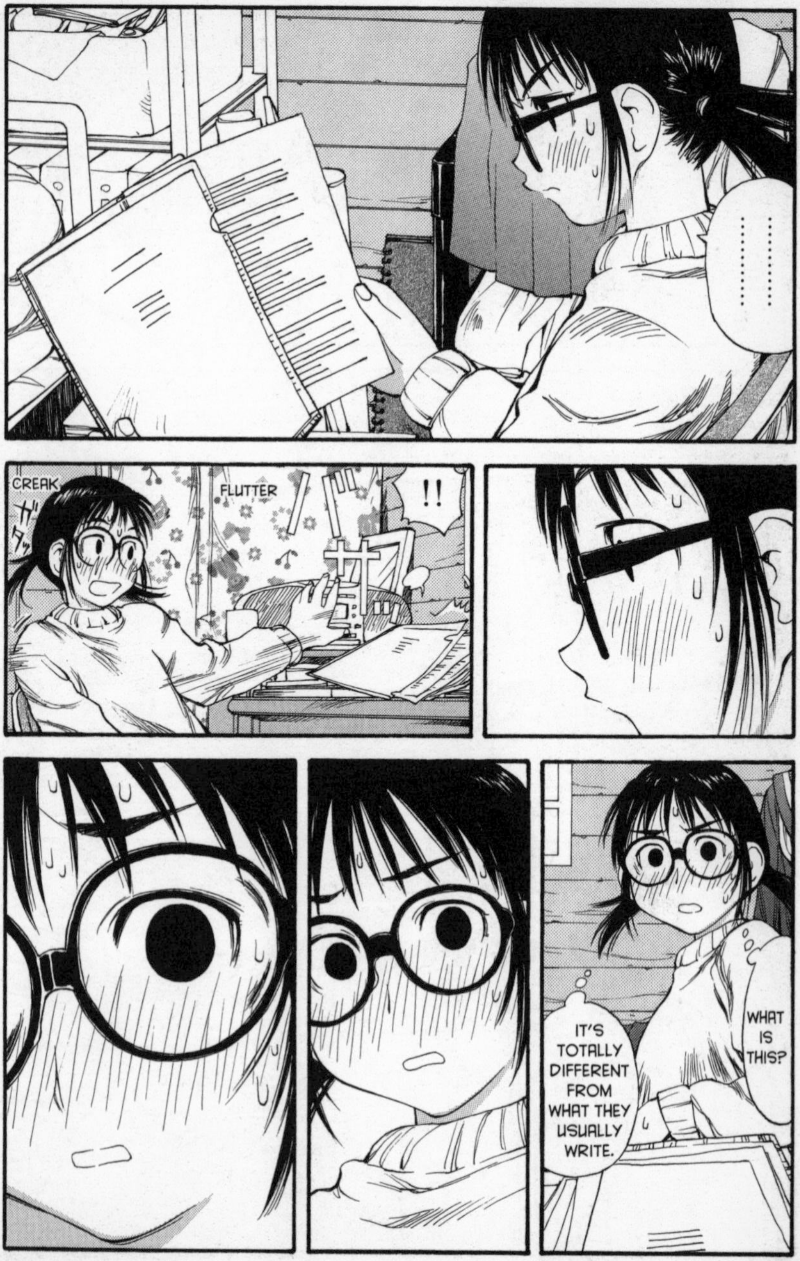
......
!!
FLUTTER
CREAK
WHAT IS THIS?
IT'S TOTALLY DIFFERENT FROM WHAT THEY USUALLY WRITE.

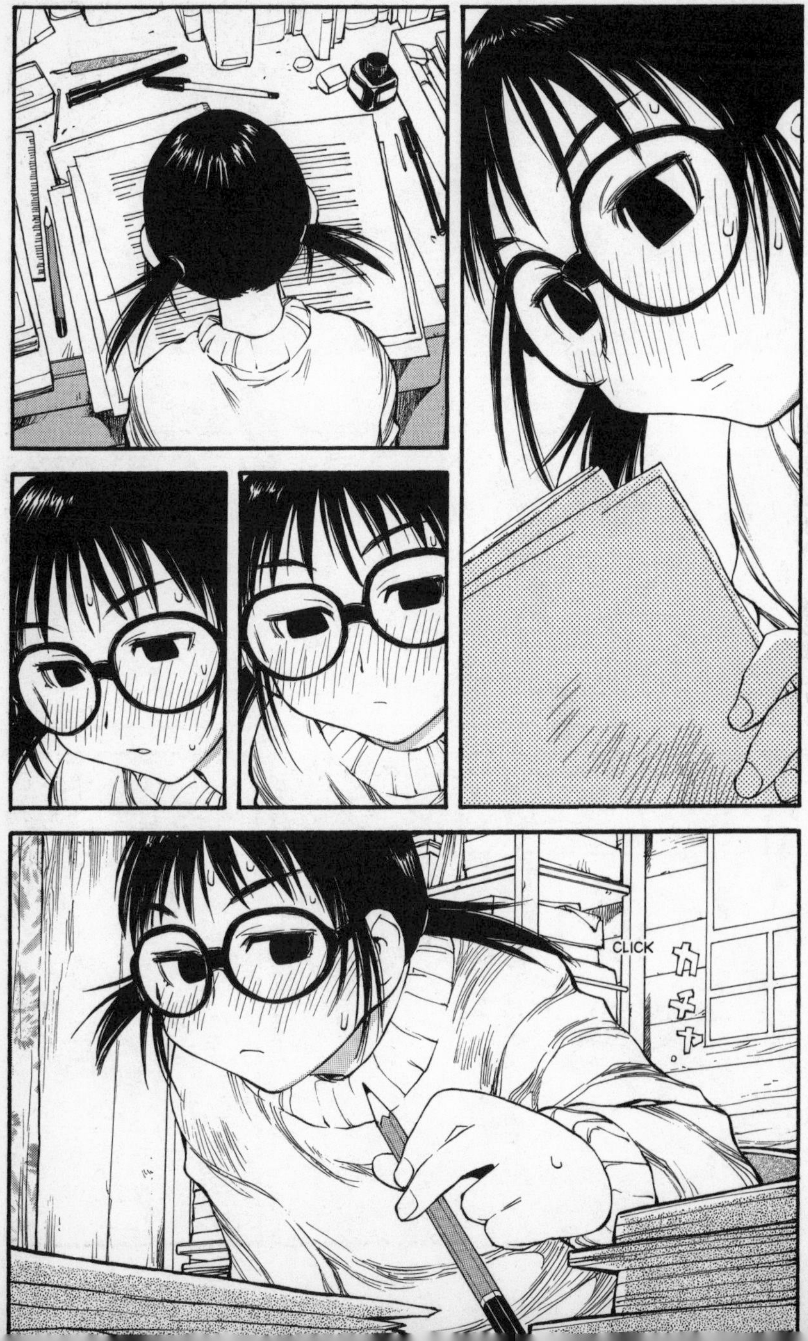
CLICK
カチャ

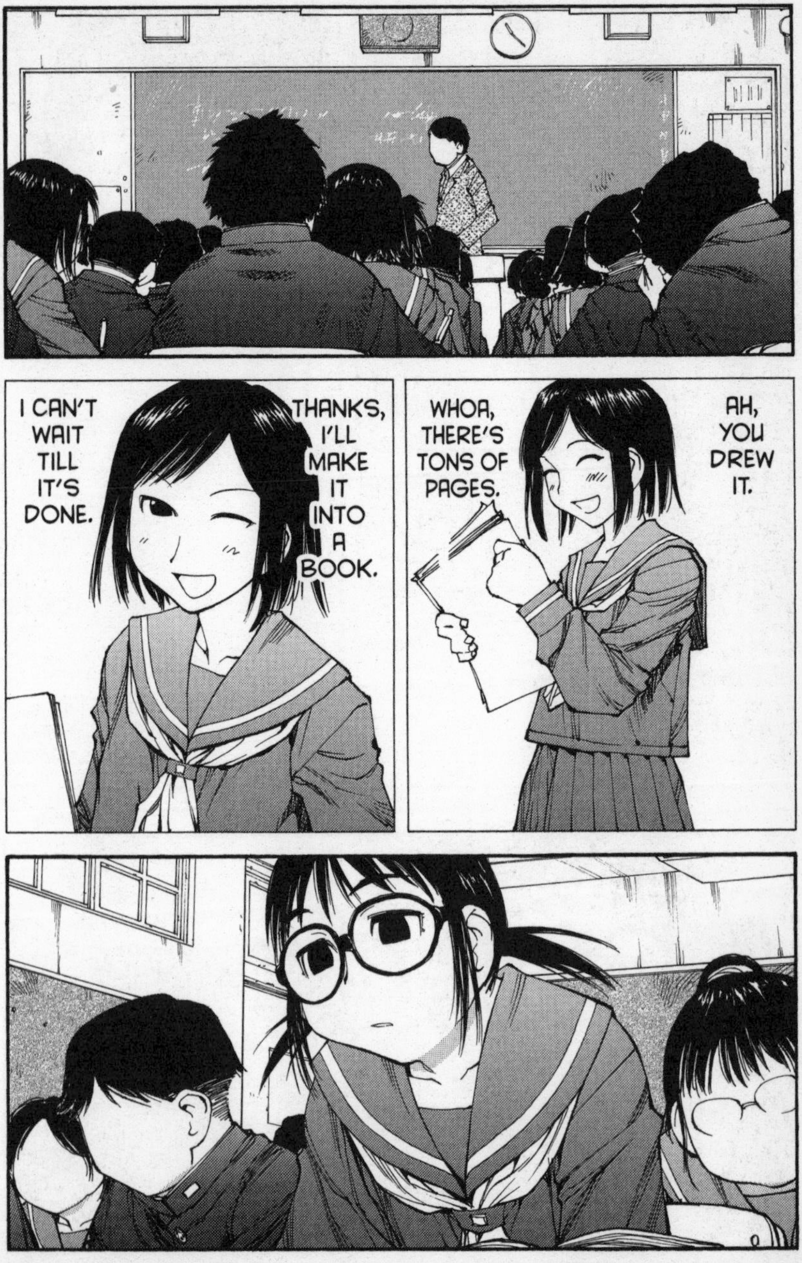
AH, YOU DREW IT.
WHOA, THERE'S TONS OF PAGES.
THANKS, I'LL MAKE IT INTO A BOOK.
I CAN'T WAIT TILL IT'S DONE.

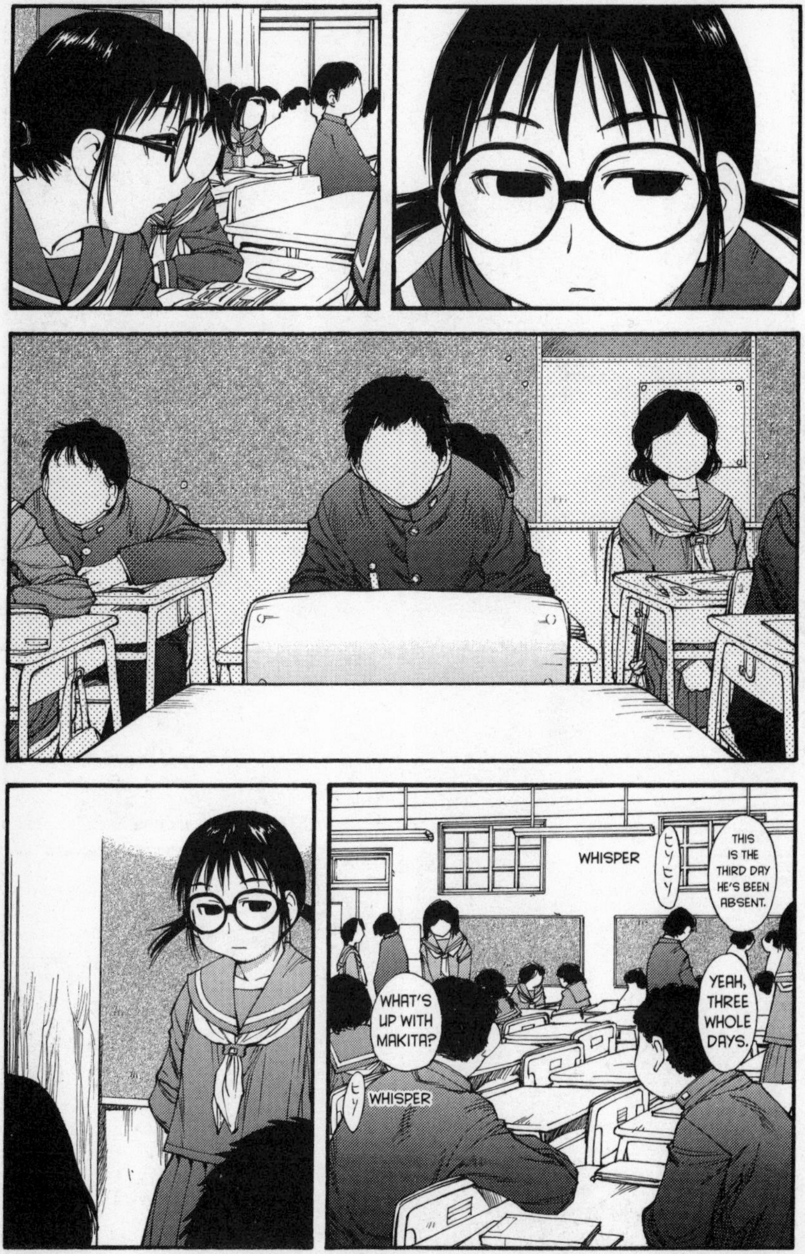
THIS IS THE THIRD DAY HE'S BEEN ABSENT.
ヒソヒソ
WHISPER
YEAH, THREE WHOLE DAYS.
WHAT'S UP WITH MAKITA?
ヒソ
WHISPER

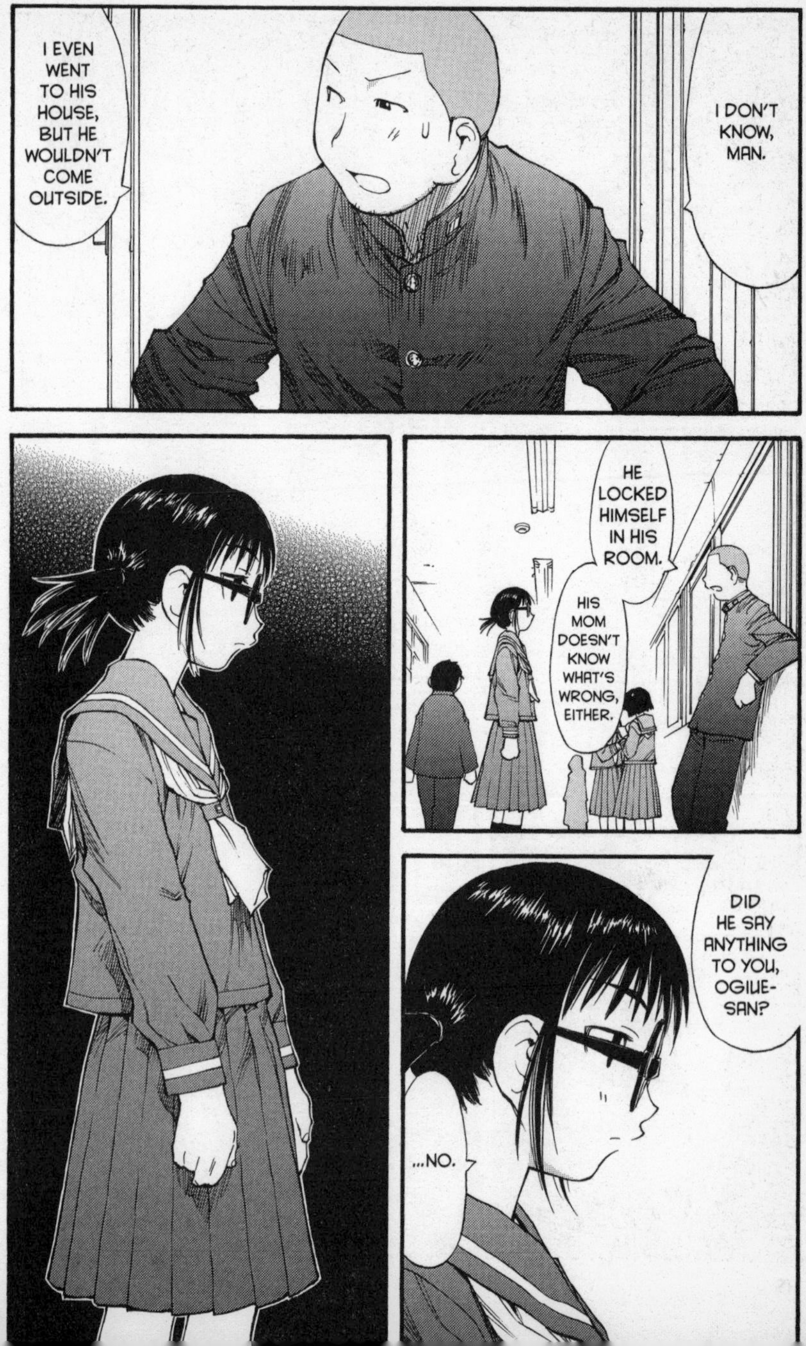
I DON'T KNOW, MAN.
I EVEN WENT TO HIS HOUSE, BUT HE WOULDN'T COME OUTSIDE.
HE LOCKED HIMSELF IN HIS ROOM.
HIS MOM DOESN'T KNOW WHAT'S WRONG, EITHER.
DID HE SAY ANYTHING TO YOU, OGIUE-SAN?
...NO.

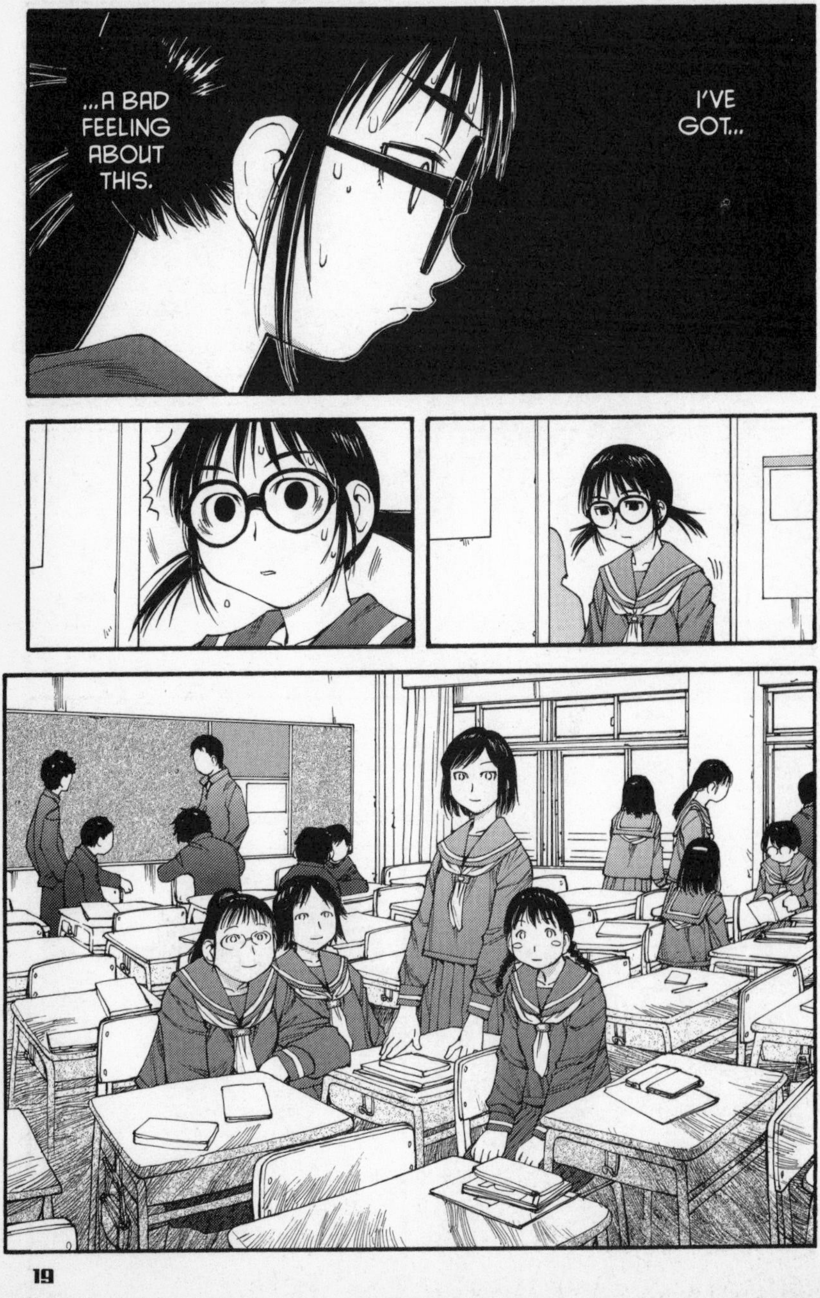
I'VE GOT...
...A BAD FEELING ABOUT THIS.

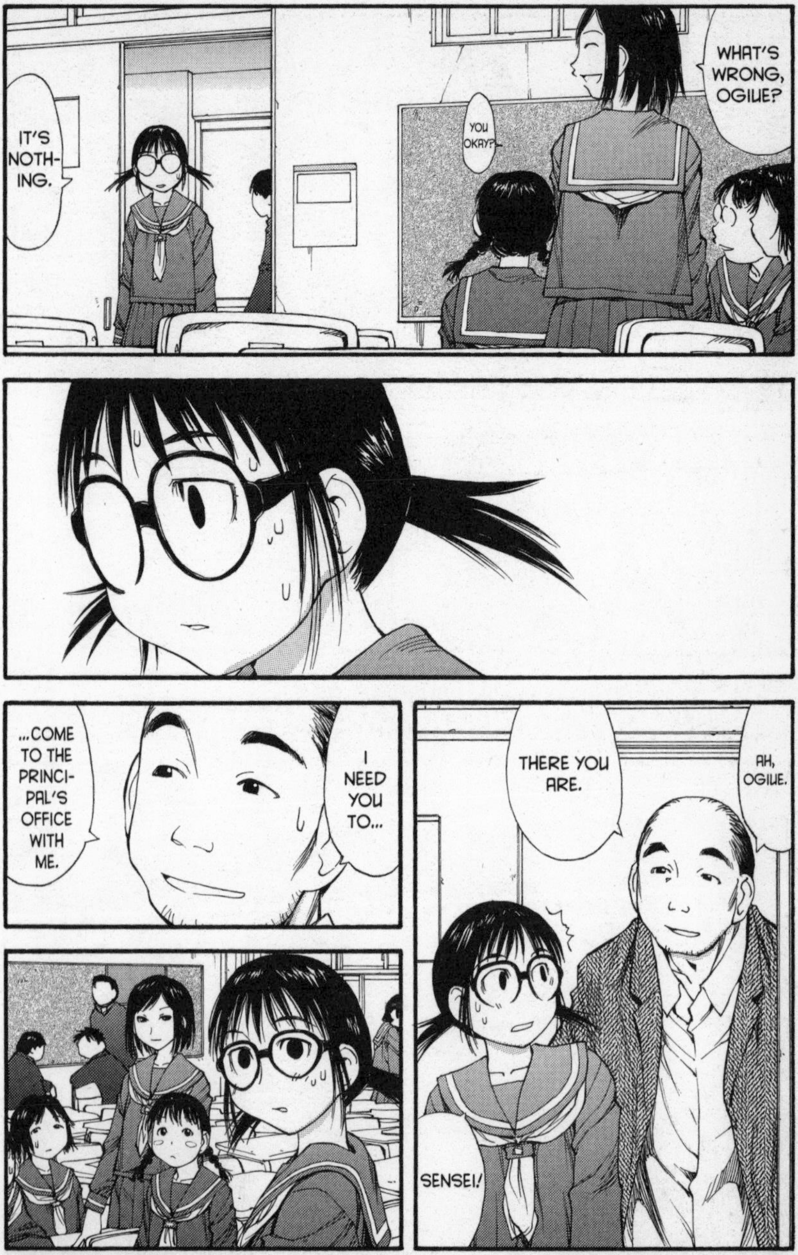
WHAT'S WRONG, OGIUE?
YOU OKAY?
IT'S NOTHING.
AH, OGIUE.
THERE YOU ARE.
SENSEI!
I NEED YOU TO...
...COME TO THE PRINCIPAL'S OFFICE WITH ME.

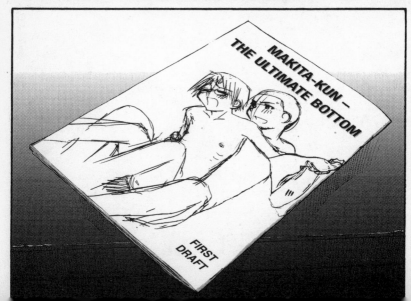

MAKITA-KUN –
THE ULTIMATE BOTTOM

FIRST
DRAFT

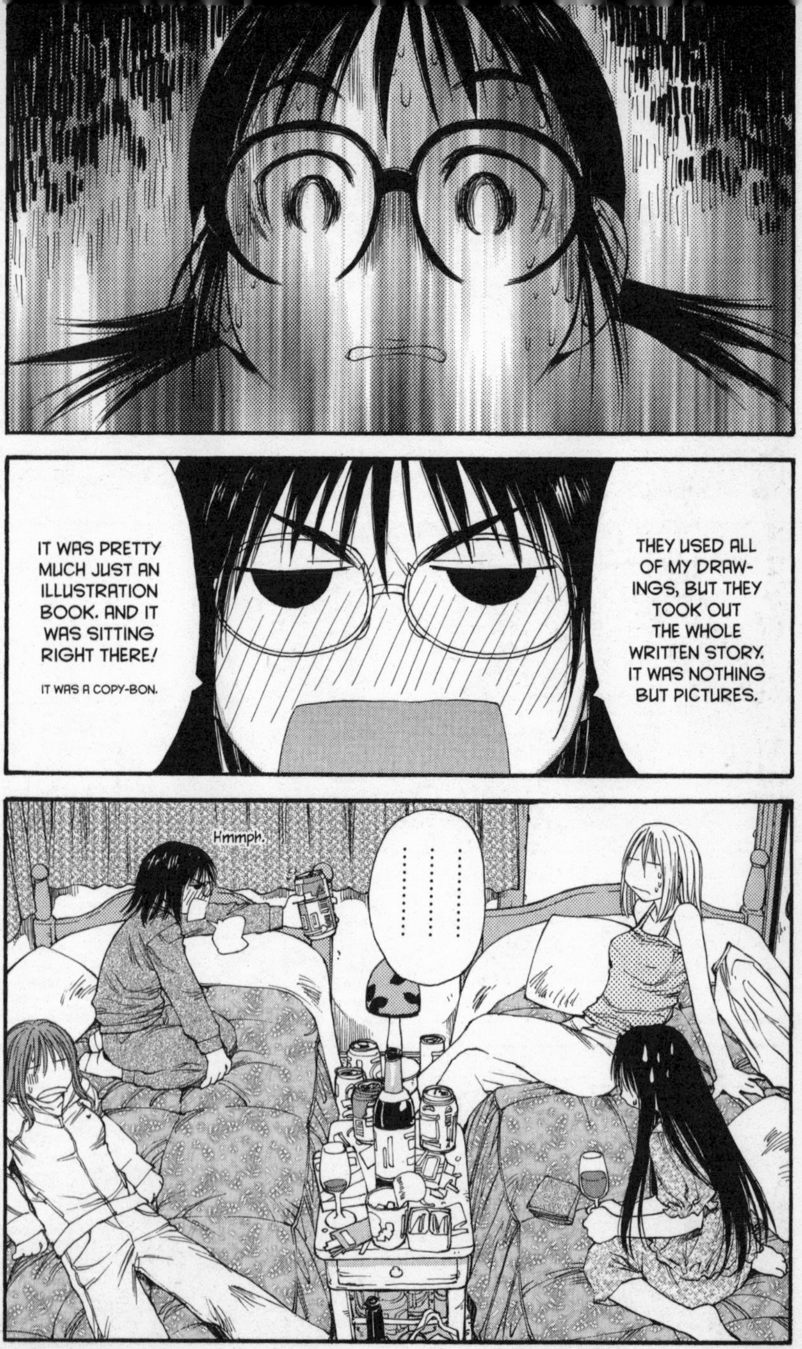
THEY USED ALL OF MY DRAWINGS, BUT THEY TOOK OUT THE WHOLE WRITTEN STORY. IT WAS NOTHING BUT PICTURES.
IT WAS PRETTY MUCH JUST AN ILLUSTRATION BOOK. AND IT WAS SITTING RIGHT THERE!
IT WAS A COPY-BON.
Hmmph.

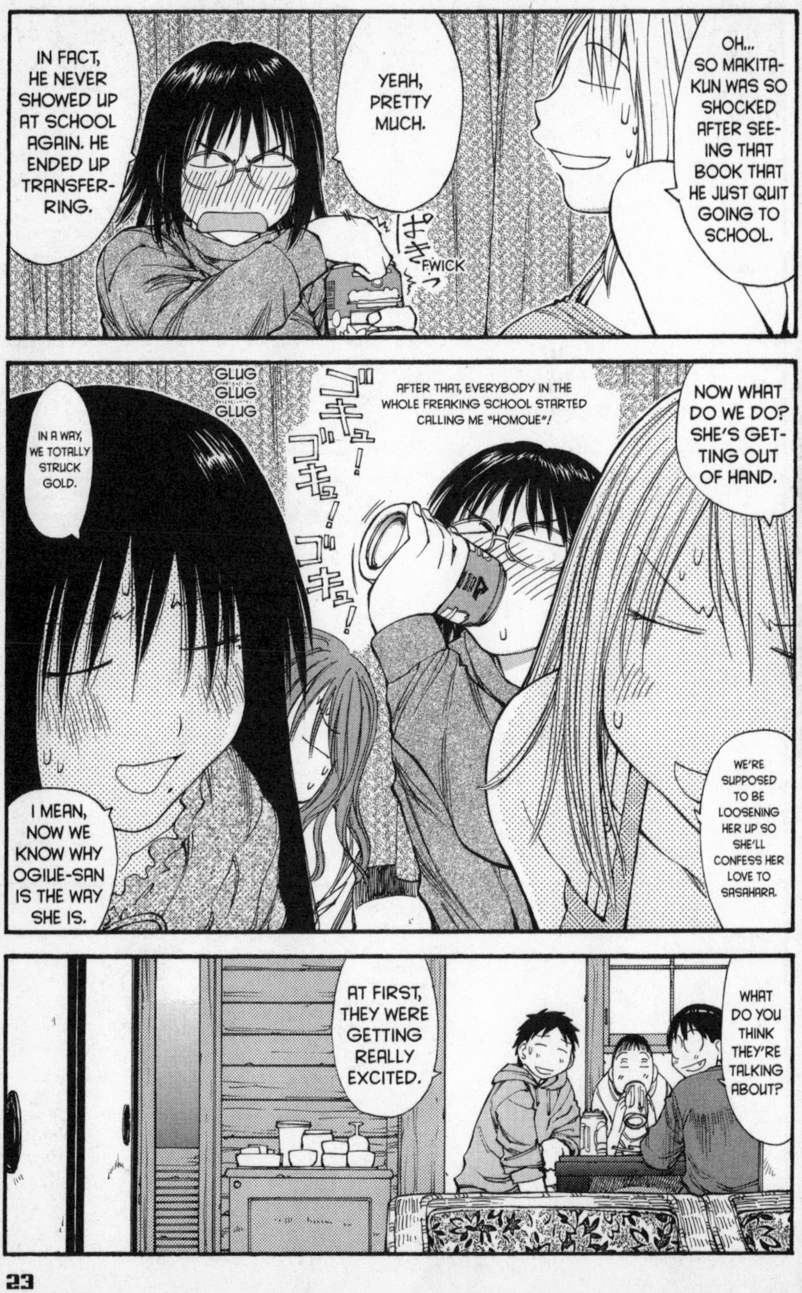
OH... SO MAKITA-KUN WAS SO SHOCKED AFTER SEEING THAT BOOK THAT HE JUST QUIT GOING TO SCHOOL.
YEAH, PRETTY MUCH.
IN FACT, HE NEVER SHOWED UP AT SCHOOL AGAIN. HE ENDED UP TRANSFERRING.
ぱきっ
FWICK
NOW WHAT DO WE DO? SHE'S GETTING OUT OF HAND.
AFTER THAT, EVERYBODY IN THE WHOLE FREAKING SCHOOL STARTED CALLING ME "HOMOUE"!
ゴキュ! ゴキュ! ゴキュ!
GLUG GLUG GLUG
IN A WAY, WE TOTALLY STRUCK GOLD.
WE'RE SUPPOSED TO BE LOOSENING HER UP SO SHE'LL CONFESS HER LOVE TO SASAHARA.
I MEAN, NOW WE KNOW WHY OGIUE-SAN IS THE WAY SHE IS.
WHAT DO YOU THINK THEY'RE TALKING ABOUT?
AT FIRST, THEY WERE GETTING REALLY EXCITED.

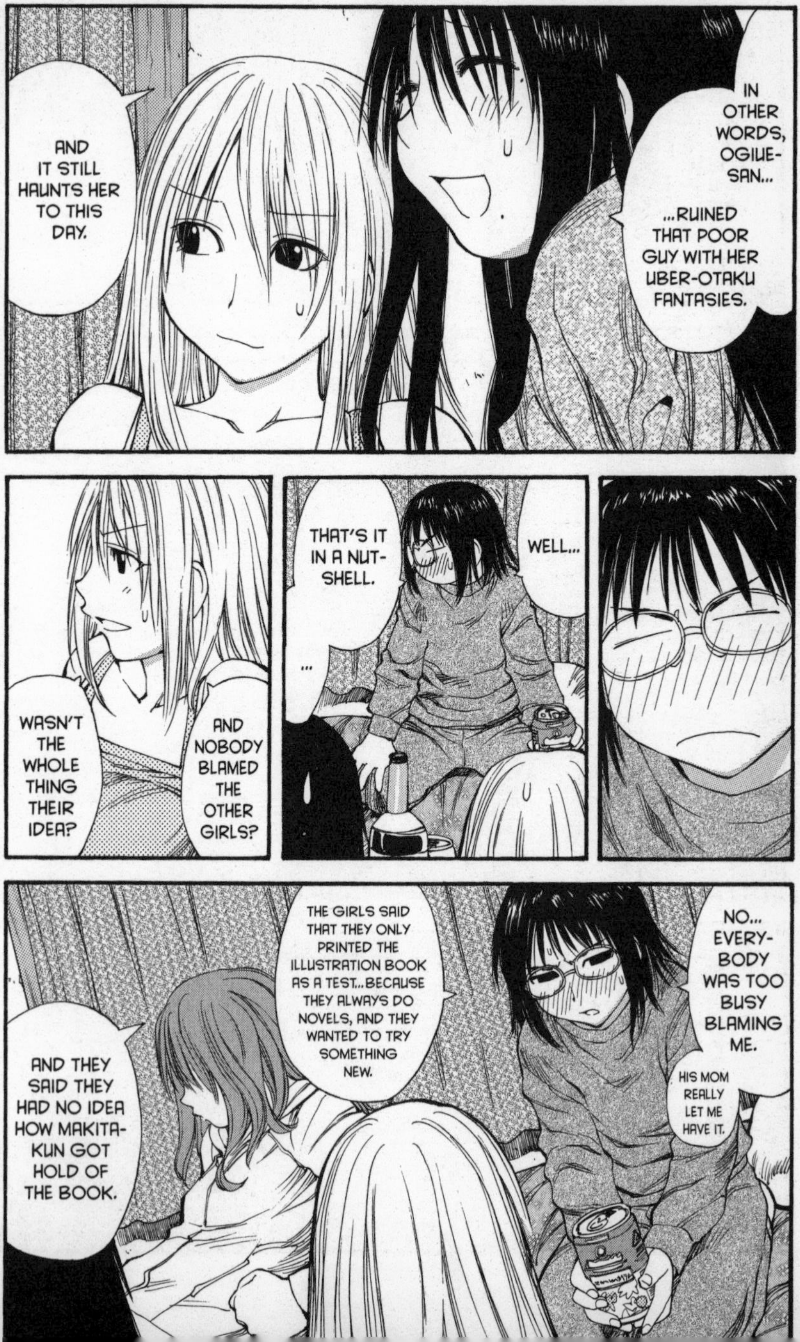
IN OTHER WORDS, OGIUE-SAN...
...RUINED THAT POOR GUY WITH HER UBER-OTAKU FANTASIES.
AND IT STILL HAUNTS HER TO THIS DAY.
WELL...
THAT'S IT IN A NUT-SHELL.
...
AND NOBODY BLAMED THE OTHER GIRLS?
WASN'T THE WHOLE THING THEIR IDEA?
NO... EVERY-BODY WAS TOO BUSY BLAMING ME.
HIS MOM REALLY LET ME HAVE IT.
THE GIRLS SAID THAT THEY ONLY PRINTED THE ILLUSTRATION BOOK AS A TEST...BECAUSE THEY ALWAYS DO NOVELS, AND THEY WANTED TO TRY SOMETHING NEW.
AND THEY SAID THEY HAD NO IDEA HOW MAKITA-KUN GOT HOLD OF THE BOOK.

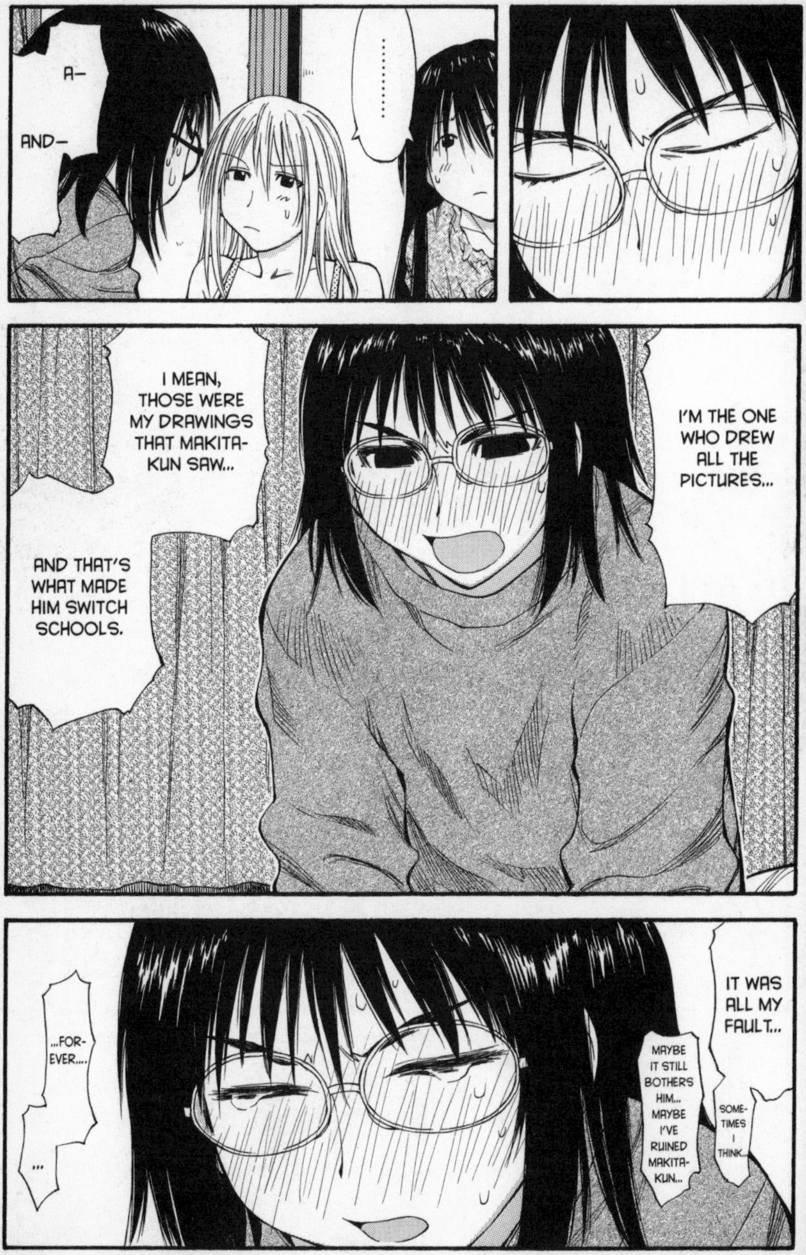

......
A—
AND—
I'M THE ONE WHO DREW ALL THE PICTURES...
I MEAN, THOSE WERE MY DRAWINGS THAT MAKITA-KUN SAW...
AND THAT'S WHAT MADE HIM SWITCH SCHOOLS.
IT WAS ALL MY FAULT...
SOMETIMES I THINK...
MAYBE IT STILL BOTHERS HIM... MAYBE I'VE RUINED MAKITA-KUN...
...FOREVER....
...

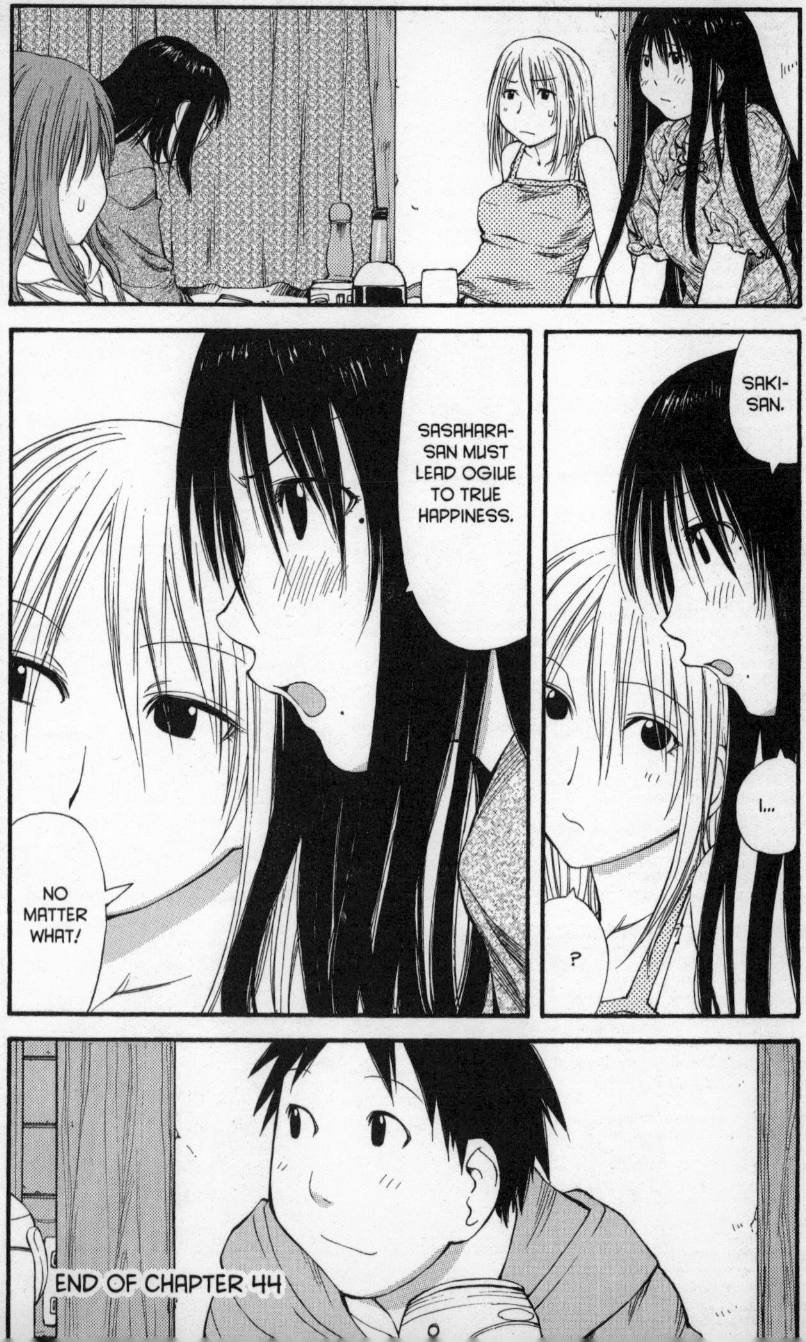
SAKI-SAN.
I...
?
SASAHARA-SAN MUST LEAD OGIUE TO TRUE HAPPINESS.
NO MATTER WHAT!
END OF CHAPTER 44

くじびき♥アンバランス
KUJIBIKI♥ UNBALANCE

72 YEAR OLD PIT VIPER [REFERRED TO AS PV BELOW] – HI, 72-YEAR-OLD PIT VIPER HERE. WAIT, I GRADUATED A LONG TIME AGO. SHOULD I REALLY BE HERE?

BENJAMIN TAKEYO [REFERRED TO AS BEN BELOW]–I GUESS IT'S OKAY, SINCE YOU COME HERE EVERY DAY ANYWAY. TODAY, WE'RE GOING TO BEGIN OUR DISCUSSION ON THE ROUGH SKETCHES OF THE CHARACTERS FROM KUJI-UN'S SECOND SEASON.

PV- I DON'T COME EVERY DAY. THESE CHARACTERS ARE TOTALLY DIFFERENT. WHO DREW THESE?

BEN- I HEARD THAT THE CREATOR, YUU KUROKI, GOT REALLY EXCITED ABOUT MESSING AROUND WITH THE CHARACTERS AND JUST WENT ALL OUT. KUROKI-SENSEI PROBABLY GOT SOME HELP FROM THE KUJI-UN CREATIVE TEAM, TOO.

PV- BUT THE SERIES IS STILL GOING ON. SHOULD KUROKI-SENSEI REALLY BE DOING THAT?

BEN- WELL, YOU KNOW WHAT HAPPENED BEFORE... AHEM, AHEM...ONLY A FEW OF THE CHARACTERS ARE REALLY POPULAR.

PV- RIGHT, BECAUSE THEY DESIGNED THE CHARACTERS USING A KUJIBIKI LOTTERY.

BEN- THAT'S RIGHT. ANYWAY, THIS IS TOKINO WE'RE LOOKING AT. HER CHARACTER HAS PROBABLY CHANGED MORE THAN ANY OTHER.

PV- SHE'S ALMOST AN ENTIRELY DIFFERENT CHARACTER. OF COURSE BEFORE SHE WAS TOTALLY NUTS, SO...

BEN- SHE HAD HER OWN LITTLE NICHE FAN GROUP, BUT I ALWAYS WONDERED ABOUT WHETHER SHE COULD REALLY MAKE IT AS THE MAIN HEROINE.

PV- YEAH, WITH THAT HAIR OF HERS.

BEN- I GUESS THAT'S WHY THEY MADE HER A REDHEAD THIS TIME. THEY REALLY WENT FOR THE DOG-EARED LOOK TO TRY TO MAKE HER MORE LOVABLE. SUPPOSEDLY, SOMEONE ELSE CAME UP WITH THE WHOLE IDEA.

PV- DID HER PERSONALITY CHANGE, TOO?

BEN- SHE'S STILL BRIGHT AND CHEERFUL LIKE SHE ALWAYS WAS, BUT THEY DID AWAY WITH HER WHOLE MUSHROOM OBSESSION. THE BIGGEST THING WAS THAT THEY TURNED HER INTO A CHILDHOOD FRIEND CHARACTER.

PV- NO KIDDING. NOW SHE REALLY SOUNDS LIKE A MAIN HEROINE.

BEN- THAT'S WHAT I'VE BEEN TRYING TO TELL YOU.

PV- BEFORE, SHE WAS A REALLY TROUBLESOME CHARACTER, I MEAN, SHE WAS IN LOVE WITH SOMEONE OTHER THAN THE HERO.

BEN- NOW SHE CAN FINALLY COMPETE WITH THE PRESIDENT. BUT HER TRANSFORMATION INTO A CHILDHOOD FRIEND CHARACTER HAPPENED MUCH LATER THAN THE OTHER CHANGES.

PV- EVEN THOUGH IT'S THE MOST IMPORTANT ONE?

BEN- THEY HAD A HARD TIME WORKING IT INTO THE SCRIPT.

PV- SO THE TOKINO CHARACTER IS MORE VULNERABLE NOW? WELL, THEY REALLY JUST GO WHEREVER THE WIND CARRIES THEM, DON'T THEY?

BEN- YEP, THAT'S HOW THEY DO THINGS.

PV- IT'S GOT ME PRETTY WORRIED. I DON'T WANT TO RELIVE MY NIGHTMARES FROM SEASON ONE.

BEN- WELL, THE STUDIO AND THE DIRECTOR ARE BOTH TOTALLY DIFFERENT, SO...

PV- YEAH, AND THEY'RE BROADCASTING THEM IN THE FALL, SO I GUESS WE DON'T HAVE TO WORRY ABOUT TYPHOONS.

(CONTINUED AT TOP)

BEN- LET'S TAKE A LOOK AT SOME OTHER CHARACTERS.

PV- WE'RE ALREADY DONE WITH TOKINO? I THOUGHT SHE'D FINALLY BECOME A CHARACTER WHO COULD COMPETE WITH THE PRESIDENT.

BEN- WE'LL HAVE TO SEE THE SHOW BEFORE WE CAN DECIDE FOR SURE. BUT NO ONE CAN REALLY COMPETE WITH THE PRESIDENT.

PV- YOU'RE THE ONE WHO SAID IT. BESIDES, THE PRESIDENT IS TOTALLY DIFFERENT NOW, TOO...

BEN- LET'S SAVE THAT FOR NEXT TIME.

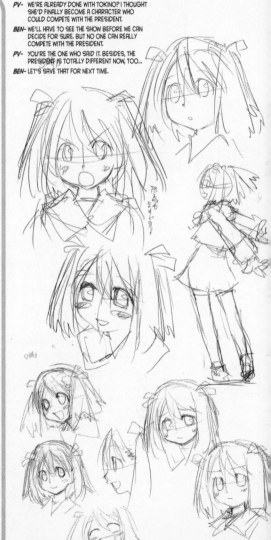

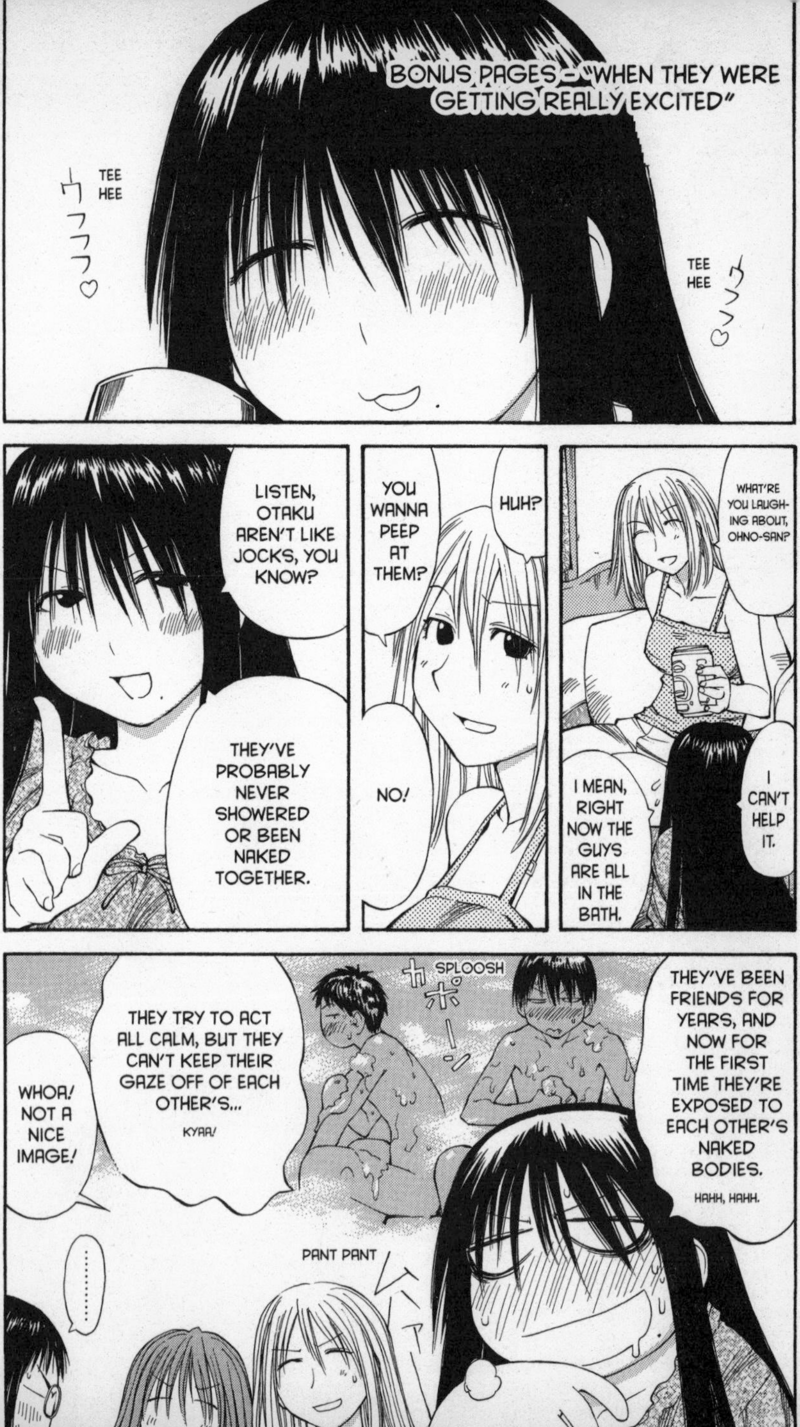
BONUS PAGES – "WHEN THEY WERE GETTING REALLY EXCITED"
TEE HEE
TEE HEE
WHAT'RE YOU LAUGHING ABOUT, OHNO-SAN?
I CAN'T HELP IT.
I MEAN, RIGHT NOW THE GUYS ARE ALL IN THE BATH.
HUH?
YOU WANNA PEEP AT THEM?
NO!
LISTEN, OTAKU AREN'T LIKE JOCKS, YOU KNOW?
THEY'VE PROBABLY NEVER SHOWERED OR BEEN NAKED TOGETHER.
THEY'VE BEEN FRIENDS FOR YEARS, AND NOW FOR THE FIRST TIME THEY'RE EXPOSED TO EACH OTHER'S NAKED BODIES.
HAHH, HAHH.
SPLOOSH
THEY TRY TO ACT ALL CALM, BUT THEY CAN'T KEEP THEIR GAZE OFF OF EACH OTHER'S...
KYAA!
WHOA! NOT A NICE IMAGE!
PANT PANT
......

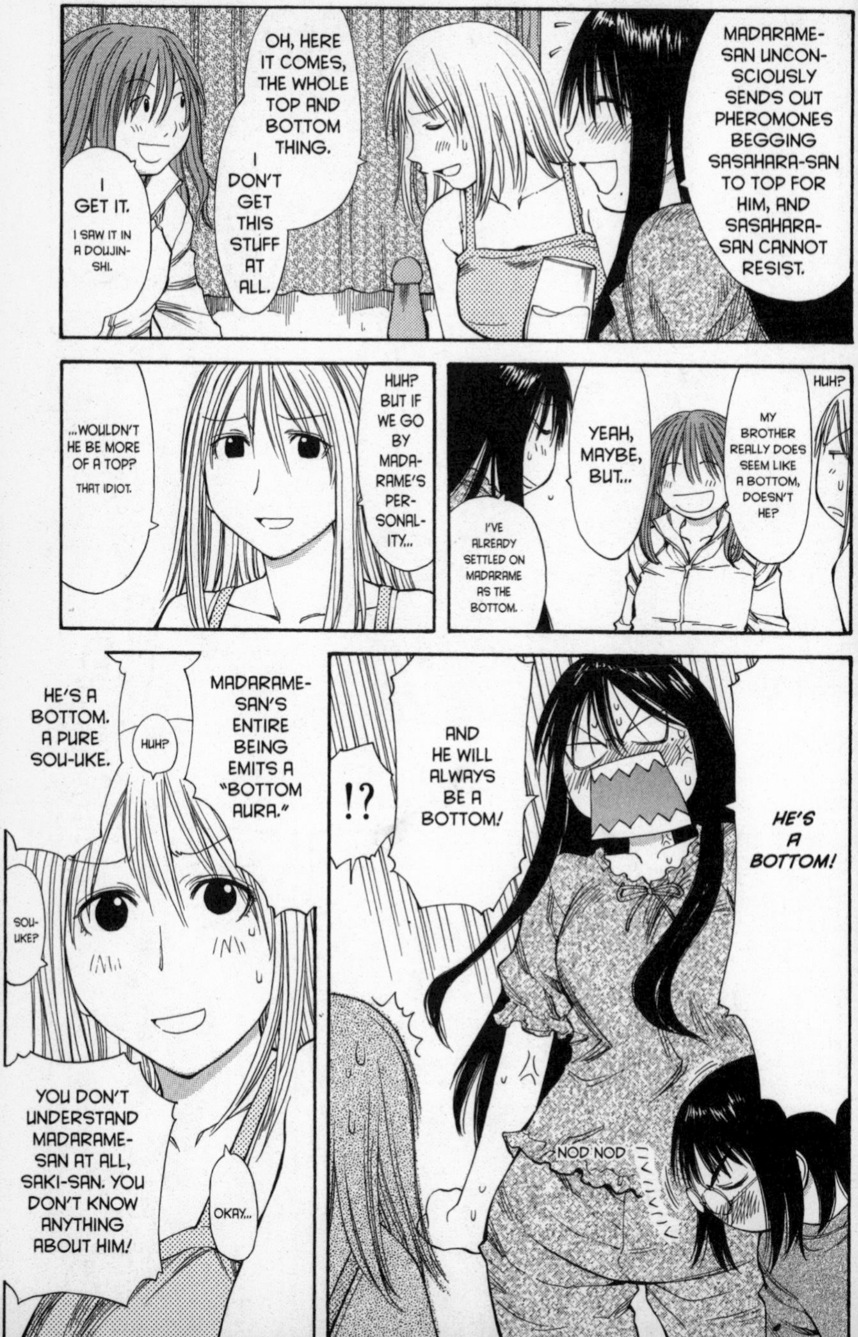
MADARAME-SAN UNCONSCIOUSLY SENDS OUT PHEROMONES BEGGING SASAHARA-SAN TO TOP FOR HIM, AND SASAHARA-SAN CANNOT RESIST.
OH, HERE IT COMES, THE WHOLE TOP AND BOTTOM THING.
I DON'T GET THIS STUFF AT ALL.
I GET IT.
I SAW IT IN A DOUJINSHI.
HUH?
MY BROTHER REALLY DOES SEEM LIKE A BOTTOM, DOESN'T HE?
YEAH, MAYBE, BUT...
I'VE ALREADY SETTLED ON MADARAME AS THE BOTTOM.
HUH? BUT IF WE GO BY MADARAME'S PERSONALITY...
...WOULDN'T HE BE MORE OF A TOP?
THAT IDIOT.
HE'S A BOTTOM!
AND HE WILL ALWAYS BE A BOTTOM!
!?
NOD NOD
MADARAME-SAN'S ENTIRE BEING EMITS A "BOTTOM AURA."
HE'S A BOTTOM. A PURE SOU-UKE.
HUH?
SOU-UKE?
YOU DON'T UNDERSTAND MADARAME-SAN AT ALL, SAKI-SAN. YOU DON'T KNOW ANYTHING ABOUT HIM!
OKAY...

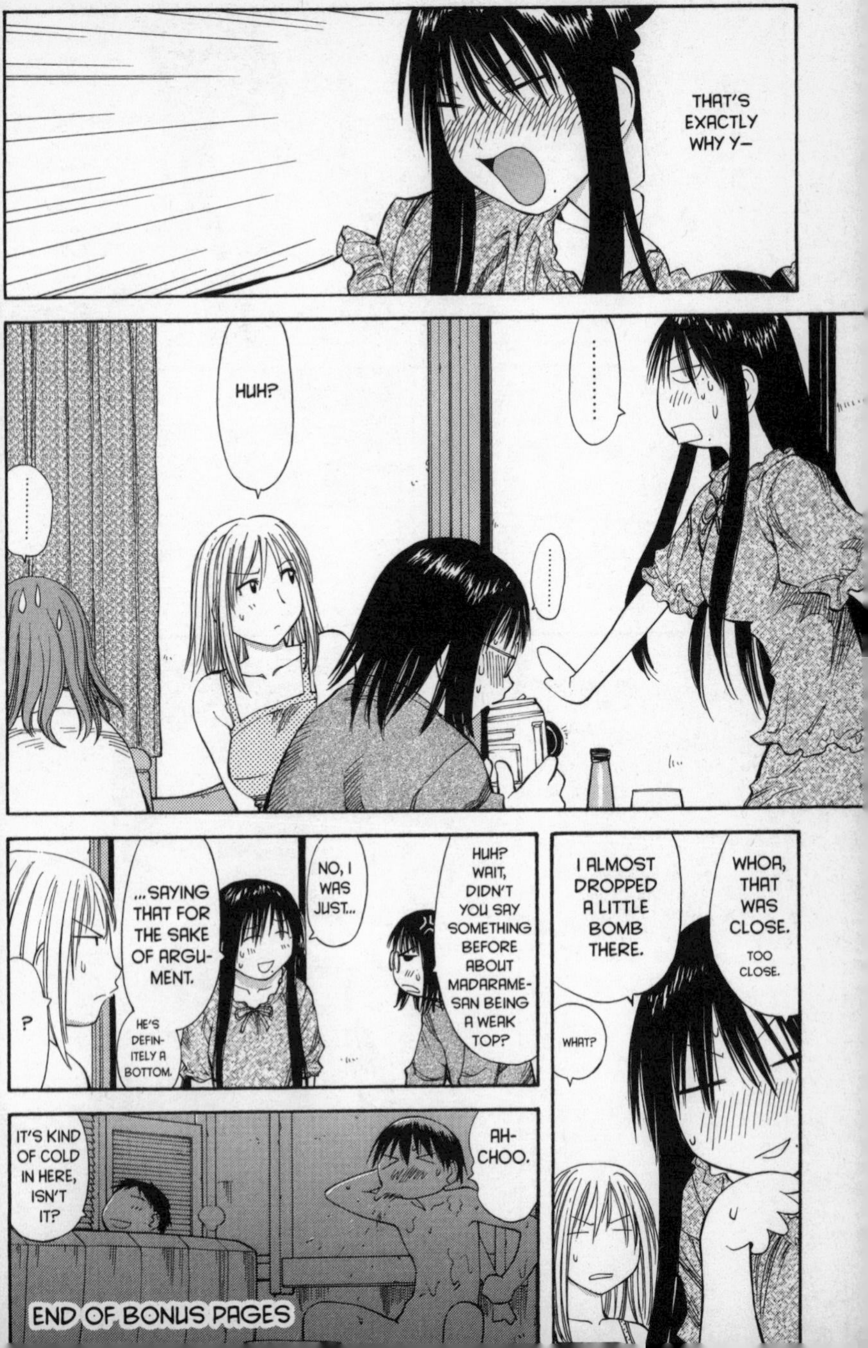

THAT'S EXACTLY WHY Y—
......
HUH?
......
......
WHOA, THAT WAS CLOSE.
TOO CLOSE.
I ALMOST DROPPED A LITTLE BOMB THERE.
WHAT?
HUH? WAIT, DIDN'T YOU SAY SOMETHING BEFORE ABOUT MADARAME-SAN BEING A WEAK TOP?
NO, I WAS JUST...
...SAYING THAT FOR THE SAKE OF ARGUMENT.
HE'S DEFINITELY A BOTTOM.
?
AH-CHOO.
IT'S KIND OF COLD IN HERE, ISN'T IT?
END OF BONUS PAGES

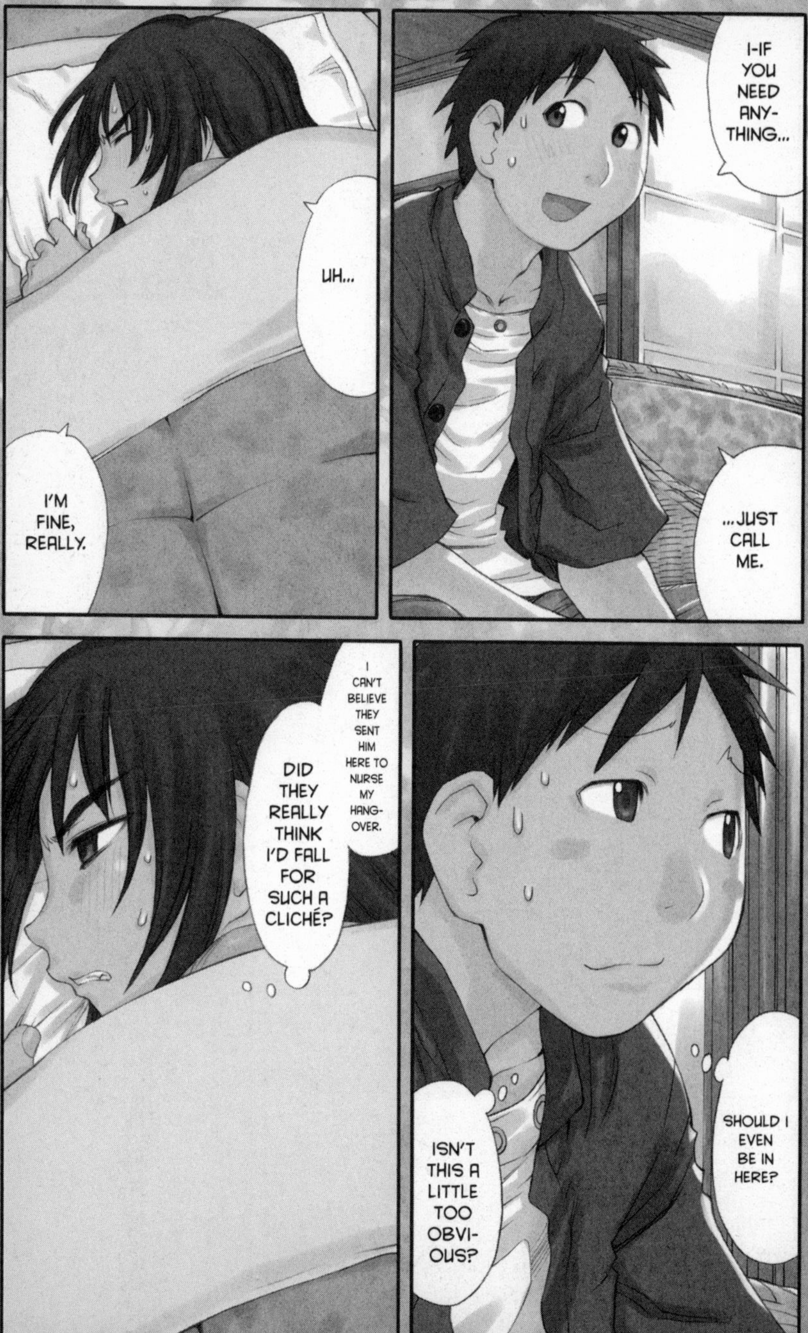
I-IF YOU NEED ANY-THING...
...JUST CALL ME.
UH...
I'M FINE, REALLY.
SHOULD I EVEN BE IN HERE?
ISN'T THIS A LITTLE TOO OBVI-OUS?
I CAN'T BELIEVE THEY SENT HIM HERE TO NURSE MY HANG-OVER.
DID THEY REALLY THINK I'D FALL FOR SUCH A CLICHÉ?

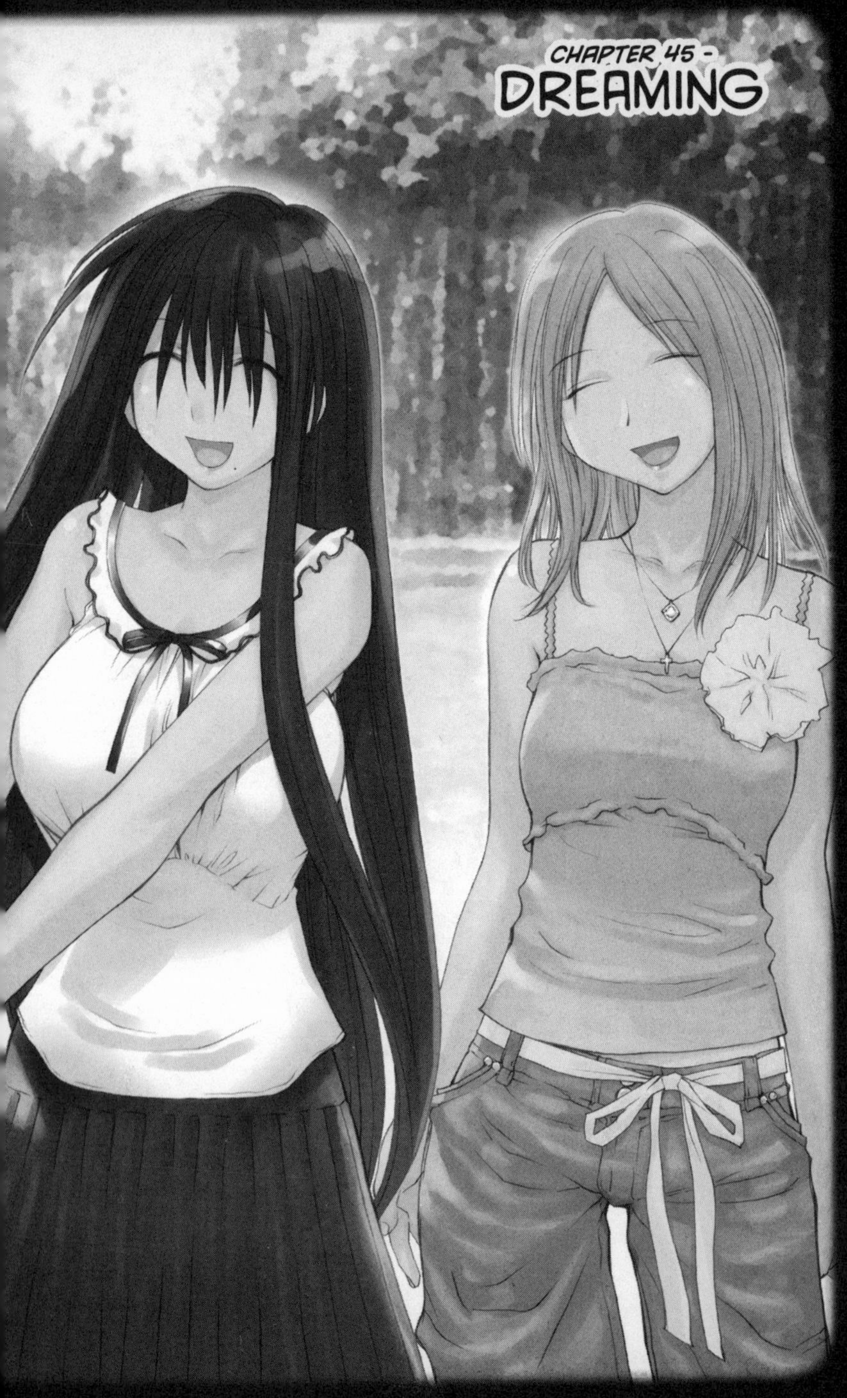
CHAPTER 45 -
DREAMING

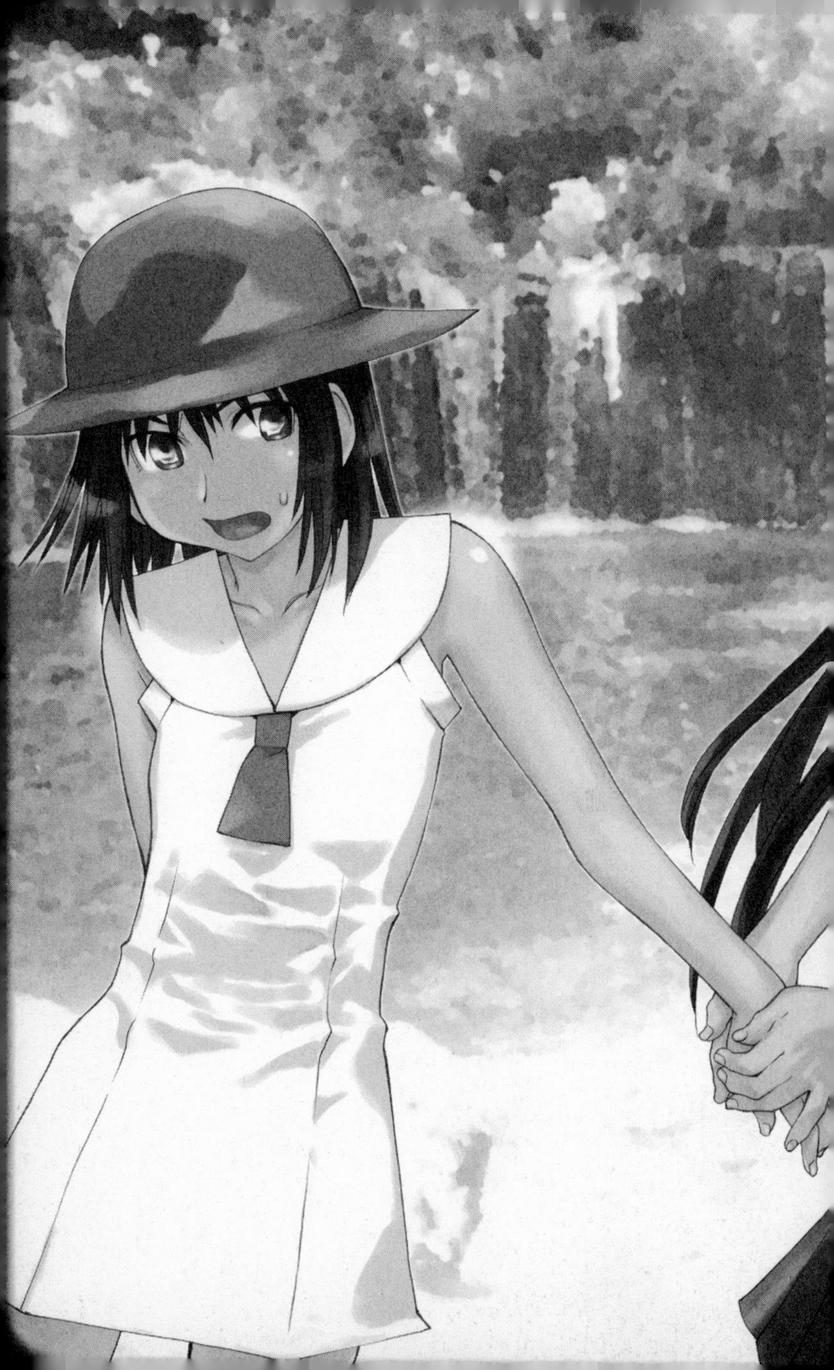

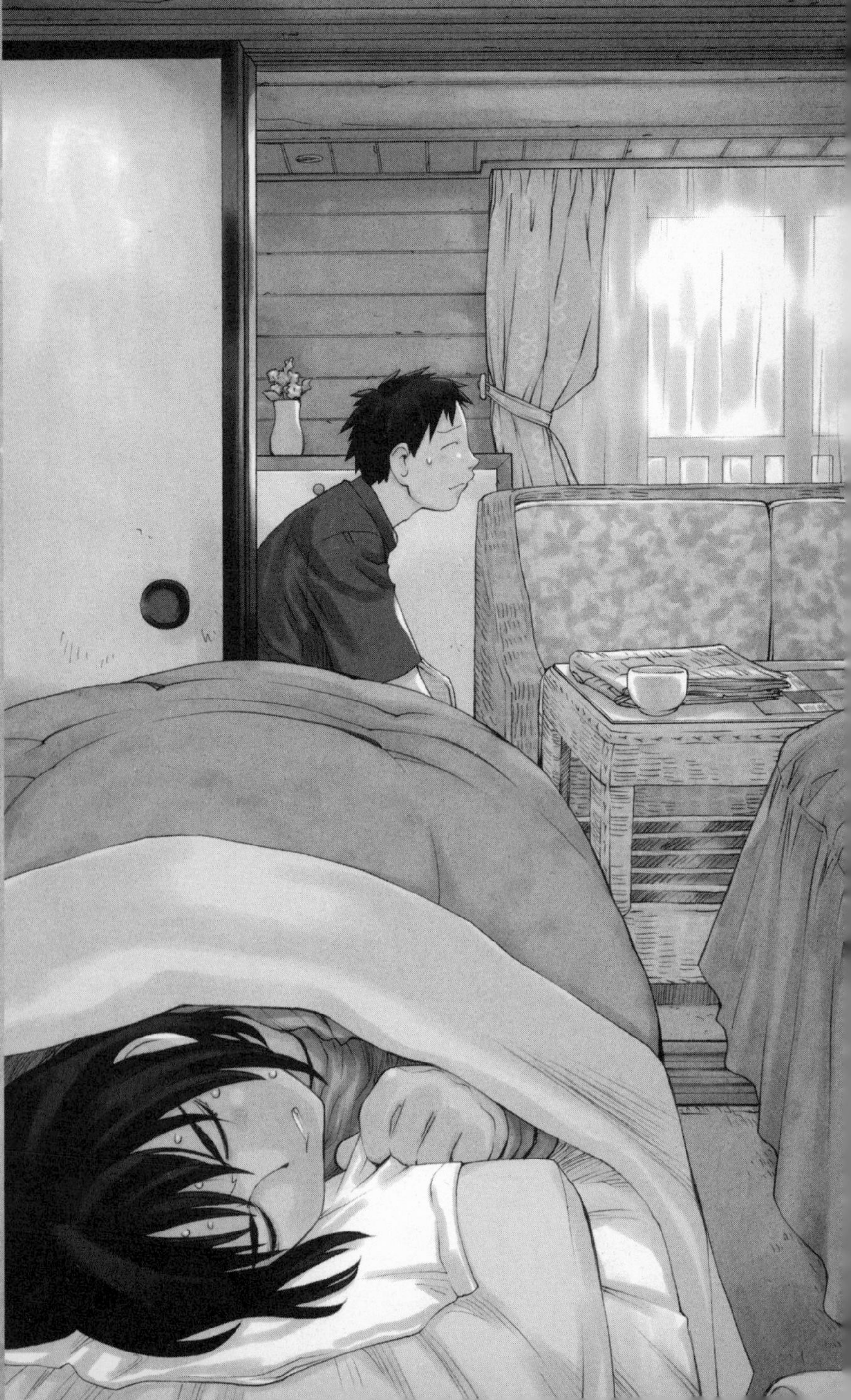

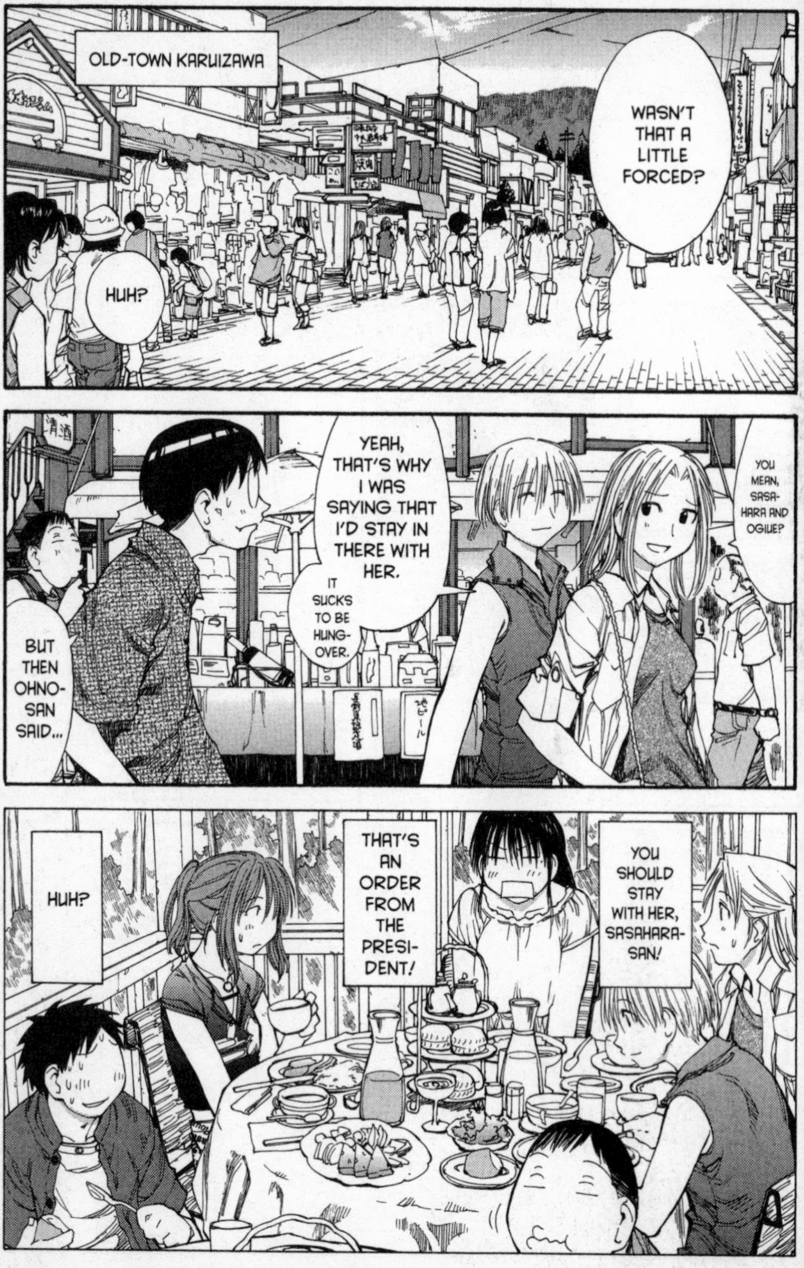
WASN'T THAT A LITTLE FORCED?
OLD-TOWN KARUIZAWA
HUH?
YOU MEAN, SASAHARA AND OGIUE?
YEAH, THAT'S WHY I WAS SAYING THAT I'D STAY IN THERE WITH HER.
IT SUCKS TO BE HUNG-OVER.
BUT THEN OHNO-SAN SAID...
YOU SHOULD STAY WITH HER, SASAHARA-SAN!
THAT'S AN ORDER FROM THE PRESIDENT!
HUH?

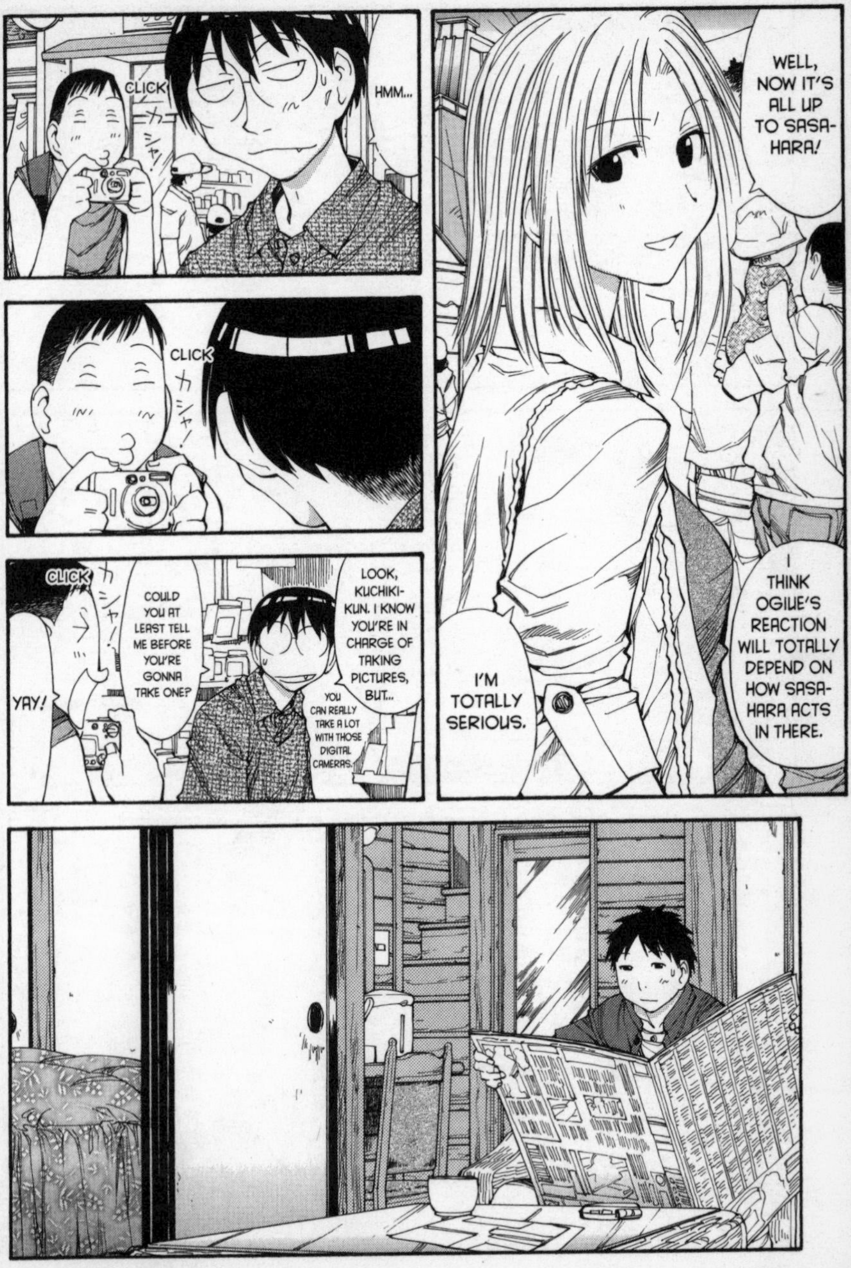
WELL, NOW IT'S ALL UP TO SASA-HARA!
I THINK OGIUE'S REACTION WILL TOTALLY DEPEND ON HOW SASA-HARA ACTS IN THERE.
I'M TOTALLY SERIOUS.
HMM...
CLICK
CLICK
カシャ!
LOOK, KUCHIKI-KUN. I KNOW YOU'RE IN CHARGE OF TAKING PICTURES, BUT...
YOU CAN REALLY TAKE A LOT WITH THOSE DIGITAL CAMERAS.
COULD YOU AT LEAST TELL ME BEFORE YOU'RE GONNA TAKE ONE?
CLICK
カシャ!
YAY!

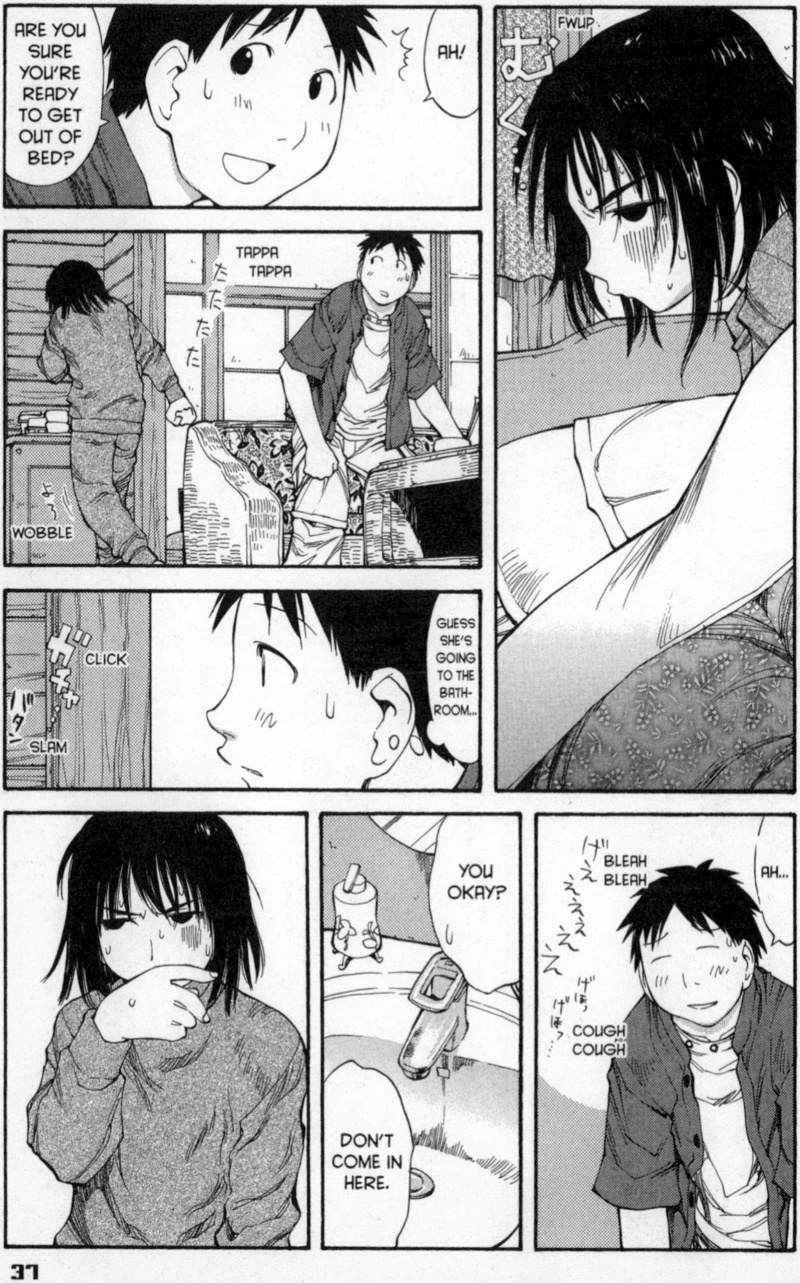

FWUP
むく…
AH!
ARE YOU SURE YOU'RE READY TO GET OUT OF BED?
TAPPA TAPPA
たたたた
よろ
WOBBLE
GUESS SHE'S GOING TO THE BATH-ROOM...
ガチャ
CLICK
バタン
SLAM
AH...
げえええええ
BLEAH BLEAH
げほ, げほっ…
COUGH COUGH
YOU OKAY?
DON'T COME IN HERE.

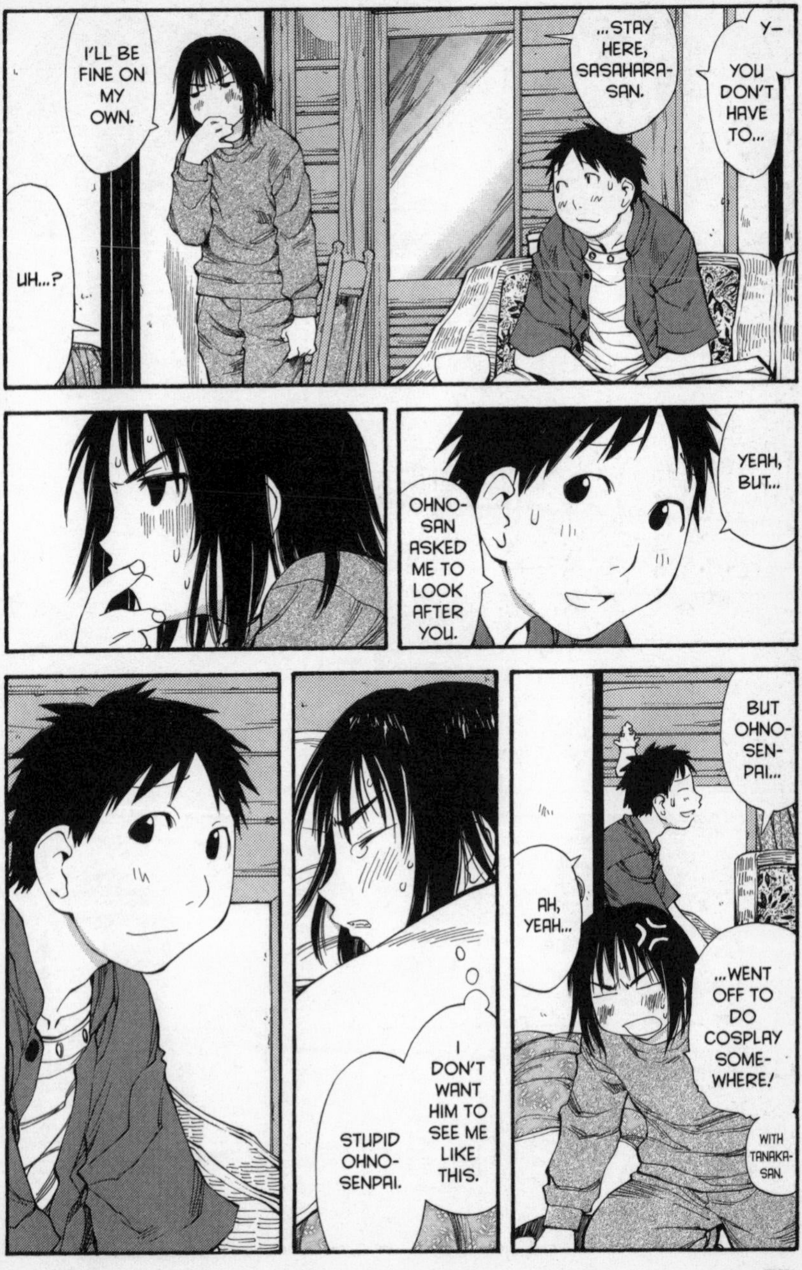
Y— YOU DON'T HAVE TO...
...STAY HERE, SASAHARA-SAN.
I'LL BE FINE ON MY OWN.
UH...?
YEAH, BUT...
OHNO-SAN ASKED ME TO LOOK AFTER YOU.
BUT OHNO-SENPAI...
...WENT OFF TO DO COSPLAY SOMEWHERE!
WITH TANAKA-SAN.
AH, YEAH...
I DON'T WANT HIM TO SEE ME LIKE THIS.
STUPID OHNO-SENPAI.

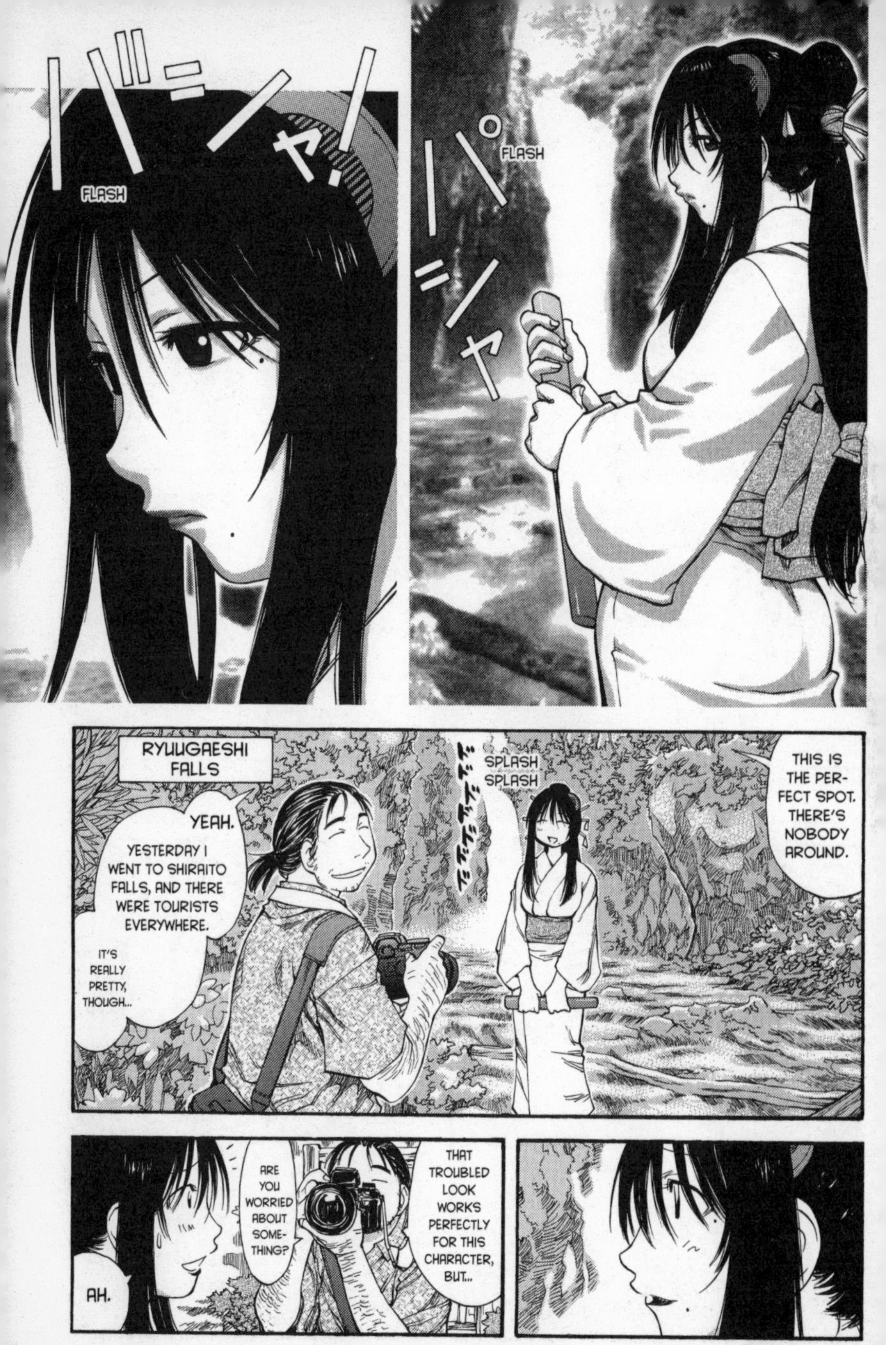
FLASH
FLASH
THIS IS THE PER-FECT SPOT. THERE'S NOBODY AROUND.
SPLASH SPLASH
RYUUGAESHI FALLS
YEAH.
YESTERDAY I WENT TO SHIRAITO FALLS, AND THERE WERE TOURISTS EVERYWHERE.
IT'S REALLY PRETTY, THOUGH...
THAT TROUBLED LOOK WORKS PERFECTLY FOR THIS CHARACTER, BUT...
ARE YOU WORRIED ABOUT SOME-THING?
AH.

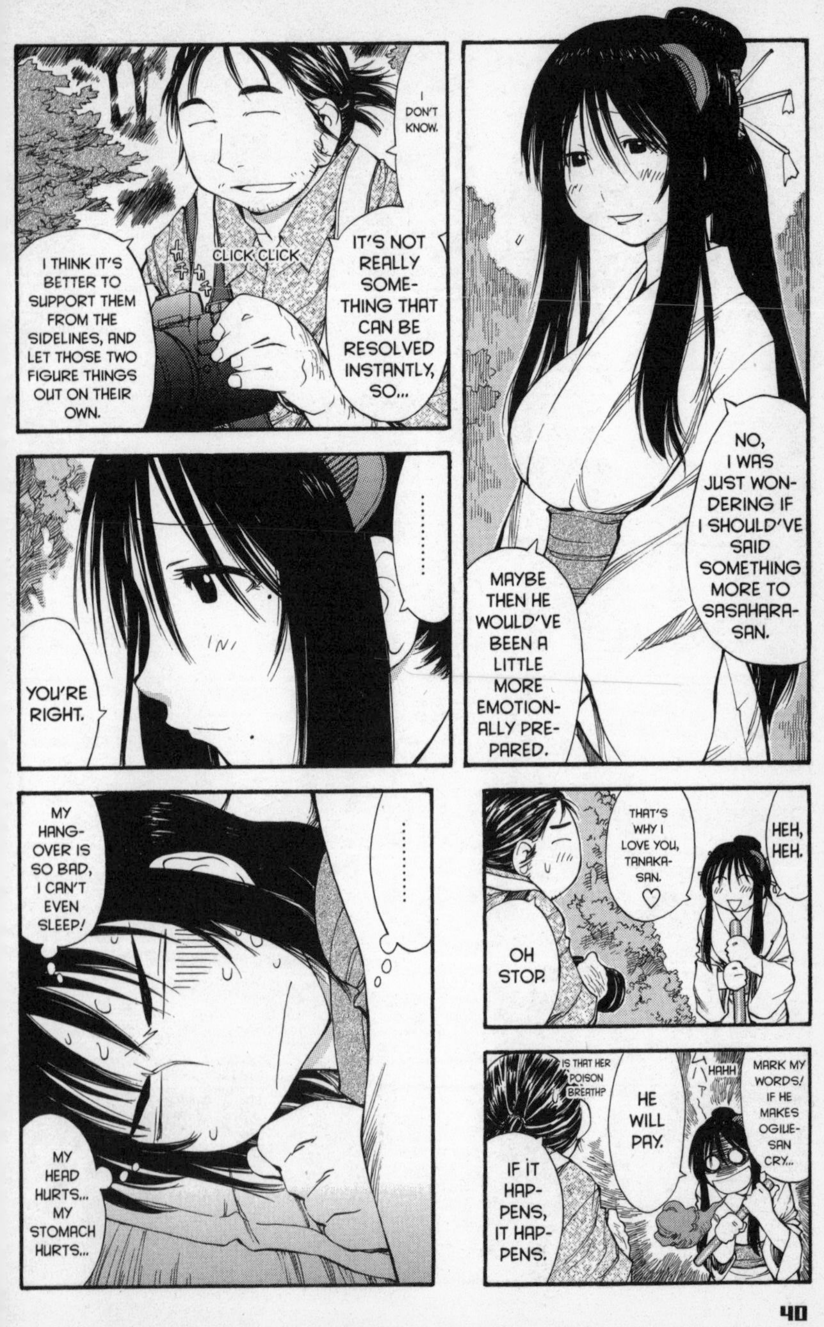
NO, I WAS JUST WONDERING IF I SHOULD'VE SAID SOMETHING MORE TO SASAHARA-SAN.
MAYBE THEN HE WOULD'VE BEEN A LITTLE MORE EMOTIONALLY PREPARED.
I DON'T KNOW.
IT'S NOT REALLY SOMETHING THAT CAN BE RESOLVED INSTANTLY, SO...
CLICK CLICK
I THINK IT'S BETTER TO SUPPORT THEM FROM THE SIDELINES, AND LET THOSE TWO FIGURE THINGS OUT ON THEIR OWN.
......
YOU'RE RIGHT.
HEH, HEH.
THAT'S WHY I LOVE YOU, TANAKA-SAN. ♡
OH STOP.
MARK MY WORDS! IF HE MAKES OGIUE-SAN CRY...
HAHH
IS THAT HER POISON BREATH?
HE WILL PAY.
IF IT HAPPENS, IT HAPPENS.
......
MY HANGOVER IS SO BAD, I CAN'T EVEN SLEEP!
MY HEAD HURTS... MY STOMACH HURTS...

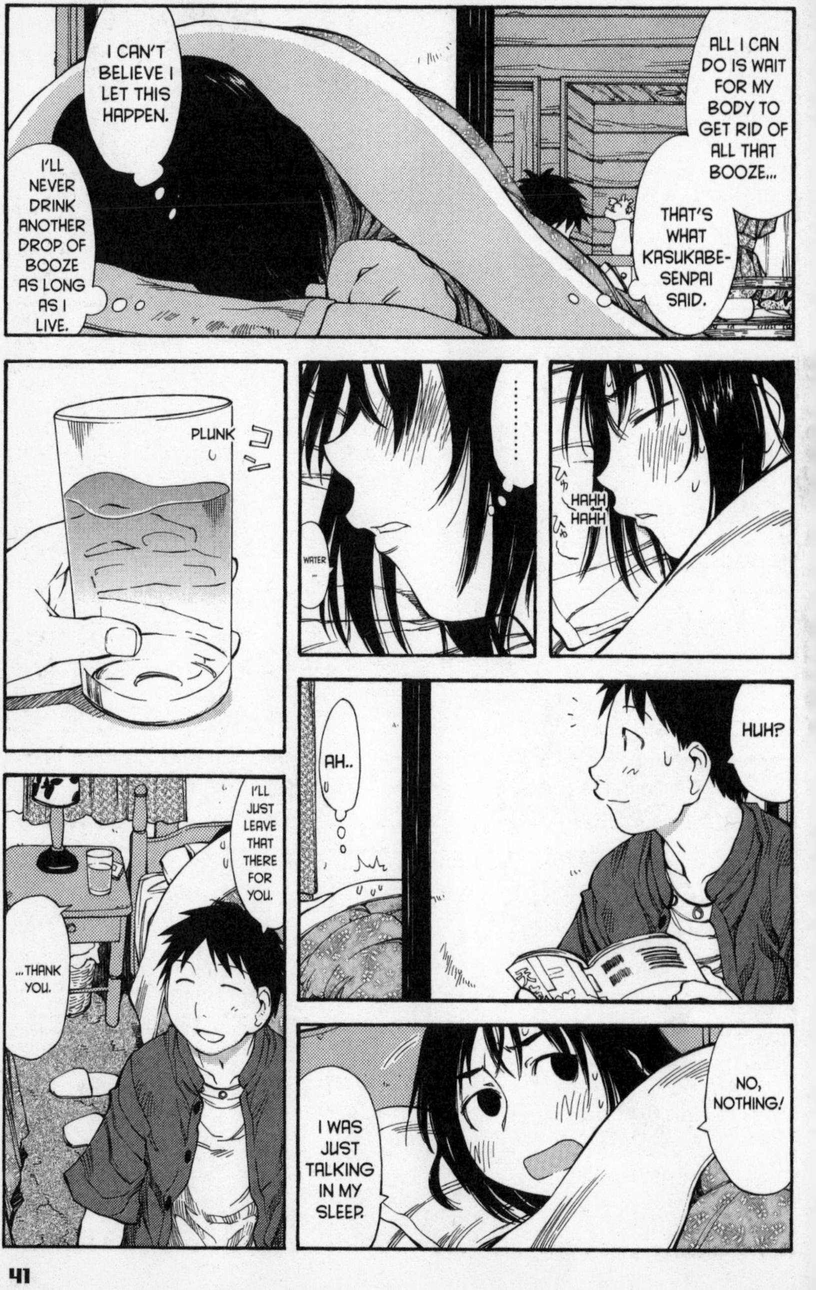
ALL I CAN DO IS WAIT FOR MY BODY TO GET RID OF ALL THAT BOOZE...
THAT'S WHAT KASUKABE-SENPAI SAID.
I CAN'T BELIEVE I LET THIS HAPPEN.
I'LL NEVER DRINK ANOTHER DROP OF BOOZE AS LONG AS I LIVE.
HAHH HAHH
......
WATER...
HUH?
AH..
NO, NOTHING!
I WAS JUST TALKING IN MY SLEEP.
PLUNK
I'LL JUST LEAVE THAT THERE FOR YOU.
...THANK YOU.

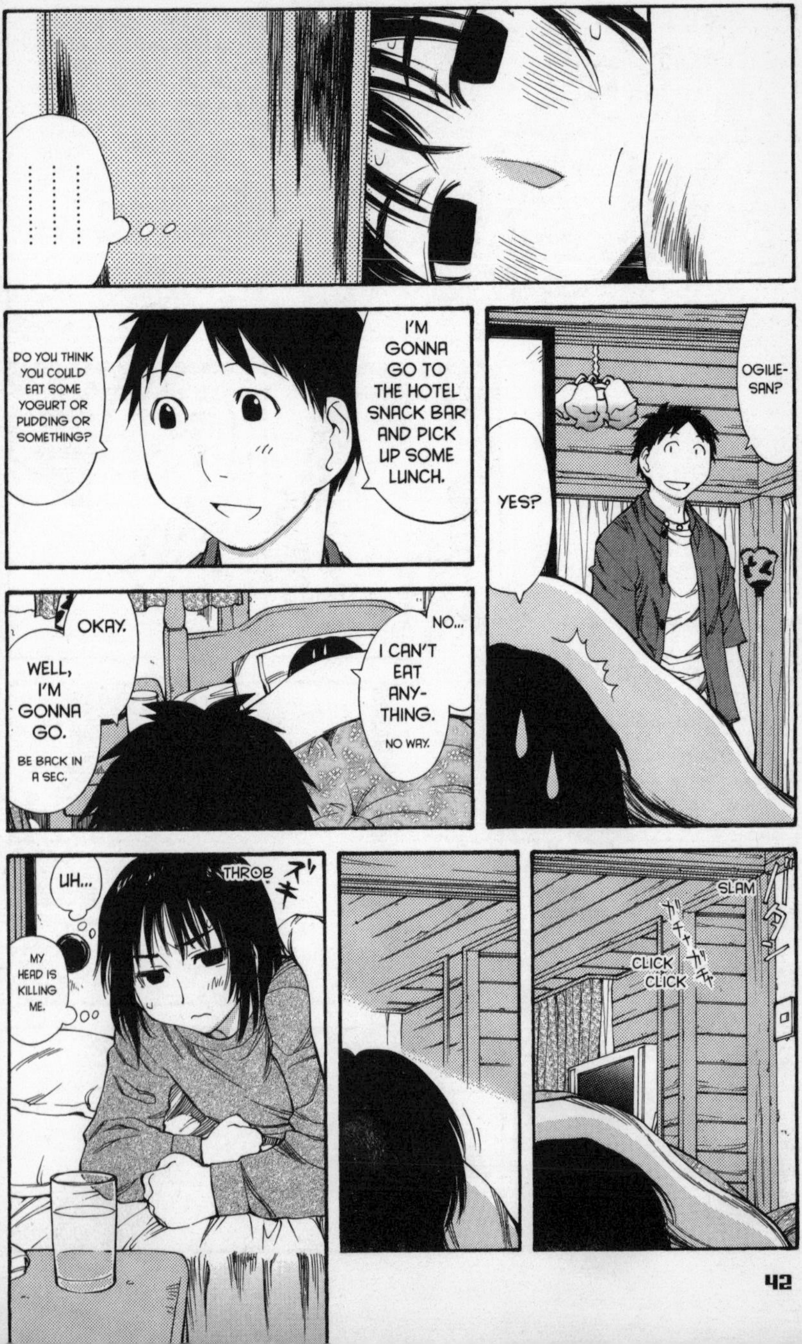
......
OGIUE-SAN?
YES?
I'M GONNA GO TO THE HOTEL SNACK BAR AND PICK UP SOME LUNCH.
DO YOU THINK YOU COULD EAT SOME YOGURT OR PUDDING OR SOMETHING?
NO...
I CAN'T EAT ANYTHING.
NO WAY.
OKAY.
WELL, I'M GONNA GO.
BE BACK IN A SEC.
SLAM
CLICK CLICK
THROB
UH...
MY HEAD IS KILLING ME.

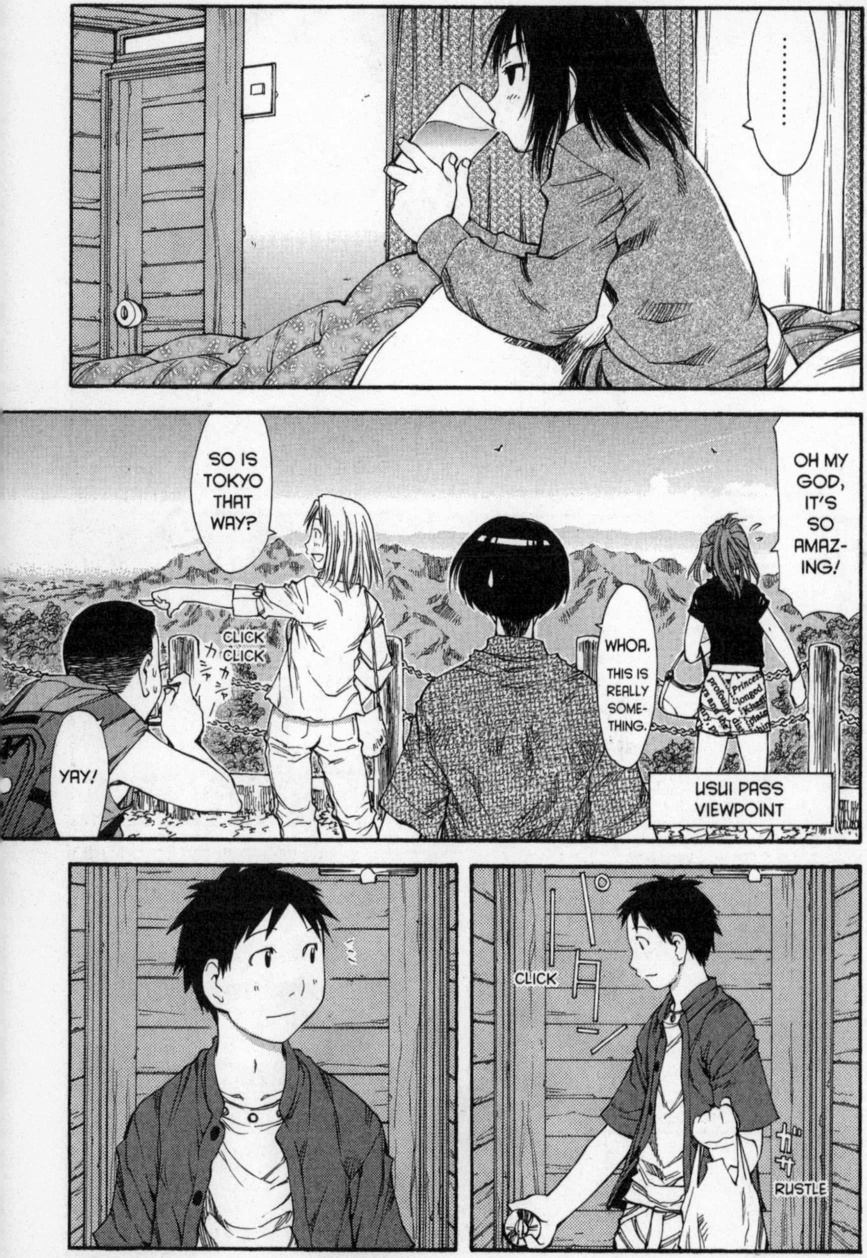
......
OH MY GOD, IT'S SO AMAZING!
WHOA. THIS IS REALLY SOMETHING.
USUI PASS VIEWPOINT
SO IS TOKYO THAT WAY?
CLICK CLICK
YAY!
CLICK
RUSTLE

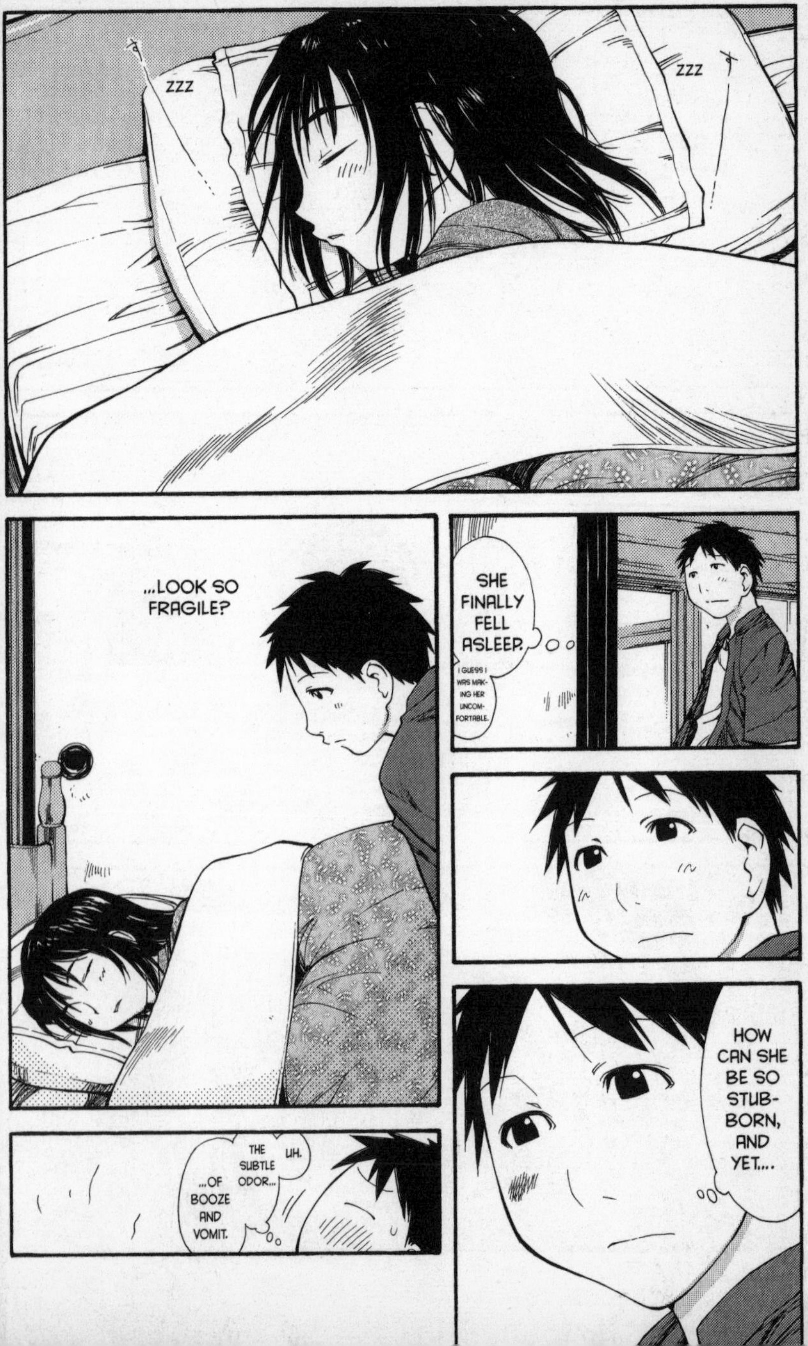
ZZZ
ZZZ
SHE FINALLY FELL ASLEEP.
I GUESS I WAS MAKING HER UNCOMFORTABLE.
HOW CAN SHE BE SO STUBBORN, AND YET....
...LOOK SO FRAGILE?
UH.
THE SUBTLE ODOR...
...OF BOOZE AND VOMIT.

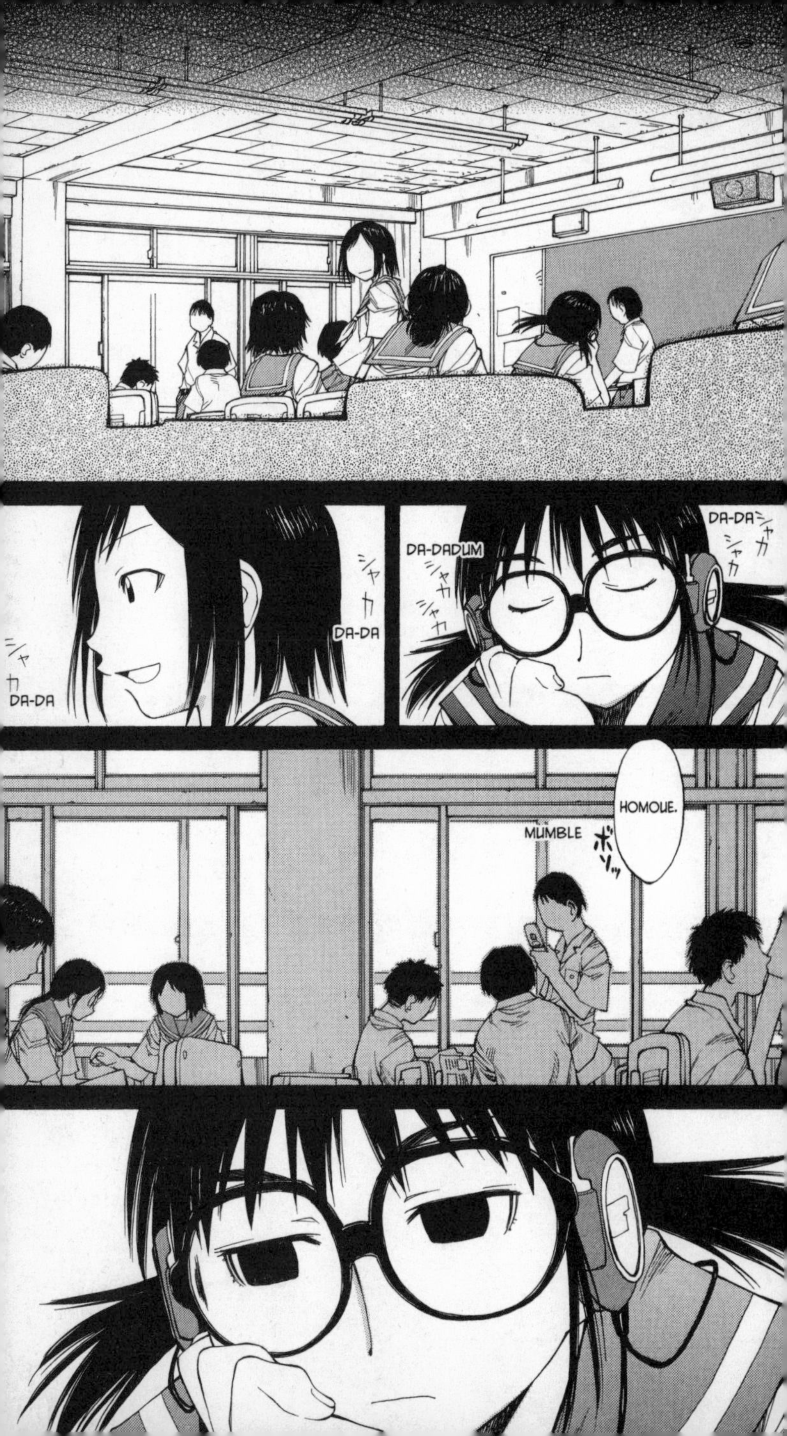
DA-DA
シャカ
シャカ
DA-DADUM
シャカ
シャカ
シャカ
DA-DA
シャカ
DA-DA
HOMOUE.
MUMBLE
ボソッ

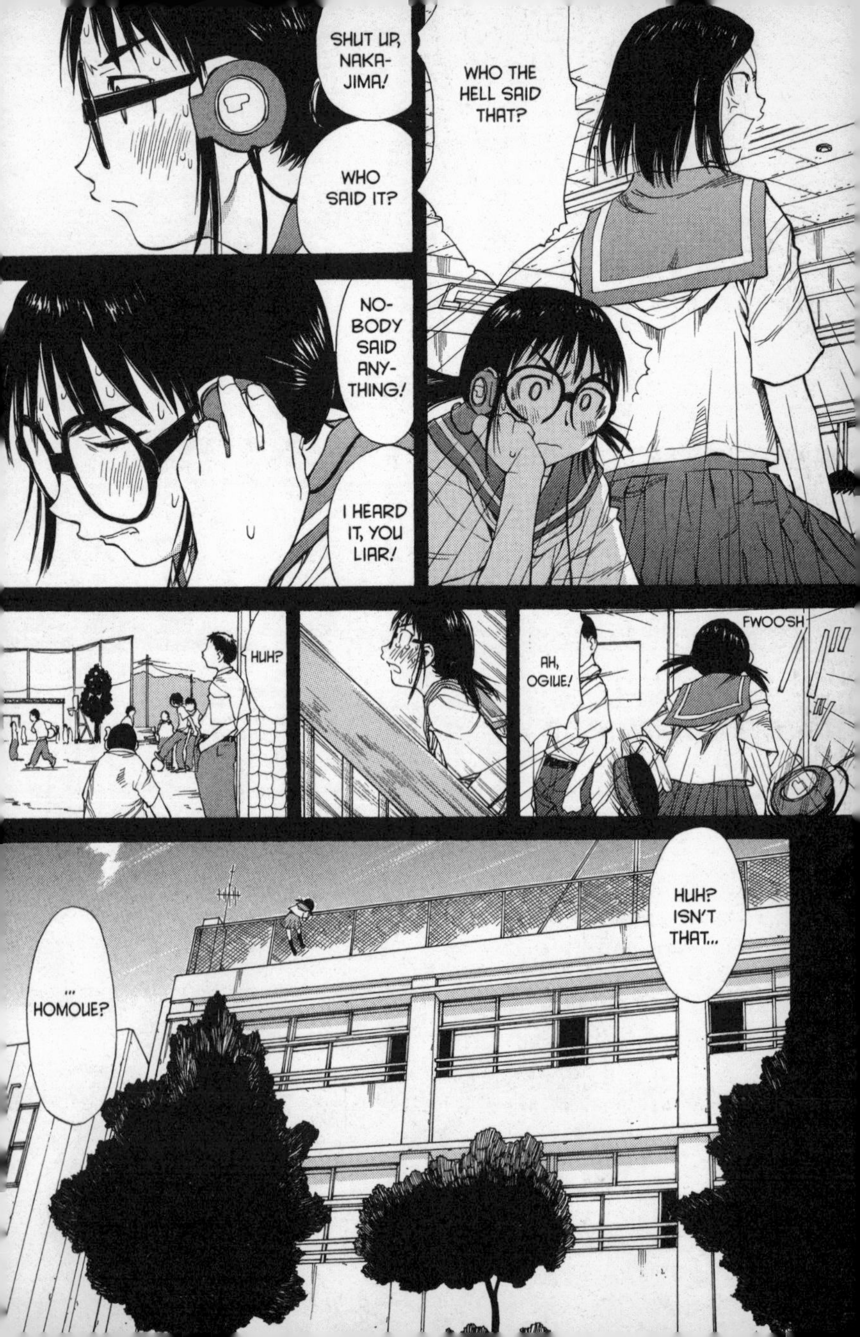
WHO THE HELL SAID THAT?
SHUT UP, NAKA-JIMA!
WHO SAID IT?
NO-BODY SAID ANY-THING!
I HEARD IT, YOU LIAR!
FWOOSH
AH, OGIUE!
HUH?
HUH? ISN'T THAT...
... HOMOUE?

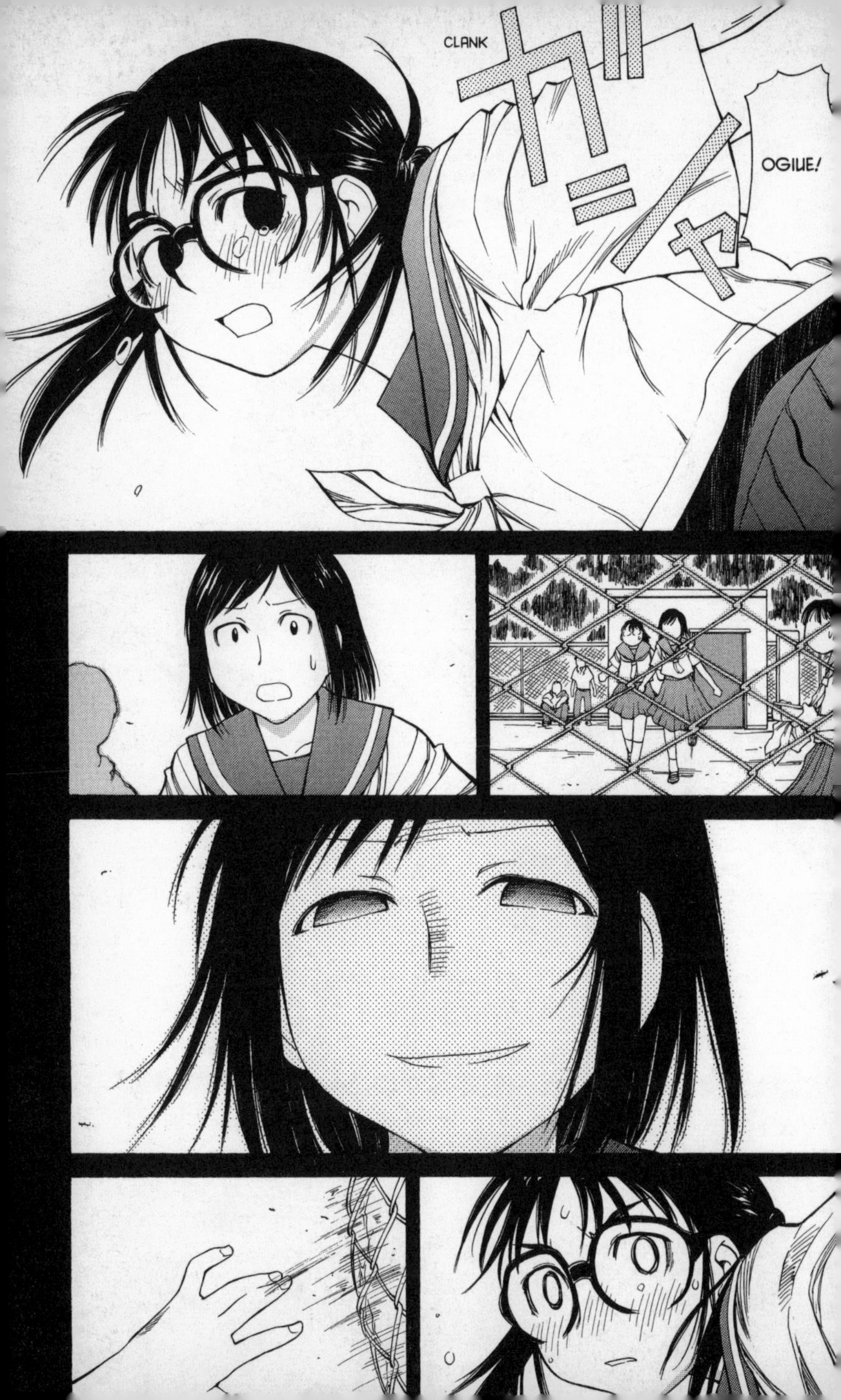
ガシャ
CLANK
OGIUE!

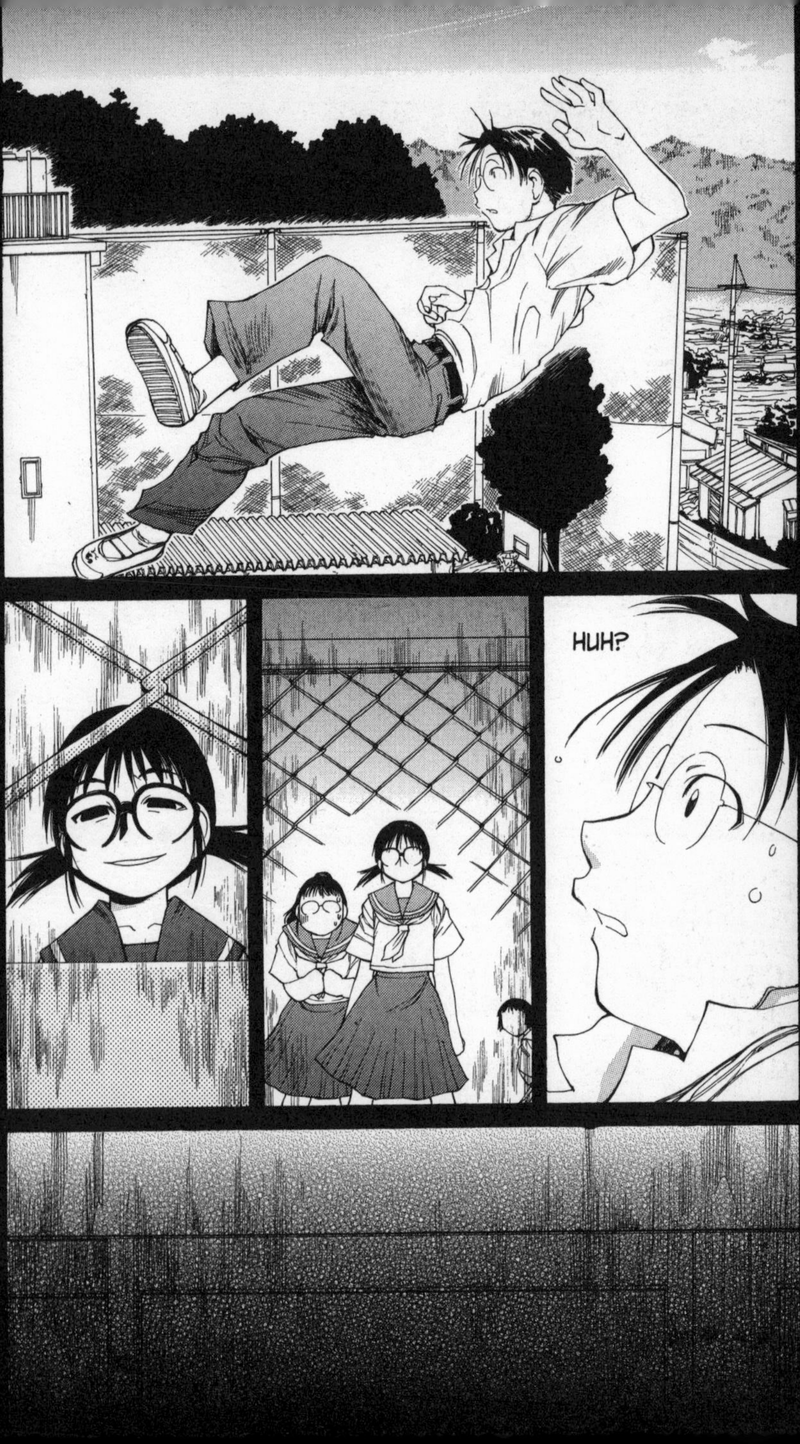
HUH?

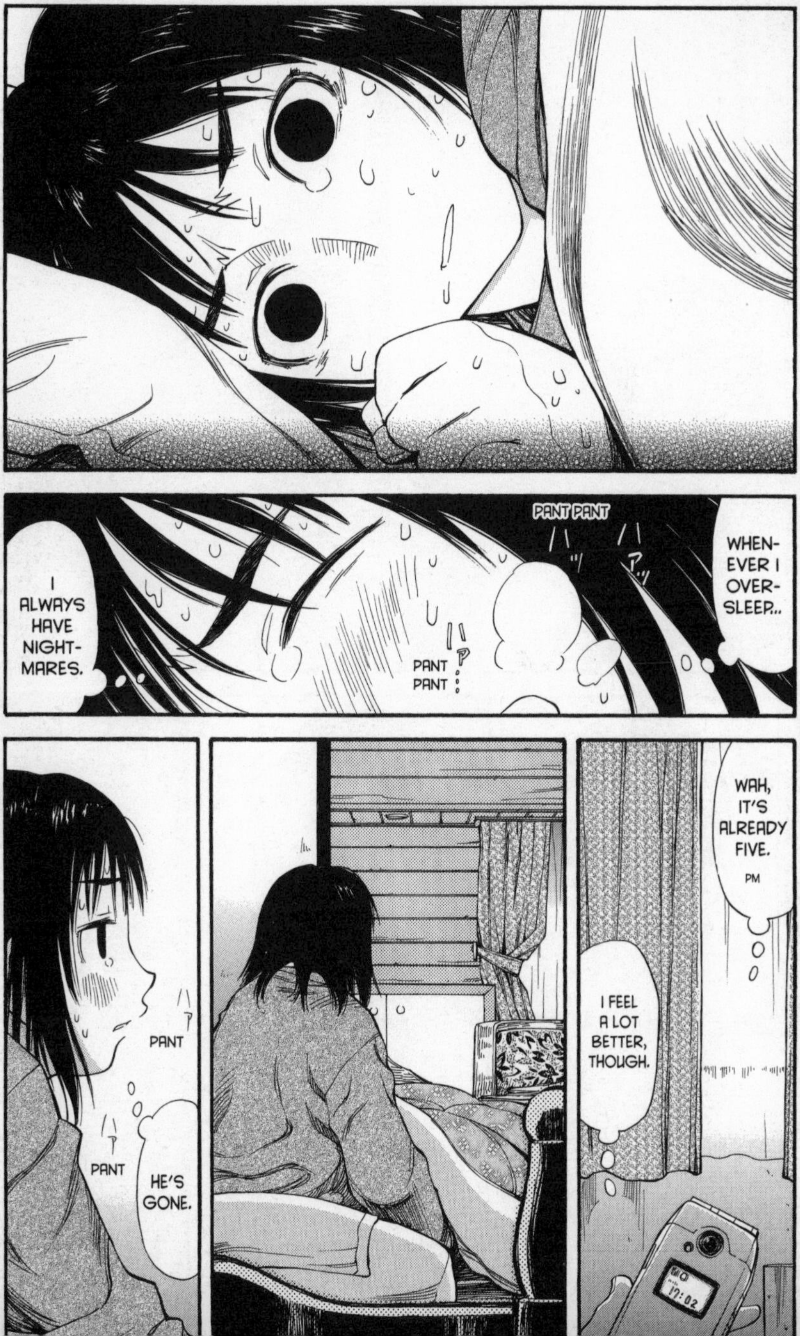
WHEN-EVER I OVER-SLEEP..
PANT PANT
PANT PANT
I ALWAYS HAVE NIGHT-MARES.
WAH, IT'S ALREADY FIVE.
PM
I FEEL A LOT BETTER, THOUGH.
17:02
PANT
PANT
HE'S GONE.

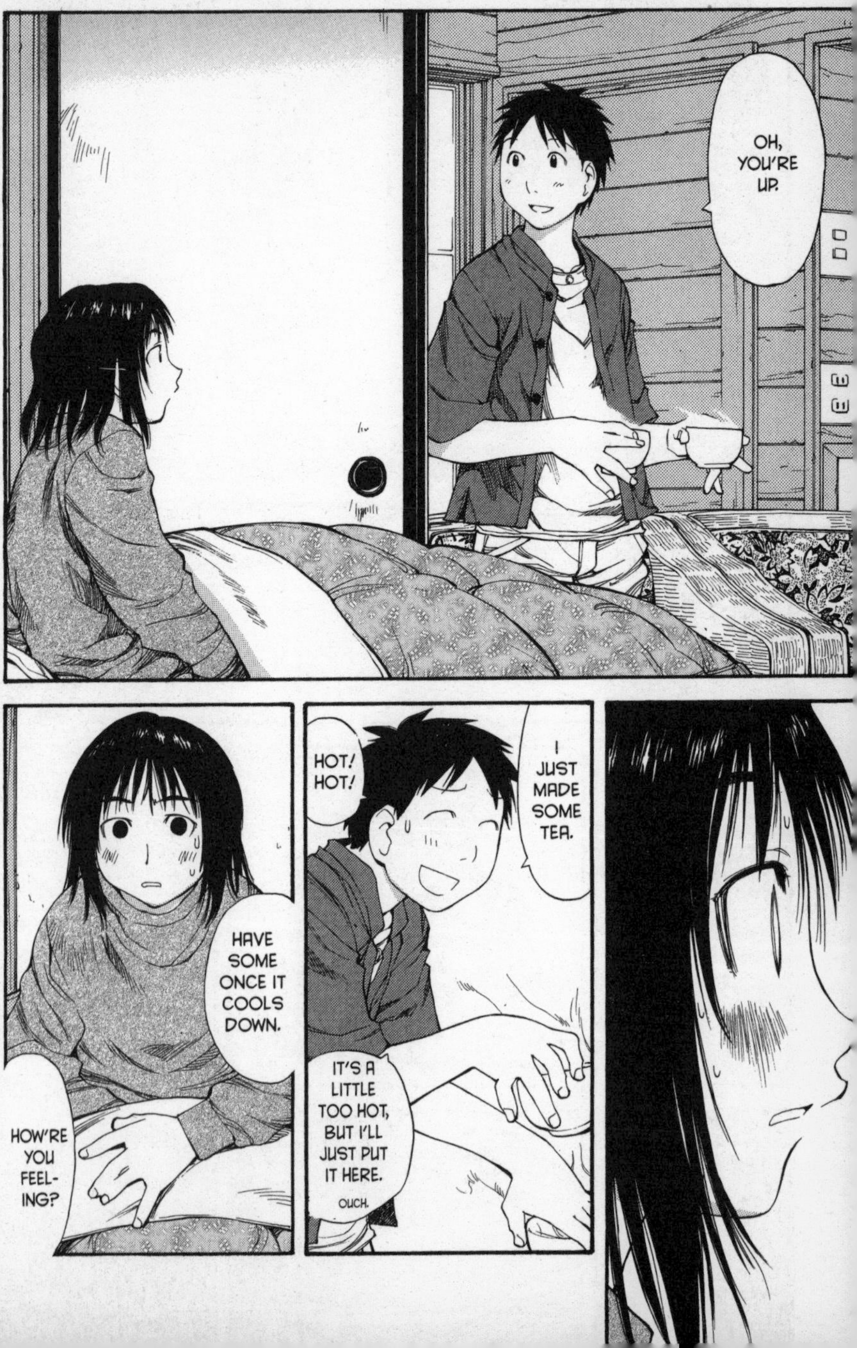
OH, YOU'RE UP.
I JUST MADE SOME TEA.
HOT! HOT!
IT'S A LITTLE TOO HOT, BUT I'LL JUST PUT IT HERE.
OUCH.
HAVE SOME ONCE IT COOLS DOWN.
HOW'RE YOU FEEL-ING?

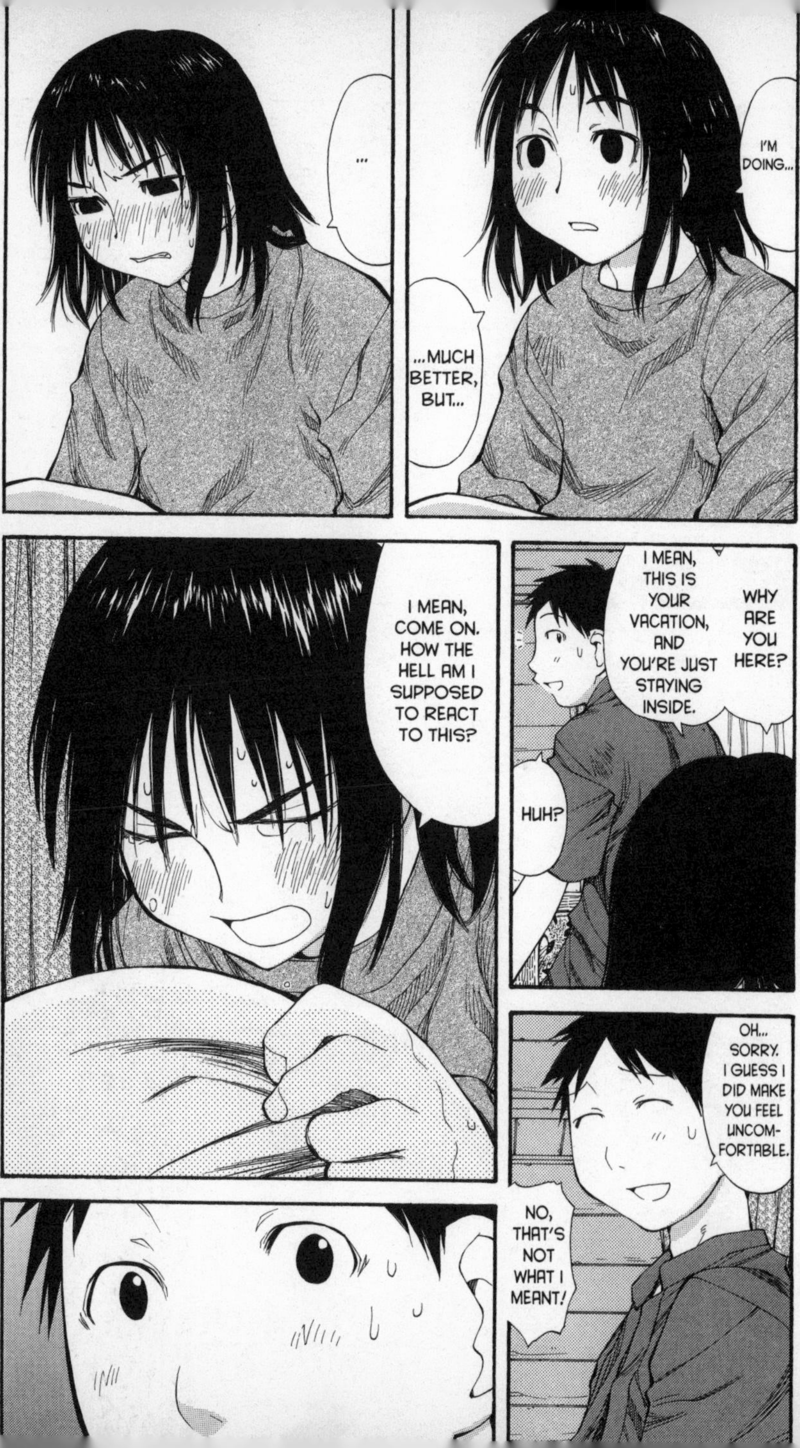
I'M DOING...
...MUCH BETTER, BUT...
...
WHY ARE YOU HERE?
I MEAN, THIS IS YOUR VACATION, AND YOU'RE JUST STAYING INSIDE.
HUH?
I MEAN, COME ON. HOW THE HELL AM I SUPPOSED TO REACT TO THIS?
OH... SORRY. I GUESS I DID MAKE YOU FEEL UNCOM-FORTABLE.
NO, THAT'S NOT WHAT I MEANT!

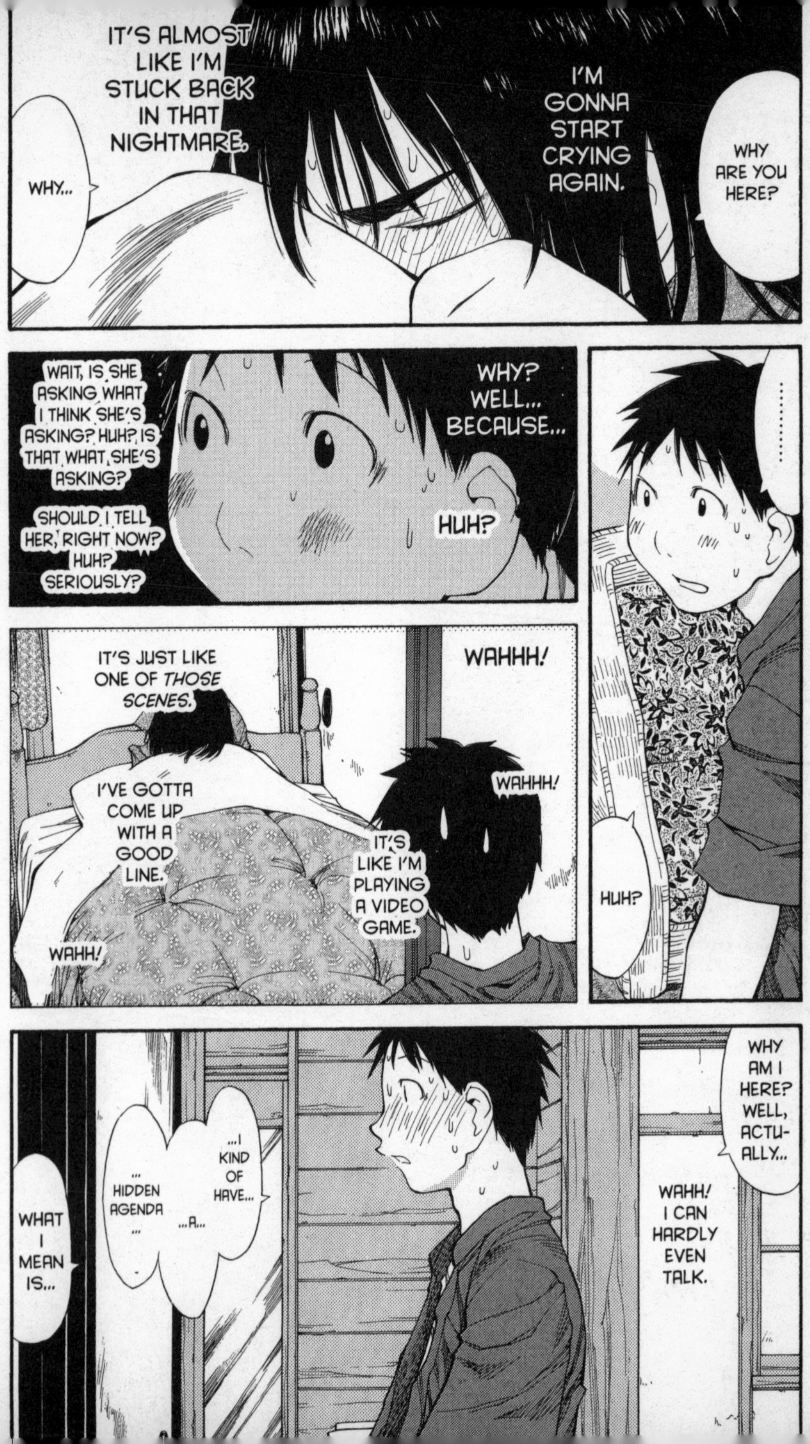
WHY ARE YOU HERE?
I'M GONNA START CRYING AGAIN.
IT'S ALMOST LIKE I'M STUCK BACK IN THAT NIGHTMARE.
WHY...
......
HUH?
WHY? WELL... BECAUSE...
HUH?
WAIT, IS SHE ASKING WHAT I THINK SHE'S ASKING? HUH? IS THAT WHAT SHE'S ASKING?
SHOULD I TELL HER, RIGHT NOW? HUH? SERIOUSLY?
WAHHH!
IT'S JUST LIKE ONE OF *THOSE* SCENES.
WAHHH!
IT'S LIKE I'M PLAYING A VIDEO GAME.
I'VE GOTTA COME UP WITH A GOOD LINE.
WAHH!
WHY AM I HERE? WELL, ACTU-ALLY...
WAHH! I CAN HARDLY EVEN TALK.
...I KIND OF HAVE...
...A...
... HIDDEN AGENDA ...
WHAT I MEAN IS...

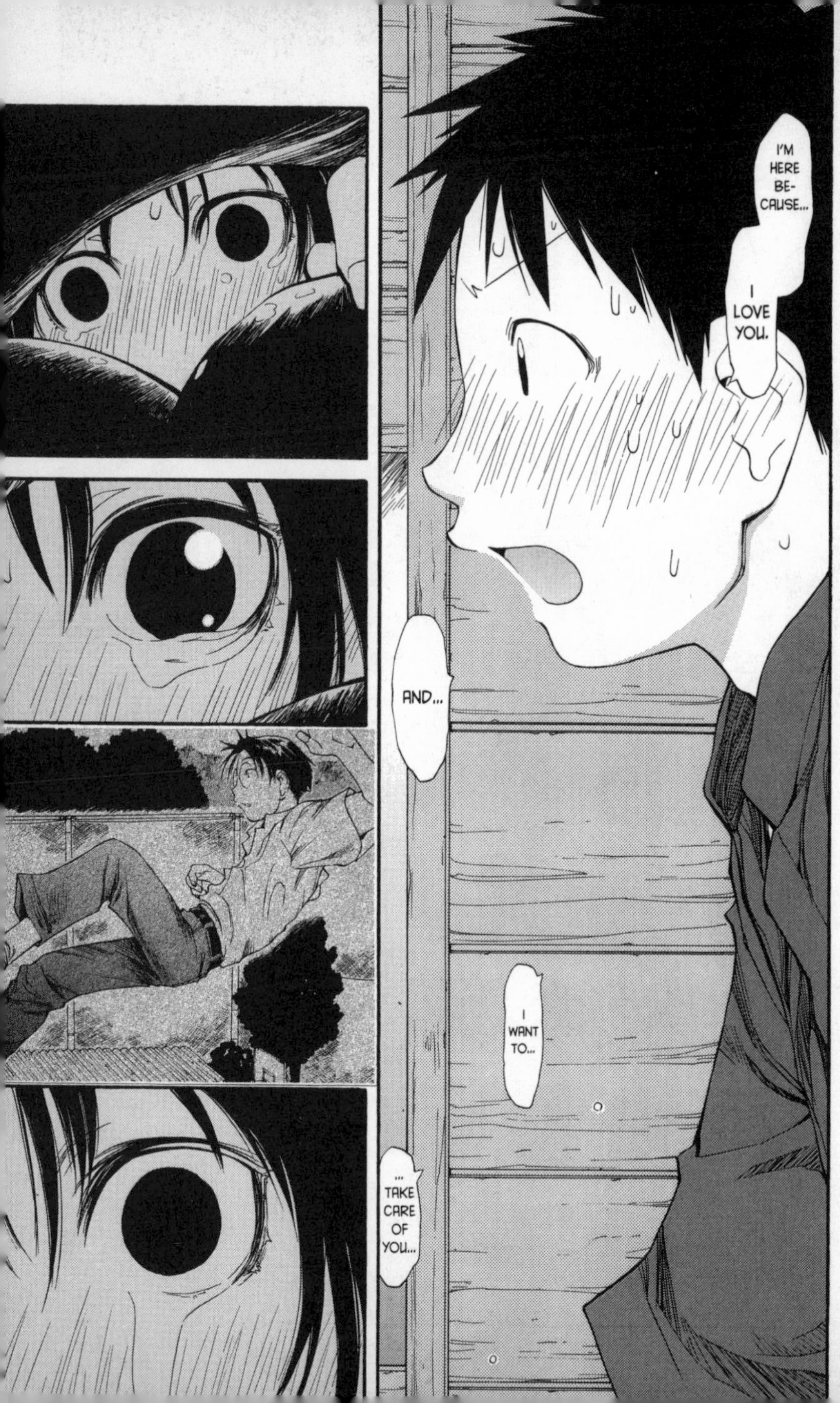
I'M HERE BE-CAUSE...
I LOVE YOU.
AND...
I WANT TO...
...TAKE CARE OF YOU...

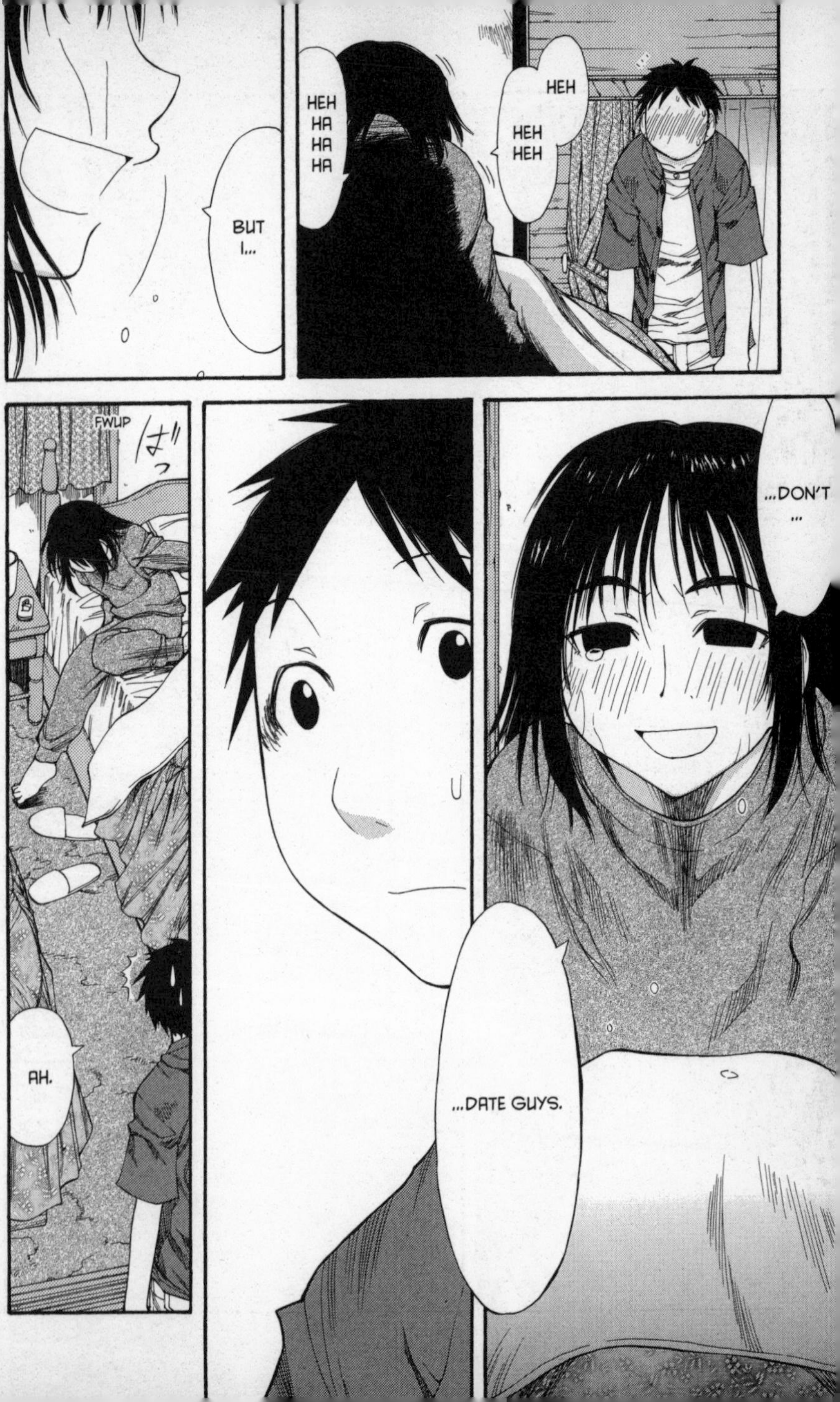
HEH
HEH HEH
HEH HA HA HA
BUT I...
...DON'T ...
...DATE GUYS.
FWUP
ばっ
AH.

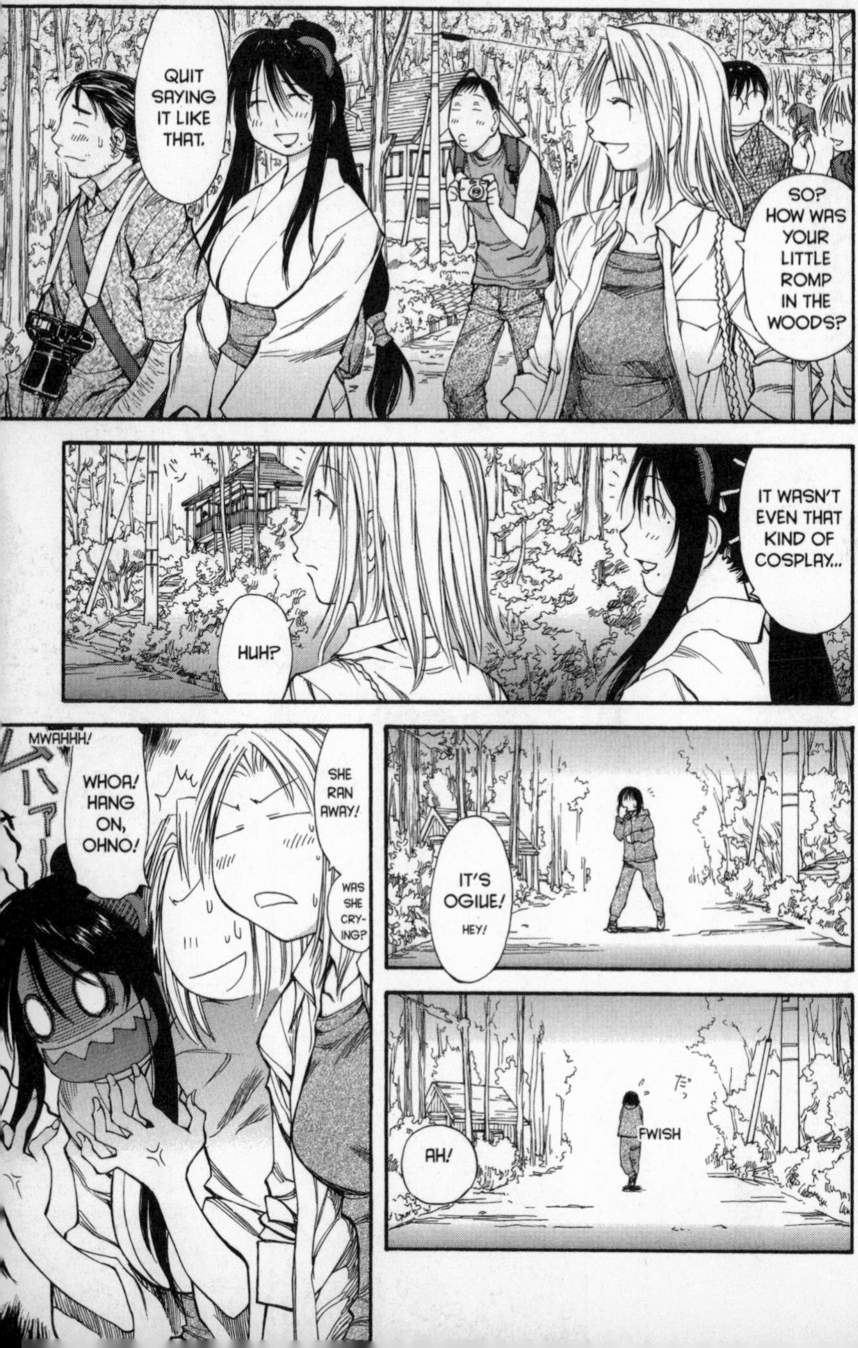
SO? HOW WAS YOUR LITTLE ROMP IN THE WOODS?
QUIT SAYING IT LIKE THAT.
IT WASN'T EVEN THAT KIND OF COSPLAY...
HUH?
IT'S OGIUE!
HEY!
AH!
FWISH
SHE RAN AWAY!
WAS SHE CRY-ING?
WHOA! HANG ON, OHNO!
MWAHHH!

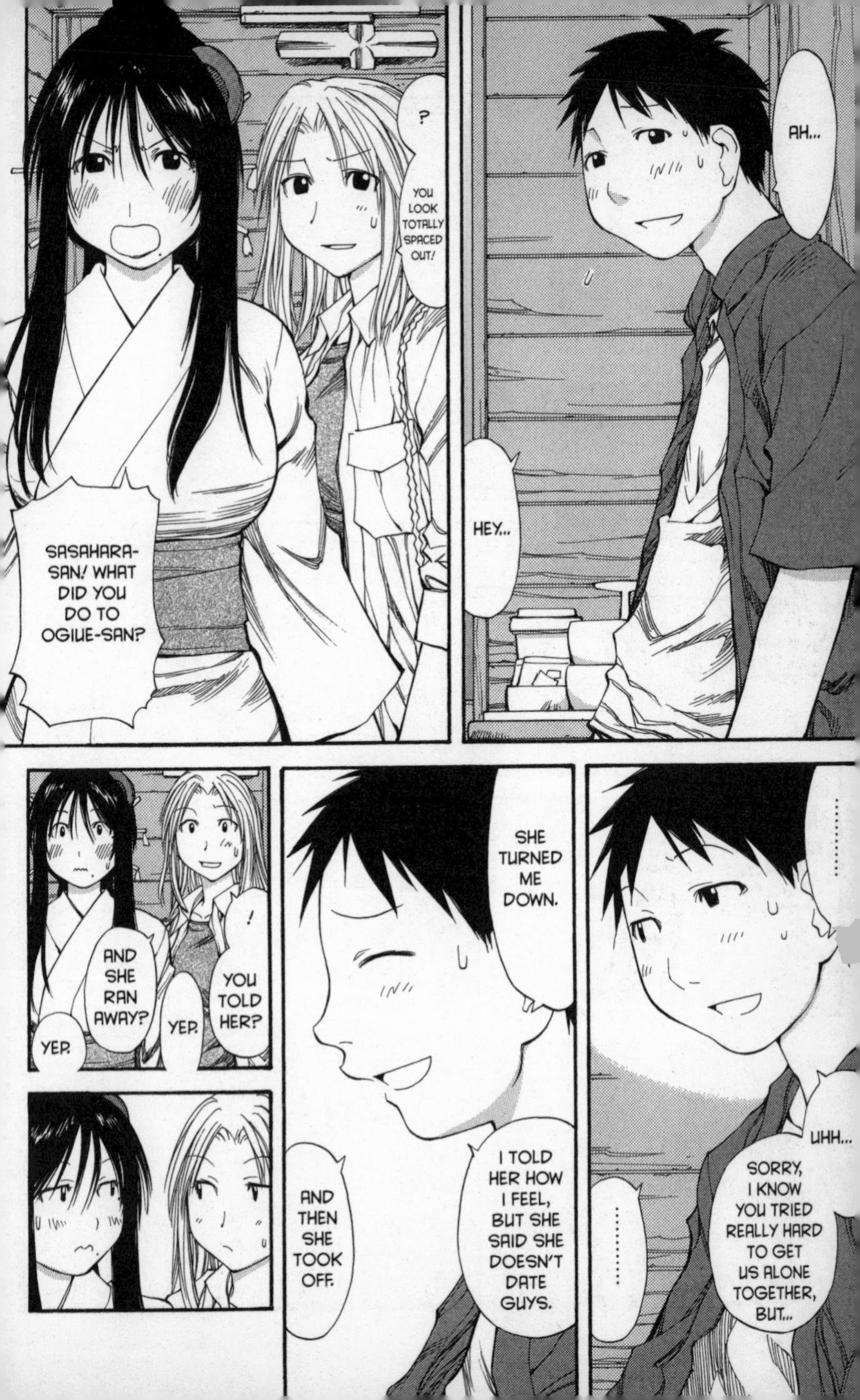
AH...
HEY...
?
YOU LOOK TOTALLY SPACED OUT!
SASAHARA-SAN! WHAT DID YOU DO TO OGIUE-SAN?
......
UHH...
SORRY, I KNOW YOU TRIED REALLY HARD TO GET US ALONE TOGETHER, BUT...
......
SHE TURNED ME DOWN.
I TOLD HER HOW I FEEL, BUT SHE SAID SHE DOESN'T DATE GUYS.
AND THEN SHE TOOK OFF.
!
YOU TOLD HER?
YEP.
AND SHE RAN AWAY?
YEP.

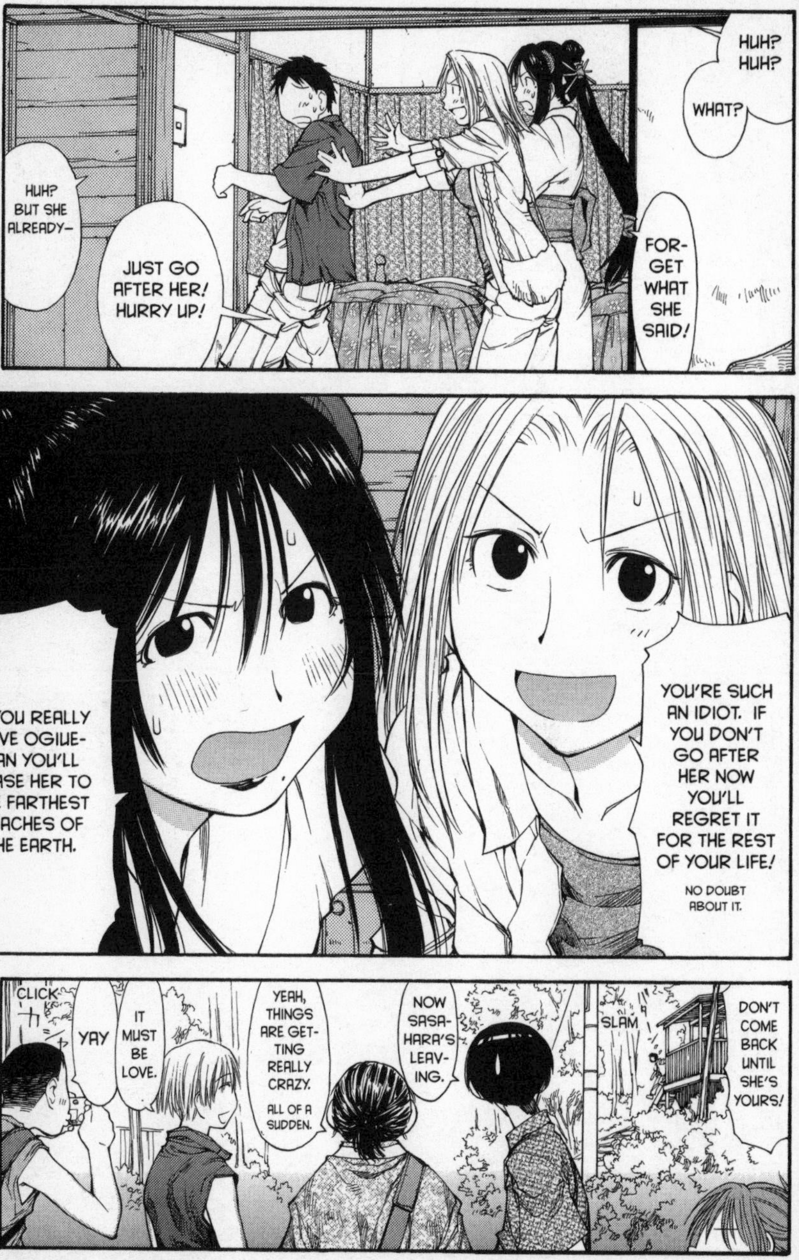
HUH? HUH?
WHAT?
FOR-GET WHAT SHE SAID!
JUST GO AFTER HER! HURRY UP!
HUH? BUT SHE ALREADY—
YOU'RE SUCH AN IDIOT. IF YOU DON'T GO AFTER HER NOW YOU'LL REGRET IT FOR THE REST OF YOUR LIFE!
NO DOUBT ABOUT IT.
IF YOU REALLY LOVE OGIUE-SAN YOU'LL CHASE HER TO THE FARTHEST REACHES OF THE EARTH.
DON'T COME BACK UNTIL SHE'S YOURS!
SLAM
NOW SASA-HARA'S LEAV-ING.
YEAH, THINGS ARE GET-TING REALLY CRAZY.
ALL OF A SUDDEN.
IT MUST BE LOVE.
YAY
CLICK

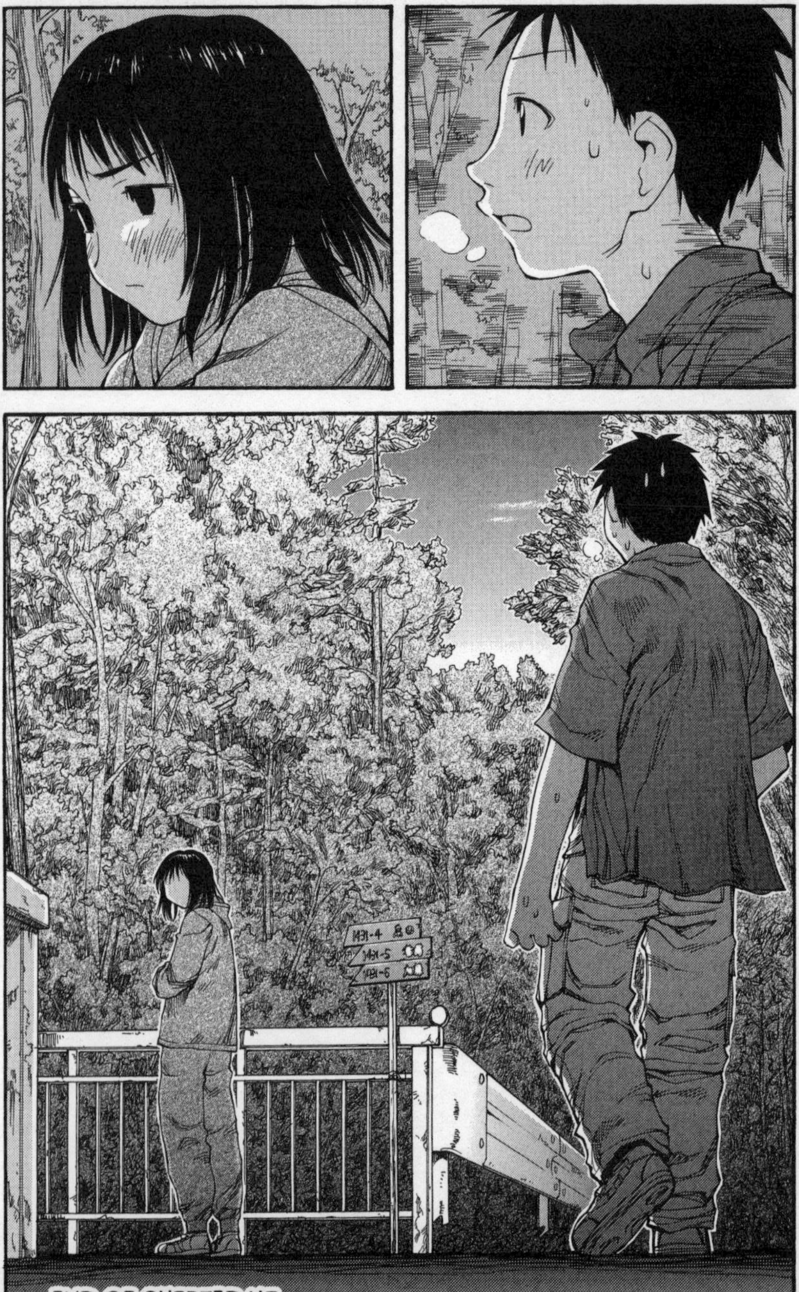
END OF CHAPTER 45

PV- IT'S THE PRESIDENT AND RISA.

BEN- YUP.

PV- SHE'S GOT BRAIDED HAIR.

BEN- SHE SURE DOES. WELL, THIS TIME THEY KNEW IT WOULD END UP AS ANIME WHEN THEY DESIGNED THE CHARACTERS.

PV- YEAH, HER WAVY HAIR FROM LAST SEASON MUST'VE BEEN A PAIN FOR THE ANIMATORS.

BEN- EXACTLY. AND NOW YOU KNOW THERE'S GONNA BE A SCENE WHERE SHE LETS HER BRAIDS LOOSE.

PV- YEAH, PROBABLY. BUT THEY'LL MAKE US WAIT. THEY'LL PROBABLY DO IT IN THE PENULTIMATE EPISODE.

BEN- DEFINITELY!

PV- OKAY, SETTLE DOWN. WHAT ABOUT THE SKETCH OF HER WITH CIRCULAR BRAIDS? THAT'S INTERESTING.

BEN- THAT WOULD LOOK COOL IN A 3D MODEL, BUT IT LOOKS LIKE THEY DECIDED ON THE OTHER STYLE.

PV- I DON'T KNOW ABOUT THAT OTAKU GLOVE.

BEN- YEAH, IT LOOKS LIKE THEY DIDN'T END UP USING THAT. THIS ROUGH SKETCH COMPILATION IS REALLY JUST THAT, A BUNCH OF SKETCHES THEY USED FOR BRAINSTORMING IDEAS. THERE'S NOT MUCH THAT THEY ACTUALLY ENDED UP USING.

PV- HOW CONFUSING. SO EVEN IF WE SEE IT HERE, IT MIGHT NOT ACTUALLY BE IN THE ANIME?

BEN- EXACTLY. FOR AN EXACT DESCRIPTION OF THE CHARACTER, YOU SHOULD REFER TO THE CHAR-ACTER DESIGN PROFILES.

PV- HMM...IT ALSO SEEMS LIKE HER PERSONALITY HAS REALLY CHANGED.

BEN- YEAH, BUT I THINK THE FOUNDATION OF HER CHARACTER IS PRETTY MUCH THE SAME. HOW-EVER, HER ATTITUDE IS COMPLETELY DIFFERENT. BEFORE, SHE WAS VERY POLITE AND FRAGILE, BUT NOW SHE SEEMS KIND OF ARROGANT AND OVERCONFIDENT.

PV- LIKE WHEN SHE SAYS, "MOVE IT!"

BEN- YEAH, NOT THAT IT'S WEIRD FOR HER TO SAY THAT OR ANYTHING. ...BUT IT JUST SEEMS LIKE SHE'S GOING BACK TO HER PAST. IN THE LAST SEASON, THEY HAD SO MANY OF THOSE COOL LITTLE "CHIHIRO-CHAN" SCENES, AND THEY KIND OF ENDED UP GOING IN THAT DIRECTION. SHE BECAME SORT OF A WEAK, DEPENDENT CHAR-ACTER, BUT IF YOU READ THE ORIGINAL MANGA, SHE'S PRETTY TOUGH.

PV- TRUE.

BEN- HOW ABOUT RISA? WHAT DO YOU THINK OF AN OLDER CHARACTER HAVING PIGTAILS LIKE THAT?

PV- BUT DON'T ALL TSUNDERE CHARACTERS HAVE PIGTAILS?

BEN- NOT ALL OF THEM. BUT ANYWAY, I ACTUALLY KIND OF LIKE THIS CHARACTER.

PV- YEAH, ...BUT HER BOOBS ARE A LITTLE...

BEN- DID YOU SAY SOMETHING?

PV- NEVER MIND.

THE BENEFITS OF TRAVEL.

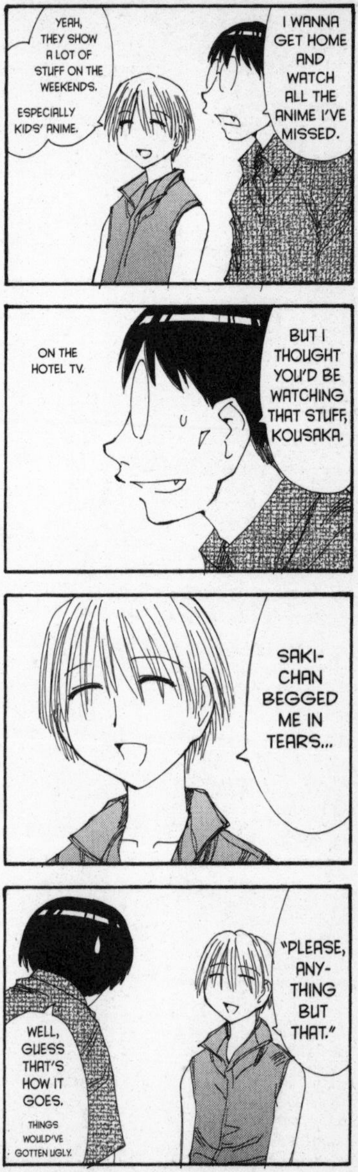
I WANNA GET HOME AND WATCH ALL THE ANIME I'VE MISSED.
YEAH, THEY SHOW A LOT OF STUFF ON THE WEEKENDS.
ESPECIALLY KIDS' ANIME.
BUT I THOUGHT YOU'D BE WATCHING THAT STUFF, KOUSAKA.
ON THE HOTEL TV.
SAKI-CHAN BEGGED ME IN TEARS...
"PLEASE, ANYTHING BUT THAT."
WELL, GUESS THAT'S HOW IT GOES.
THINGS WOULD'VE GOTTEN UGLY.

THIS TRIP'S MOST MEMORABLE MOMENT.

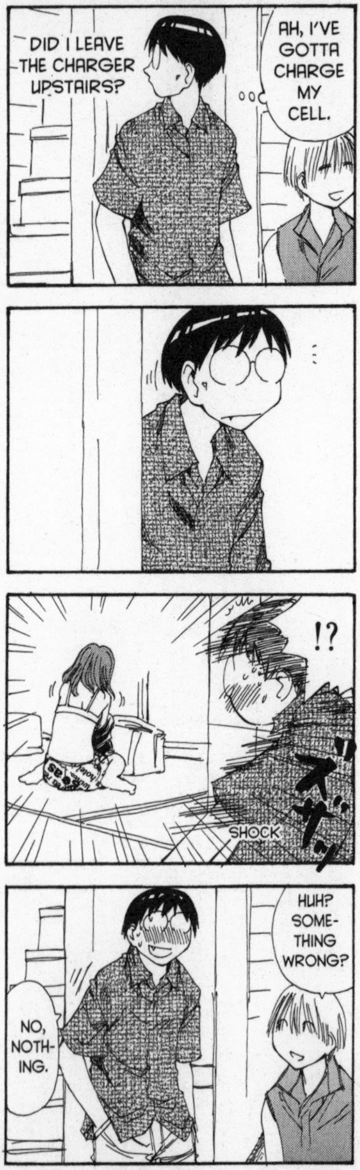
AH, I'VE GOTTA CHARGE MY CELL.
DID I LEAVE THE CHARGER UPSTAIRS?
!?
SHOCK
HUH? SOMETHING WRONG?
NO, NOTHING.

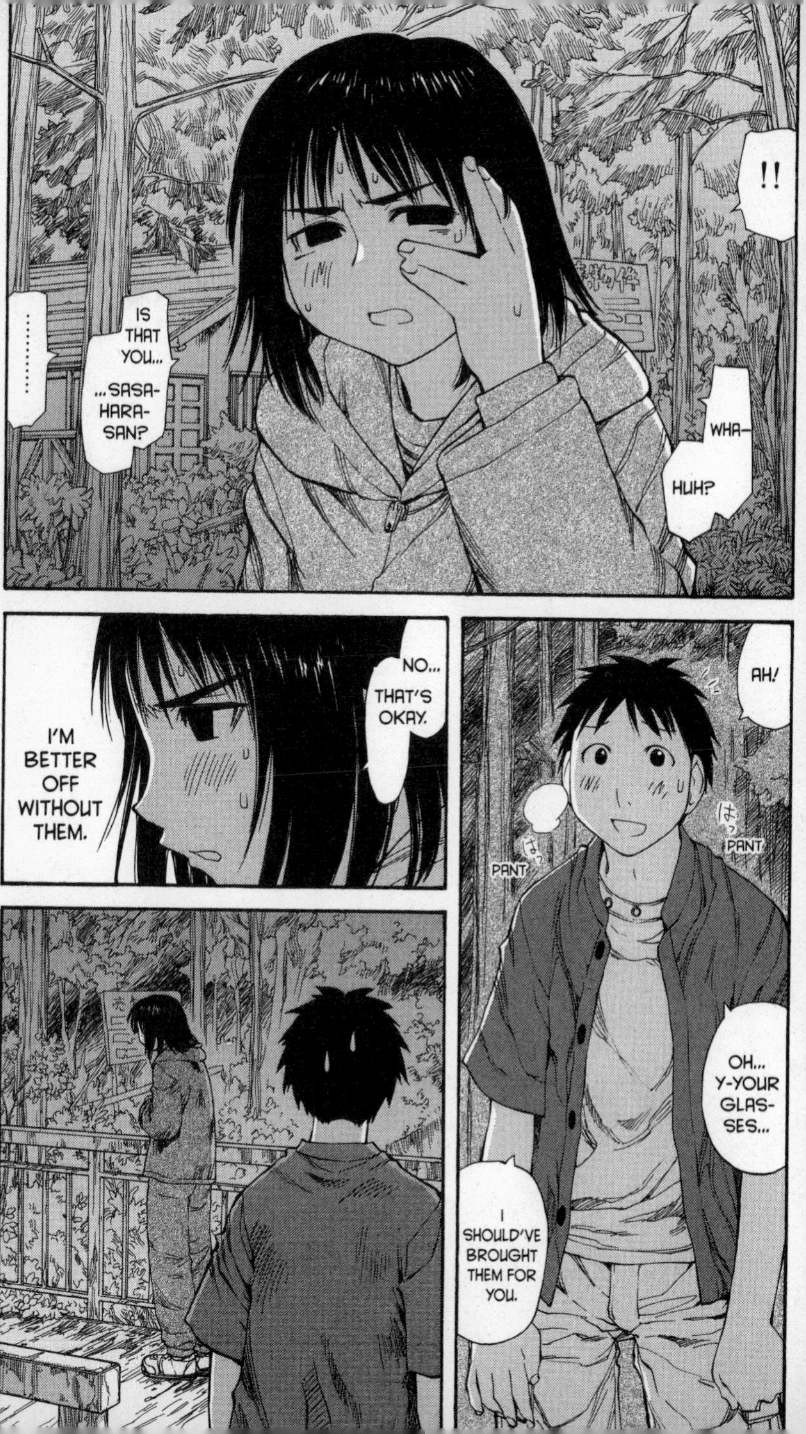
!!
IS THAT YOU... ...SASA-HARA-SAN?
WHA-
HUH?
......
AH!
はっ PANT
はっ PANT
OH... Y-YOUR GLAS-SES...
I SHOULD'VE BROUGHT THEM FOR YOU.
NO... THAT'S OKAY.
I'M BETTER OFF WITHOUT THEM.

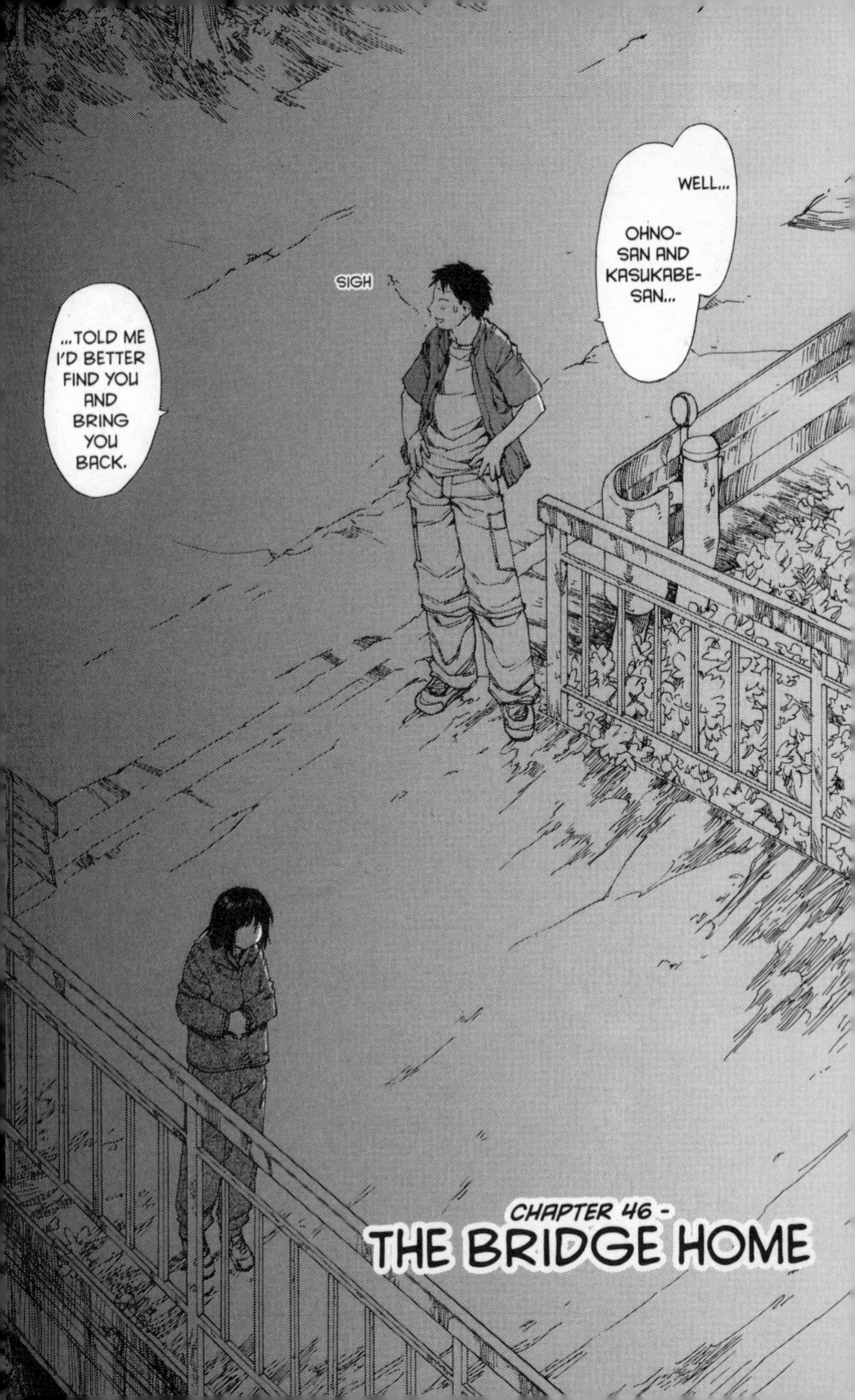
WELL...
OHNO-SAN AND KASUKABE-SAN...
SIGH
...TOLD ME I'D BETTER FIND YOU AND BRING YOU BACK.
CHAPTER 46 -
THE BRIDGE HOME

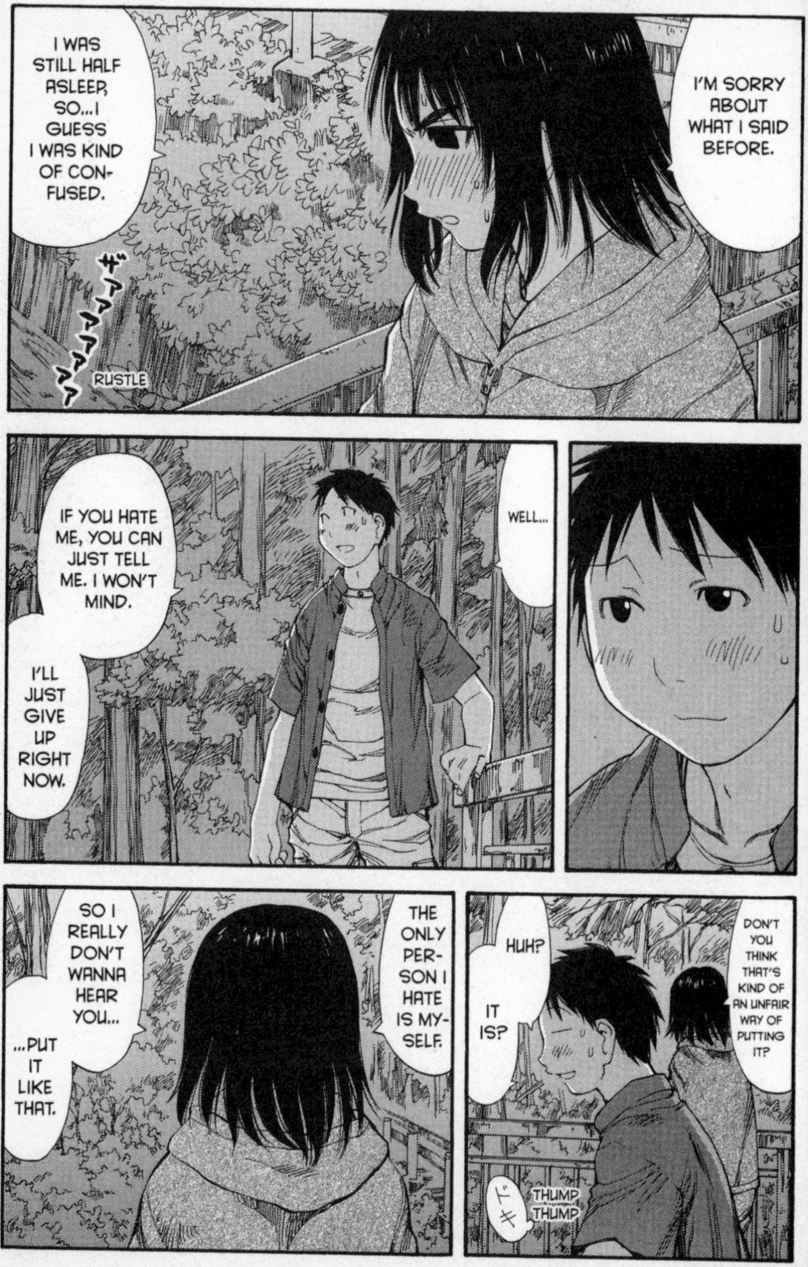

I'M SORRY ABOUT WHAT I SAID BEFORE.
I WAS STILL HALF ASLEEP, SO...I GUESS I WAS KIND OF CON-FUSED.
ザァァァァァァ
RUSTLE
WELL...
IF YOU HATE ME, YOU CAN JUST TELL ME. I WON'T MIND.
I'LL JUST GIVE UP RIGHT NOW.
DON'T YOU THINK THAT'S KIND OF AN UNFAIR WAY OF PUTTING IT?
HUH?
IT IS?
ドキ
THUMP THUMP
THE ONLY PERSON I HATE IS MY-SELF.
SO I REALLY DON'T WANNA HEAR YOU...
...PUT IT LIKE THAT.

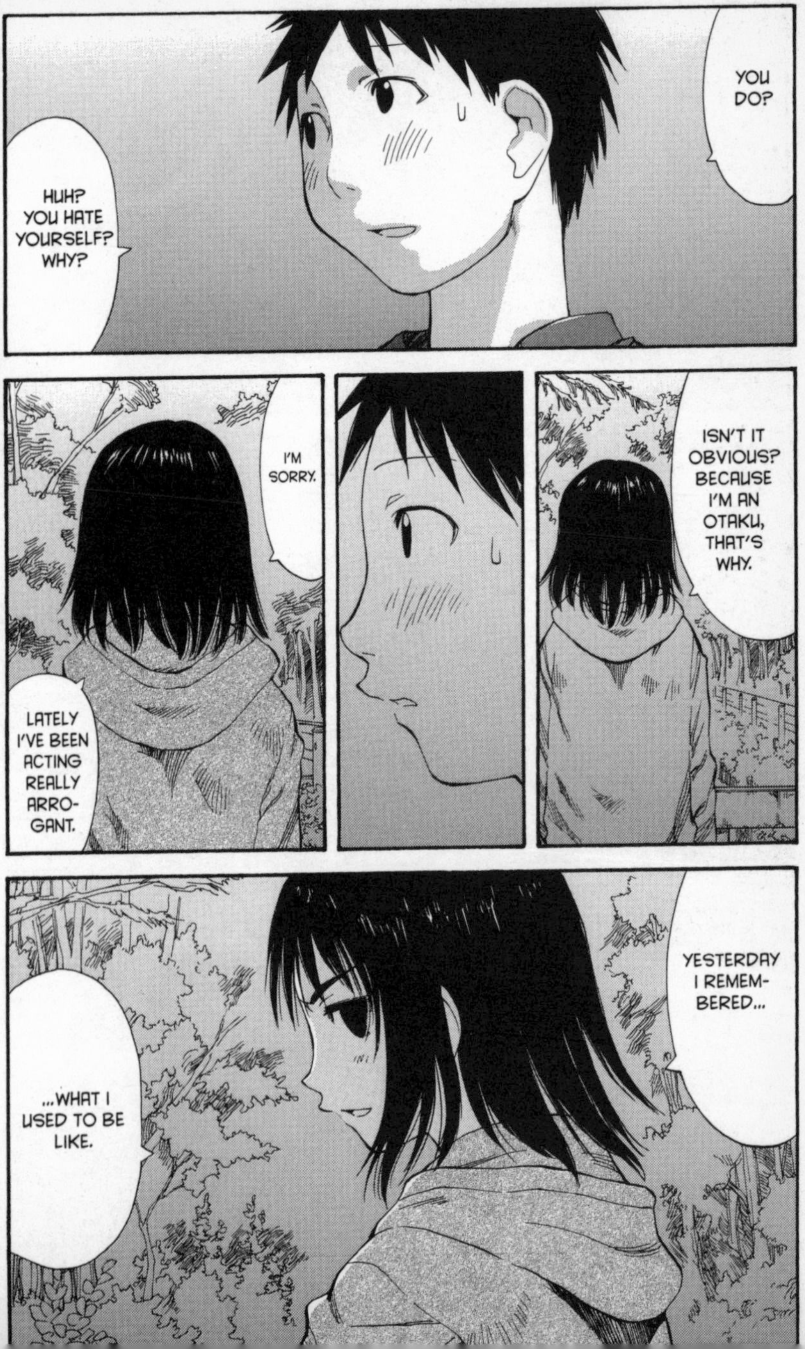
YOU DO?
HUH? YOU HATE YOURSELF? WHY?
ISN'T IT OBVIOUS? BECAUSE I'M AN OTAKU, THAT'S WHY.
I'M SORRY.
LATELY I'VE BEEN ACTING REALLY ARRO-GANT.
YESTERDAY I REMEM-BERED...
...WHAT I USED TO BE LIKE.

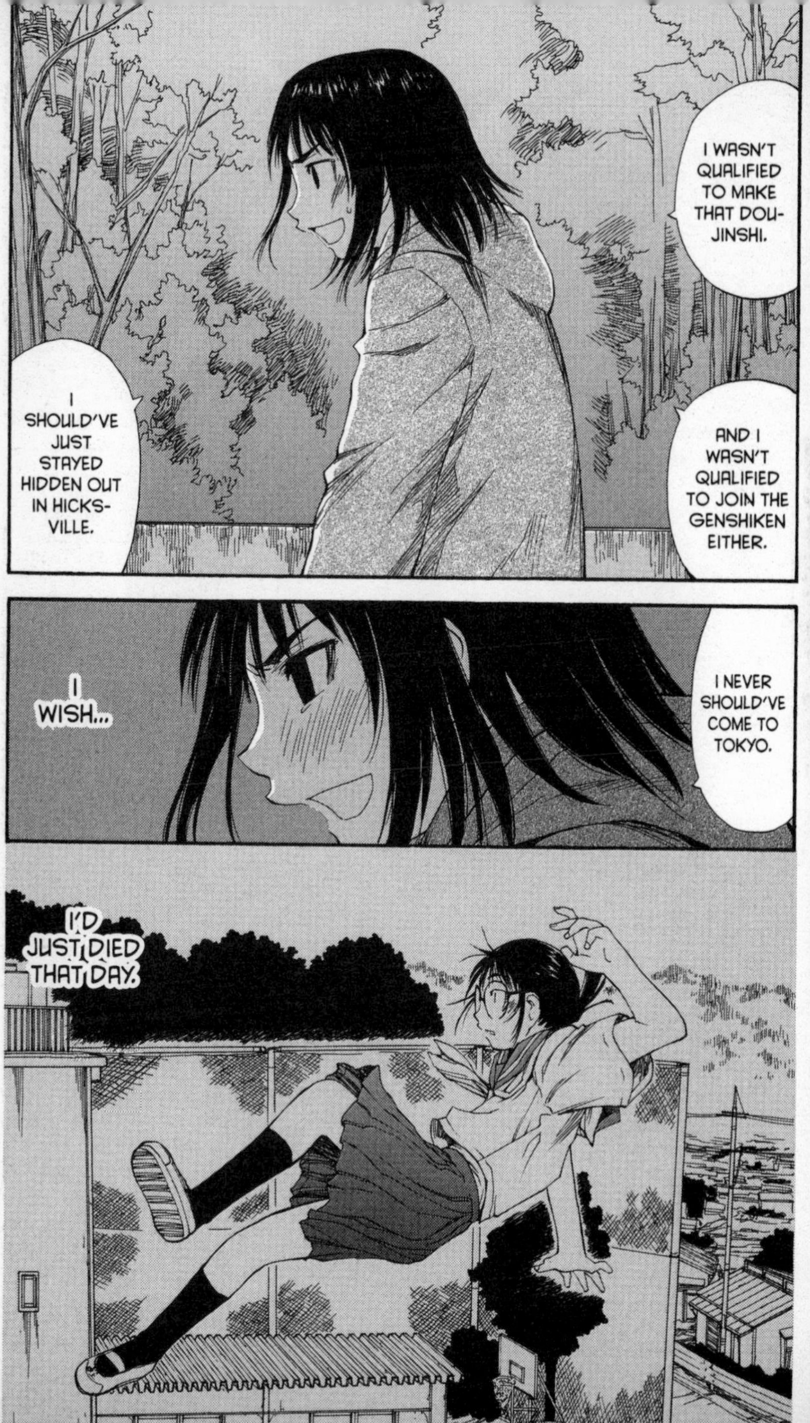
I WASN'T QUALIFIED TO MAKE THAT DOUJINSHI.
AND I WASN'T QUALIFIED TO JOIN THE GENSHIKEN EITHER.
I SHOULD'VE JUST STAYED HIDDEN OUT IN HICKSVILLE.
I NEVER SHOULD'VE COME TO TOKYO.
I WISH...
I'D JUST DIED THAT DAY.

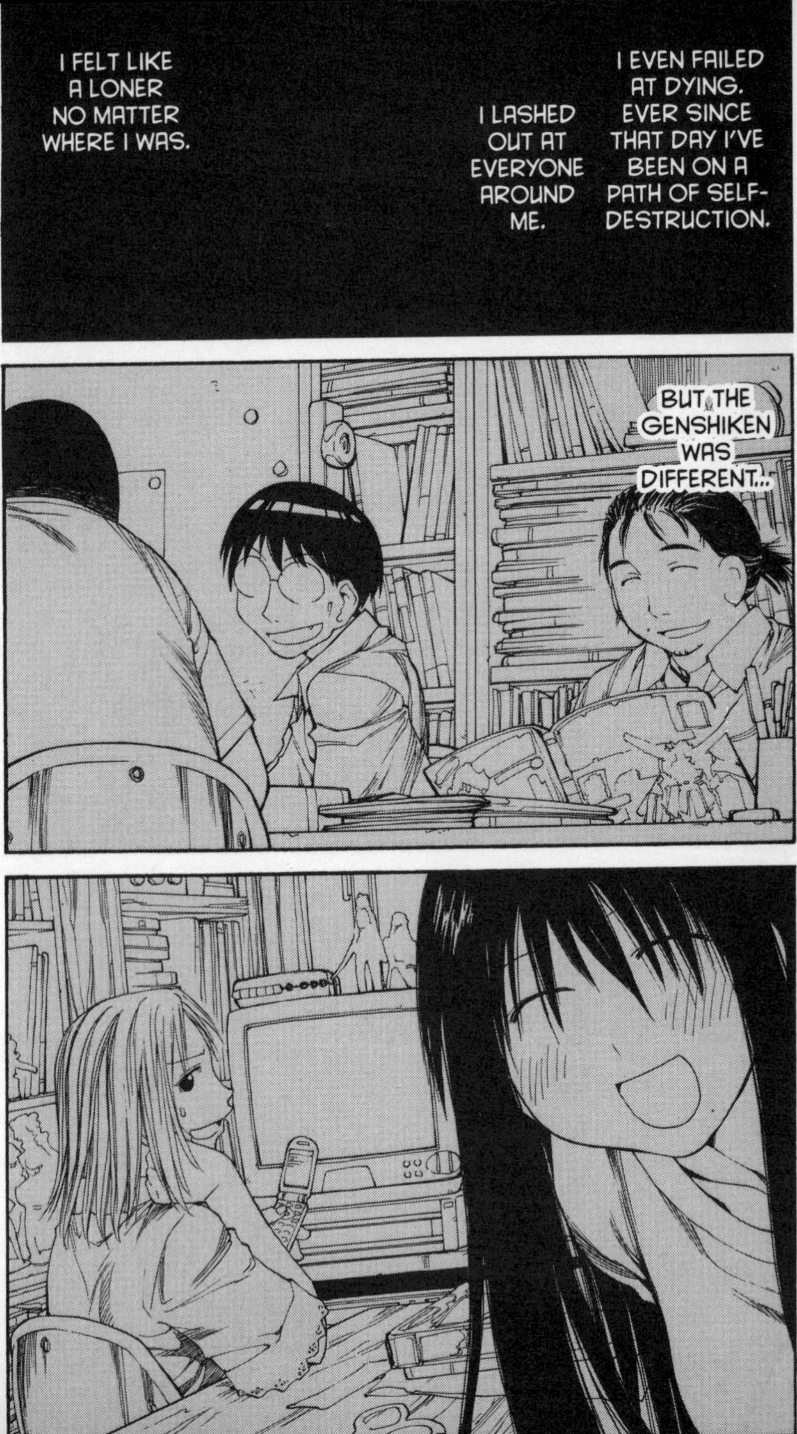
I EVEN FAILED AT DYING. EVER SINCE THAT DAY I'VE BEEN ON A PATH OF SELF-DESTRUCTION.
I LASHED OUT AT EVERYONE AROUND ME.
I FELT LIKE A LONER NO MATTER WHERE I WAS.
BUT THE GENSHIKEN WAS DIFFERENT...

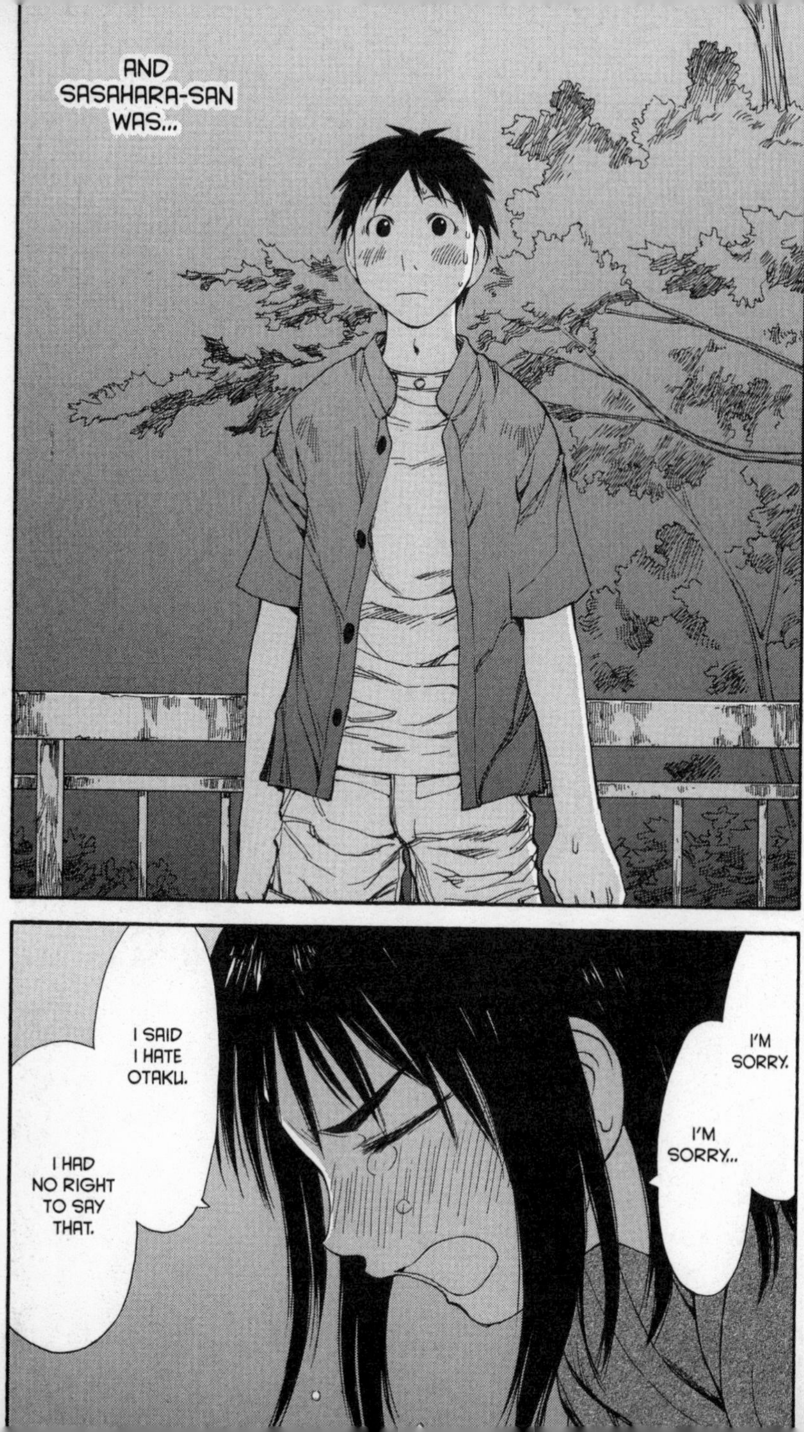
AND SASAHARA-SAN WAS...
I'M SORRY.
I'M SORRY...
I SAID I HATE OTAKU.
I HAD NO RIGHT TO SAY THAT.

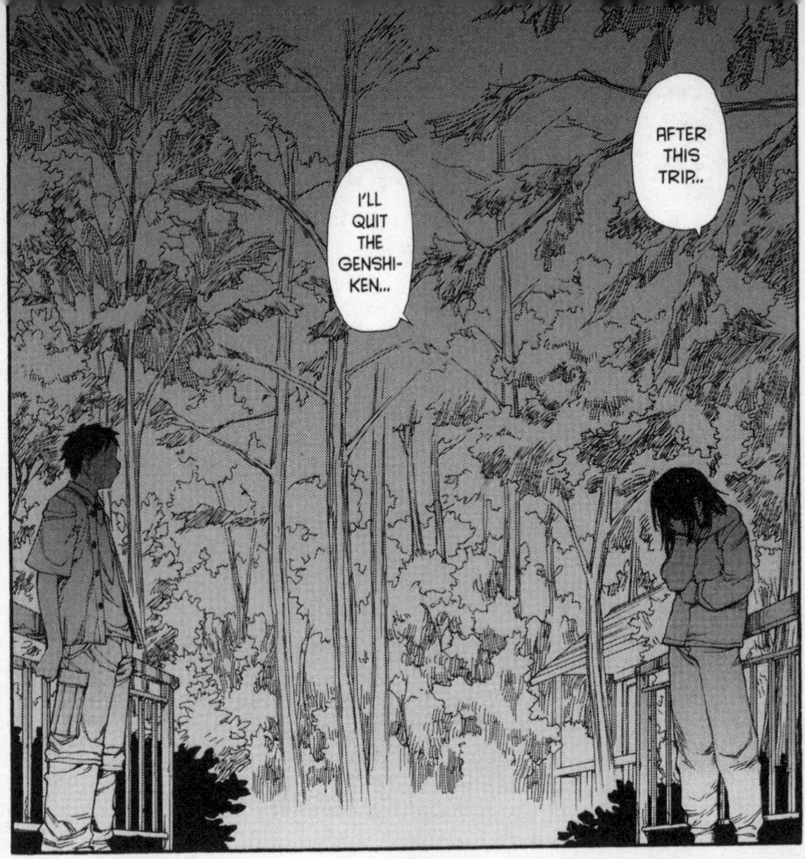
AFTER THIS TRIP...
I'LL QUIT THE GENSHIKEN...

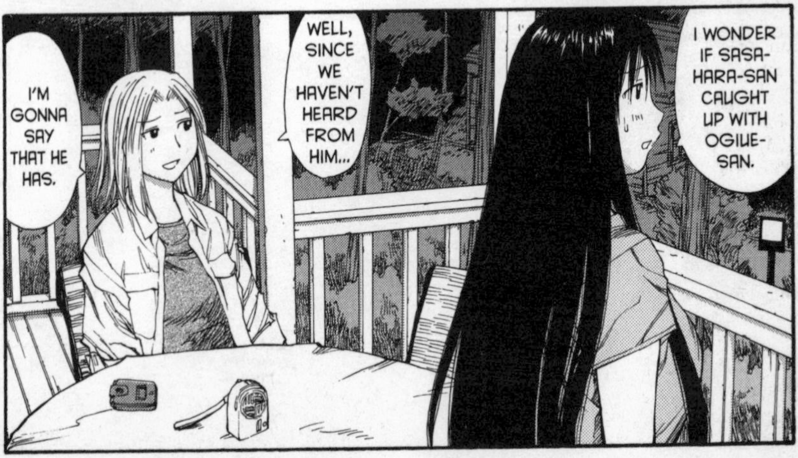
I WONDER IF SASA-HARA-SAN CAUGHT UP WITH OGIUE-SAN.
WELL, SINCE WE HAVEN'T HEARD FROM HIM...
I'M GONNA SAY THAT HE HAS.

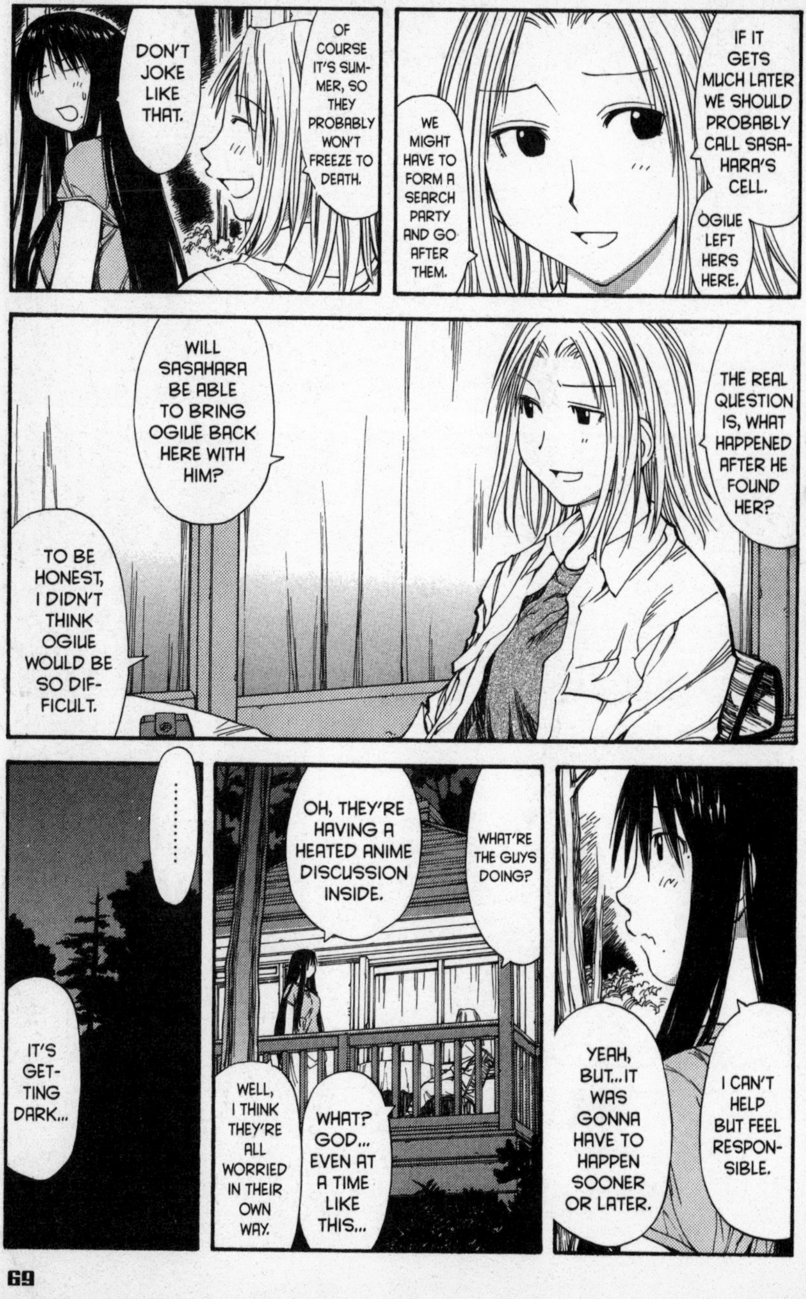
IF IT GETS MUCH LATER WE SHOULD PROBABLY CALL SASAHARA'S CELL.
OGIUE LEFT HERS HERE.
WE MIGHT HAVE TO FORM A SEARCH PARTY AND GO AFTER THEM.
OF COURSE IT'S SUMMER, SO THEY PROBABLY WON'T FREEZE TO DEATH.
DON'T JOKE LIKE THAT.
THE REAL QUESTION IS, WHAT HAPPENED AFTER HE FOUND HER?
WILL SASAHARA BE ABLE TO BRING OGIUE BACK HERE WITH HIM?
TO BE HONEST, I DIDN'T THINK OGIUE WOULD BE SO DIFFICULT.
I CAN'T HELP BUT FEEL RESPONSIBLE.
YEAH, BUT...IT WAS GONNA HAVE TO HAPPEN SOONER OR LATER.
WHAT'RE THE GUYS DOING?
OH, THEY'RE HAVING A HEATED ANIME DISCUSSION INSIDE.
WHAT? GOD... EVEN AT A TIME LIKE THIS...
WELL, I THINK THEY'RE ALL WORRIED IN THEIR OWN WAY.
....
IT'S GETTING DARK...

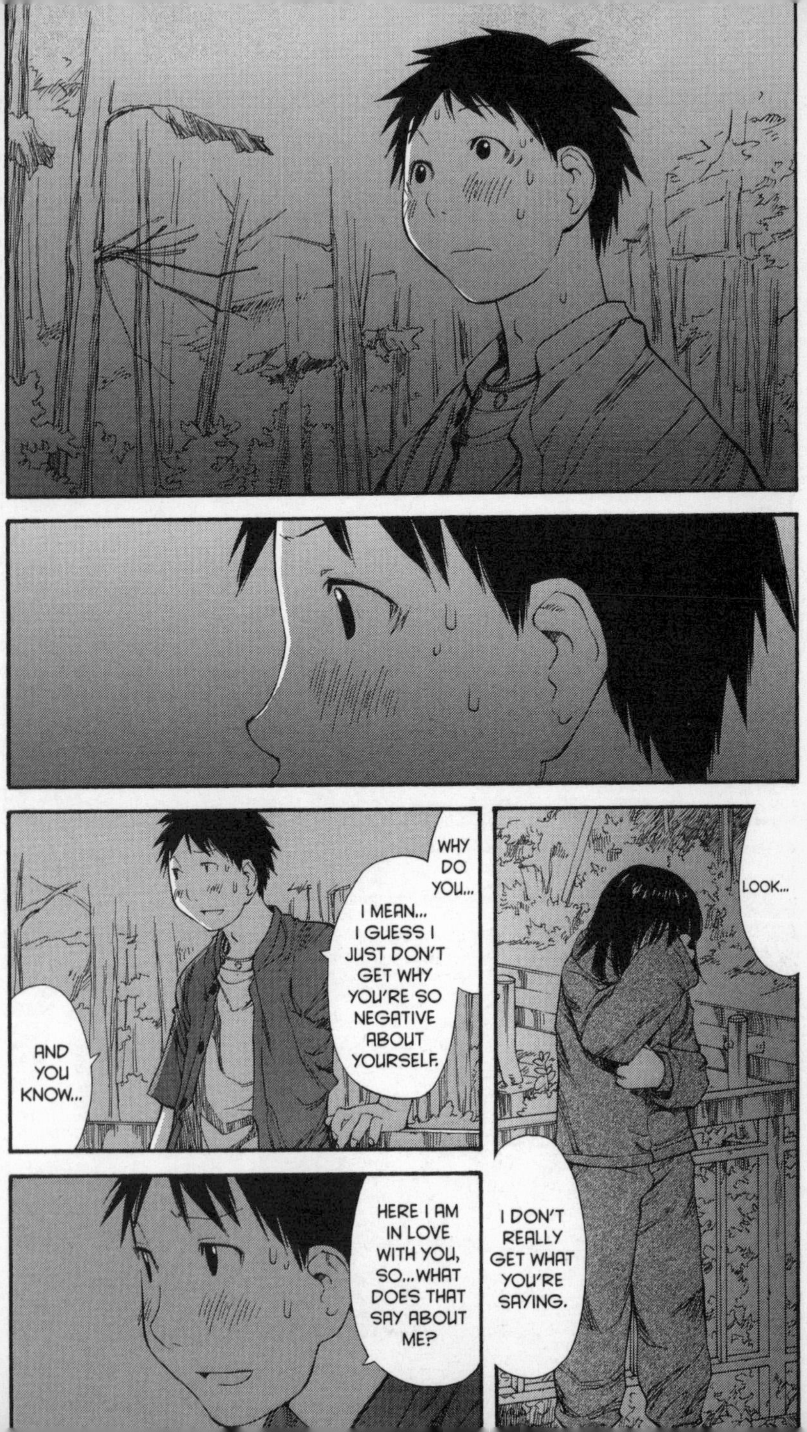
LOOK...
I DON'T REALLY GET WHAT YOU'RE SAYING.
WHY DO YOU...
I MEAN... I GUESS I JUST DON'T GET WHY YOU'RE SO NEGATIVE ABOUT YOURSELF.
AND YOU KNOW...
HERE I AM IN LOVE WITH YOU, SO...WHAT DOES THAT SAY ABOUT ME?

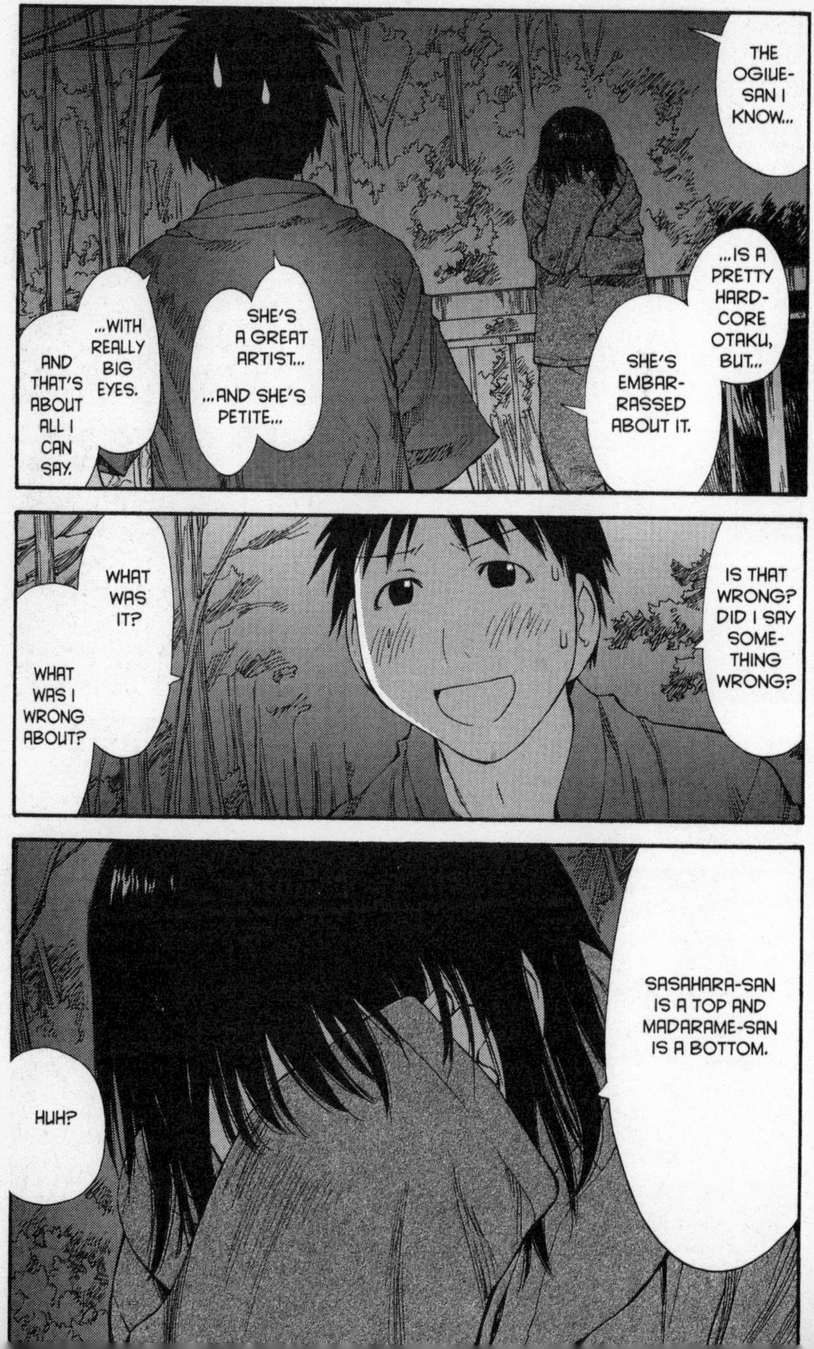
THE OGIUE-SAN I KNOW...
...IS A PRETTY HARD-CORE OTAKU, BUT...
SHE'S EMBARRASSED ABOUT IT.
SHE'S A GREAT ARTIST...
...AND SHE'S PETITE...
...WITH REALLY BIG EYES.
AND THAT'S ABOUT ALL I CAN SAY.
IS THAT WRONG? DID I SAY SOMETHING WRONG?
WHAT WAS IT?
WHAT WAS I WRONG ABOUT?
SASAHARA-SAN IS A TOP AND MADARAME-SAN IS A BOTTOM.
HUH?

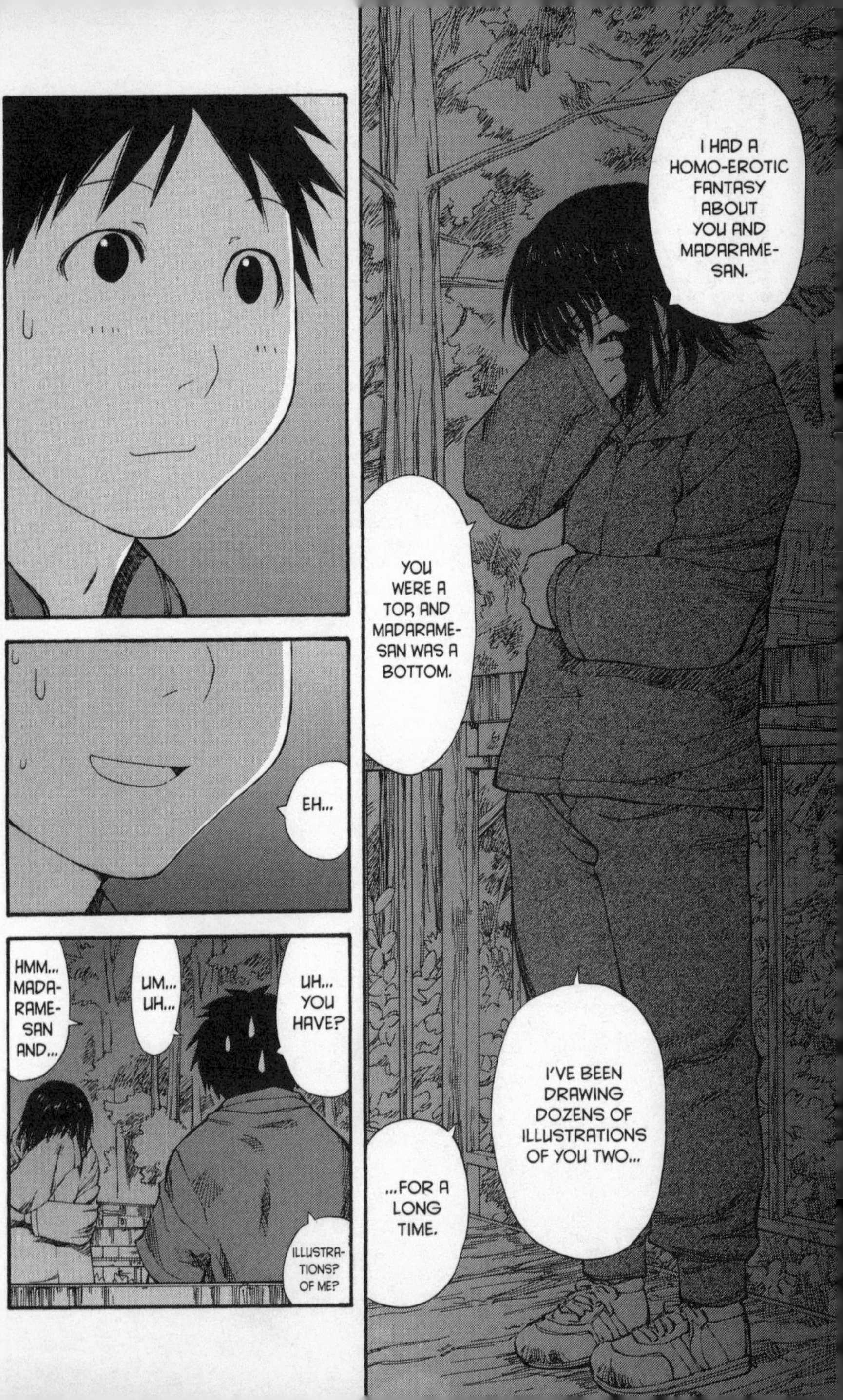
I HAD A HOMO-EROTIC FANTASY ABOUT YOU AND MADARAME-SAN.
YOU WERE A TOP, AND MADARAME-SAN WAS A BOTTOM.
I'VE BEEN DRAWING DOZENS OF ILLUSTRATIONS OF YOU TWO...
...FOR A LONG TIME.
EH...
UH... YOU HAVE?
UM... UH...
HMM... MADARAME-SAN AND...
ILLUSTRATIONS? OF ME?

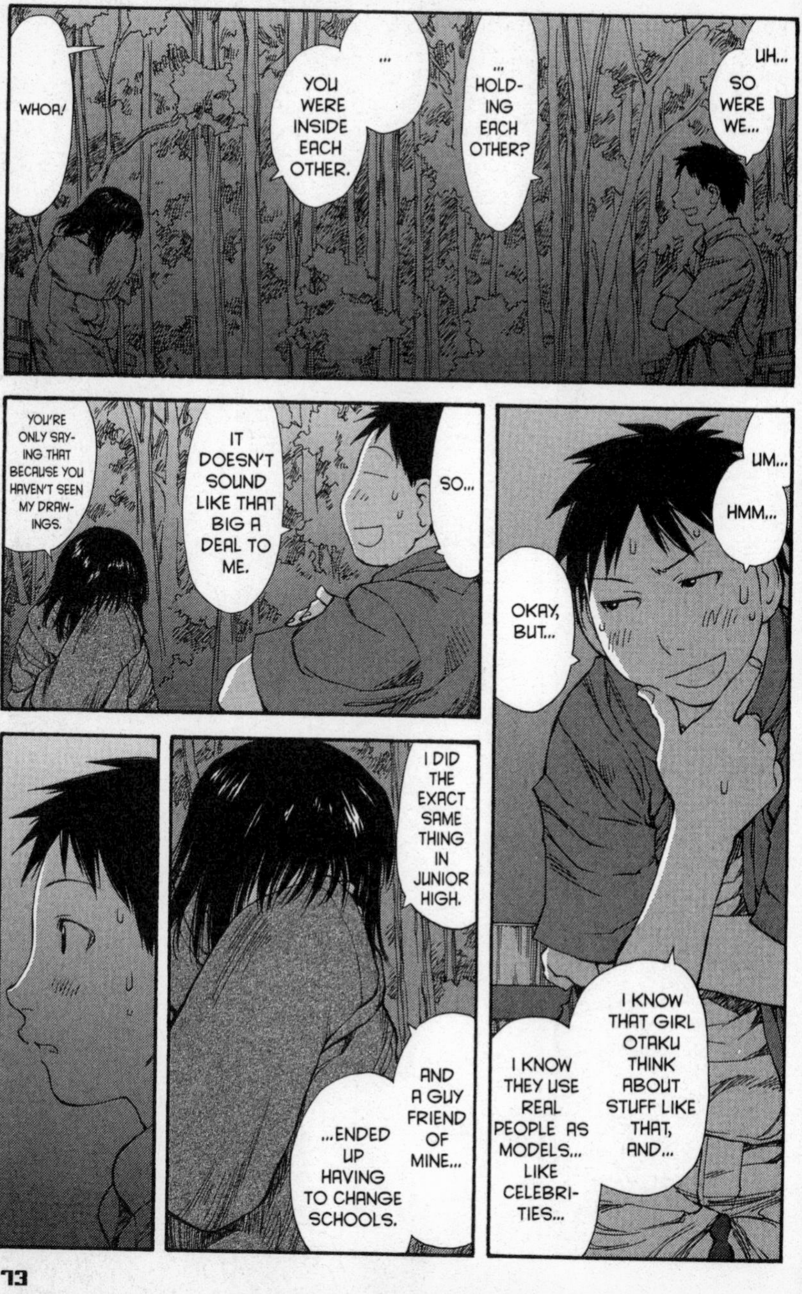
UH... SO WERE WE...
... HOLDING EACH OTHER?
... YOU WERE INSIDE EACH OTHER.
WHOA!
UM... HMM...
OKAY, BUT...
I KNOW THAT GIRL OTAKU THINK ABOUT STUFF LIKE THAT, AND...
I KNOW THEY USE REAL PEOPLE AS MODELS... LIKE CELEBRITIES...
SO...
IT DOESN'T SOUND LIKE THAT BIG A DEAL TO ME.
YOU'RE ONLY SAYING THAT BECAUSE YOU HAVEN'T SEEN MY DRAWINGS.
I DID THE EXACT SAME THING IN JUNIOR HIGH.
AND A GUY FRIEND OF MINE...
...ENDED UP HAVING TO CHANGE SCHOOLS.

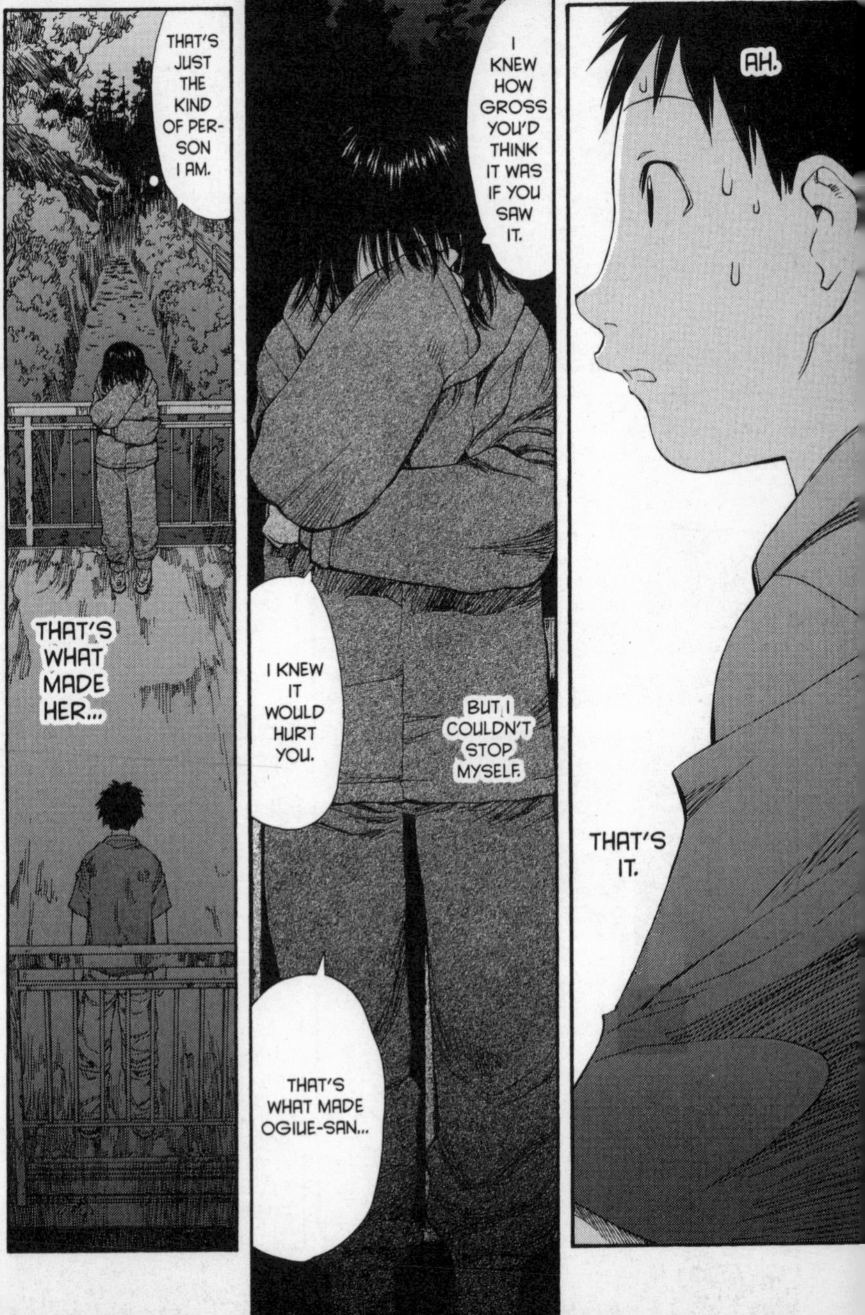
AH.
THAT'S IT.
I KNEW HOW GROSS YOU'D THINK IT WAS IF YOU SAW IT.
I KNEW IT WOULD HURT YOU.
BUT I COULDN'T STOP MYSELF.
THAT'S WHAT MADE OGIUE-SAN...
THAT'S JUST THE KIND OF PERSON I AM.
THAT'S WHAT MADE HER...

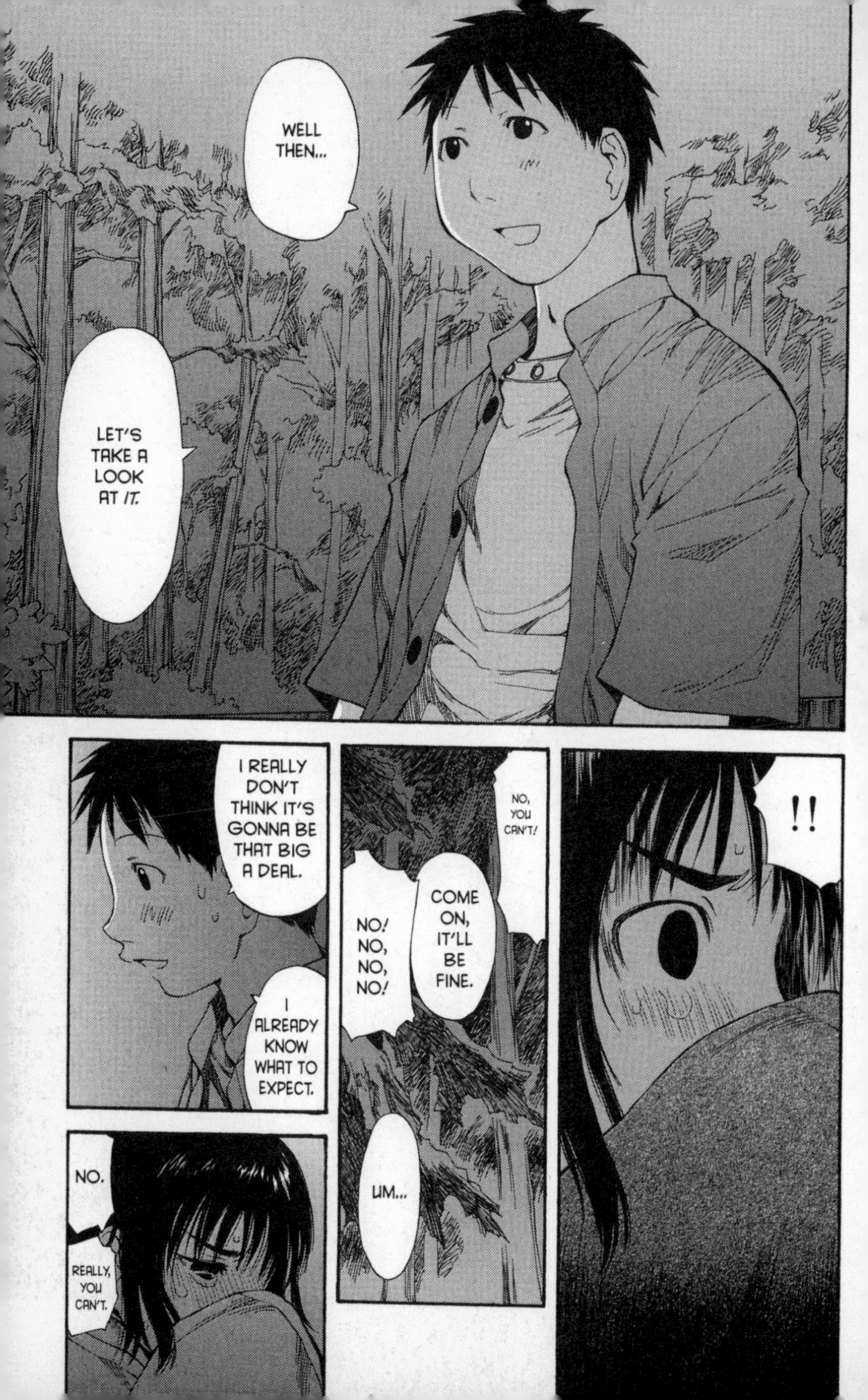
WELL THEN...
LET'S TAKE A LOOK AT *IT.*
!!
NO, YOU CAN'T!
COME ON, IT'LL BE FINE.
NO! NO, NO, NO!
UM...
I REALLY DON'T THINK IT'S GONNA BE THAT BIG A DEAL.
I ALREADY KNOW WHAT TO EXPECT.
NO.
REALLY, YOU CAN'T.

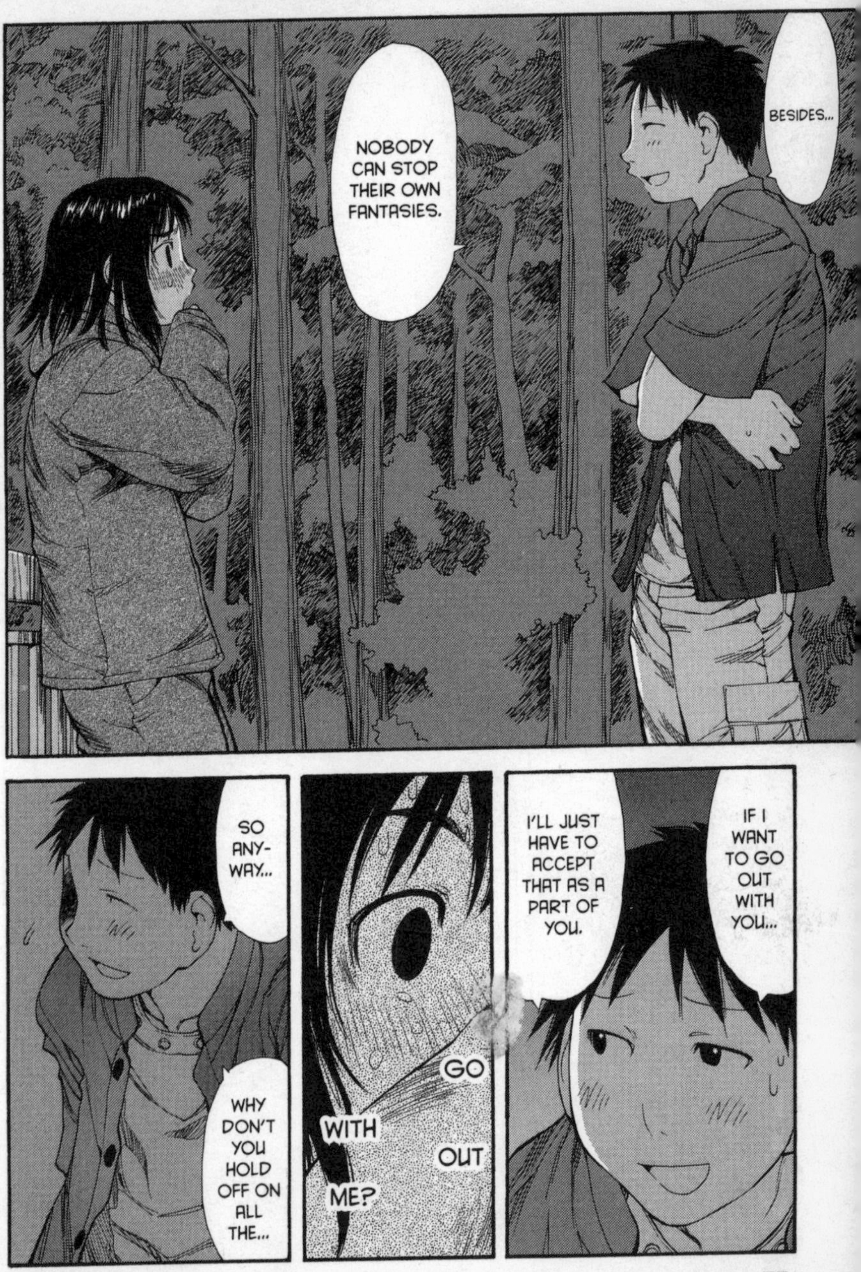
BESIDES...
NOBODY CAN STOP THEIR OWN FANTASIES.
IF I WANT TO GO OUT WITH YOU...
I'LL JUST HAVE TO ACCEPT THAT AS A PART OF YOU.
GO OUT WITH ME?
SO ANYWAY...
WHY DON'T YOU HOLD OFF ON ALL THE...

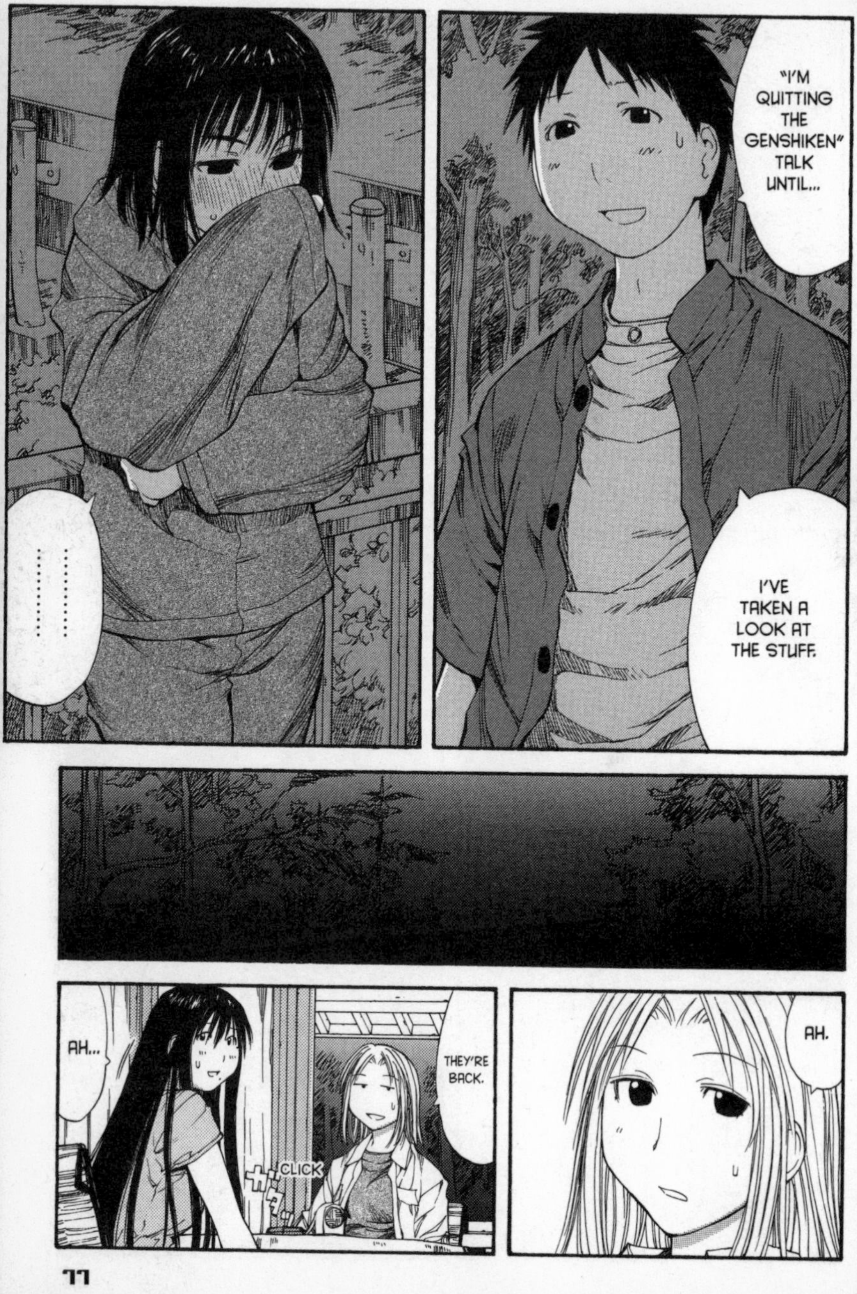
"I'M QUITTING THE GENSHIKEN" TALK UNTIL...
I'VE TAKEN A LOOK AT THE STUFF.
......
AH.
THEY'RE BACK.
AH...
CLICK

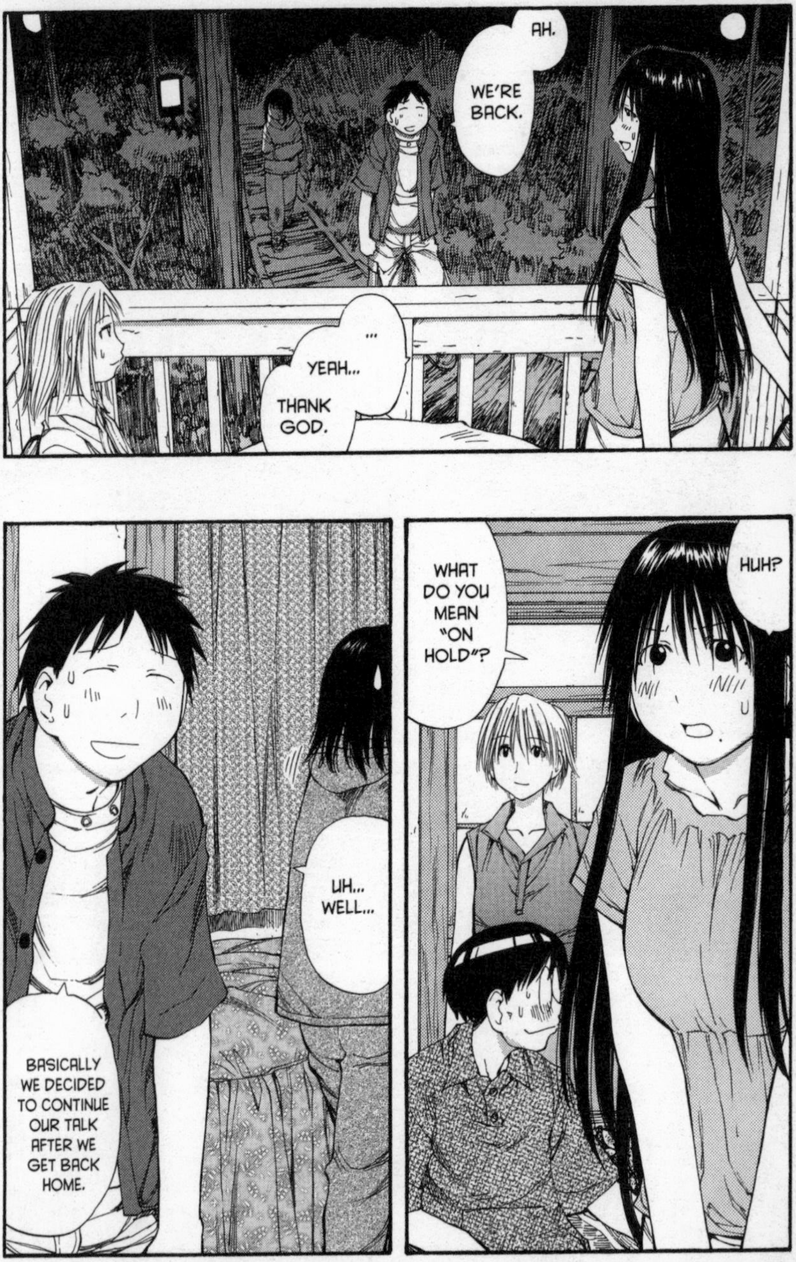
AH.
WE'RE BACK.
... YEAH... THANK GOD.
HUH?
WHAT DO YOU MEAN "ON HOLD"?
UH... WELL...
BASICALLY WE DECIDED TO CONTINUE OUR TALK AFTER WE GET BACK HOME.

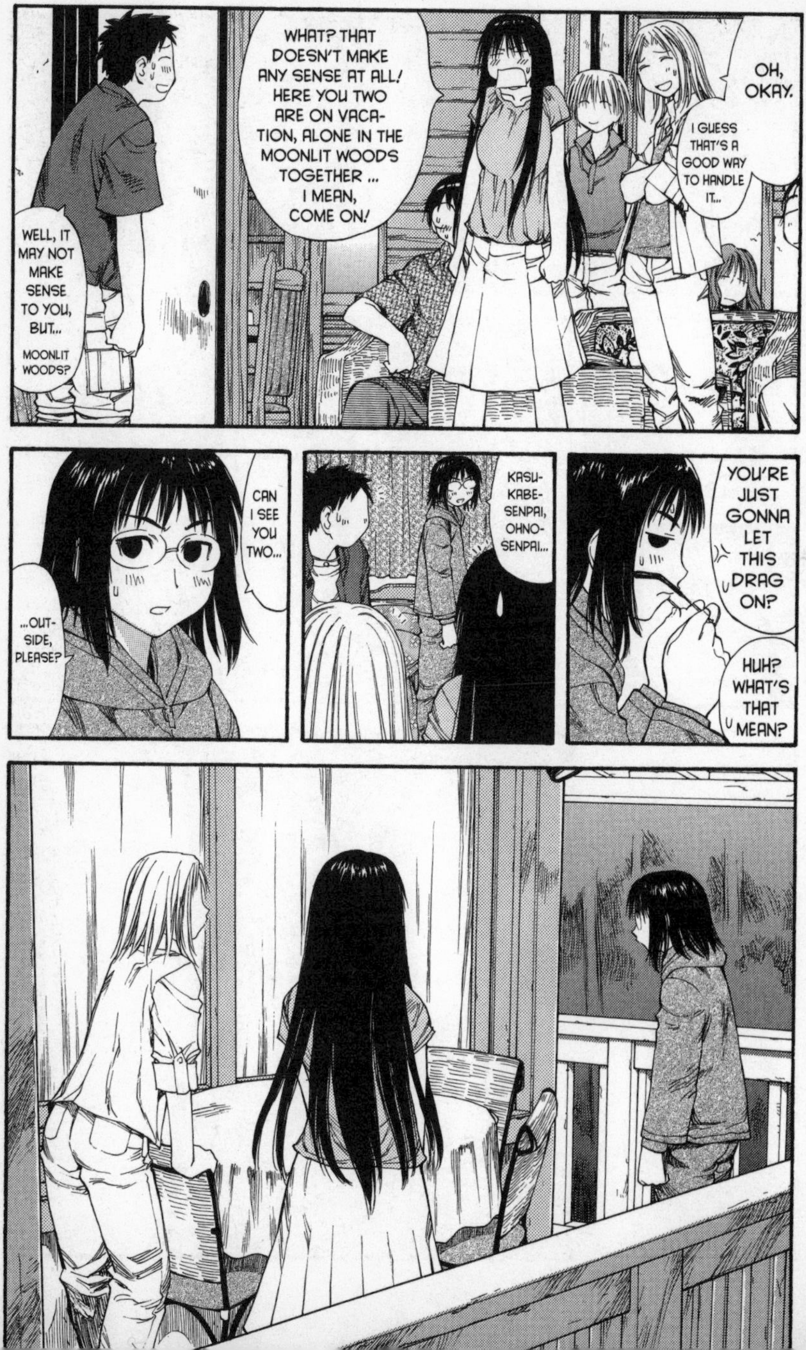
OH, OKAY.
I GUESS THAT'S A GOOD WAY TO HANDLE IT...
WHAT? THAT DOESN'T MAKE ANY SENSE AT ALL! HERE YOU TWO ARE ON VACATION, ALONE IN THE MOONLIT WOODS TOGETHER ... I MEAN, COME ON!
WELL, IT MAY NOT MAKE SENSE TO YOU, BUT...
MOONLIT WOODS?
YOU'RE JUST GONNA LET THIS DRAG ON?
HUH? WHAT'S THAT MEAN?
KASUKABE-SENPAI, OHNO-SENPAI...
CAN I SEE YOU TWO...
...OUTSIDE, PLEASE?

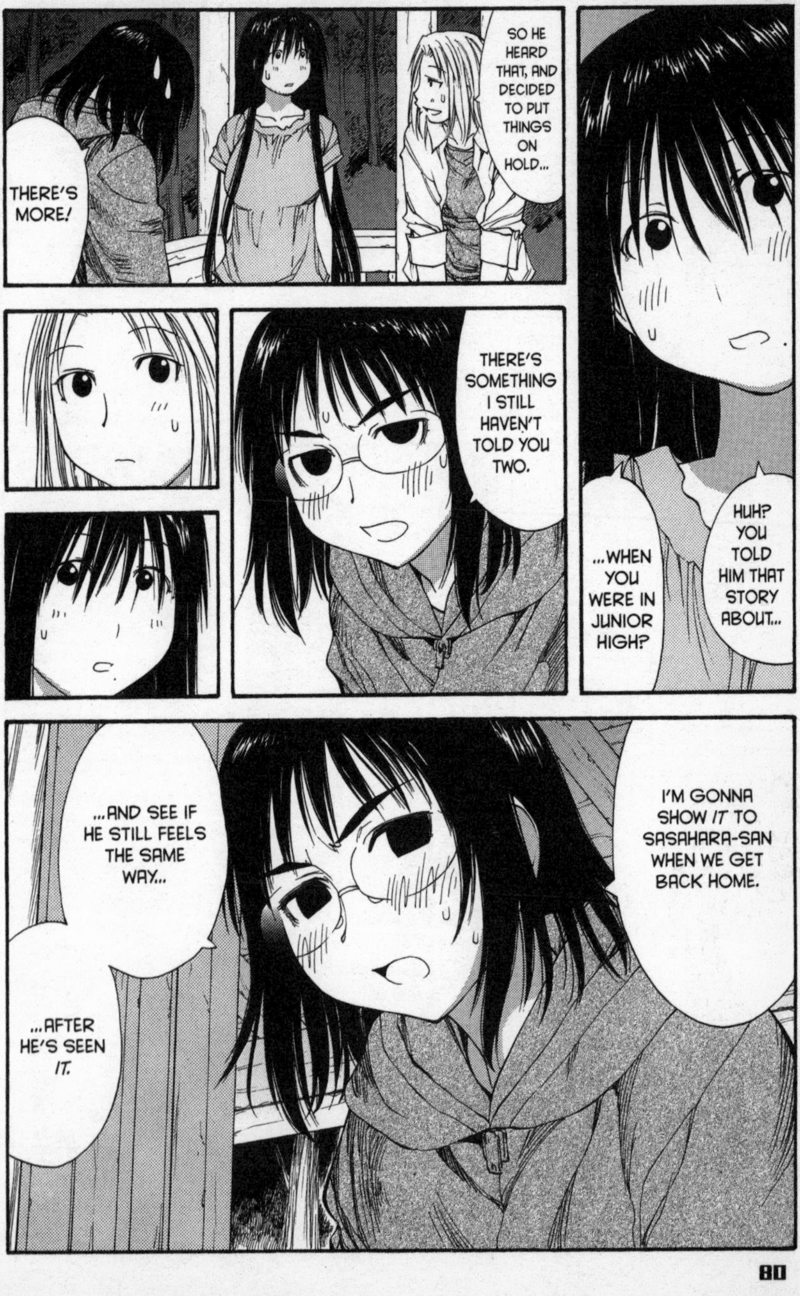
HUH? YOU TOLD HIM THAT STORY ABOUT...
...WHEN YOU WERE IN JUNIOR HIGH?
SO HE HEARD THAT, AND DECIDED TO PUT THINGS ON HOLD...
THERE'S MORE!
THERE'S SOMETHING I STILL HAVEN'T TOLD YOU TWO.
I'M GONNA SHOW *IT* TO SASAHARA-SAN WHEN WE GET BACK HOME.
...AND SEE IF HE STILL FEELS THE SAME WAY...
...AFTER HE'S SEEN *IT*.

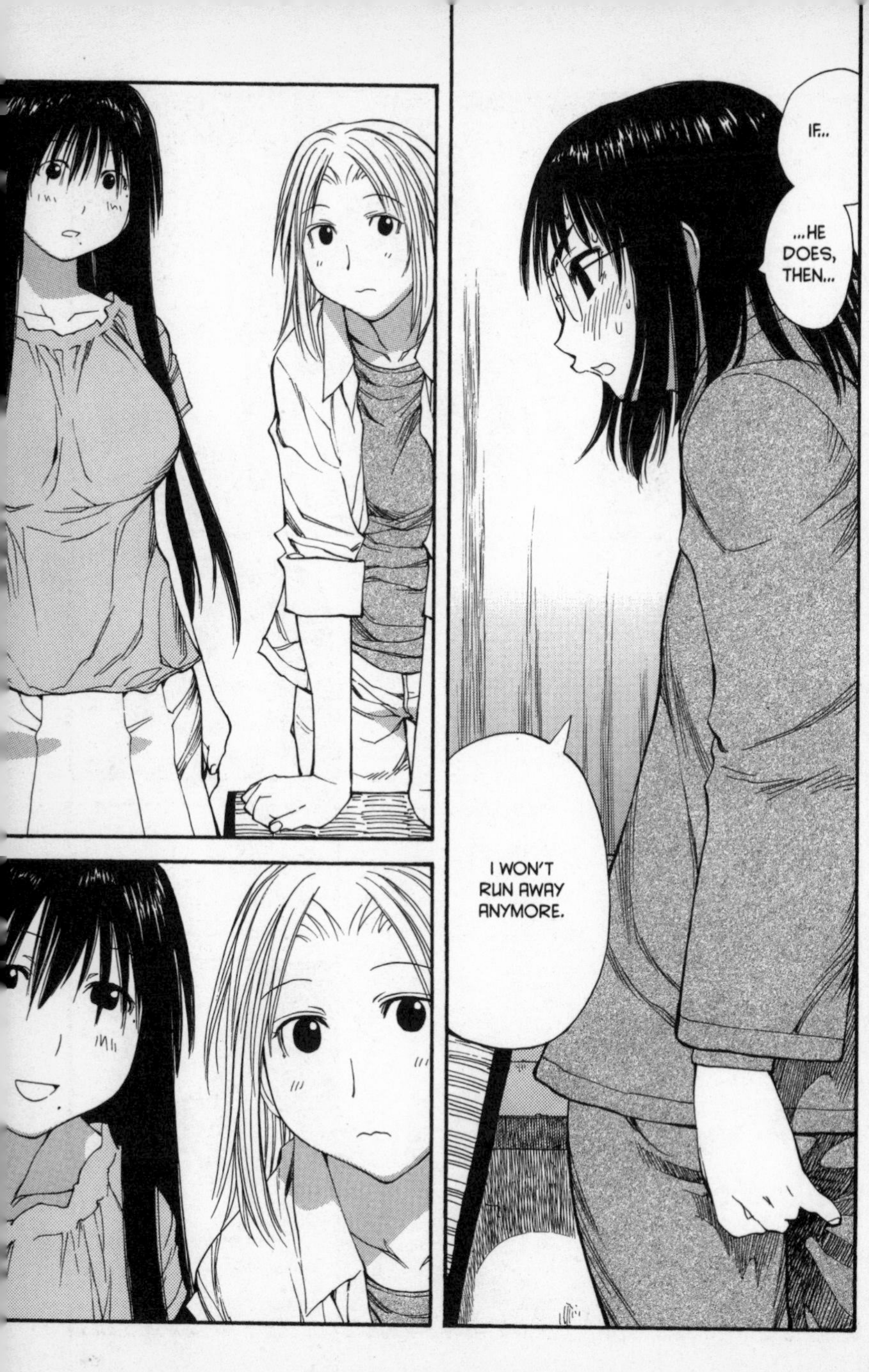
IF...
...HE DOES, THEN...
I WON'T RUN AWAY ANYMORE.

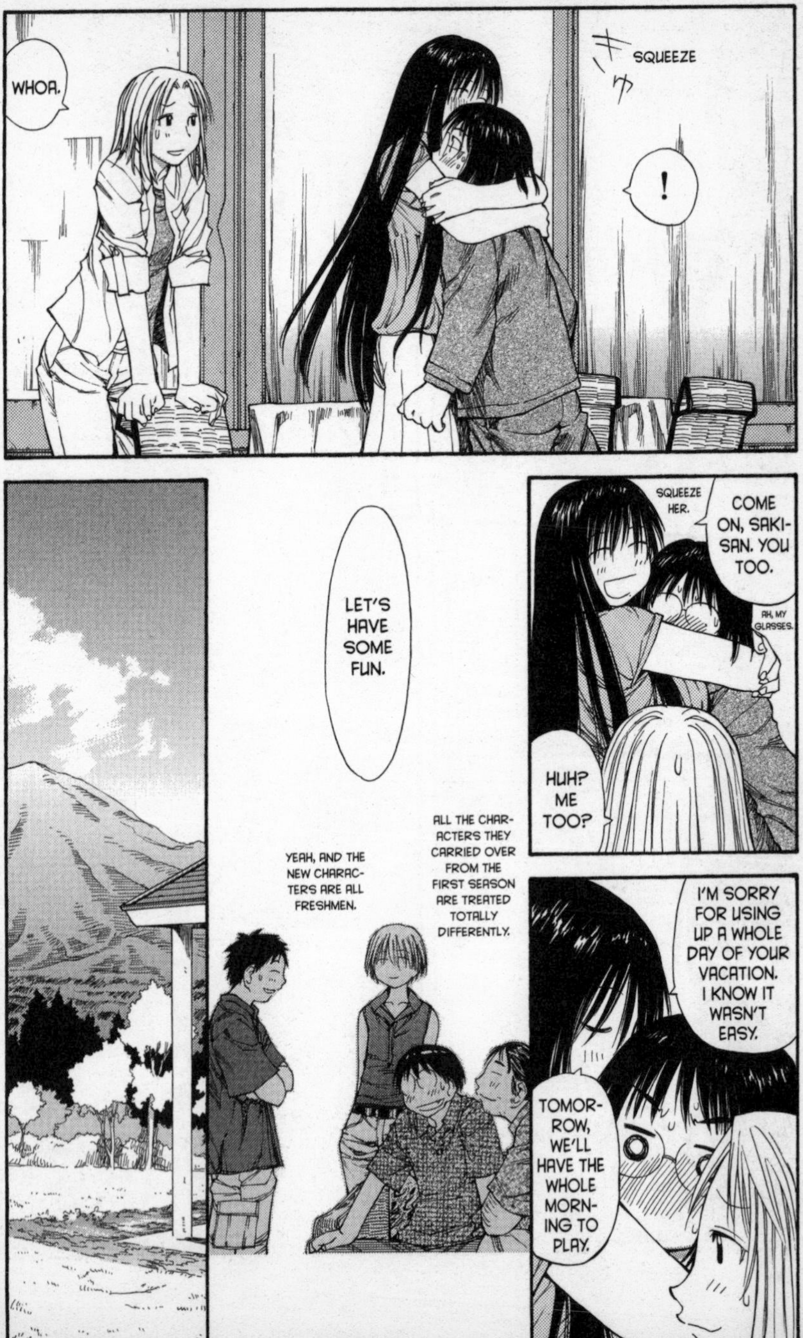
きゅ
SQUEEZE
!
WHOA.
SQUEEZE HER.
COME ON, SAKI-SAN. YOU TOO.
AH, MY GLASSES.
HUH? ME TOO?
I'M SORRY FOR USING UP A WHOLE DAY OF YOUR VACATION. I KNOW IT WASN'T EASY.
TOMORROW, WE'LL HAVE THE WHOLE MORNING TO PLAY.
LET'S HAVE SOME FUN.
ALL THE CHARACTERS THEY CARRIED OVER FROM THE FIRST SEASON ARE TREATED TOTALLY DIFFERENTLY.
YEAH, AND THE NEW CHARACTERS ARE ALL FRESHMEN.

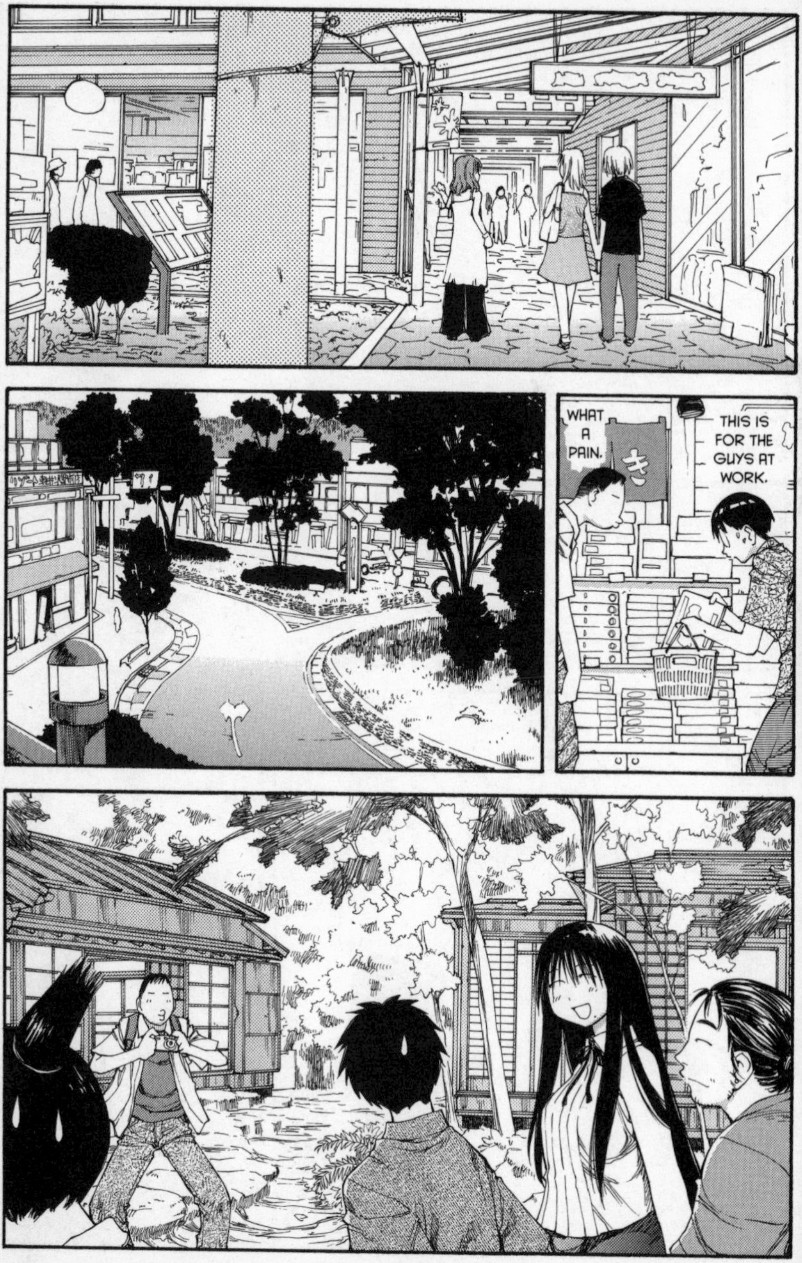
THIS IS FOR THE GUYS AT WORK.
WHAT A PAIN.
き

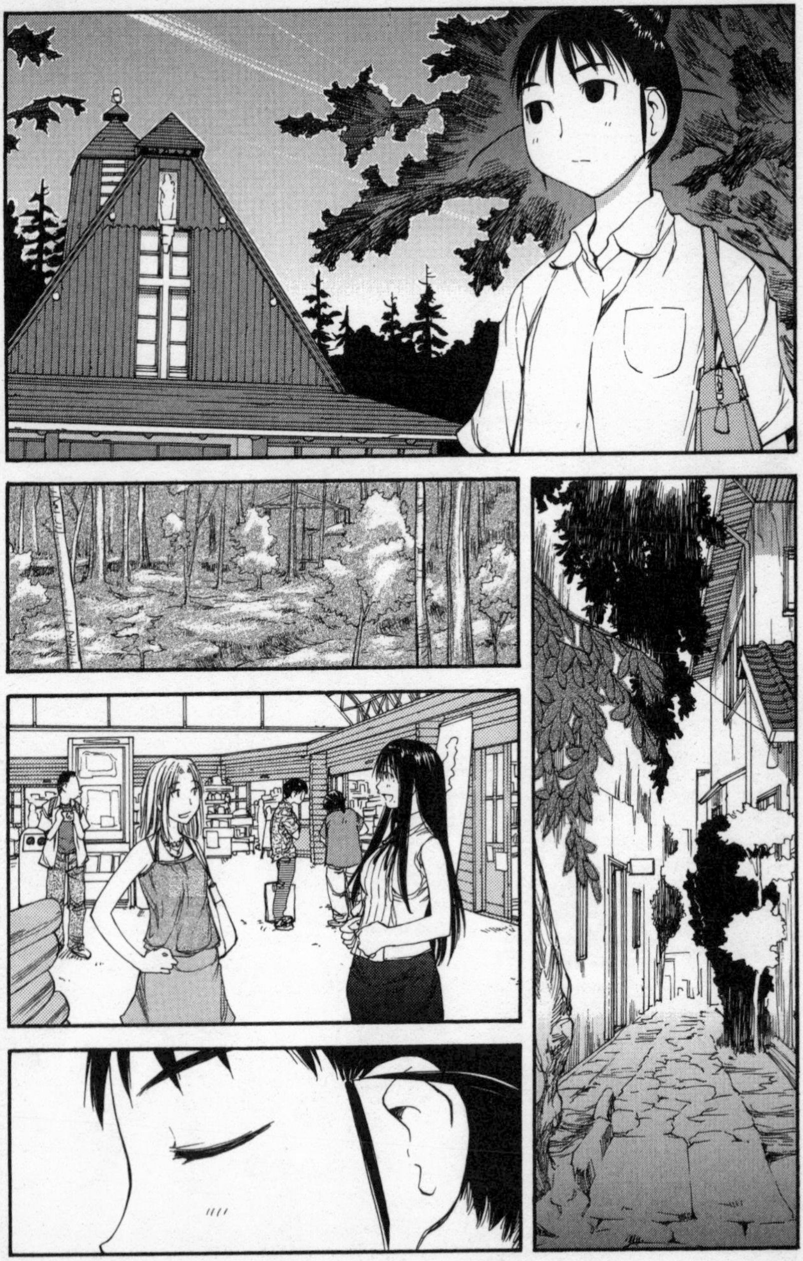

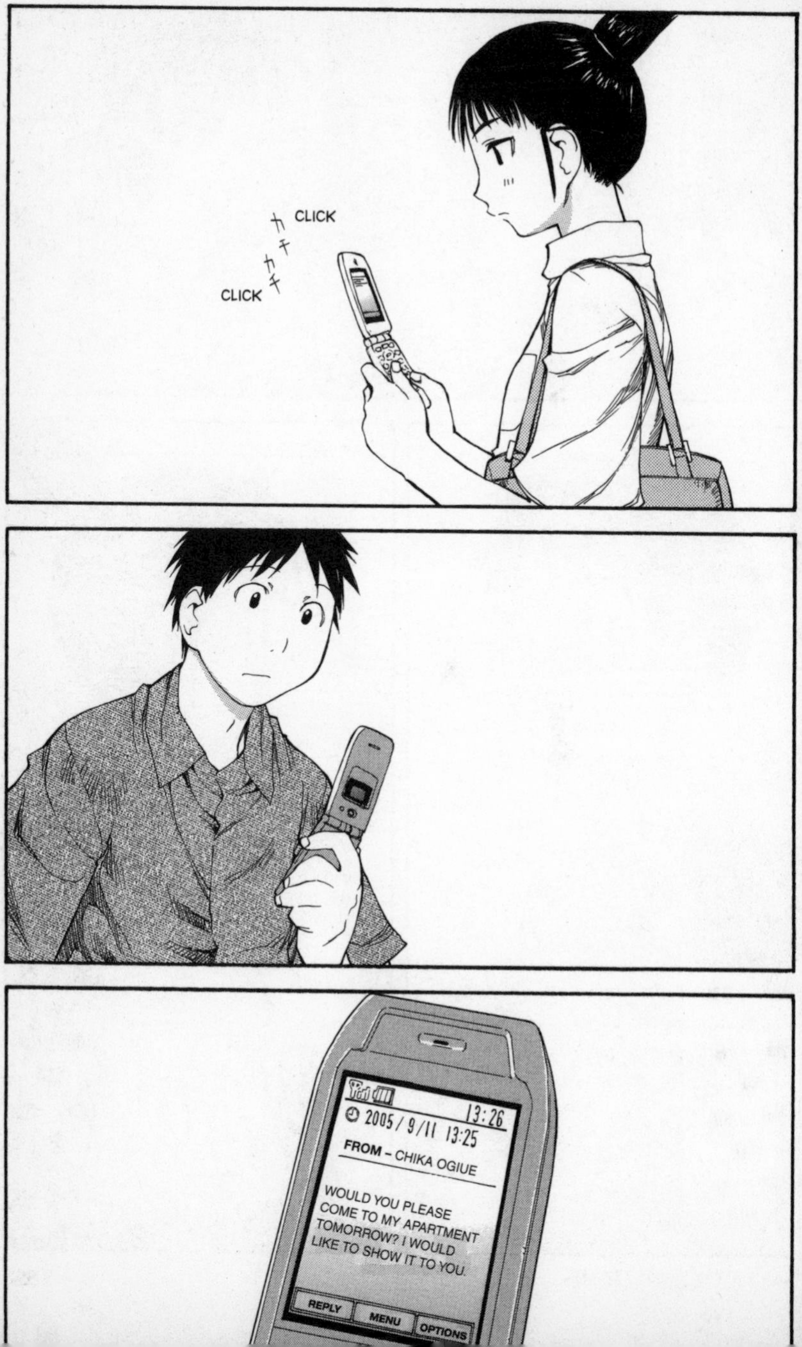
CLICK
カチ
カチ
CLICK
13:26
2005/9/11 13:25
FROM – CHIKA OGIUE
WOULD YOU PLEASE COME TO MY APARTMENT TOMORROW? I WOULD LIKE TO SHOW IT TO YOU.
REPLY
MENU
OPTIONS

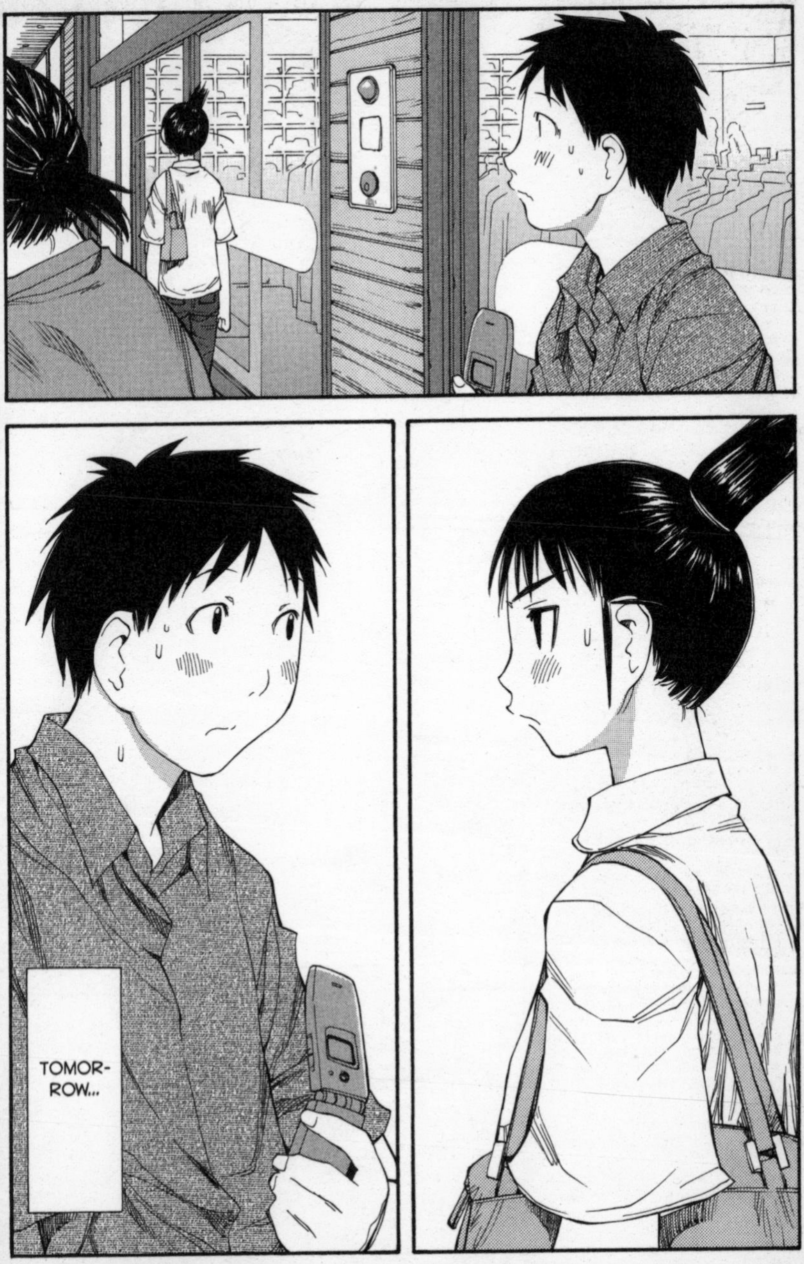
TOMOR-
ROW...

END OF CHAPTER 46

BEN- RENKO HAS BEEN UPGRADED TO A MAIN CHARACTER.

PV- WELL, I GUESS THAT'S TO BE EXPECTED. IN THE LAST SEASON THE RENKO/PRESIDENT STORY LINE WAS SUCH A MAINSTAY.

BEN- LOOK AT HER EXPRESSION, SHE'S NOT SURPRISED.

PV- BUT HER AS A PROFESSOR CHARACTER? THAT'S TOO PERFECT.

BEN- WITH YAMADA AS HER ASSISTANT.

PV- BUT I BET THEY'RE NOT ACTUALLY GONNA USE HER WHITE LAB COAT AND CAT EARS FROM THIS SKETCH.
THE OFFICIAL CHARACTER DESIGN PROFILE SHOWS HER IN A SCHOOL UNIFORM...HEH, HEH.

BEN- BUT APPARENTLY, SHE WILL BE WEARING THE LAB COAT IN SOME SCENES.

PV- ...

BEN- WHAT?

PV- THOSE CAT EARS...

BEN- SO THAT'S WHAT YOU'RE INTERESTED IN. BUT I HEARD THAT IN SOME SCENES, SHE ACTUALLY WILL USE HER PONYTAIL RIBBON TO MAKE CAT EARS.

PV- I WANT THE REAL THING.

BEN- TRYING TO SOUND LIKE A PERVERT ISN'T GONNA CHANGE ANYTHING. LOOK WHAT THEY'VE DONE TO YAMADA. PRETTY INTERESTING.

PV- INTERESTING? HOW CAN YOU EVEN SAY THAT? IT'S A TOTAL RIPOFF.

BEN- THIS IS SUPPOSED TO BE A PARODY. DON'T GO THROWING THE WORD RIPOFF AROUND SO LIGHTLY.

PV- BUT THEY'LL NEVER USE HER LIKE THIS, WILL THEY?

BEN- YEAH, I DON'T THINK WE EVER SEE HER LIKE THIS IN THE MAIN SERIES.

PV- IT IS KIND OF CONVENIENT TO HAVE AT LEAST ONE MAD SCIENTIST CHARACTER AROUND. THAT WAY YOU CAN HAVE ALL KINDS OF CRAZY STORIES.

BEN- YOU MEAN LIKE SERGEANT KURYURYU? THE MAIN FOCUS OF THIS SEASON SEEMS TO BE CHARACTER DRIVEN-STORIES RATHER THAN HIGH-CONCEPT STUFF.

PV- WHAT? YOU MEAN THEY WON'T HAVE KOYUKI TAKE A "MATURITY POTION" AND SUDDENLY BECOME AN ADULT? OR A MAGIC WAND THAT TURNS THE PRESIDENT INTO A WITCH?

BEN- WELL, I WOULD LIKE TO SEE THAT.

PV- RIGHT?

BEN- BUT WHAT I REALLY WANT IS A PORN GAME USING THESE TWO CHARACTERS.

PV- DON'T EVEN GO THERE.

BEN- WHERE YOU CAN TOTALLY CHANGE THE CHARACTERS.

PV- I SAID DON'T GO THERE.

HOLDING HANDS...

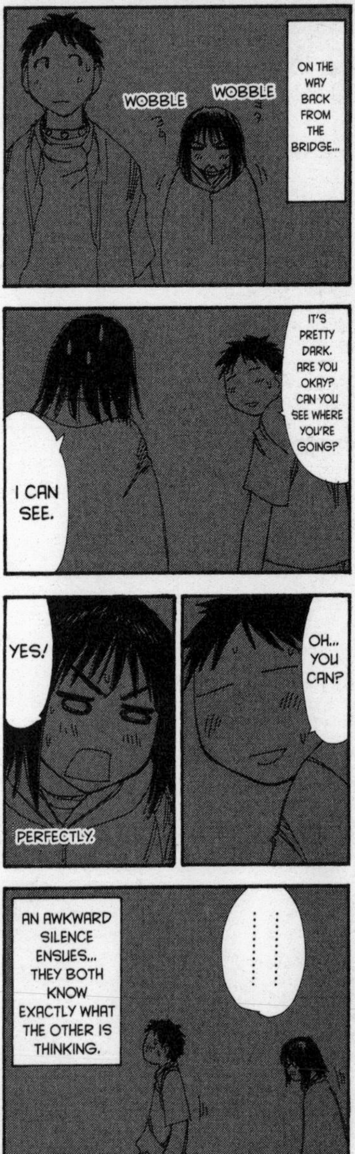
ON THE WAY BACK FROM THE BRIDGE...
WOBBLE
WOBBLE
IT'S PRETTY DARK. ARE YOU OKAY? CAN YOU SEE WHERE YOU'RE GOING?
I CAN SEE.
OH... YOU CAN?
YES!
PERFECTLY.
......
AN AWKWARD SILENCE ENSUES... THEY BOTH KNOW EXACTLY WHAT THE OTHER IS THINKING.

THE MEETING

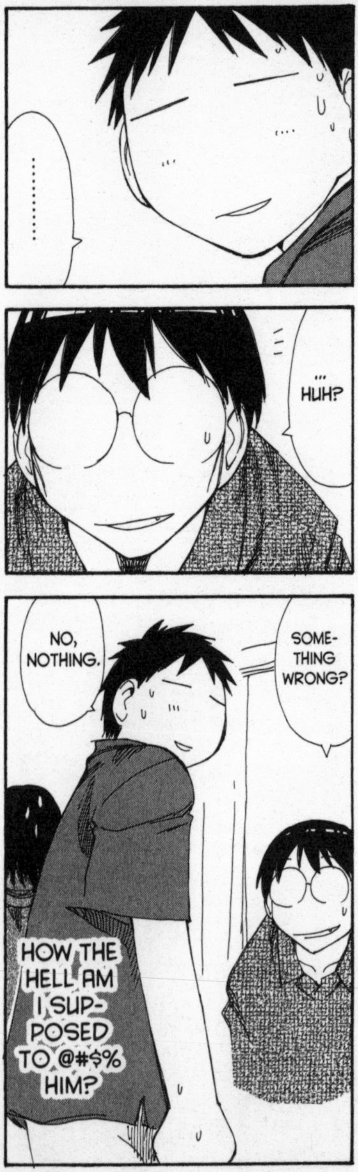
......
... HUH?
SOME-THING WRONG?
NO, NOTHING.
HOW THE HELL AM I SUP-POSED TO @#$% HIM?

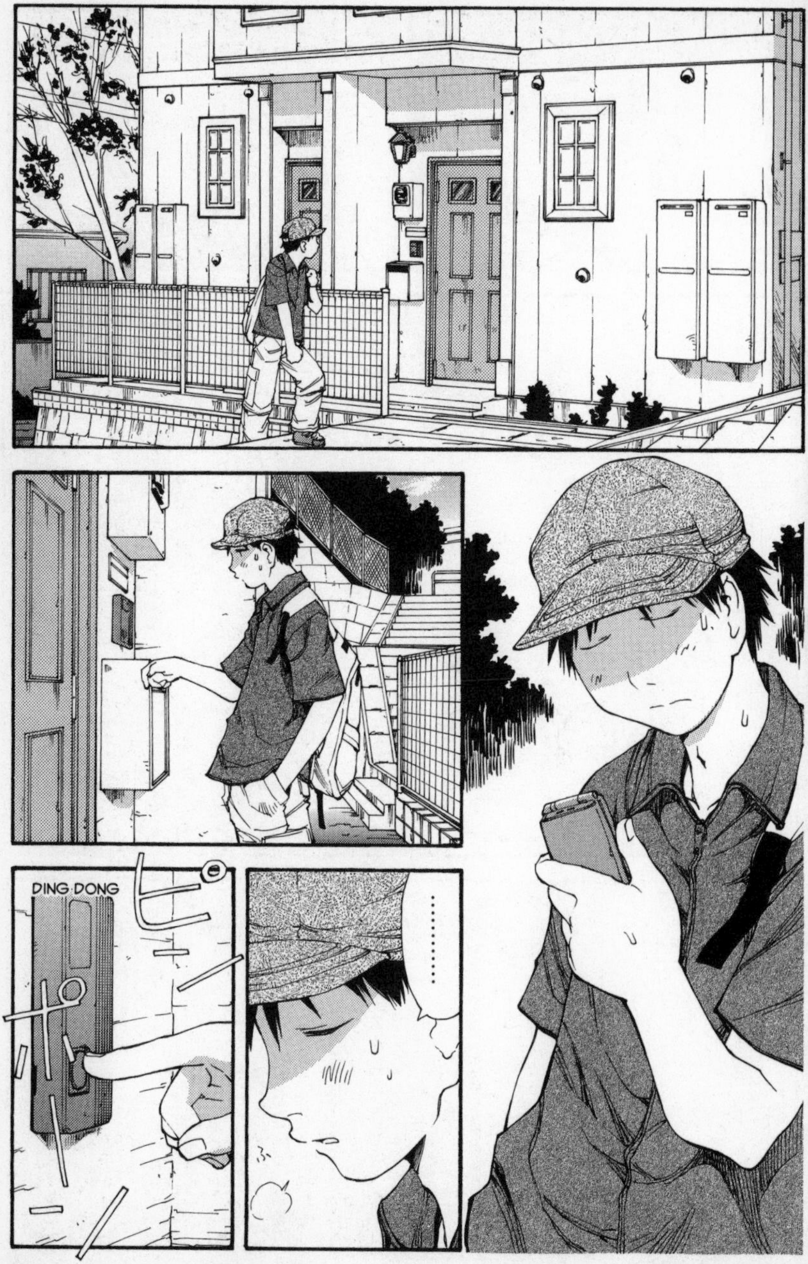
……
DING DONG

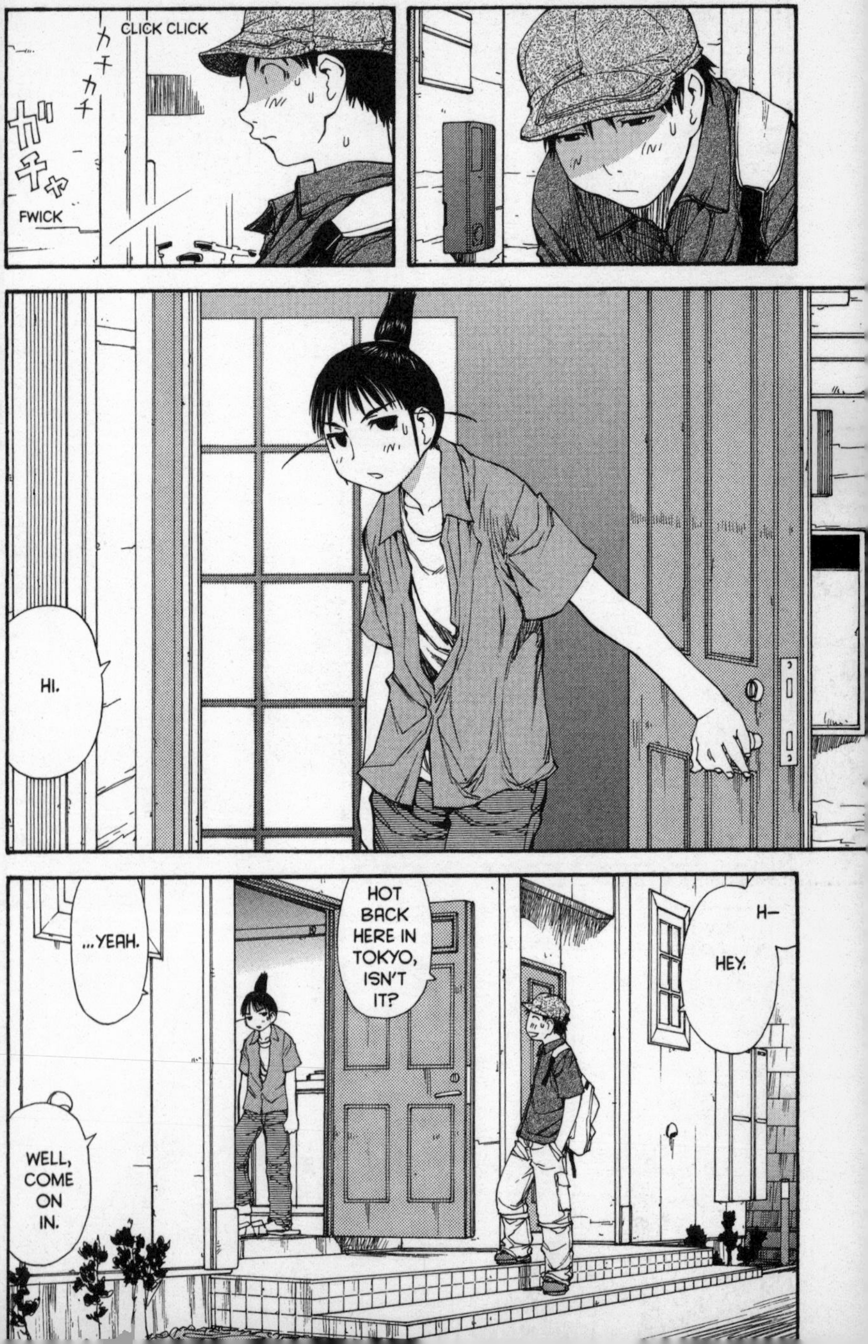
CLICK CLICK
カチカチ
ガチャ
FWICK
HI.
H— HEY.
HOT BACK HERE IN TOKYO, ISN'T IT?
...YEAH.
WELL, COME ON IN.

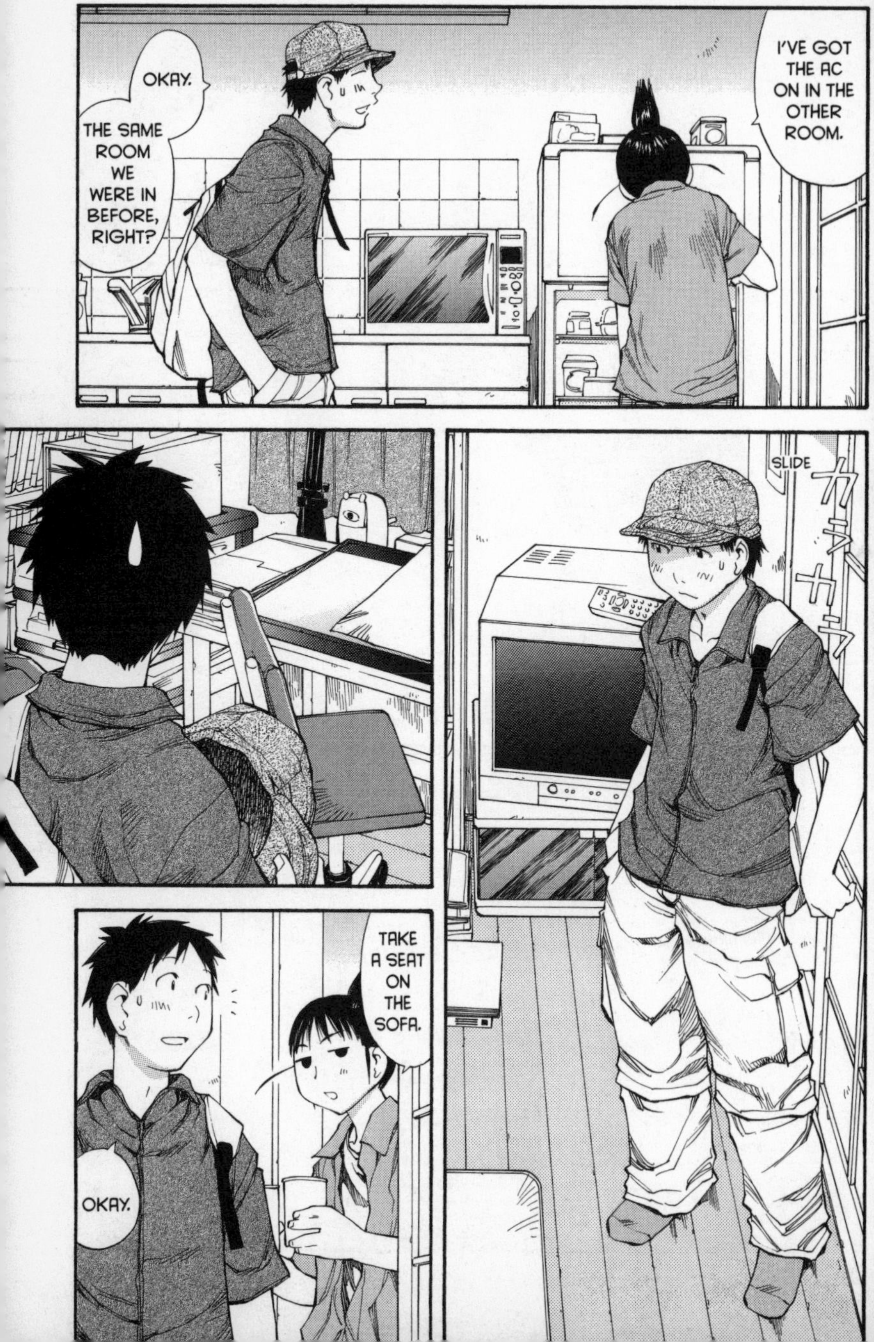
I'VE GOT THE AC ON IN THE OTHER ROOM.
OKAY.
THE SAME ROOM WE WERE IN BEFORE, RIGHT?
SLIDE
カラカラ
TAKE A SEAT ON THE SOFA.
OKAY.

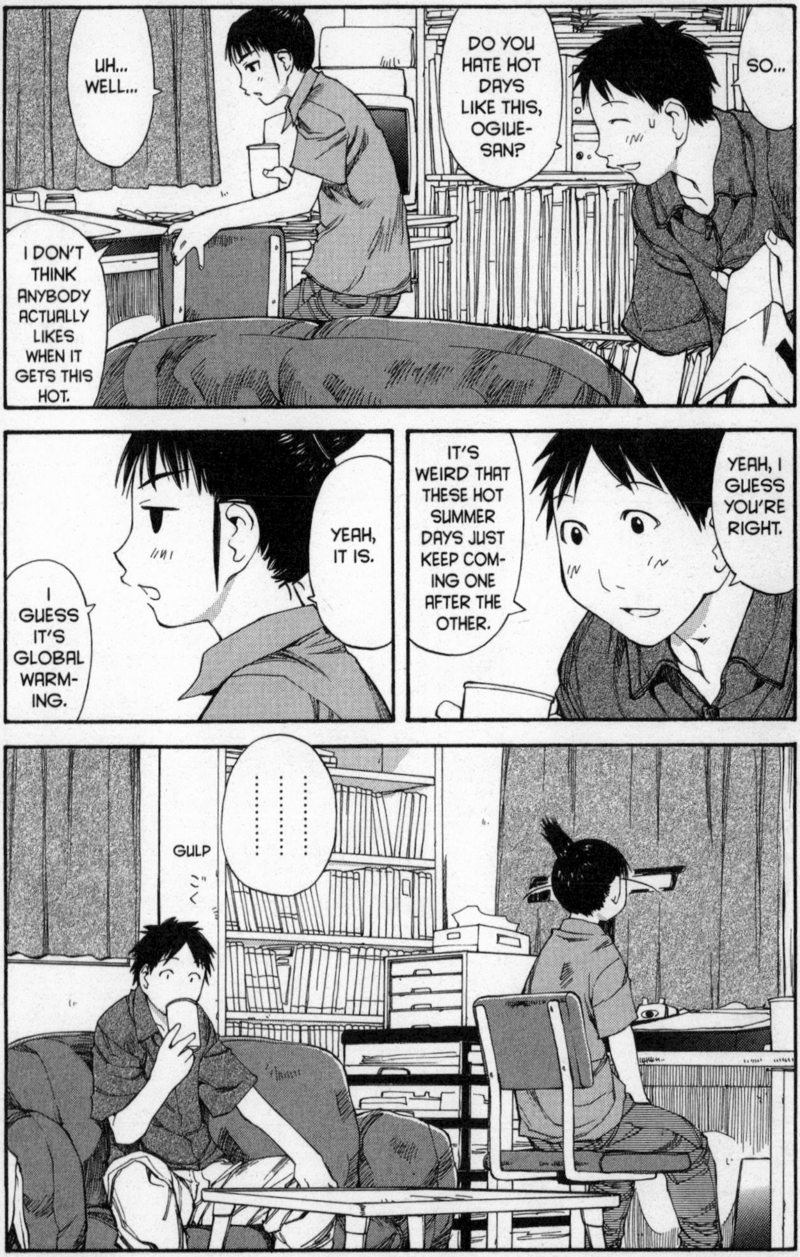
SO...
DO YOU HATE HOT DAYS LIKE THIS, OGIUE-SAN?
UH... WELL...
I DON'T THINK ANYBODY ACTUALLY LIKES WHEN IT GETS THIS HOT.
YEAH, I GUESS YOU'RE RIGHT.
IT'S WEIRD THAT THESE HOT SUMMER DAYS JUST KEEP COMING ONE AFTER THE OTHER.
YEAH, IT IS.
I GUESS IT'S GLOBAL WARMING.
......
GULP
ごく

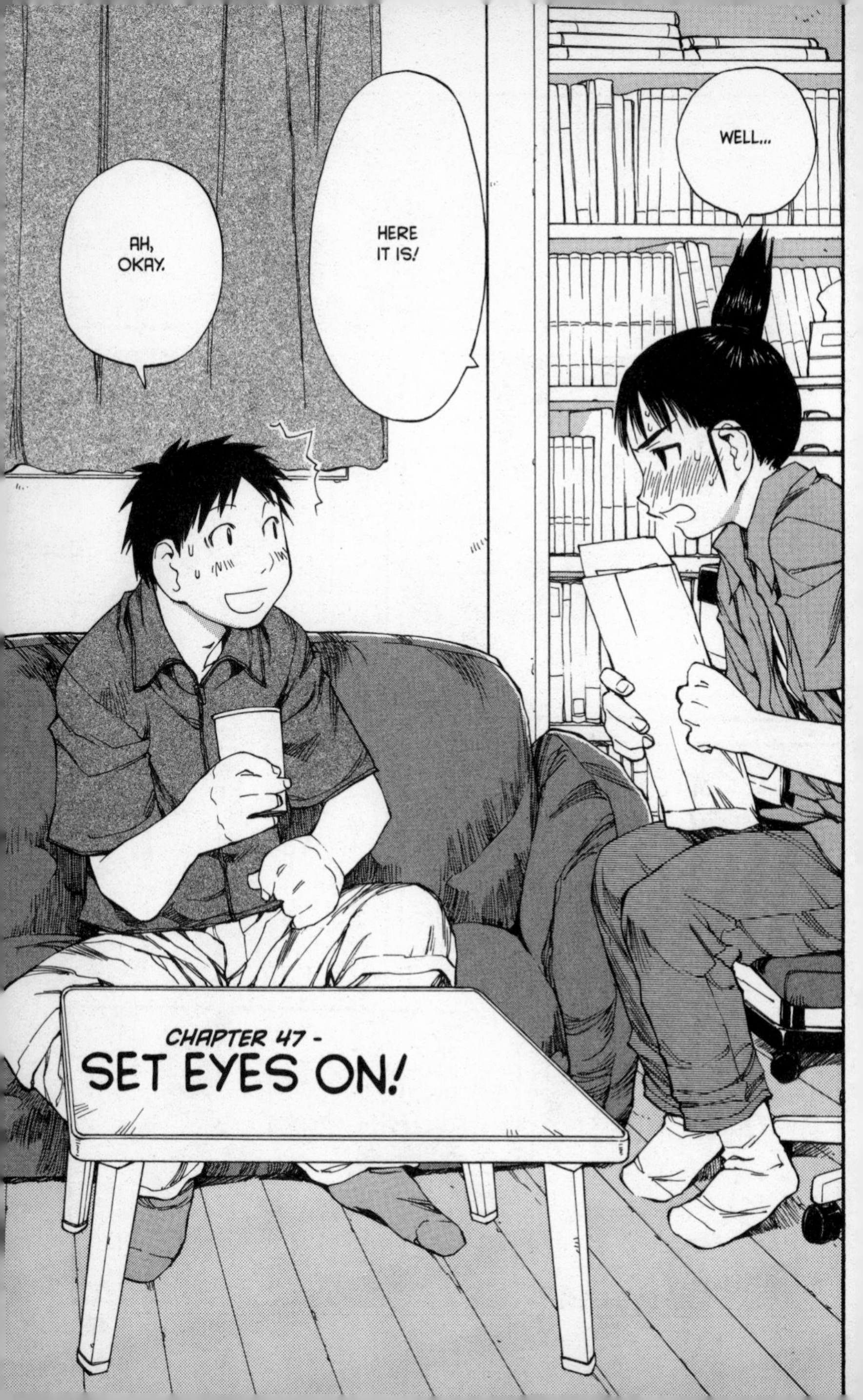
WELL...
HERE IT IS!
AH, OKAY.
CHAPTER 47 -
SET EYES ON!

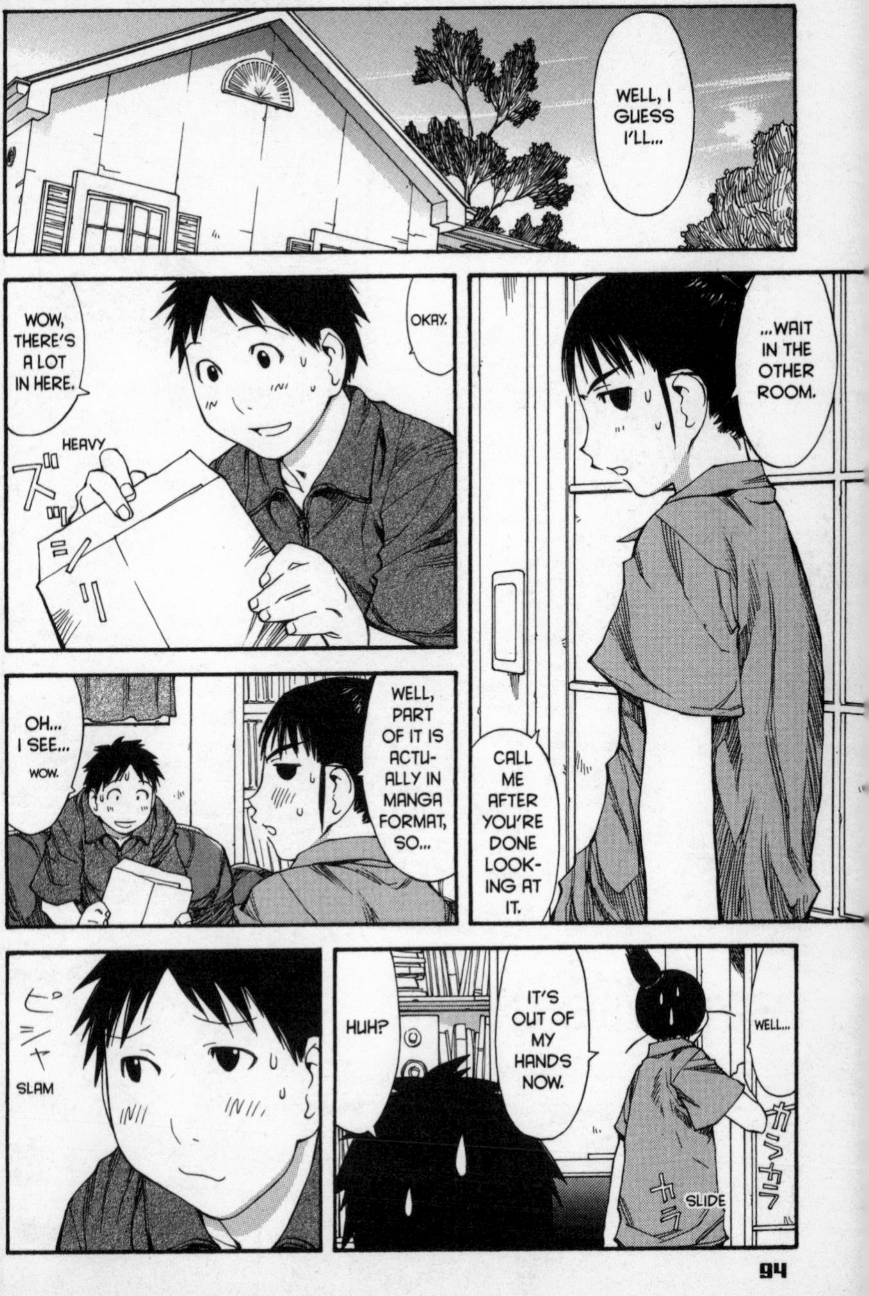
WELL, I GUESS I'LL...
...WAIT IN THE OTHER ROOM.
CALL ME AFTER YOU'RE DONE LOOKING AT IT.
OKAY.
WOW, THERE'S A LOT IN HERE.
HEAVY
WELL, PART OF IT IS ACTUALLY IN MANGA FORMAT, SO...
OH... I SEE... WOW.
WELL...
SLIDE
IT'S OUT OF MY HANDS NOW.
HUH?
SLAM

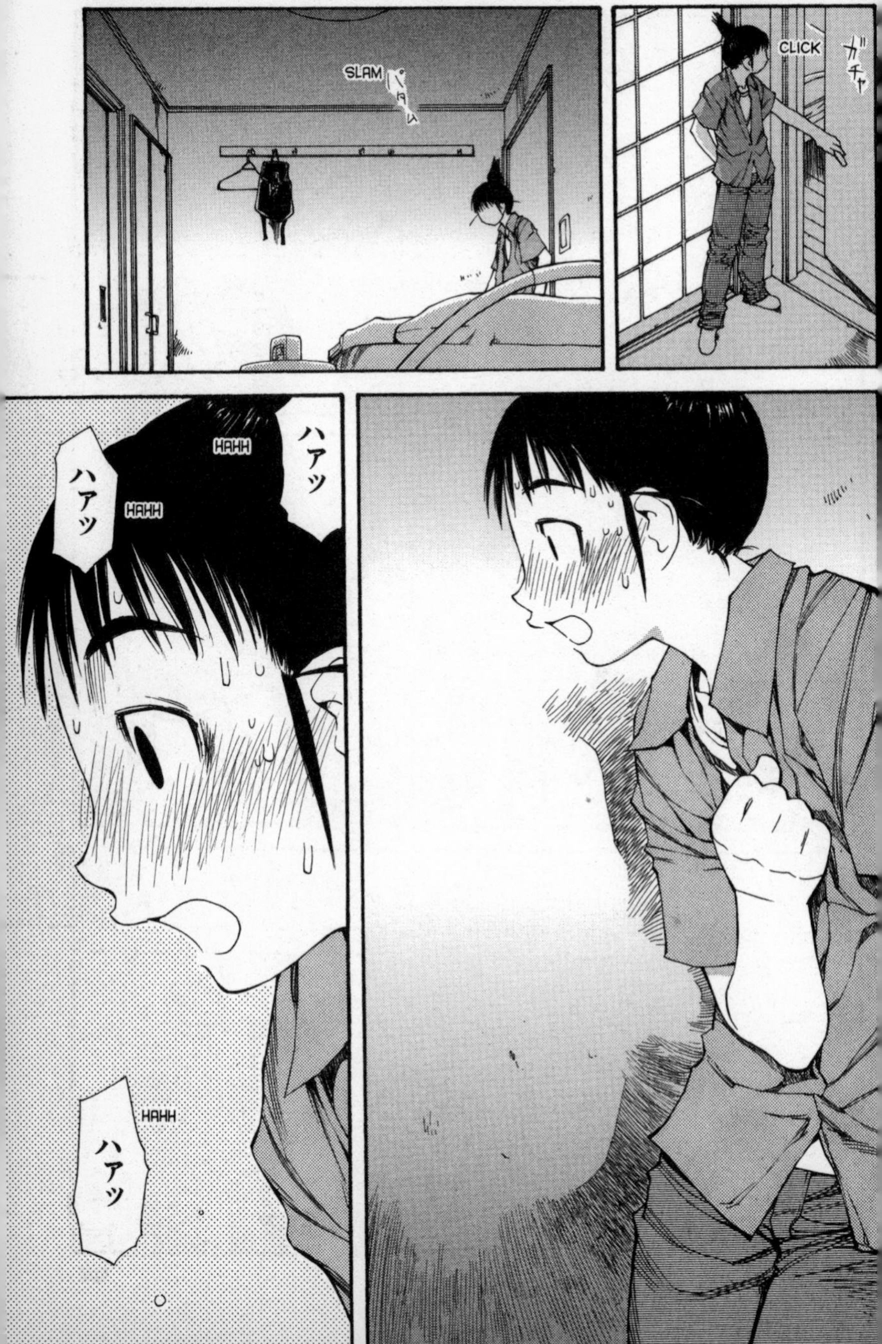
CLICK
ガチャ
SLAM
バタム
HAHH
ハアッ
HAHH
ハアッ
HAHH
ハアッ

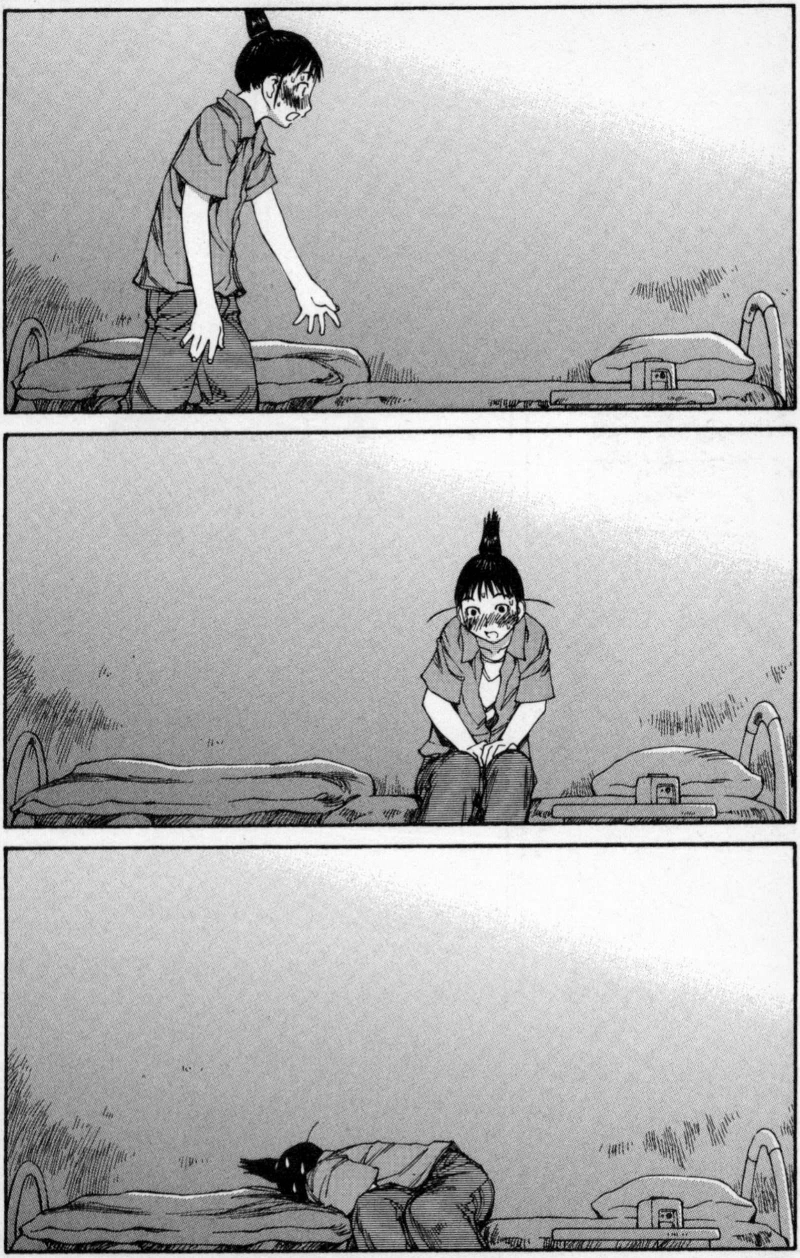

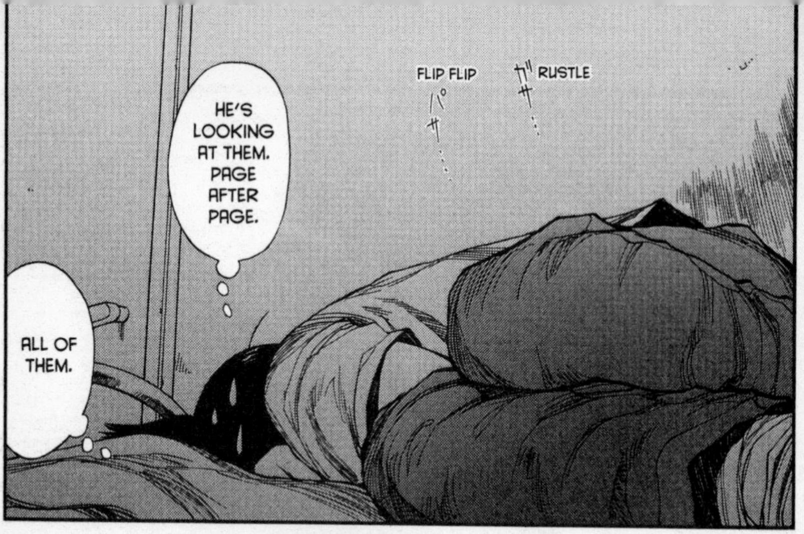
ガサ…
RUSTLE
パサ…
FLIP FLIP
HE'S LOOKING AT THEM. PAGE AFTER PAGE.
ALL OF THEM.
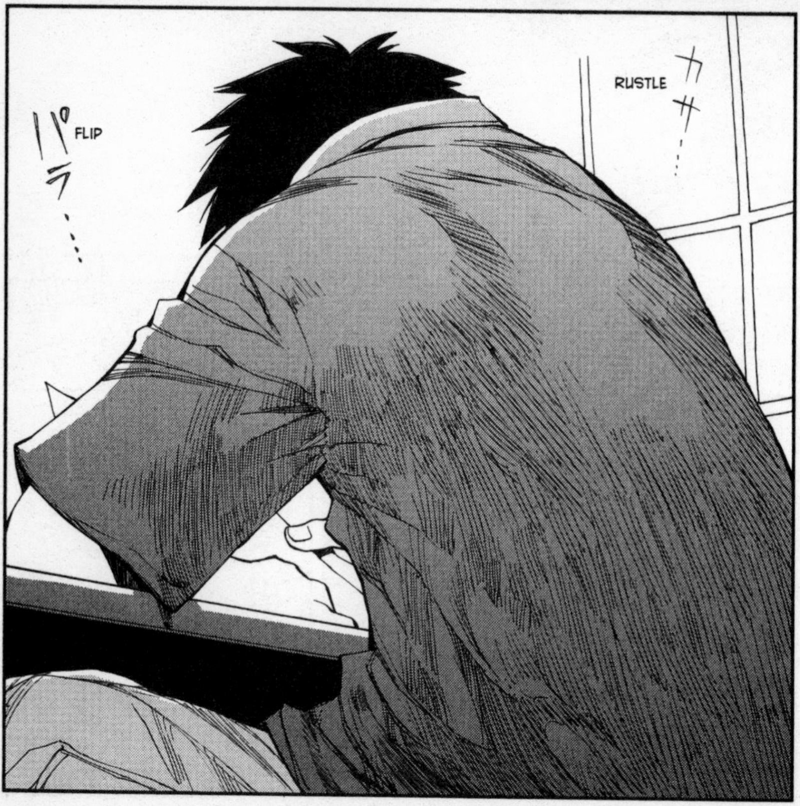
カサ…
RUSTLE
パラ…
FLIP

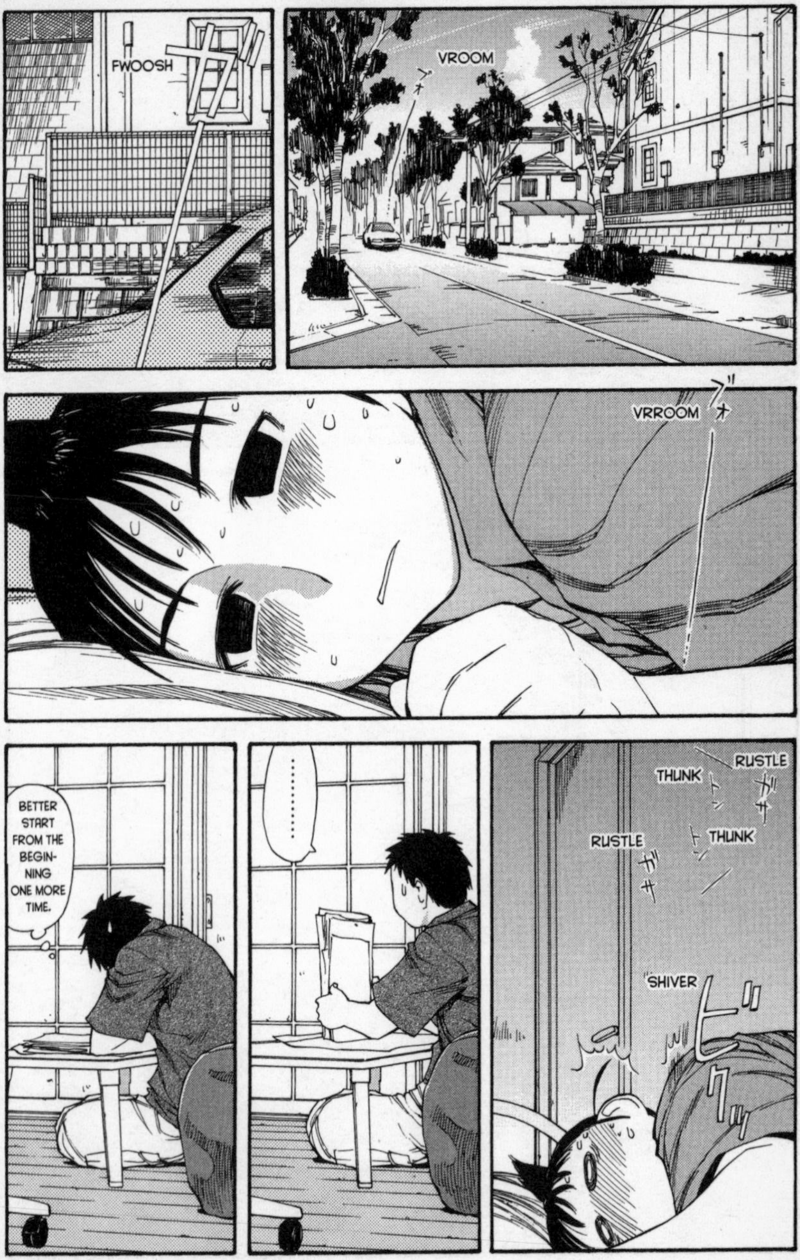
VROOM
FWOOSH
VRROOM
RUSTLE
THUNK
THUNK
RUSTLE
SHIVER
......
BETTER START FROM THE BEGIN-NING ONE MORE TIME.

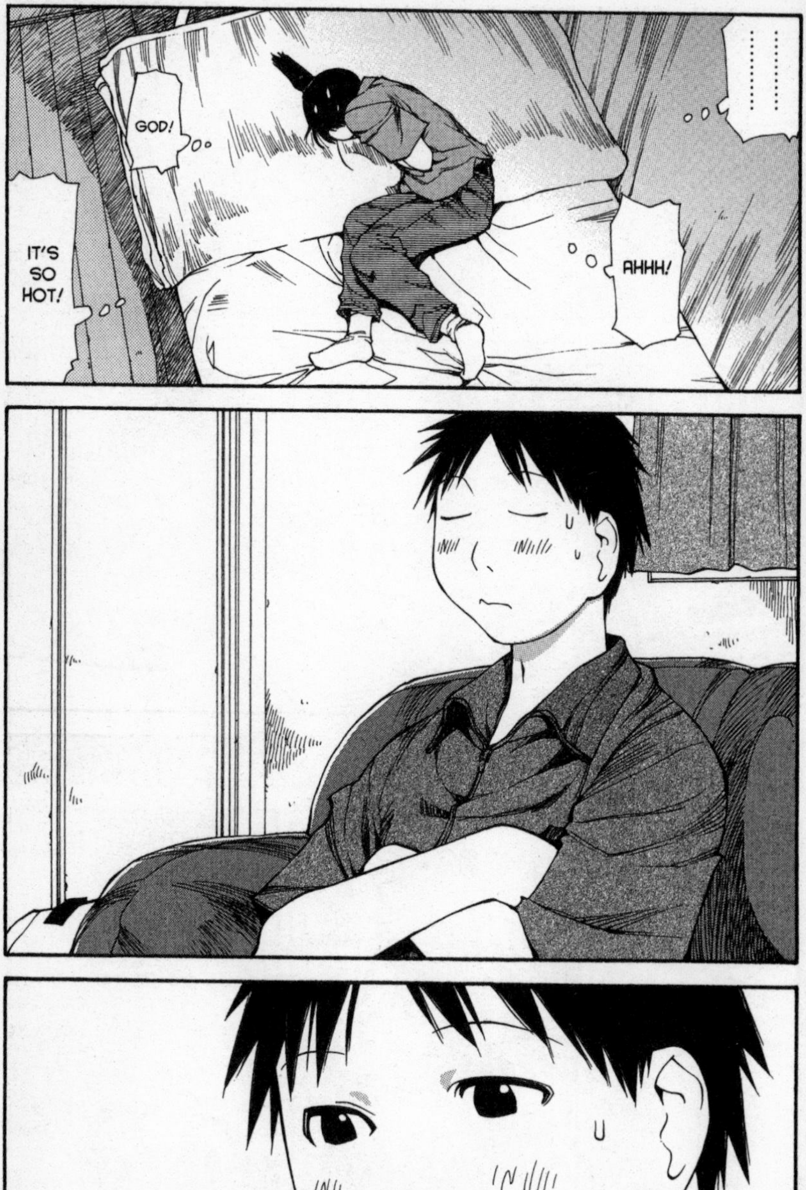
……
AHHH!
GOD!
IT'S SO HOT!

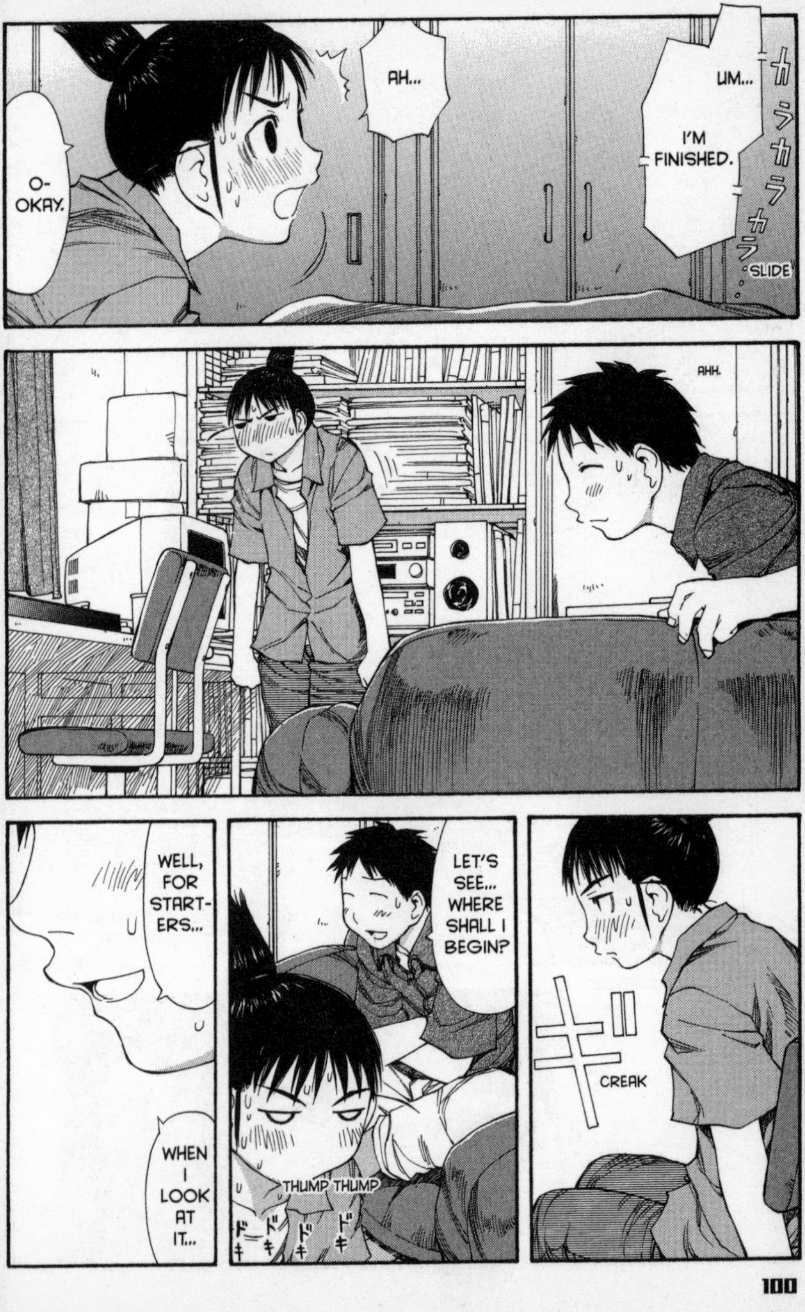
UM...
I'M FINISHED.
カラカラ
SLIDE
AH...
O-OKAY.
AHH.
ギ
CREAK
LET'S SEE... WHERE SHALL I BEGIN?
THUMP THUMP
ドキドキドキドキ
WELL, FOR STARTERS...
WHEN I LOOK AT IT...

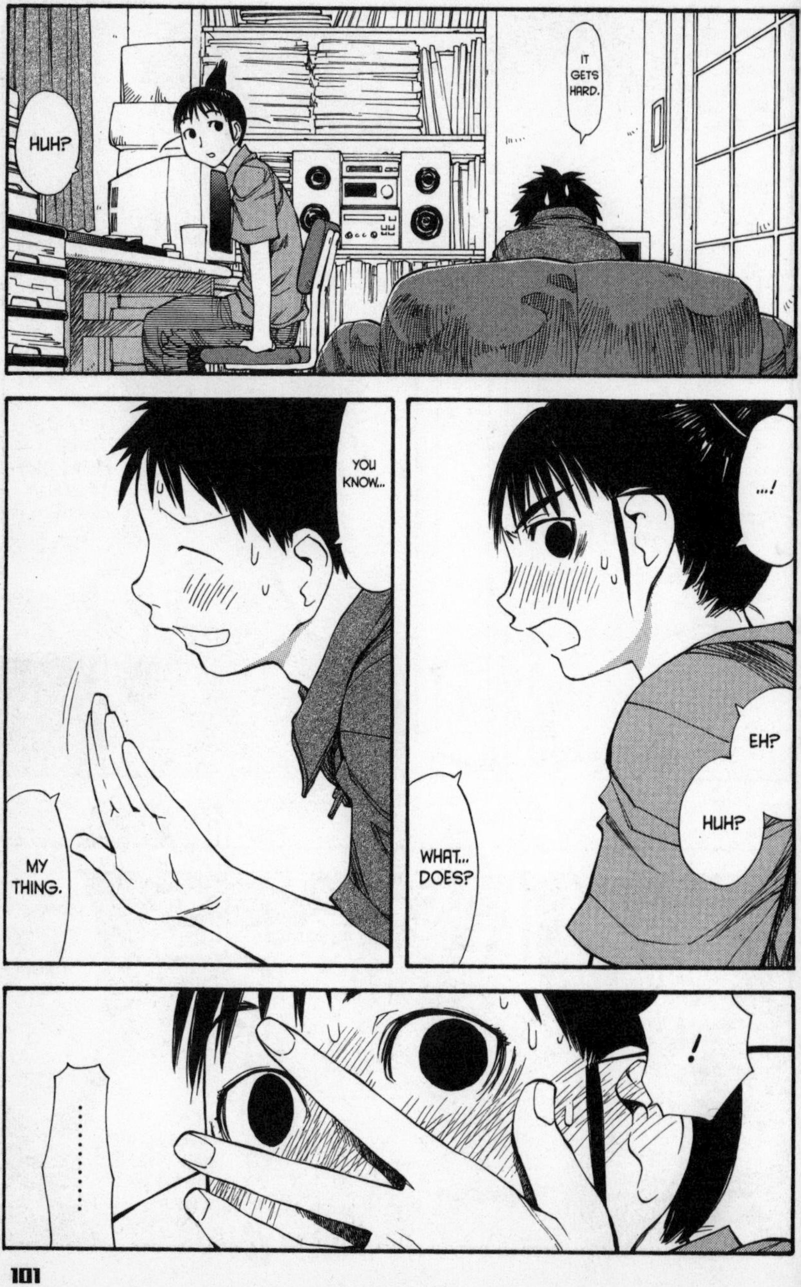
IT GETS HARD.
HUH?
...!
EH?
HUH?
WHAT... DOES?
YOU KNOW...
MY THING.
!
......

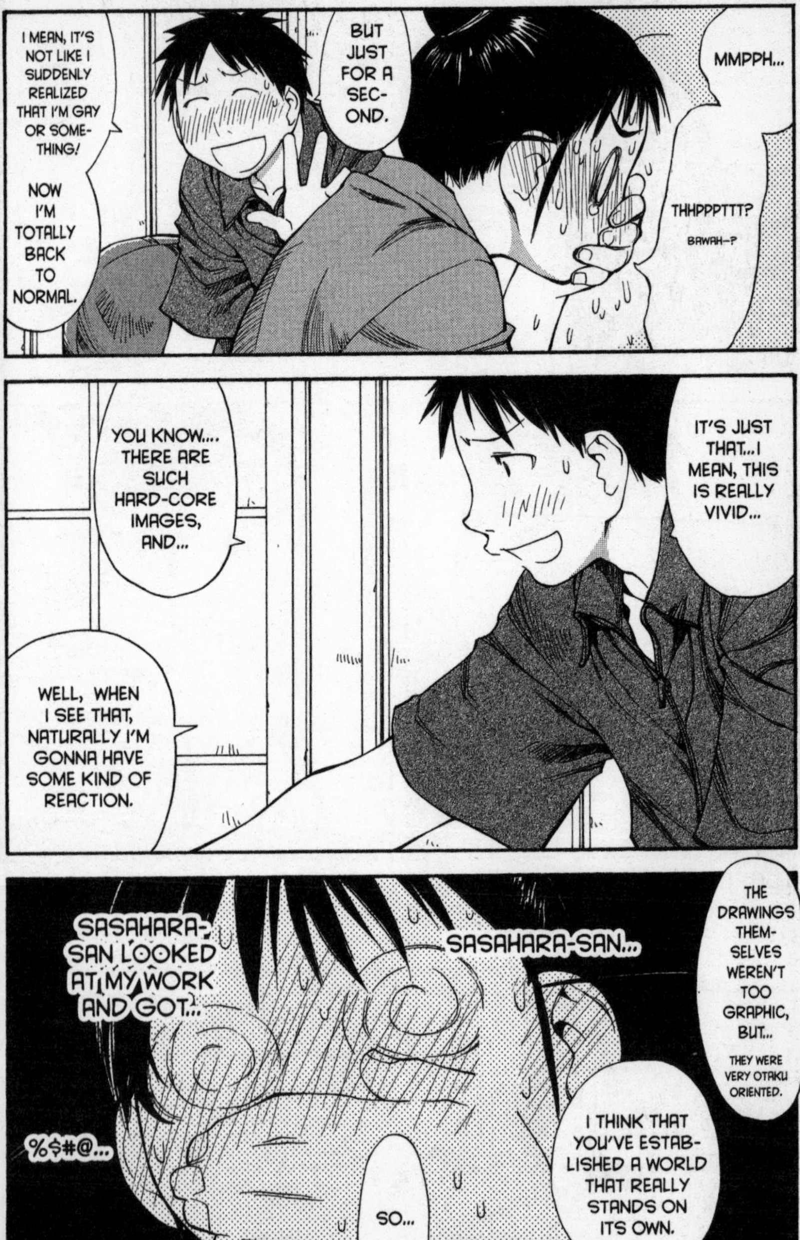
MMPPH...
THHPPPTTT?
BAWAH--?
BUT JUST FOR A SECOND.
I MEAN, IT'S NOT LIKE I SUDDENLY REALIZED THAT I'M GAY OR SOMETHING!
NOW I'M TOTALLY BACK TO NORMAL.
IT'S JUST THAT...I MEAN, THIS IS REALLY VIVID...
YOU KNOW.... THERE ARE SUCH HARD-CORE IMAGES, AND...
WELL, WHEN I SEE THAT, NATURALLY I'M GONNA HAVE SOME KIND OF REACTION.
THE DRAWINGS THEMSELVES WEREN'T TOO GRAPHIC, BUT...
THEY WERE VERY OTAKU ORIENTED.
SASAHARA-SAN...
SASAHARA-SAN LOOKED AT MY WORK AND GOT...
I THINK THAT YOU'VE ESTABLISHED A WORLD THAT REALLY STANDS ON ITS OWN.
SO...
%$#@...

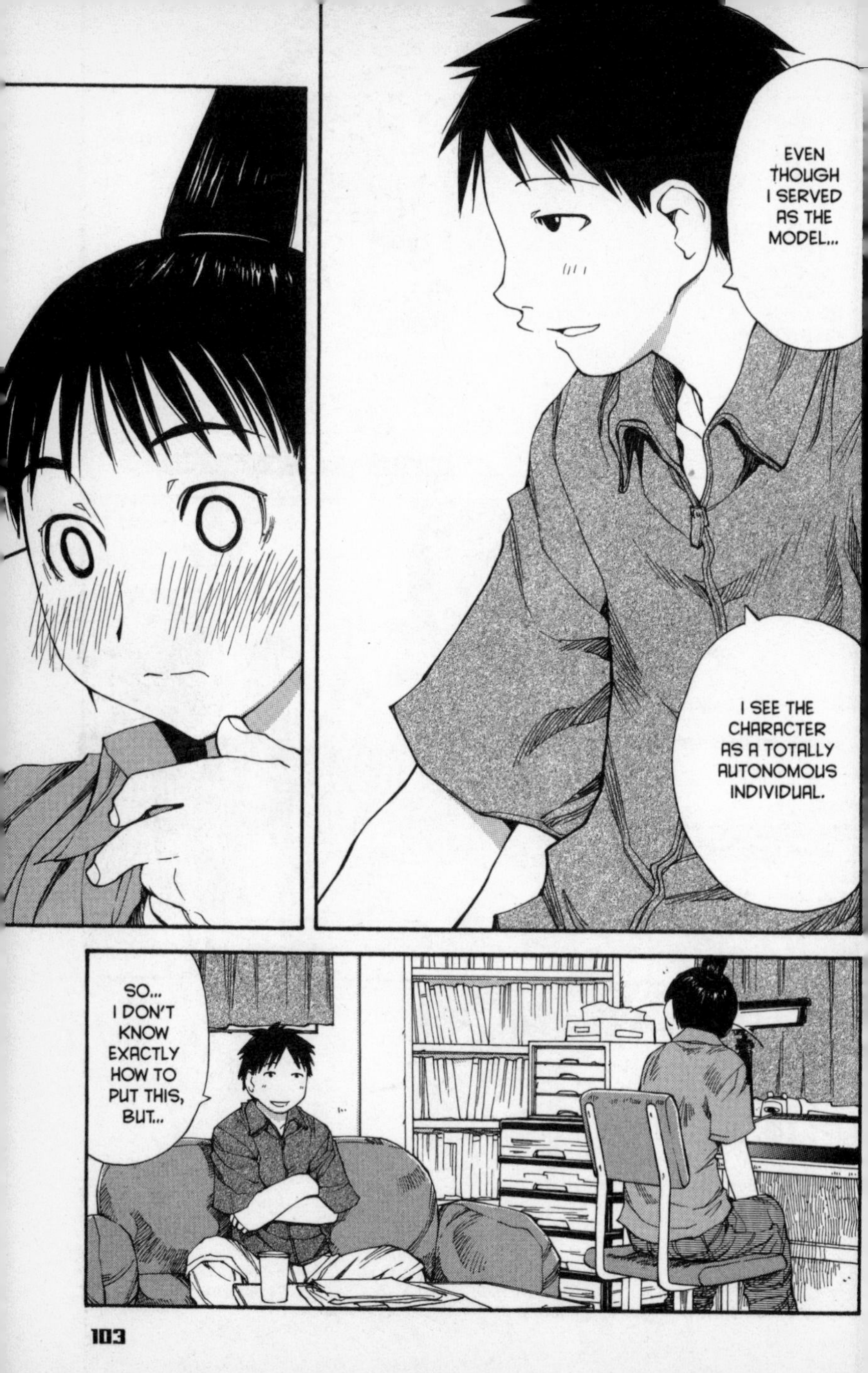
EVEN THOUGH I SERVED AS THE MODEL...
I SEE THE CHARACTER AS A TOTALLY AUTONOMOUS INDIVIDUAL.
SO... I DON'T KNOW EXACTLY HOW TO PUT THIS, BUT...

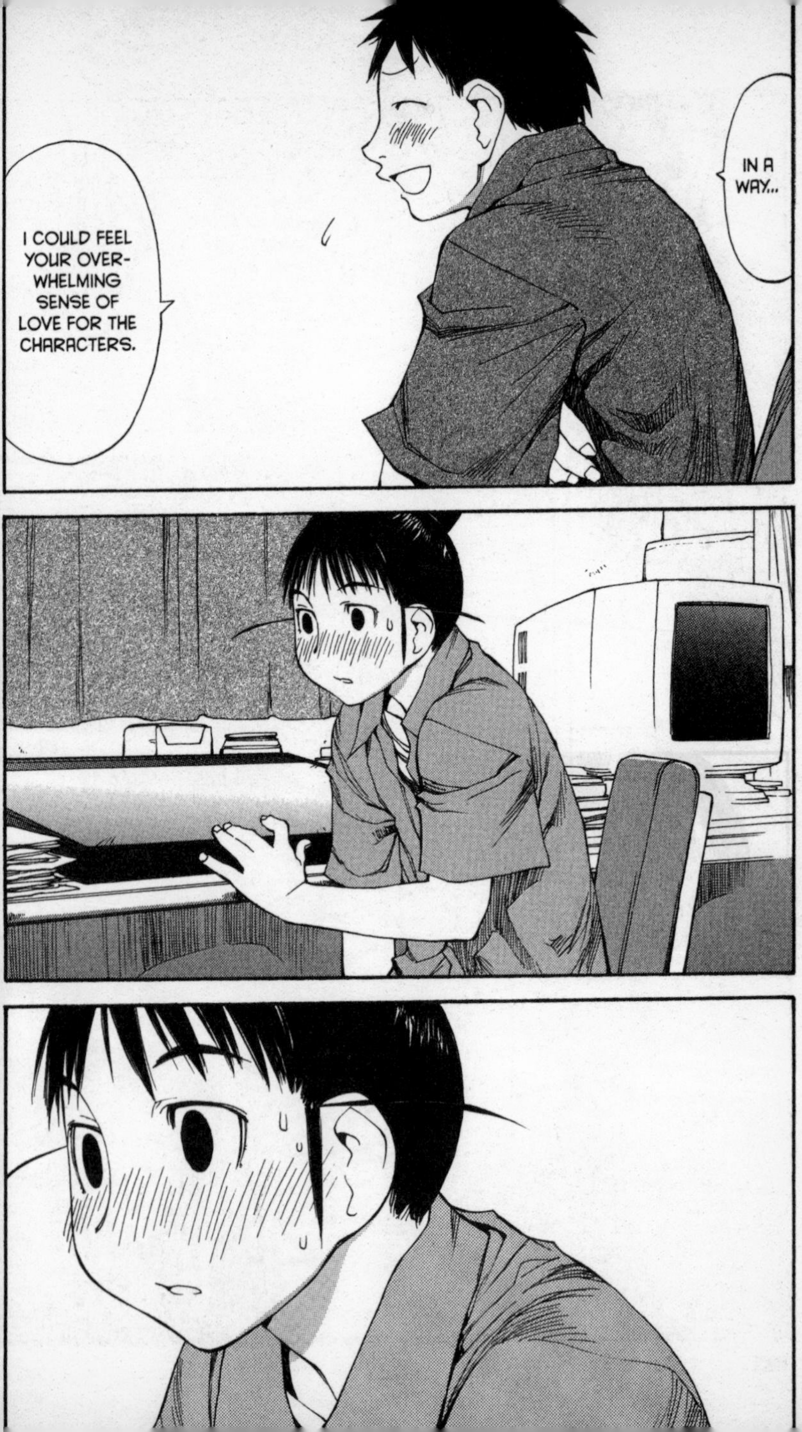
IN A WAY...
I COULD FEEL YOUR OVER-WHELMING SENSE OF LOVE FOR THE CHARACTERS.

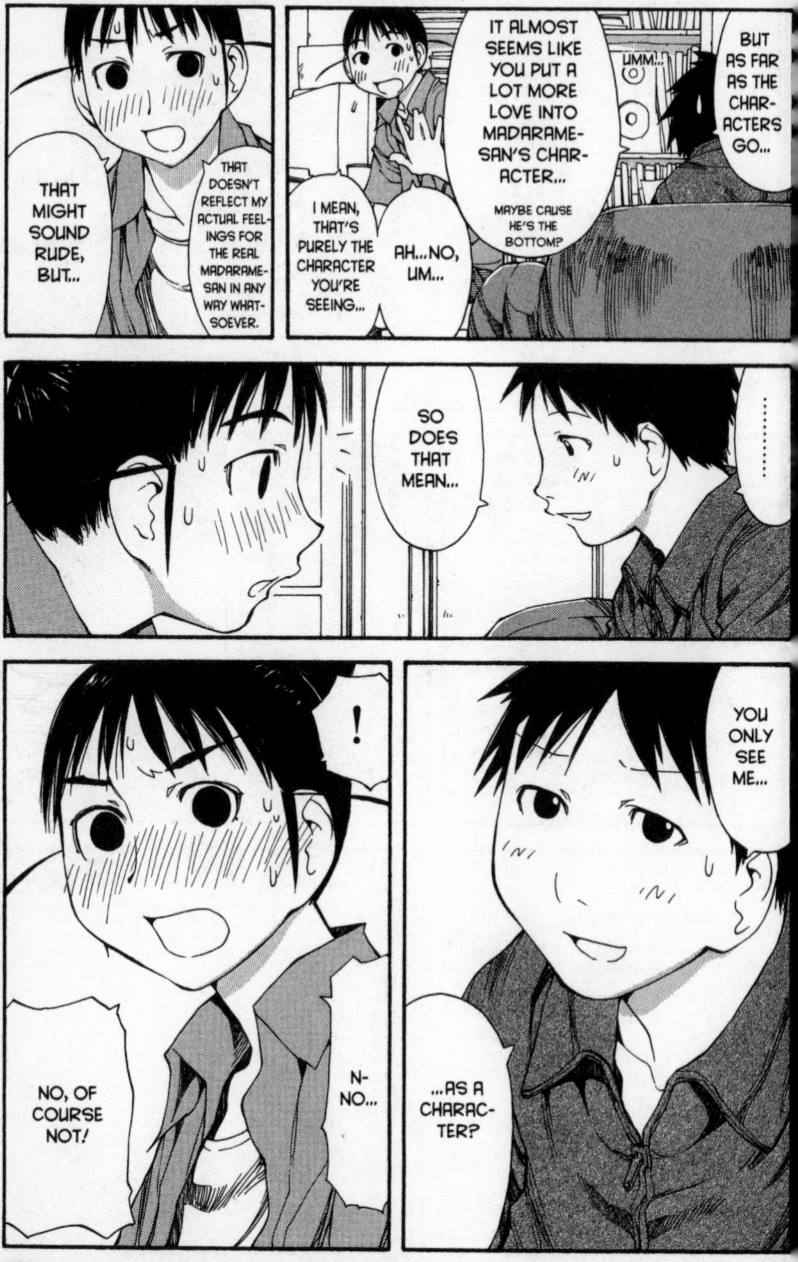
BUT AS FAR AS THE CHARACTERS GO...
UMM...
IT ALMOST SEEMS LIKE YOU PUT A LOT MORE LOVE INTO MADARAME-SAN'S CHARACTER...
MAYBE CAUSE HE'S THE BOTTOM?
AH...NO, UM...
I MEAN, THAT'S PURELY THE CHARACTER YOU'RE SEEING...
THAT DOESN'T REFLECT MY ACTUAL FEELINGS FOR THE REAL MADARAME-SAN IN ANY WAY WHATSOEVER.
THAT MIGHT SOUND RUDE, BUT...
......
SO DOES THAT MEAN...
YOU ONLY SEE ME...
...AS A CHARACTER?
!
N-NO...
NO, OF COURSE NOT!

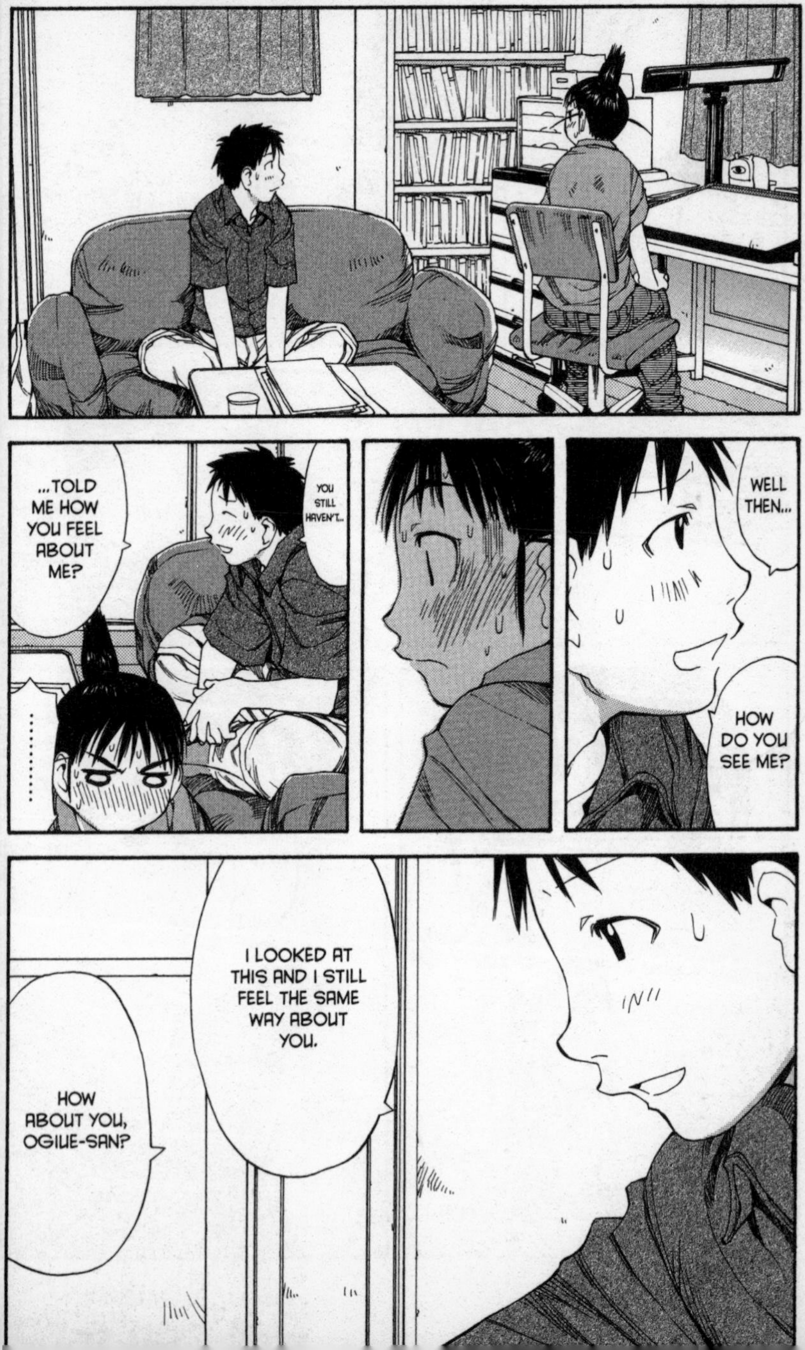
WELL THEN...
HOW DO YOU SEE ME?
YOU STILL HAVEN'T...
...TOLD ME HOW YOU FEEL ABOUT ME?
....
I LOOKED AT THIS AND I STILL FEEL THE SAME WAY ABOUT YOU.
HOW ABOUT YOU, OGIUE-SAN?

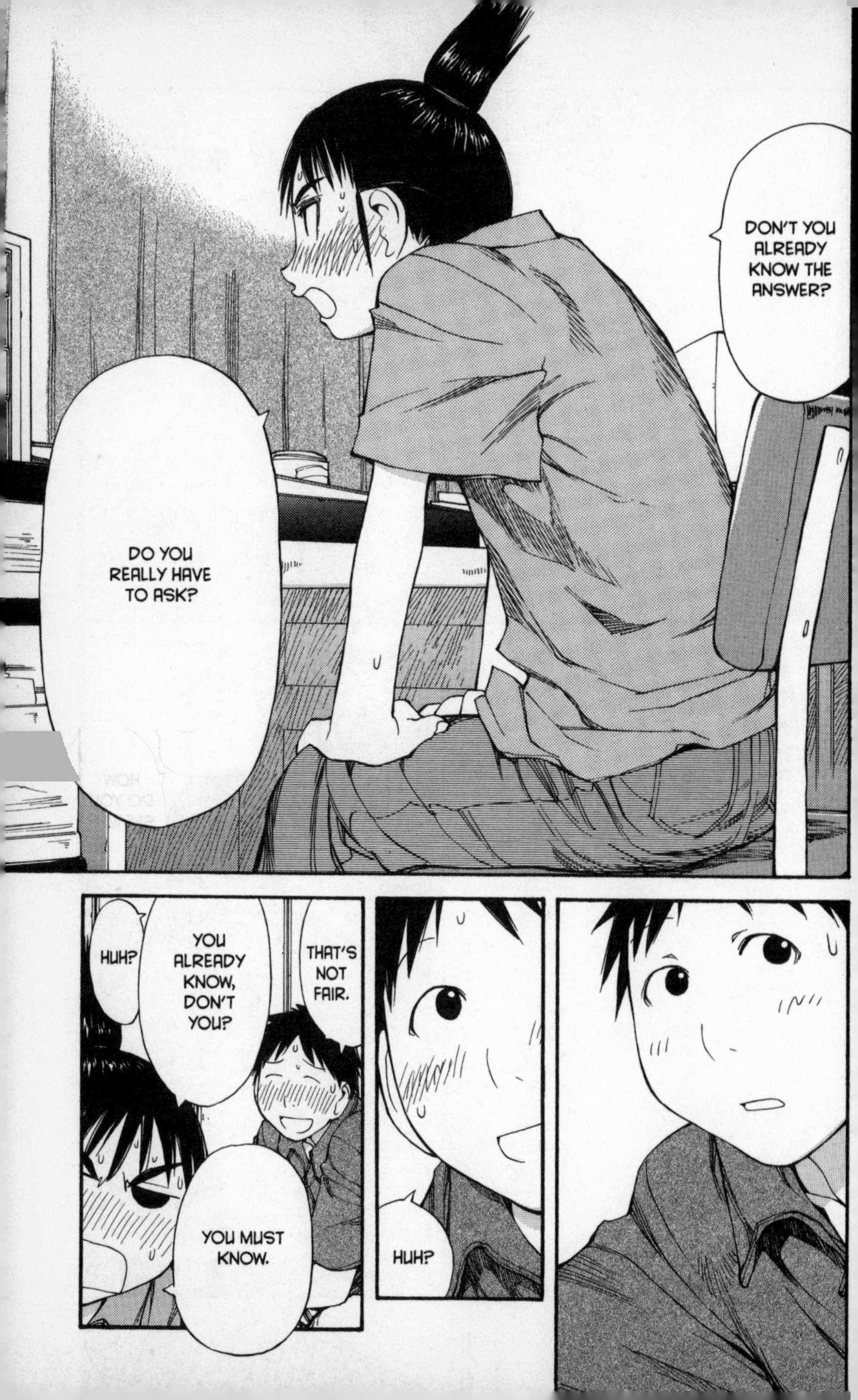
DON'T YOU ALREADY KNOW THE ANSWER?
DO YOU REALLY HAVE TO ASK?
HUH?
THAT'S NOT FAIR.
YOU ALREADY KNOW, DON'T YOU?
HUH?
YOU MUST KNOW.

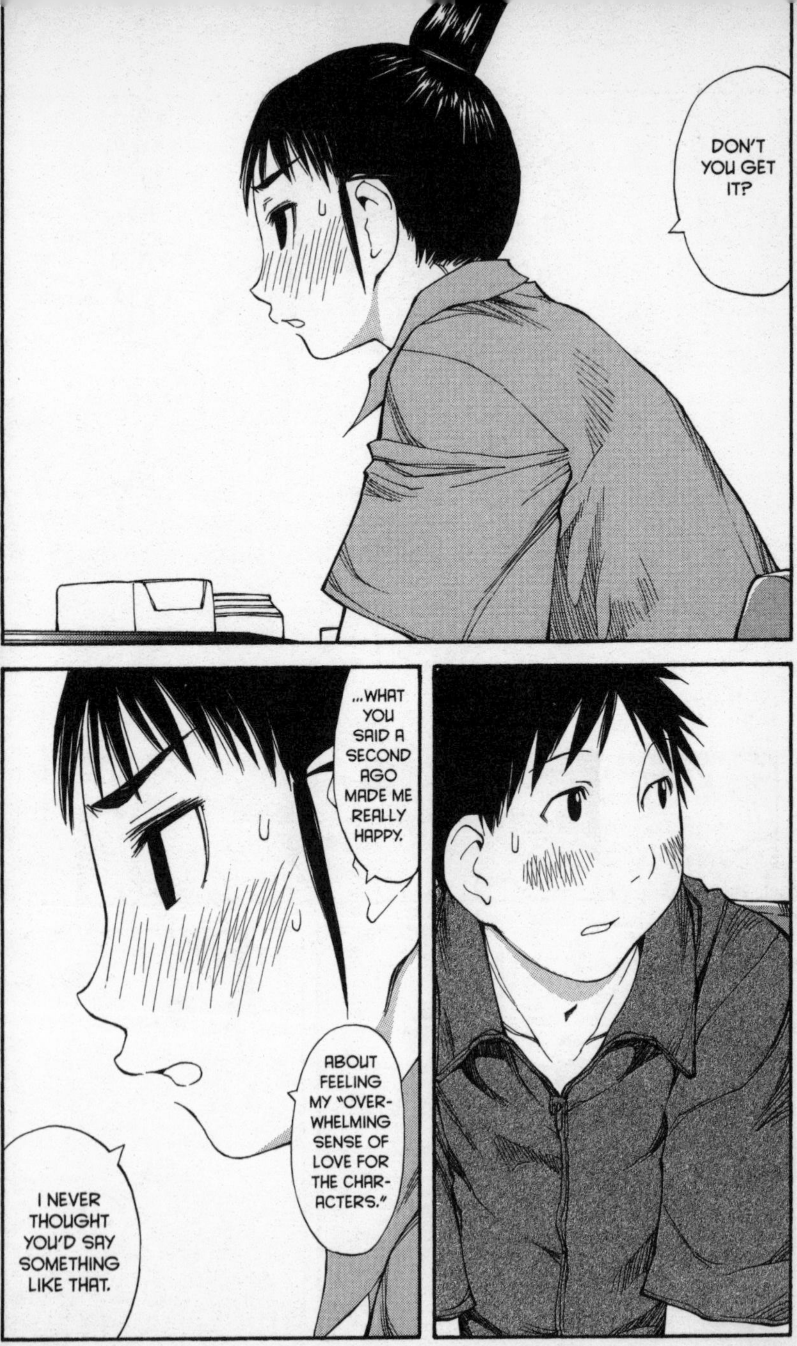
DON'T YOU GET IT?
...WHAT YOU SAID A SECOND AGO MADE ME REALLY HAPPY.
ABOUT FEELING MY "OVER-WHELMING SENSE OF LOVE FOR THE CHAR-ACTERS."
I NEVER THOUGHT YOU'D SAY SOMETHING LIKE THAT.

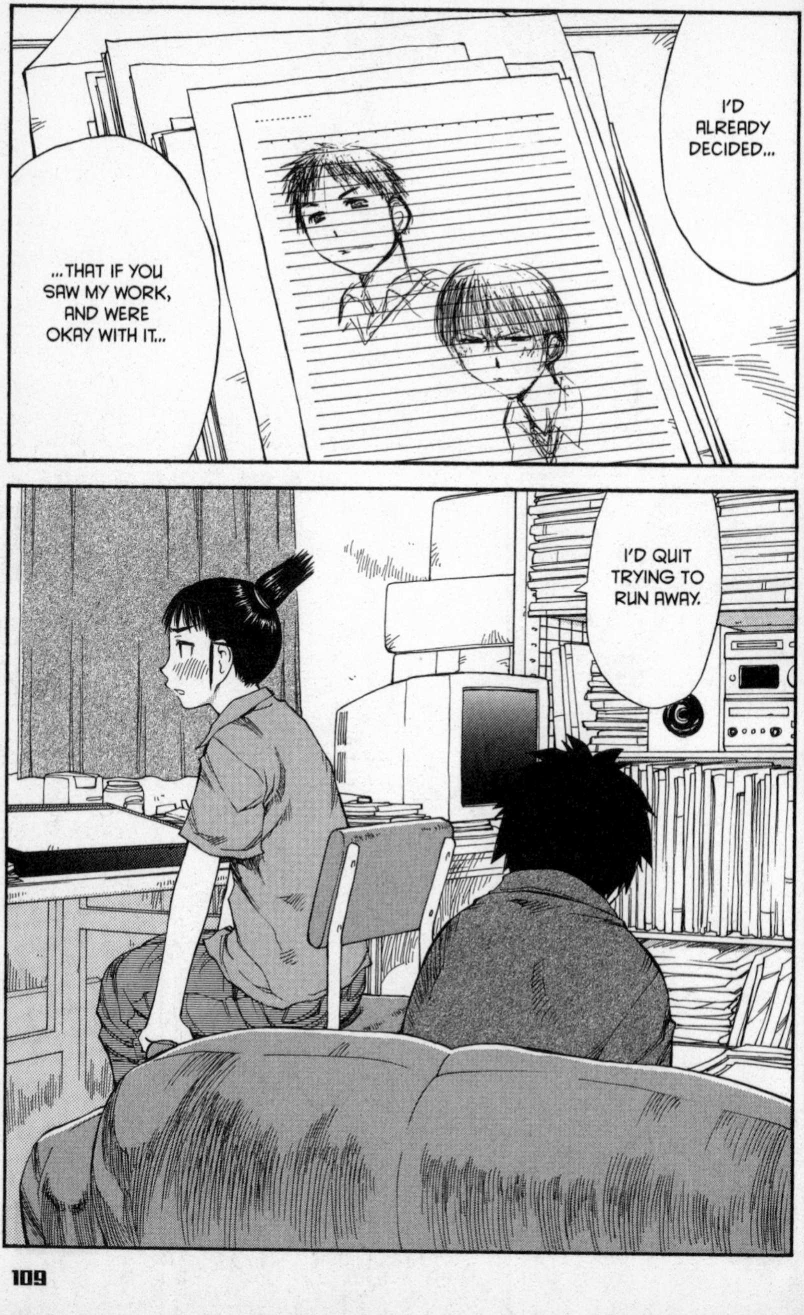
I'D ALREADY DECIDED...
...THAT IF YOU SAW MY WORK, AND WERE OKAY WITH IT...
I'D QUIT TRYING TO RUN AWAY.

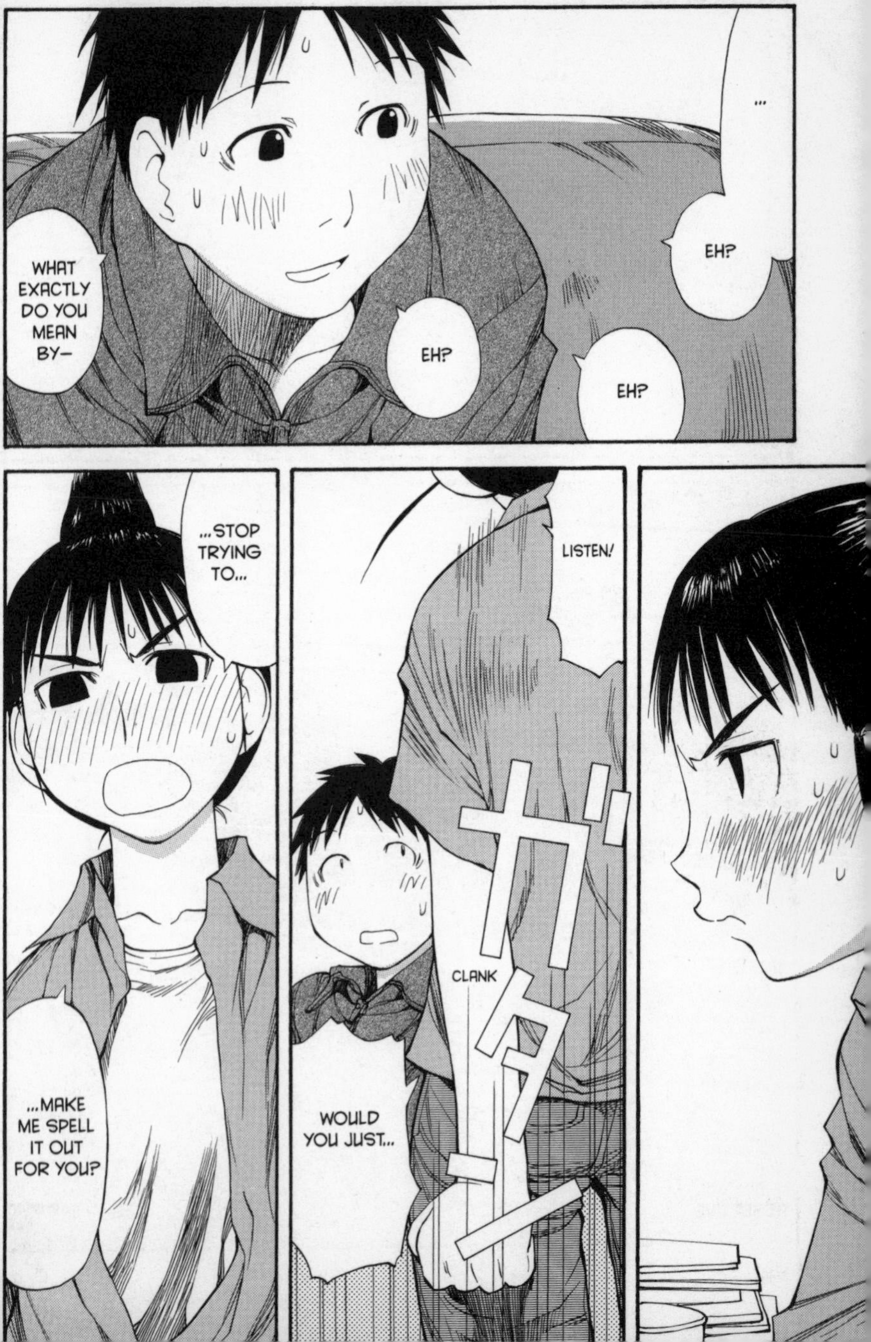
...
EH?
EH?
EH?
WHAT EXACTLY DO YOU MEAN BY—
LISTEN!
ガタ
CLANK
WOULD YOU JUST...
...STOP TRYING TO...
...MAKE ME SPELL IT OUT FOR YOU?

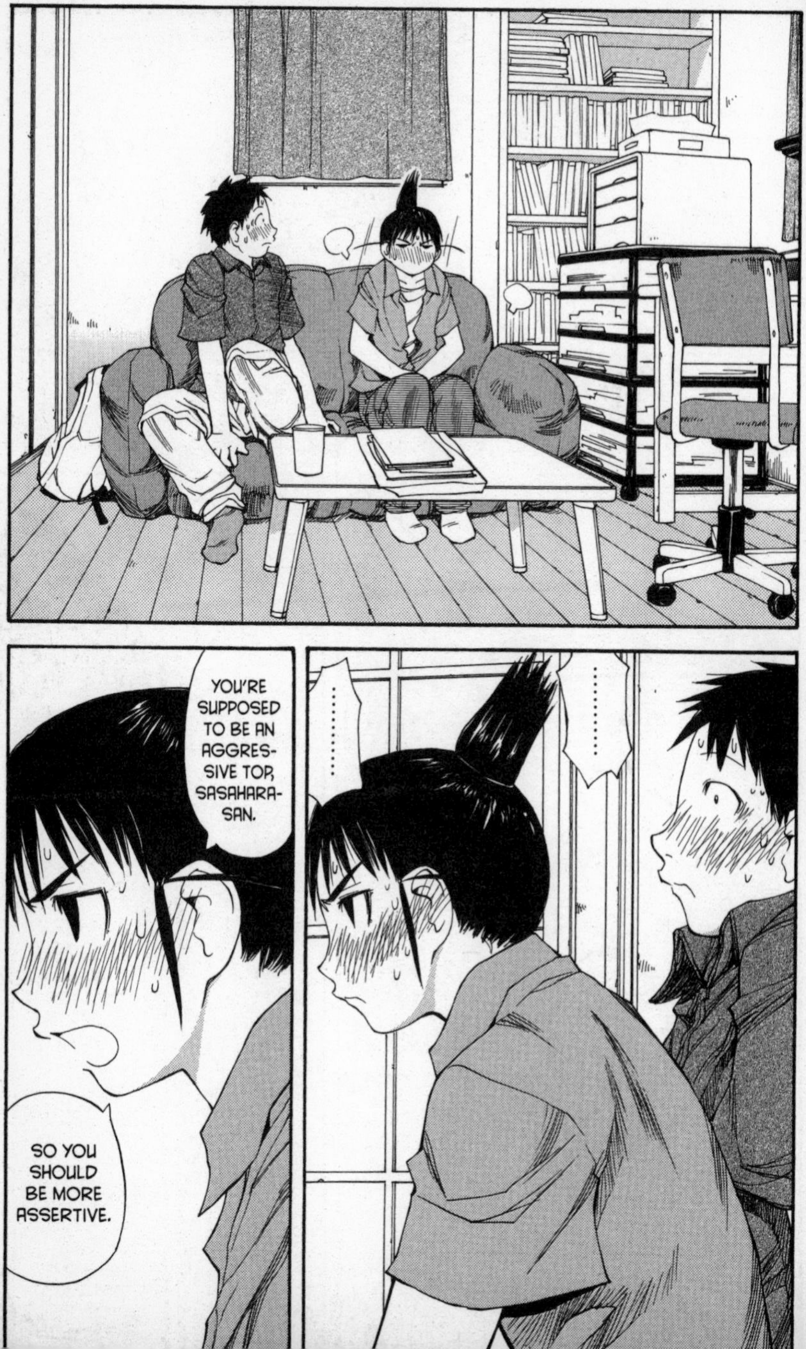

......
......
YOU'RE SUPPOSED TO BE AN AGGRES-SIVE TOP, SASAHARA-SAN.
SO YOU SHOULD BE MORE ASSERTIVE.

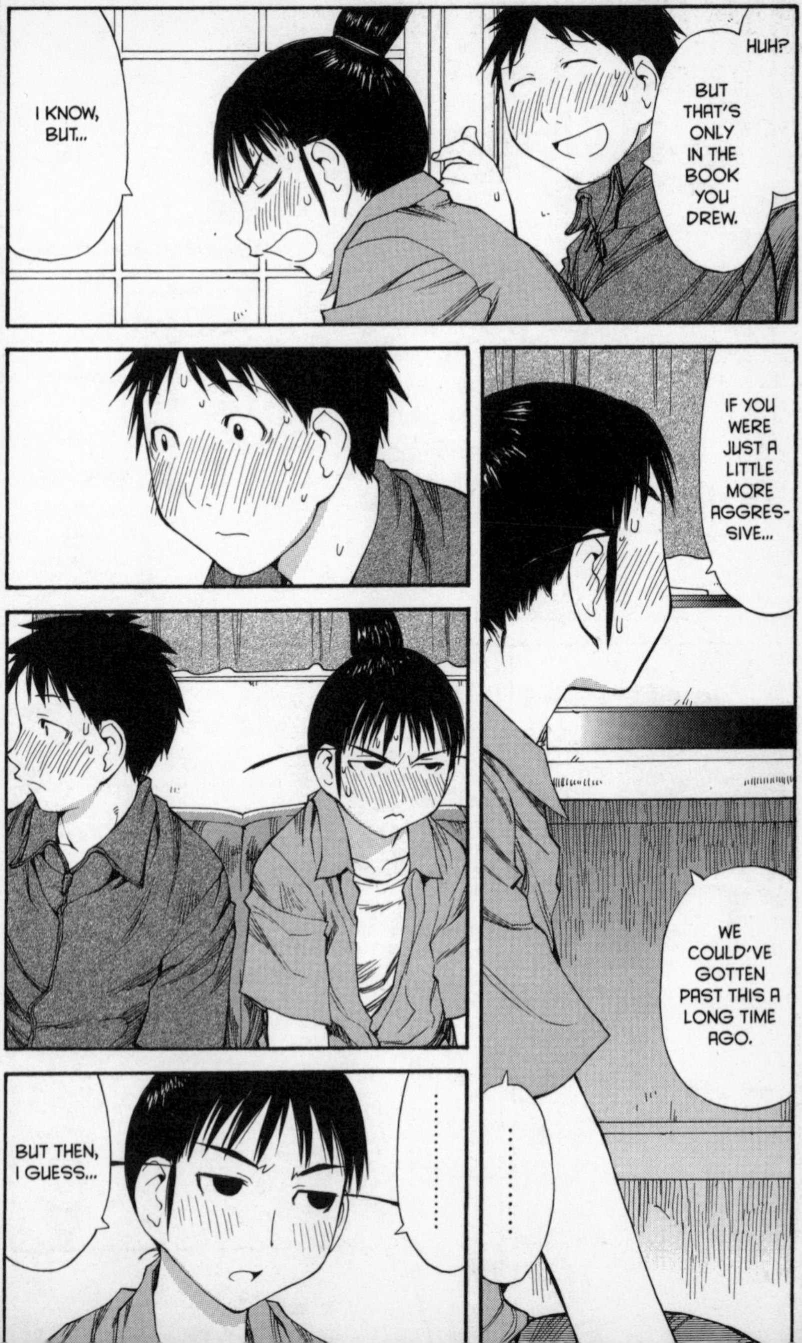
HUH?
BUT THAT'S ONLY IN THE BOOK YOU DREW.
I KNOW, BUT...
IF YOU WERE JUST A LITTLE MORE AGGRES-SIVE...
WE COULD'VE GOTTEN PAST THIS A LONG TIME AGO.
......
......
BUT THEN, I GUESS...

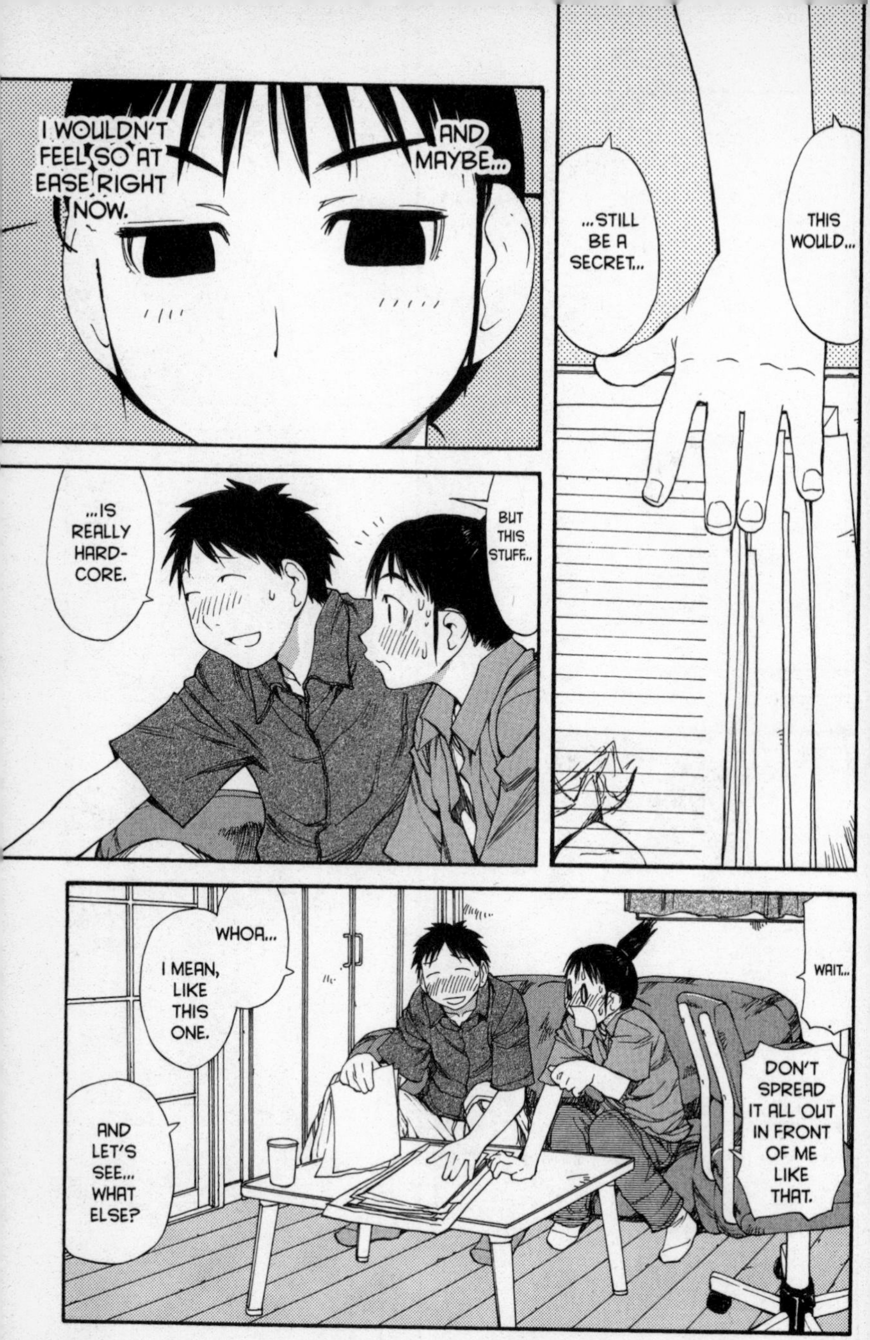
THIS WOULD...
...STILL BE A SECRET...
AND MAYBE...
I WOULDN'T FEEL SO AT EASE RIGHT NOW.
BUT THIS STUFF...
...IS REALLY HARD-CORE.
WAIT...
DON'T SPREAD IT ALL OUT IN FRONT OF ME LIKE THAT.
WHOA...
I MEAN, LIKE THIS ONE.
AND LET'S SEE... WHAT ELSE?

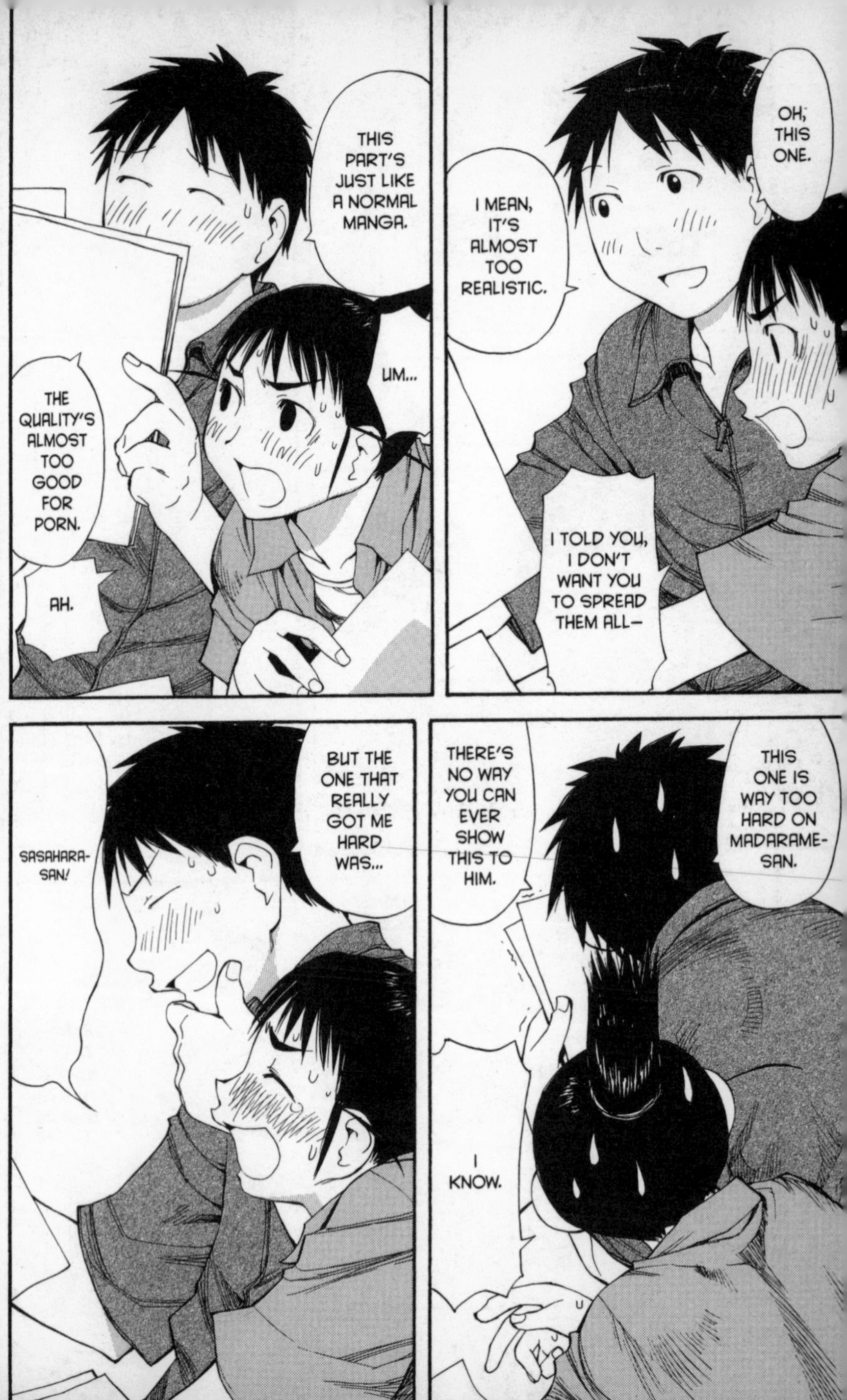
OH, THIS ONE.
I MEAN, IT'S ALMOST TOO REALISTIC.
I TOLD YOU, I DON'T WANT YOU TO SPREAD THEM ALL—
THIS PART'S JUST LIKE A NORMAL MANGA.
UM...
THE QUALITY'S ALMOST TOO GOOD FOR PORN.
AH.
THIS ONE IS WAY TOO HARD ON MADARAME-SAN.
THERE'S NO WAY YOU CAN EVER SHOW THIS TO HIM.
I KNOW.
BUT THE ONE THAT REALLY GOT ME HARD WAS...
SASAHARA-SAN!

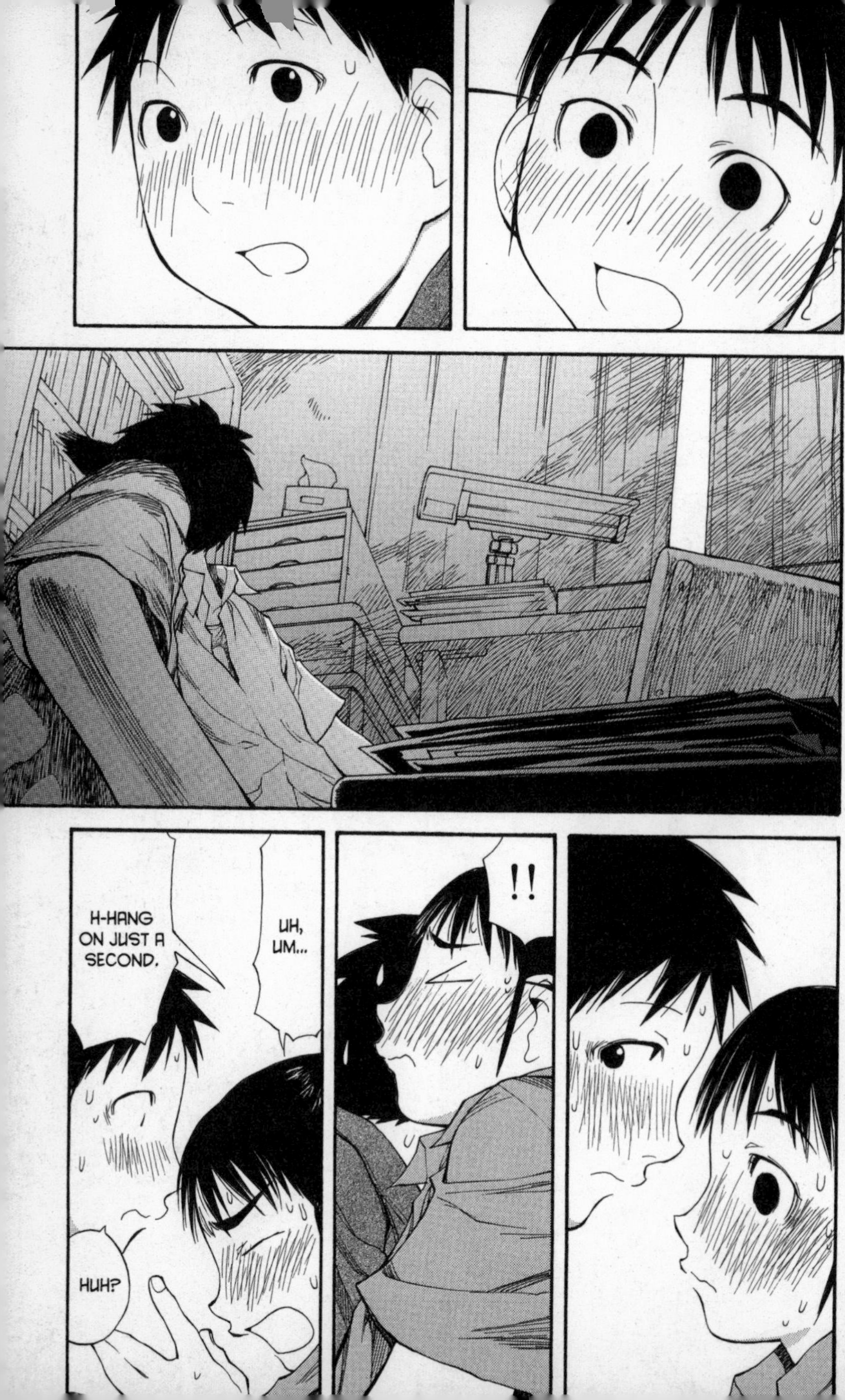
!!
UH, UM...
H-HANG ON JUST A SECOND.
HUH?

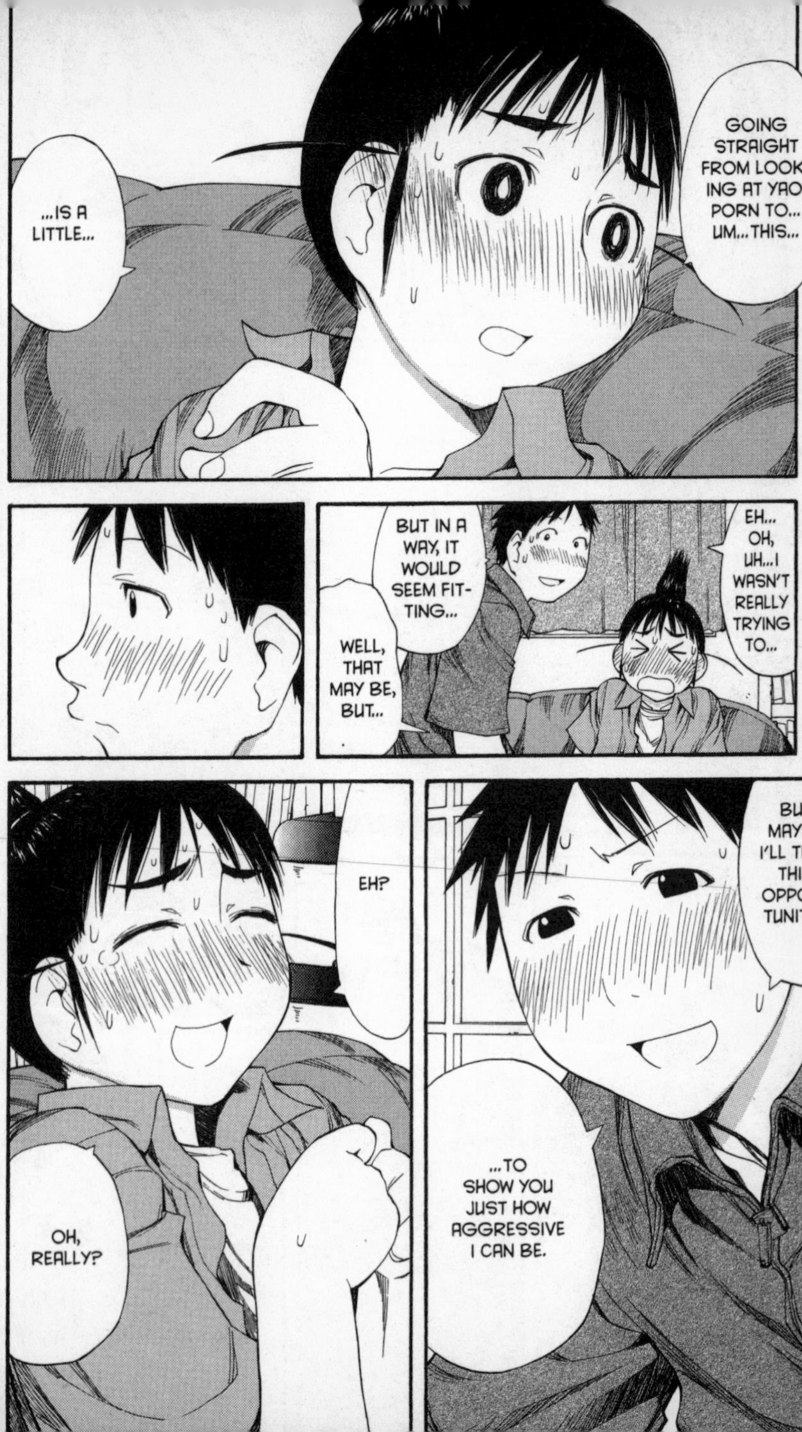
GOING STRAIGHT FROM LOOKING AT YAOI PORN TO... UM...THIS...
...IS A LITTLE...
EH... OH, UH...I WASN'T REALLY TRYING TO...
BUT IN A WAY, IT WOULD SEEM FITTING...
WELL, THAT MAY BE, BUT...
BUT MAYBE I'LL TAKE THIS OPPORTUNITY...
...TO SHOW YOU JUST HOW AGGRESSIVE I CAN BE.
EH?
OH, REALLY?

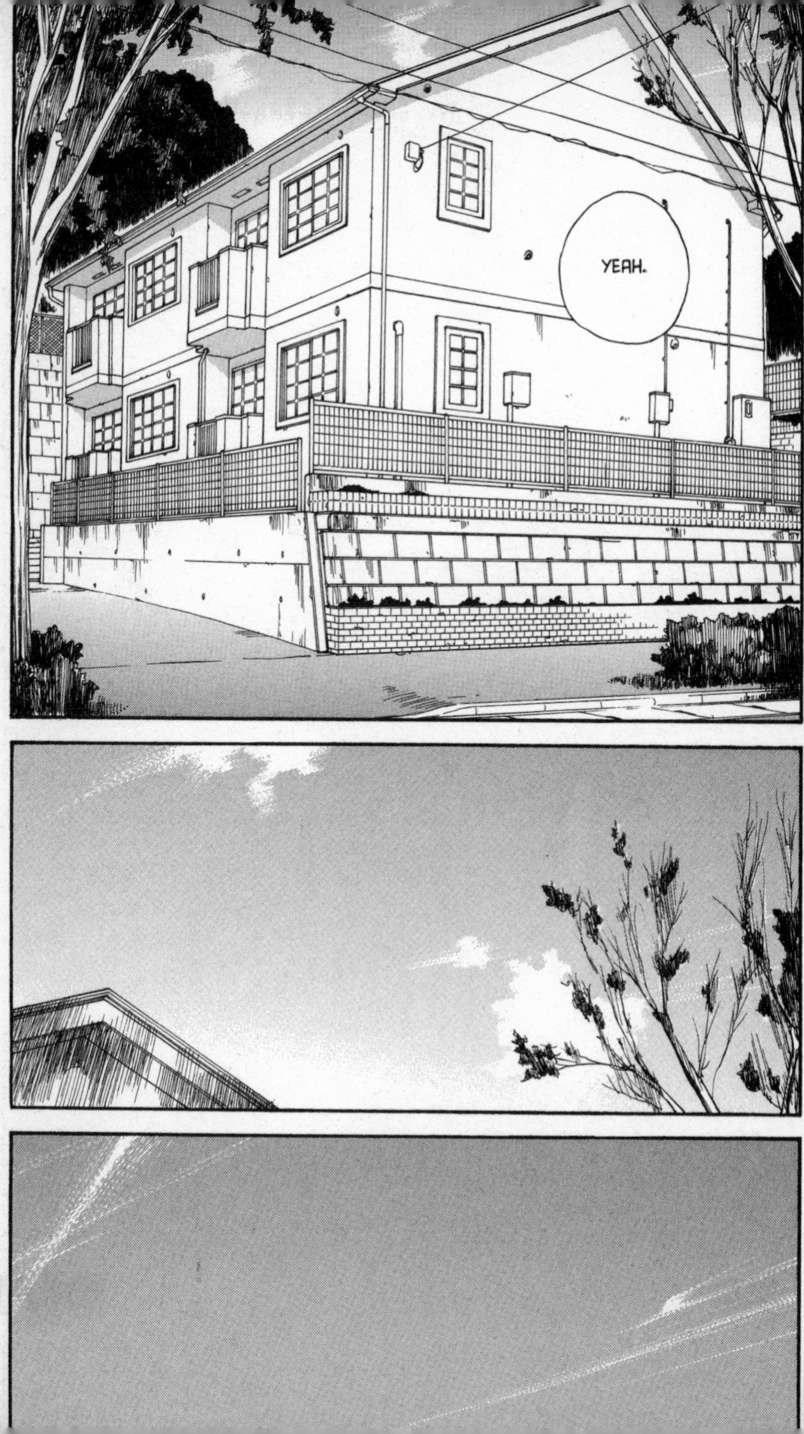
YEAH.

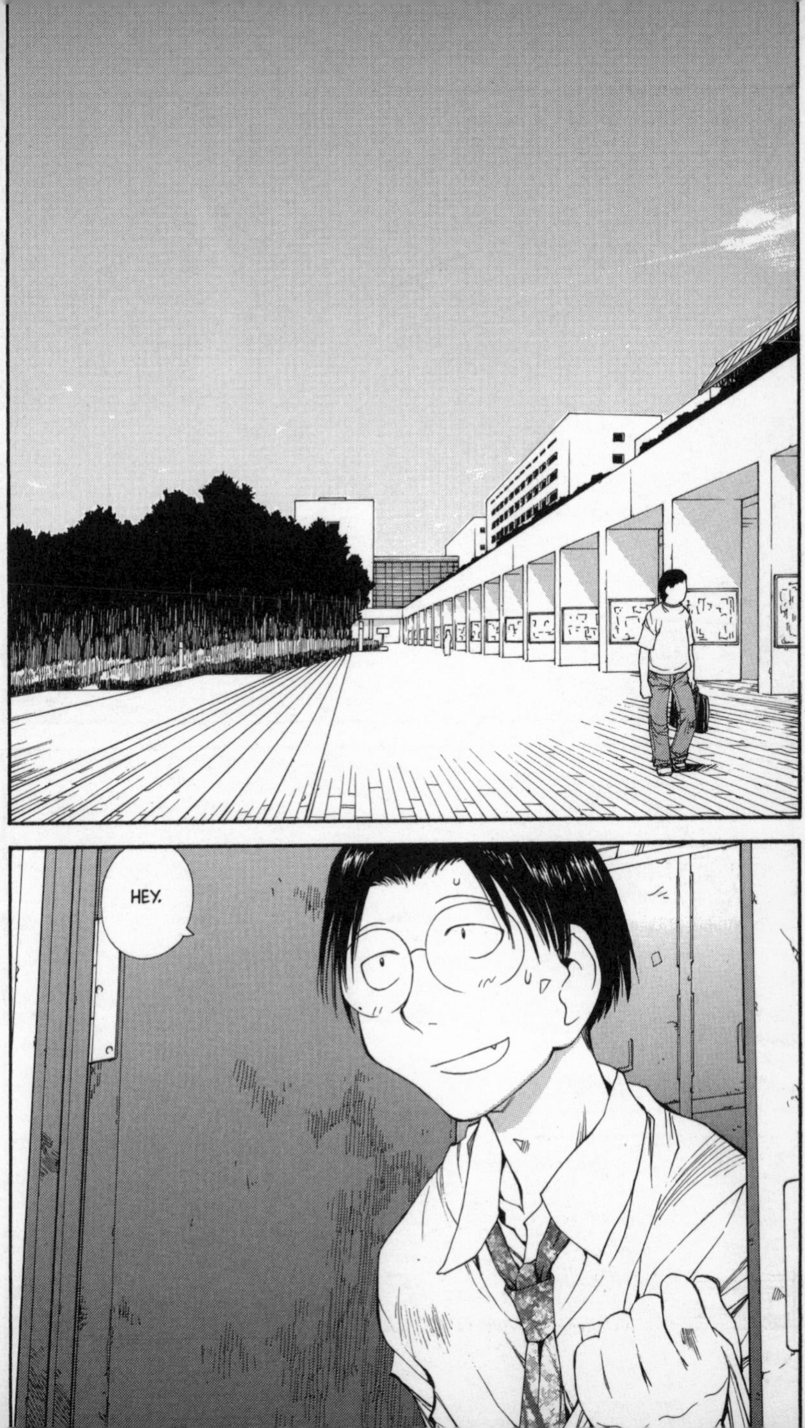
HEY.

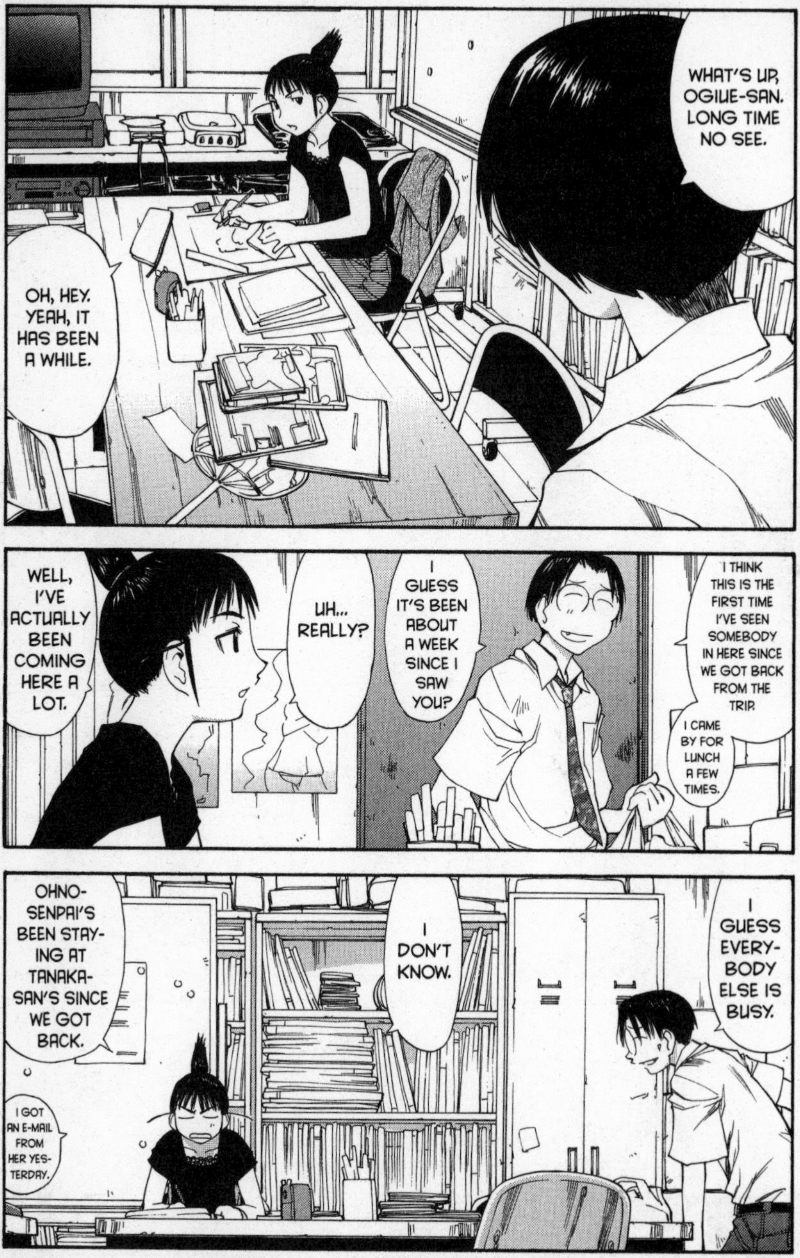
WHAT'S UP, OGIUE-SAN. LONG TIME NO SEE.
OH, HEY. YEAH, IT HAS BEEN A WHILE.
I THINK THIS IS THE FIRST TIME I'VE SEEN SOMEBODY IN HERE SINCE WE GOT BACK FROM THE TRIP.
I CAME BY FOR LUNCH A FEW TIMES.
I GUESS IT'S BEEN ABOUT A WEEK SINCE I SAW YOU?
UH... REALLY?
WELL, I'VE ACTUALLY BEEN COMING HERE A LOT.
I GUESS EVERYBODY ELSE IS BUSY.
I DON'T KNOW.
OHNO-SENPAI'S BEEN STAYING AT TANAKA-SAN'S SINCE WE GOT BACK.
I GOT AN E-MAIL FROM HER YESTERDAY.

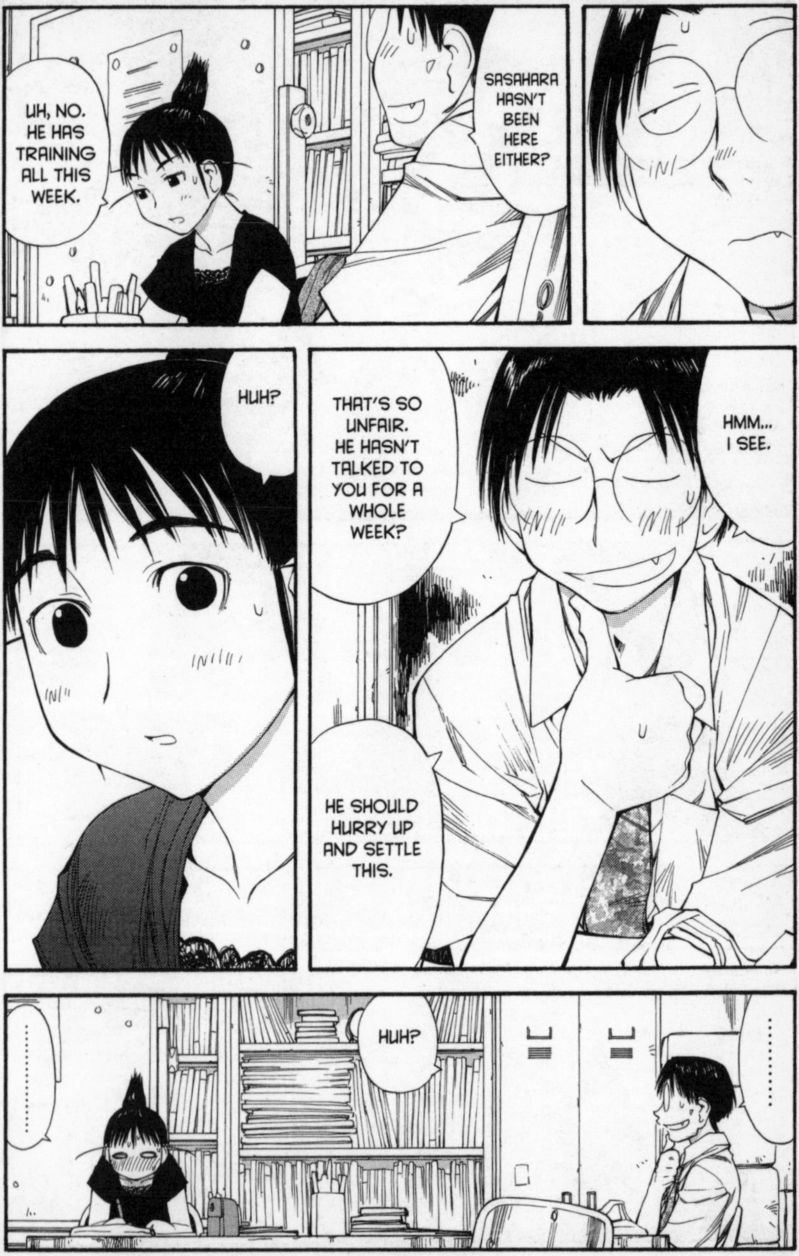
SASAHARA HASN'T BEEN HERE EITHER?
UH, NO. HE HAS TRAINING ALL THIS WEEK.
HMM... I SEE.
THAT'S SO UNFAIR. HE HASN'T TALKED TO YOU FOR A WHOLE WEEK?
HE SHOULD HURRY UP AND SETTLE THIS.
HUH?
......
HUH?
......

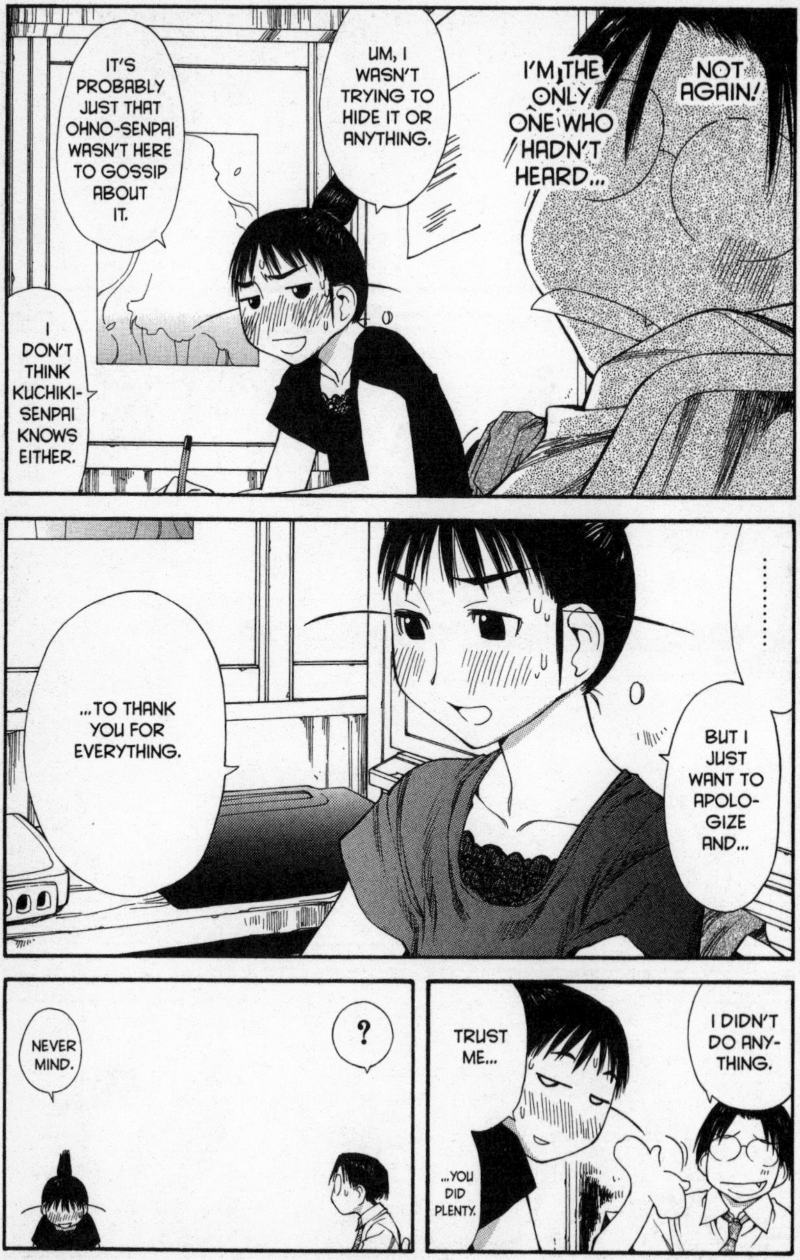
NOT AGAIN!
I'M THE ONLY ONE WHO HADN'T HEARD...
UM, I WASN'T TRYING TO HIDE IT OR ANYTHING.
IT'S PROBABLY JUST THAT OHNO-SENPAI WASN'T HERE TO GOSSIP ABOUT IT.
I DON'T THINK KUCHIKI-SENPAI KNOWS EITHER.
......
BUT I JUST WANT TO APOLOGIZE AND...
...TO THANK YOU FOR EVERYTHING.
I DIDN'T DO ANYTHING.
TRUST ME...
...YOU DID PLENTY.
?
NEVER MIND.

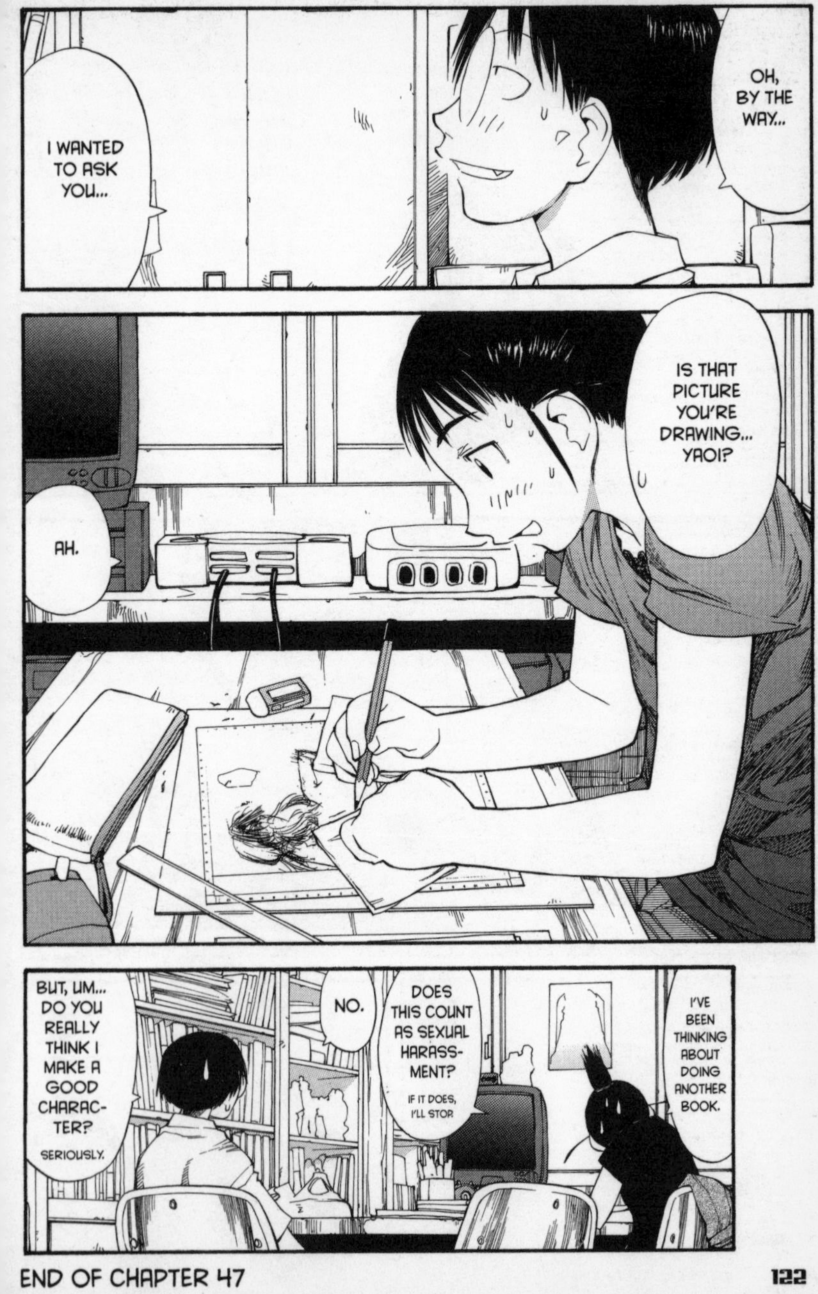
OH, BY THE WAY...
I WANTED TO ASK YOU...
IS THAT PICTURE YOU'RE DRAWING... YAOI?
AH.
I'VE BEEN THINKING ABOUT DOING ANOTHER BOOK.
DOES THIS COUNT AS SEXUAL HARASS-MENT?
IF IT DOES, I'LL STOP.
NO.
BUT, UM... DO YOU REALLY THINK I MAKE A GOOD CHARAC-TER?
SERIOUSLY.

KUJIBIKI ♥ UNBALANCE

BEN- KOYUKI HAS PUSHED HER OLDER SISTER KOMA-KI ASIDE, AND BECOME A MAIN CHARACTER.

PV- WELL, SHE IS AN IMPORTANT LITTLE-SISTER CHARACTER. IT WAS A GOOD WAY TO KEEP THINGS BALANCED.

BEN- NOW SHE HAS PSYCHIC POWERS.

PV- SO IT TURNS OUT THAT THE WEAKEST CHARACTER OF ALL HAD A DORMANT SUPERPOWER BURIED DEEP WITHIN HER. THAT'S A CLASSIC STORY-TELLING TOOL. IT'S THE OLD "IYABON RULE."

BEN- UM, YOU'RE TOTALLY USING THAT WRONG, BUT ANYWAY... YOU SEEM TO BE TAKING THIS PRETTY CALMLY. IT SEEMS THAT HER CHARACTER HAS AGED QUITE A BIT, AND SHE'S BECOME AN ELEMENTARY-SCHOOL STUDENT. WHAT DO YOU THINK ABOUT THAT?

PV- YEAH WELL, SHE USED TO BE A PRESCHOOLER, RIGHT? I MEAN, COME ON. DON'T YOU THINK THAT'S A LITTLE SICK?

BEN- WHAT IS? I MEAN, IS HAVING HER AS AN ELEMENTARY SCHOOL STUDENT ANY LESS SICK?

PV- MAYBE THEY CHANGED IT BECAUSE THEY THOUGHT THEY'D GONE TOO FAR.

BEN- ARE YOU TALKING ABOUT THE GAME?

PV- WELL, THERE WILL BE PLENTY OF DOUJINSHI'S EXPLORING THIS ANYWAY, SO I'LL JUST MAKE DO WITH THOSE.

BEN- GOOD LUCK.

PV- THE WAY SHE RUNS IS REALLY CUTE.

BEN- ARE YOU IGNORING ME?

PV- HOW ABOUT SHINOBU?

BEN- WELL, FIRST THEY WERE GOING TO HAVE HER AS A MAIN CHARACTER, BUT ONCE THEY MADE TOKINO INTO A CHILDHOOD FRIEND CHARACTER, SHINOBU'S ROLE KIND OF BECAME SUPERFLUOUS, SO SHE WAS DOWNGRADED TO A SUPPORTING CHARACTER.

PV- POOR THING.

BEN- BUT NOW SHE'S A MUCH SIMPLER CHARACTER. SHE NO LONGER HAS A SPLIT PERSONALITY. INSTEAD SHE JUST HIDES HER TRUE SELF. PLUS, NOW A BIG PART OF HER CHARACTER IS THAT SHE REALLY LOVES HER LITTLE BROTHER.

PV- OH, SO IN OTHER WORDS, THIS TIME MOST OF THE CHARACTERS ARE REALLY INTO CHIHIRO.

BEN- YES. BEFORE, WE HAD CHIHIRO AS THE MAIN CHARACTER, BUT NONE OF THE OTHER CHARACTERS WERE IN LOVE WITH HIM. SO, THEY ENDED UP WITH THIS HAREM-STYLE STORY THAT DIDN'T QUITE WORK.

PV- BUT THERE WAS STILL THE PRESIDENT...

BEN- YEAH, JUST HER AND KOMAKI.

PV- WHEN YOU THINK ABOUT IT, IT'S PRETTY CRAZY. WHAT WAS YUU KUROKI THINKING?

BEN- THAT'S PROBABLY WHY THEY DECIDED TO CHANGE SO MUCH THIS TIME.

PV- BUT THE MANGA IS STILL GOING.

BEN- YEAH, THAT'S PROBABLY WHY THEY CAME UP WITH ALL THOSE NEW CHARACTERS.

PV- OH, WE TALKED ABOUT THAT BEFORE, DIDN'T WE?

BEN- YER...BY THE WAY, DOESN'T THAT PECULIAR CREATURE THEY DREW ON THE BOTTOM KIND OF LOOK LIKE YOU, PIT VIPER?

PV- YEAH, BUT I DON'T BECOME SUPER GORGEOUS WHEN I TAKE MY GLASSES OFF.

BEN- WHOA, I DIDN'T EXPECT YOU TO ANSWER SO SERIOUSLY.

SHOULD I JUST PUNCH HIM?

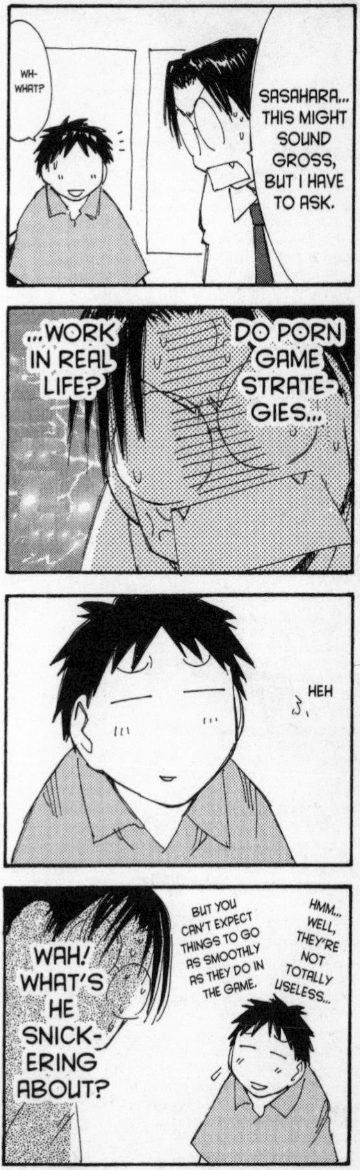
SASAHARA... THIS MIGHT SOUND GROSS, BUT I HAVE TO ASK.
WH-WHAT?
DO PORN GAME STRATE-GIES...
...WORK IN REAL LIFE?
HEH
HMM... WELL, THEY'RE NOT TOTALLY USELESS...
BUT YOU CAN'T EXPECT THINGS TO GO AS SMOOTHLY AS THEY DO IN THE GAME.
WAH! WHAT'S HE SNICK-ERING ABOUT?

REAL

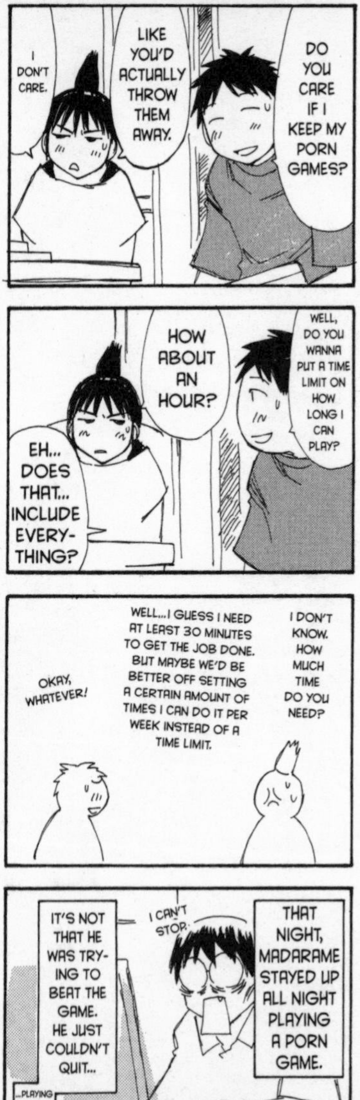
DO YOU CARE IF I KEEP MY PORN GAMES?
LIKE YOU'D ACTUALLY THROW THEM AWAY.
I DON'T CARE.
WELL, DO YOU WANNA PUT A TIME LIMIT ON HOW LONG I CAN PLAY?
HOW ABOUT AN HOUR?
EH... DOES THAT... INCLUDE EVERY-THING?
I DON'T KNOW. HOW MUCH TIME DO YOU NEED?
WELL...I GUESS I NEED AT LEAST 30 MINUTES TO GET THE JOB DONE. BUT MAYBE WE'D BE BETTER OFF SETTING A CERTAIN AMOUNT OF TIMES I CAN DO IT PER WEEK INSTEAD OF A TIME LIMIT.
OKAY, WHATEVER!
THAT NIGHT, MADARAME STAYED UP ALL NIGHT PLAYING A PORN GAME.
I CAN'T STOP.
IT'S NOT THAT HE WAS TRY-ING TO BEAT THE GAME. HE JUST COULDN'T QUIT...
...PLAYING "NYABO-RYABO ALTER-NATIVE."

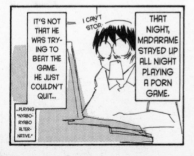

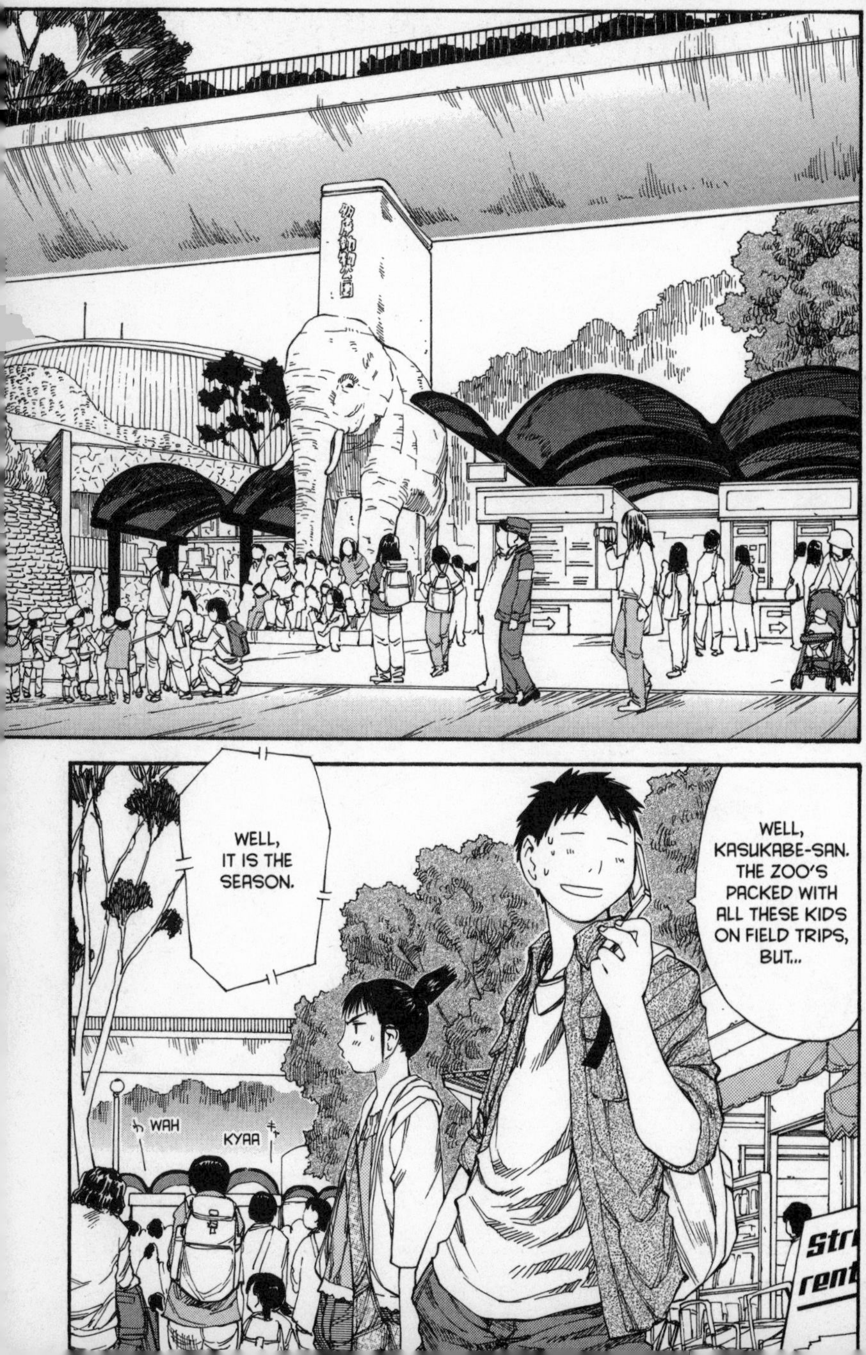
WELL, KASUKABE-SAN. THE ZOO'S PACKED WITH ALL THESE KIDS ON FIELD TRIPS, BUT...
WELL, IT IS THE SEASON.
KYAA
WAH

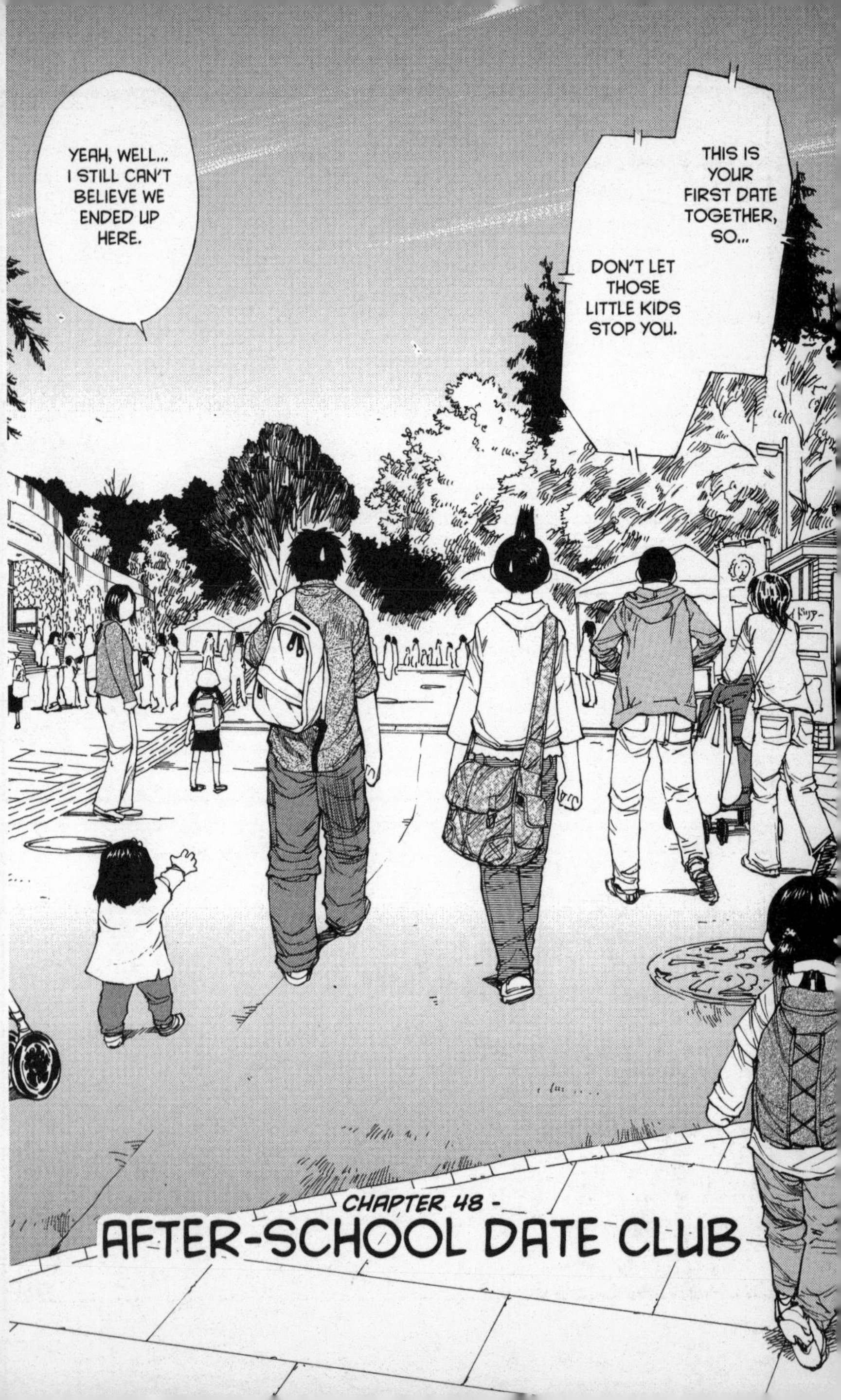
THIS IS YOUR FIRST DATE TOGETHER, SO...
DON'T LET THOSE LITTLE KIDS STOP YOU.
YEAH, WELL... I STILL CAN'T BELIEVE WE ENDED UP HERE.
CHAPTER 48 -
AFTER-SCHOOL DATE CLUB

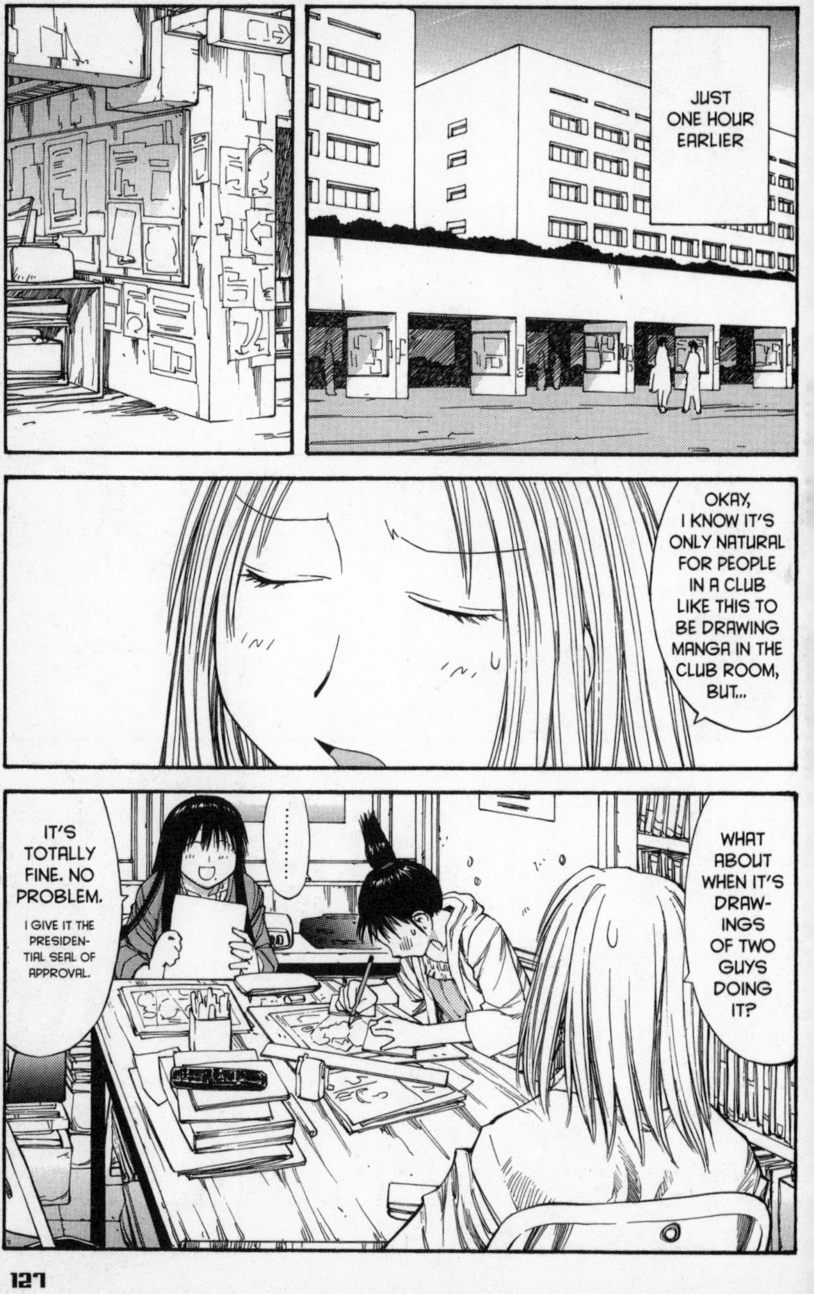
JUST ONE HOUR EARLIER
OKAY, I KNOW IT'S ONLY NATURAL FOR PEOPLE IN A CLUB LIKE THIS TO BE DRAWING MANGA IN THE CLUB ROOM, BUT...
WHAT ABOUT WHEN IT'S DRAW-INGS OF TWO GUYS DOING IT?
......
IT'S TOTALLY FINE. NO PROBLEM.
I GIVE IT THE PRESIDEN-TIAL SEAL OF APPROVAL.

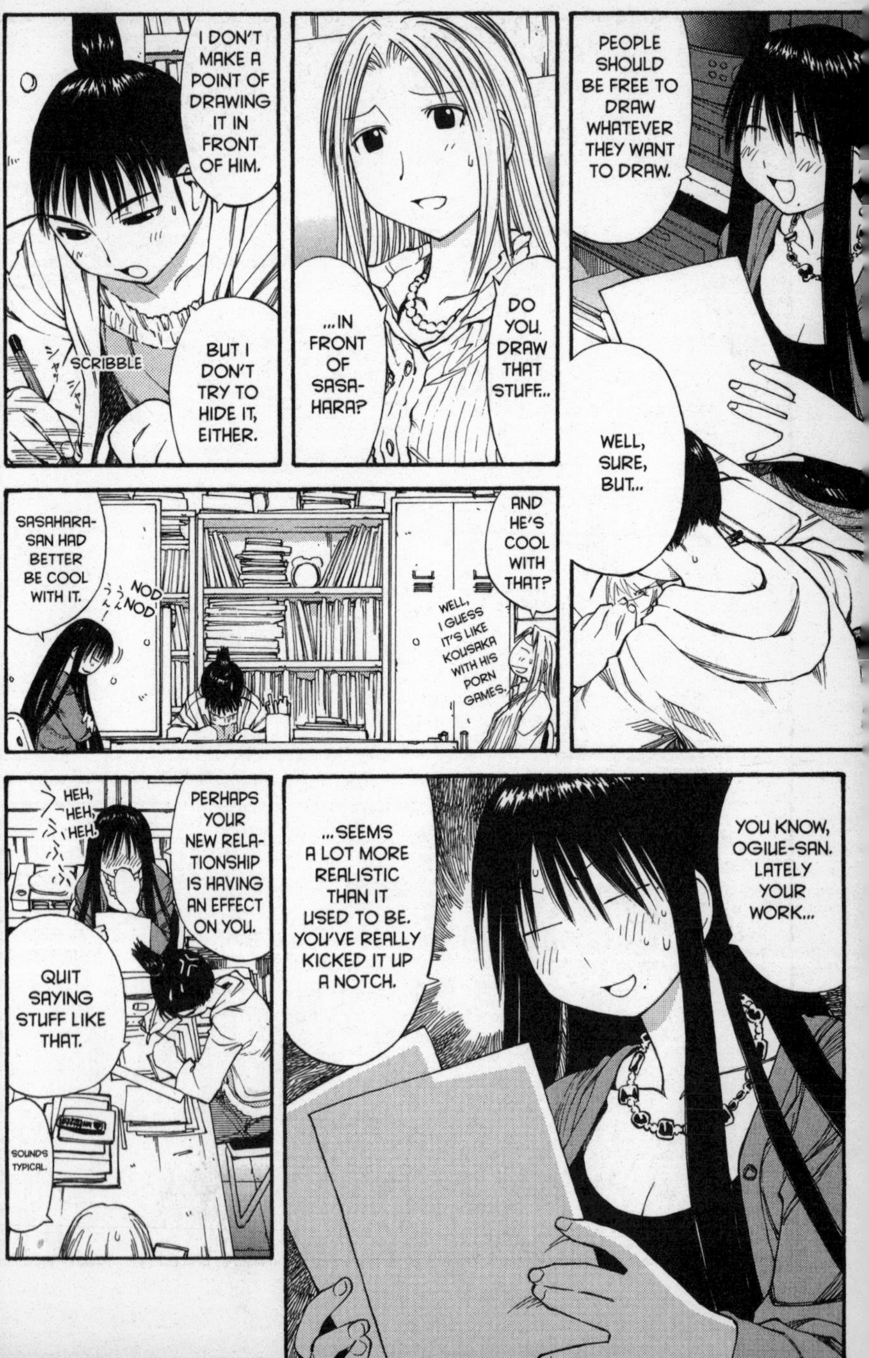
PEOPLE SHOULD BE FREE TO DRAW WHATEVER THEY WANT TO DRAW.
WELL, SURE, BUT...
DO YOU DRAW THAT STUFF...
...IN FRONT OF SASAHARA?
I DON'T MAKE A POINT OF DRAWING IT IN FRONT OF HIM.
BUT I DON'T TRY TO HIDE IT, EITHER.
SCRIBBLE
AND HE'S COOL WITH THAT?
WELL, I GUESS IT'S LIKE KOUSAKA WITH HIS PORN GAMES.
SASAHARA-SAN HAD BETTER BE COOL WITH IT.
NOD NOD
YOU KNOW, OGIUE-SAN. LATELY YOUR WORK...
...SEEMS A LOT MORE REALISTIC THAN IT USED TO BE. YOU'VE REALLY KICKED IT UP A NOTCH.
PERHAPS YOUR NEW RELATIONSHIP IS HAVING AN EFFECT ON YOU.
HEH, HEH, HEH.
QUIT SAYING STUFF LIKE THAT.
SOUNDS TYPICAL.

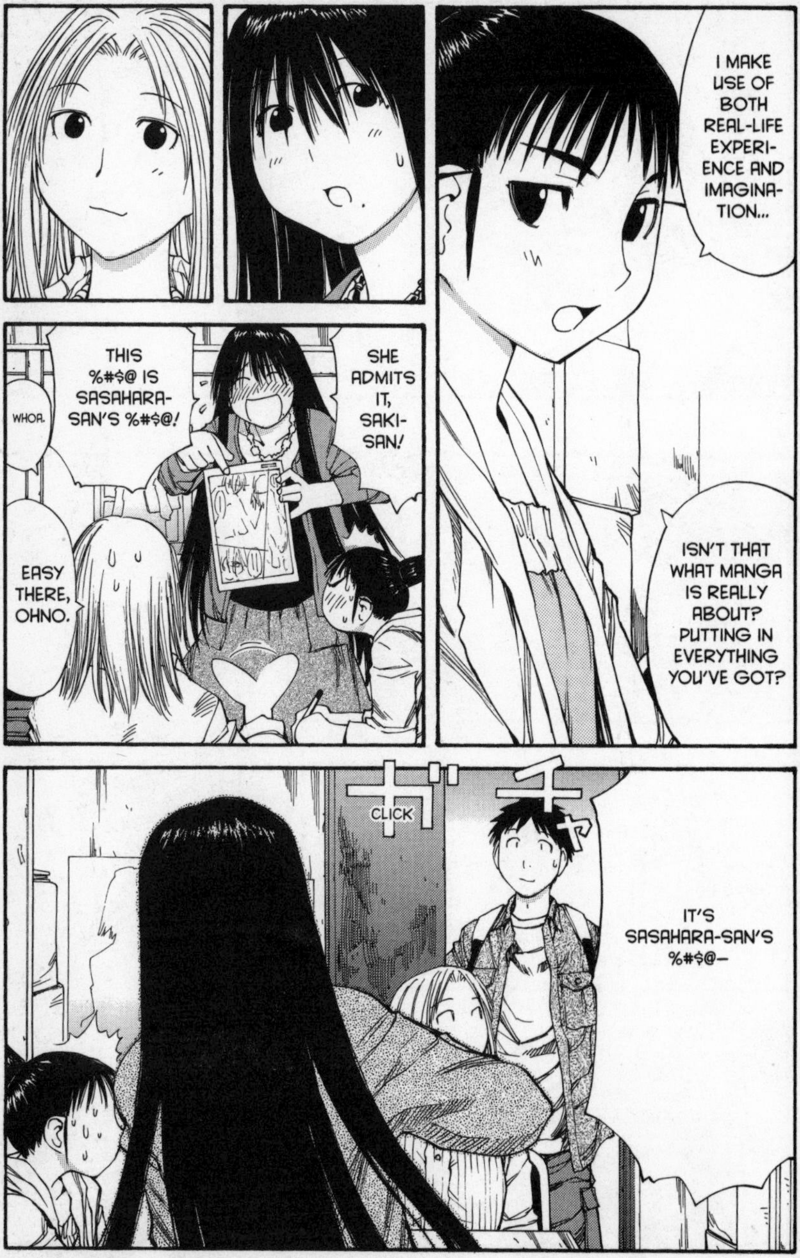
I MAKE USE OF BOTH REAL-LIFE EXPERI-ENCE AND IMAGINA-TION...
ISN'T THAT WHAT MANGA IS REALLY ABOUT? PUTTING IN EVERYTHING YOU'VE GOT?
SHE ADMITS IT, SAKI-SAN!
THIS %#$@ IS SASAHARA-SAN'S %#$@!
WHOA.
EASY THERE, OHNO.
ガチャ
CLICK
IT'S SASAHARA-SAN'S %#$@—

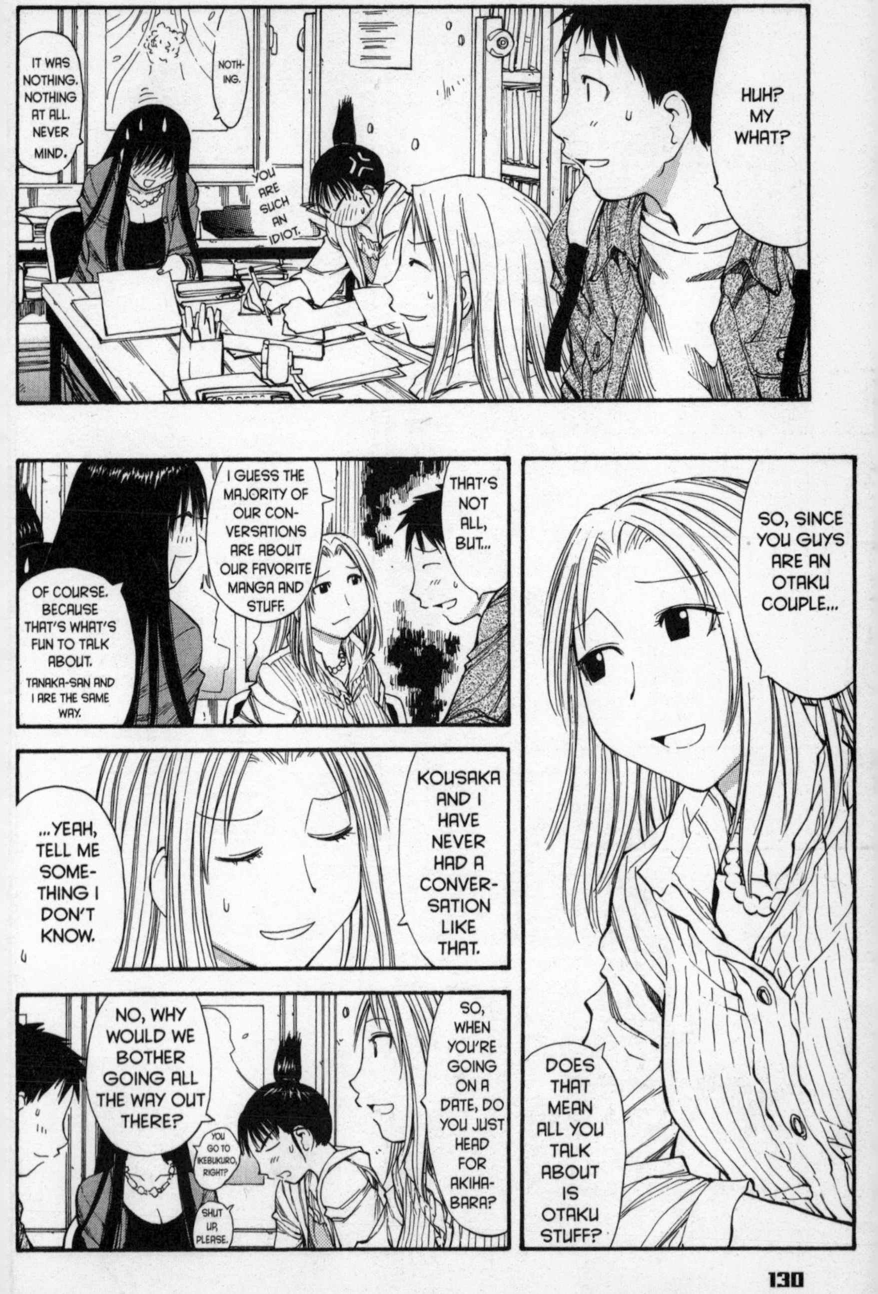
HUH? MY WHAT?
NOTH-ING.
IT WAS NOTHING. NOTHING AT ALL. NEVER MIND.
YOU ARE SUCH AN IDIOT.
SO, SINCE YOU GUYS ARE AN OTAKU COUPLE...
DOES THAT MEAN ALL YOU TALK ABOUT IS OTAKU STUFF?
THAT'S NOT ALL, BUT...
I GUESS THE MAJORITY OF OUR CON-VERSATIONS ARE ABOUT OUR FAVORITE MANGA AND STUFF.
OF COURSE. BECAUSE THAT'S WHAT'S FUN TO TALK ABOUT.
TANAKA-SAN AND I ARE THE SAME WAY.
KOUSAKA AND I HAVE NEVER HAD A CONVER-SATION LIKE THAT.
...YEAH, TELL ME SOME-THING I DON'T KNOW.
SO, WHEN YOU'RE GOING ON A DATE, DO YOU JUST HEAD FOR AKIHA-BARA?
NO, WHY WOULD WE BOTHER GOING ALL THE WAY OUT THERE?
YOU GO TO IKEBUKURO, RIGHT?
SHUT UP, PLEASE.

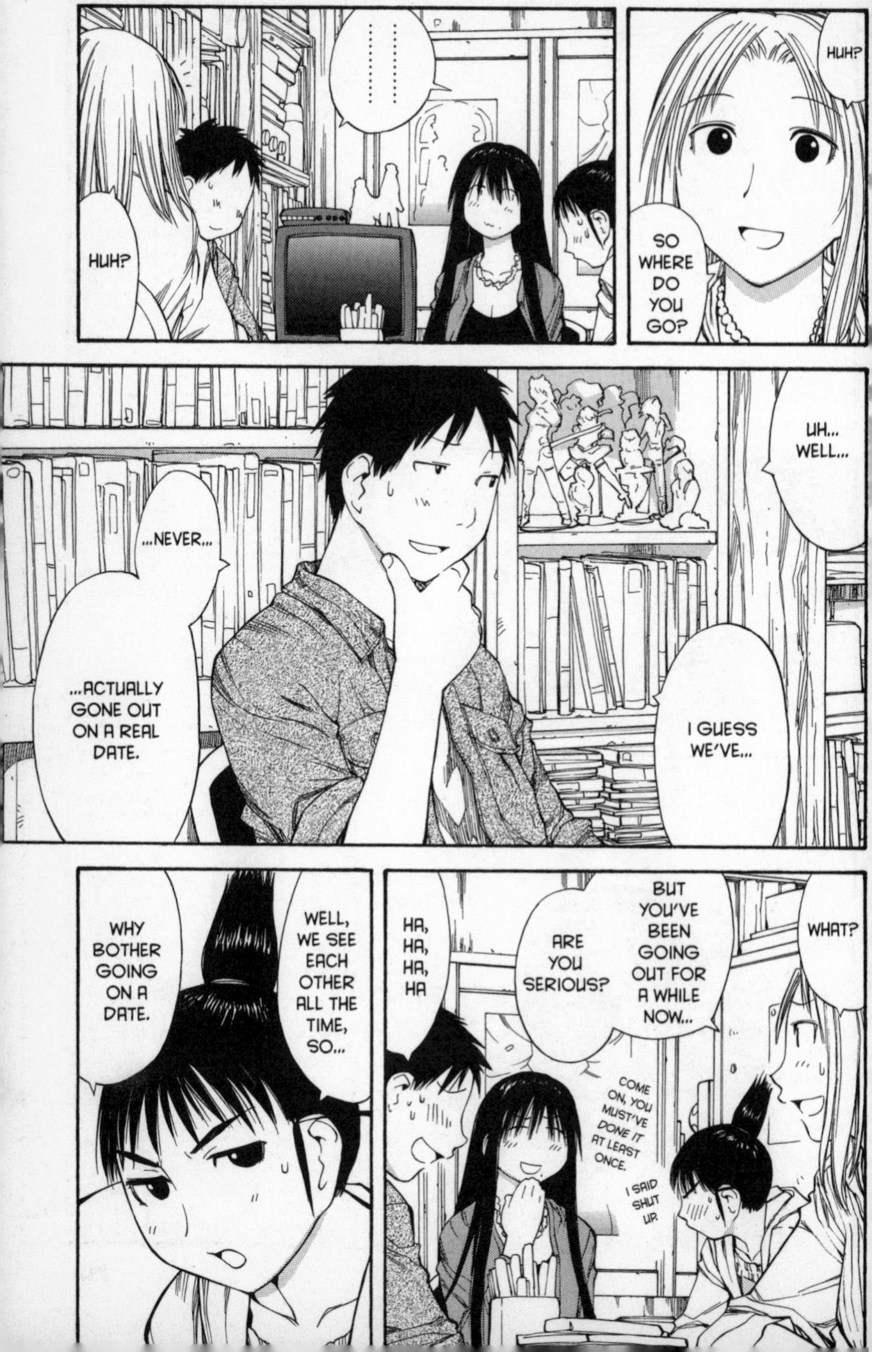
HUH?
SO WHERE DO YOU GO?
......
HUH?
UH... WELL...
I GUESS WE'VE...
...NEVER...
...ACTUALLY GONE OUT ON A REAL DATE.
WHAT?
BUT YOU'VE BEEN GOING OUT FOR A WHILE NOW...
ARE YOU SERIOUS?
COME ON, YOU MUST'VE DONE IT AT LEAST ONCE.
I SAID SHUT UP.
HA, HA, HA, HA
WELL, WE SEE EACH OTHER ALL THE TIME, SO...
WHY BOTHER GOING ON A DATE.

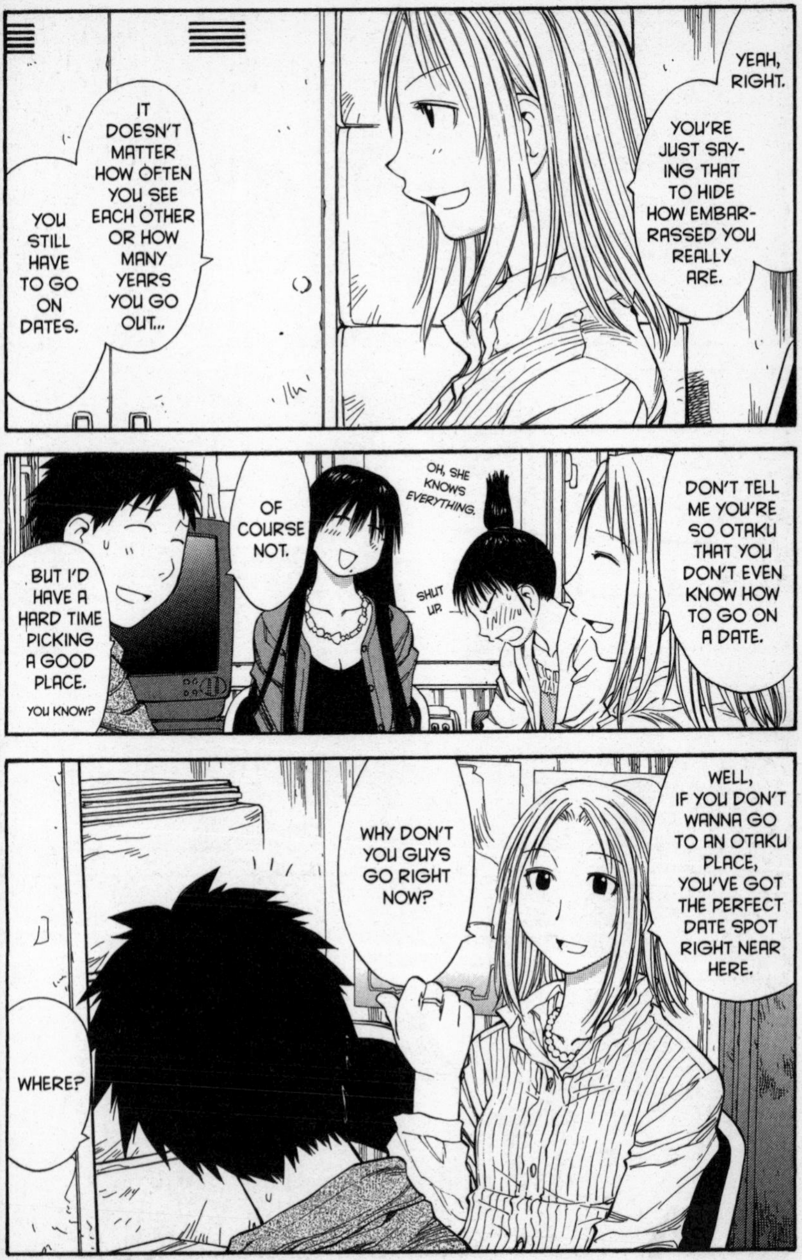
YEAH, RIGHT.
YOU'RE JUST SAYING THAT TO HIDE HOW EMBARRASSED YOU REALLY ARE.
IT DOESN'T MATTER HOW OFTEN YOU SEE EACH OTHER OR HOW MANY YEARS YOU GO OUT...
YOU STILL HAVE TO GO ON DATES.
DON'T TELL ME YOU'RE SO OTAKU THAT YOU DON'T EVEN KNOW HOW TO GO ON A DATE.
OH, SHE KNOWS EVERYTHING.
SHUT UP.
OF COURSE NOT.
BUT I'D HAVE A HARD TIME PICKING A GOOD PLACE.
YOU KNOW?
WELL, IF YOU DON'T WANNA GO TO AN OTAKU PLACE, YOU'VE GOT THE PERFECT DATE SPOT RIGHT NEAR HERE.
WHY DON'T YOU GUYS GO RIGHT NOW?
WHERE?

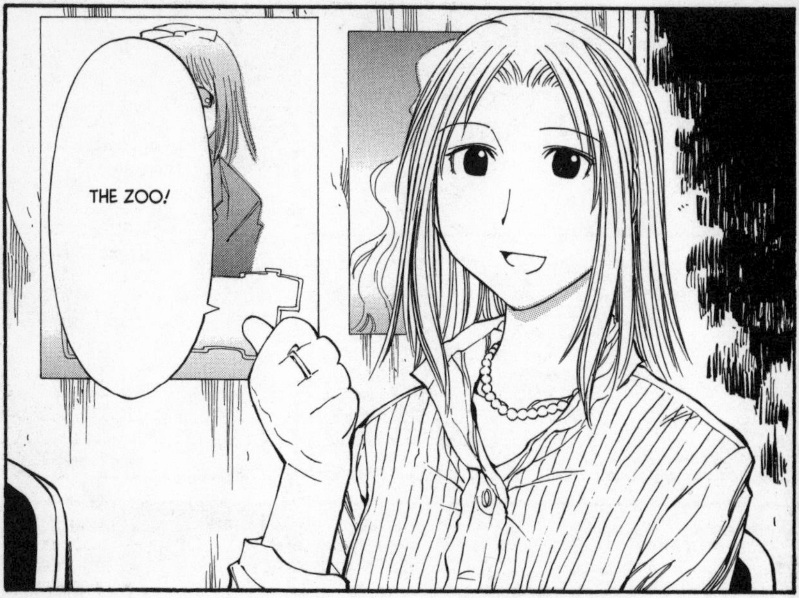
THE ZOO!

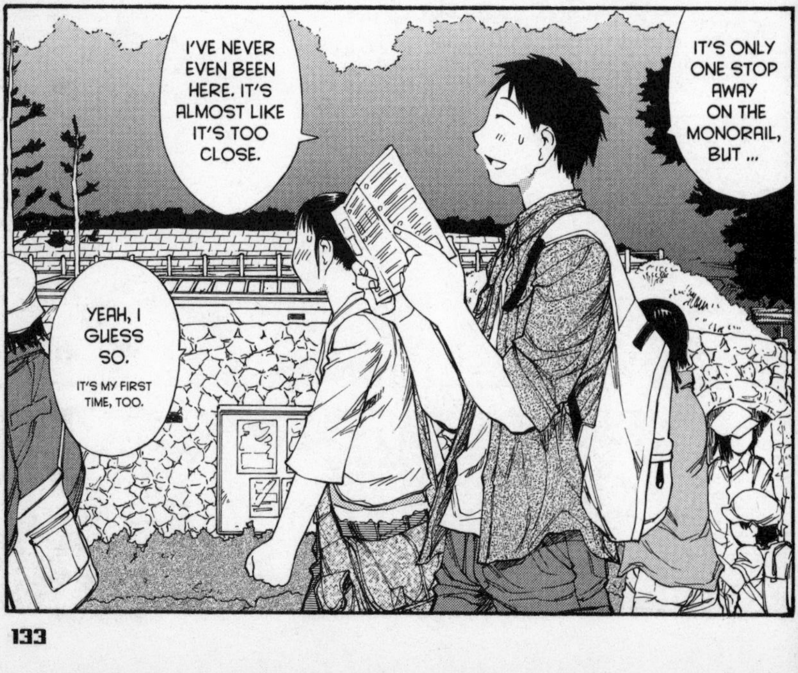
IT'S ONLY ONE STOP AWAY ON THE MONORAIL, BUT ...
I'VE NEVER EVEN BEEN HERE. IT'S ALMOST LIKE IT'S TOO CLOSE.
YEAH, I GUESS SO.
IT'S MY FIRST TIME, TOO.

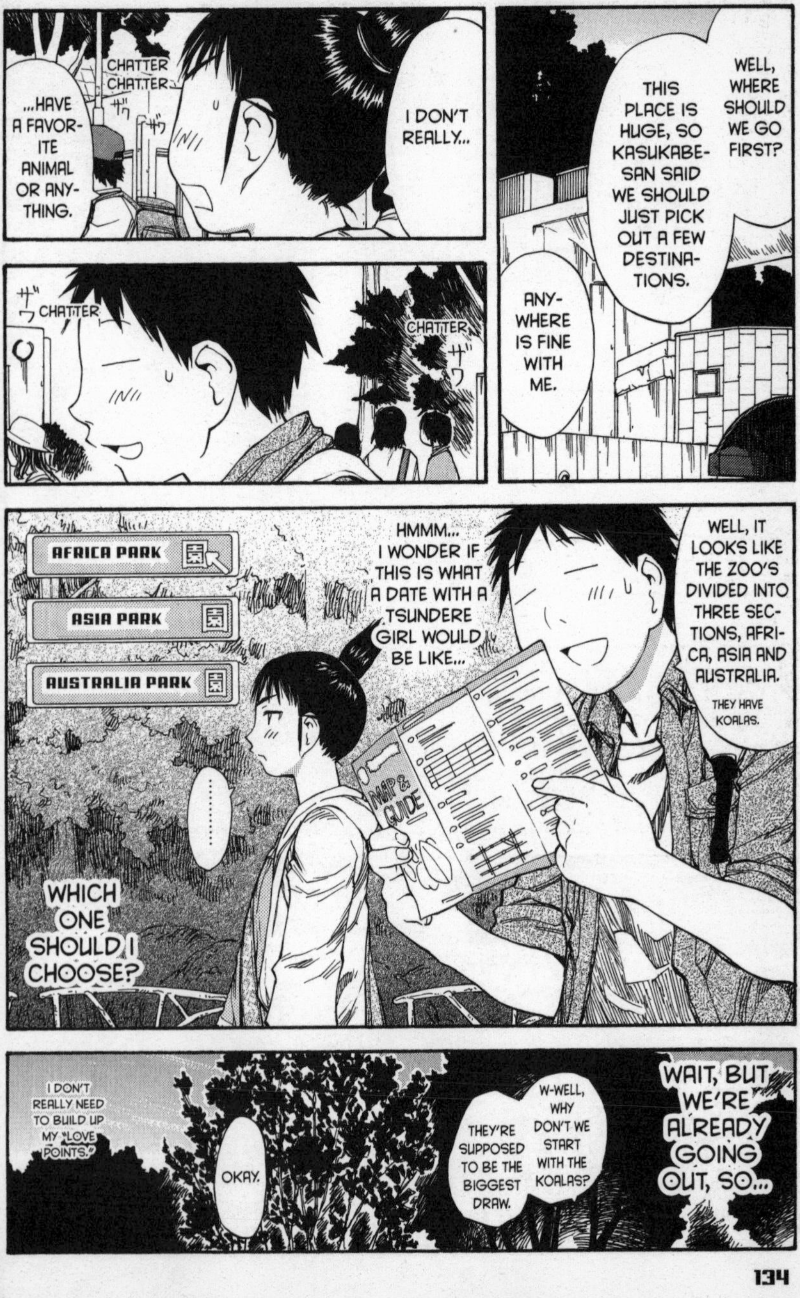
WELL, WHERE SHOULD WE GO FIRST?
THIS PLACE IS HUGE, SO KASUKABE-SAN SAID WE SHOULD JUST PICK OUT A FEW DESTINATIONS.
ANYWHERE IS FINE WITH ME.
I DON'T REALLY...
CHATTER CHATTER
...HAVE A FAVORITE ANIMAL OR ANYTHING.
CHATTER
CHATTER
WELL, IT LOOKS LIKE THE ZOO'S DIVIDED INTO THREE SECTIONS, AFRICA, ASIA AND AUSTRALIA.
THEY HAVE KOALAS.
HMMM... I WONDER IF THIS IS WHAT A DATE WITH A TSUNDERE GIRL WOULD BE LIKE...
AFRICA PARK
ASIA PARK
AUSTRALIA PARK
MAP & GUIDE
......
WHICH ONE SHOULD I CHOOSE?
WAIT, BUT WE'RE ALREADY GOING OUT, SO...
W-WELL, WHY DON'T WE START WITH THE KOALAS?
THEY'RE SUPPOSED TO BE THE BIGGEST DRAW.
OKAY.
I DON'T REALLY NEED TO BUILD UP MY "LOVE POINTS."

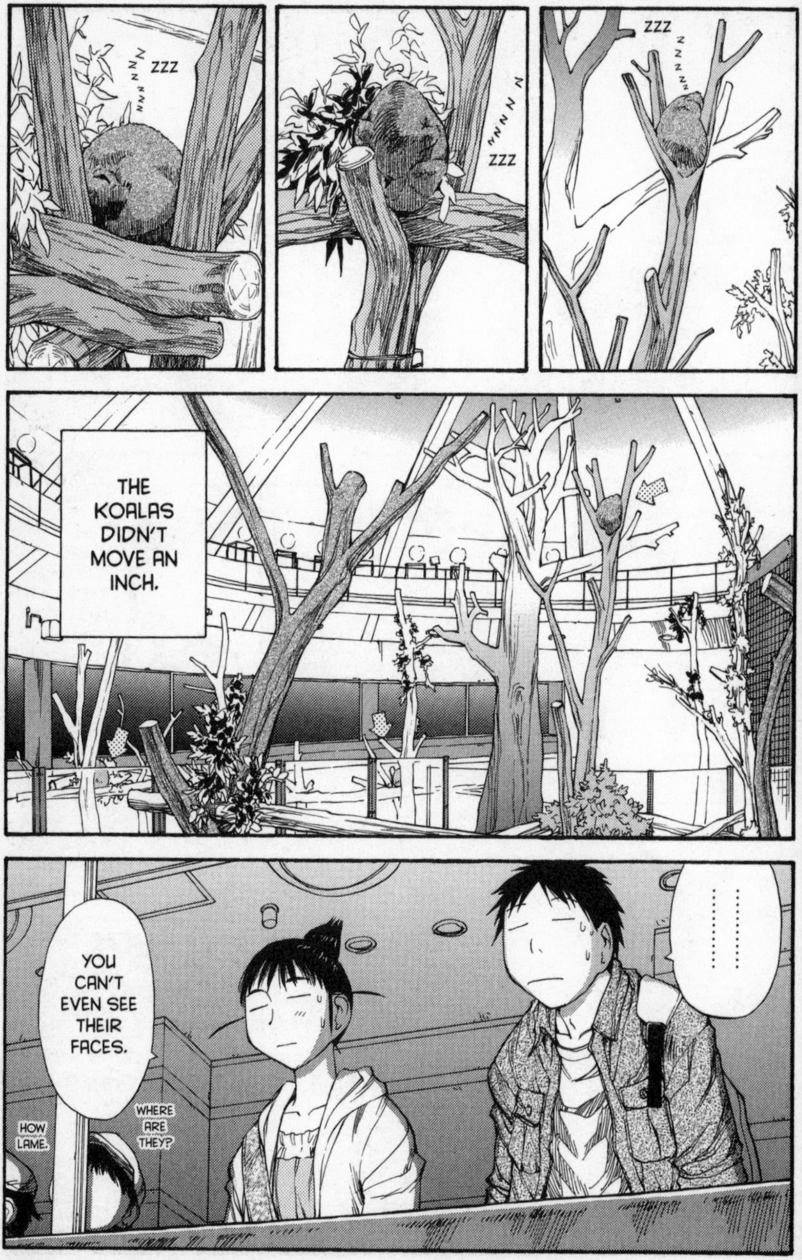
ZZZ
ZZZZ
ZZZZ
ZZZ
ZZZZ
ZZZ
THE KOALAS DIDN'T MOVE AN INCH.
......
YOU CAN'T EVEN SEE THEIR FACES.
WHERE ARE THEY?
HOW LAME.

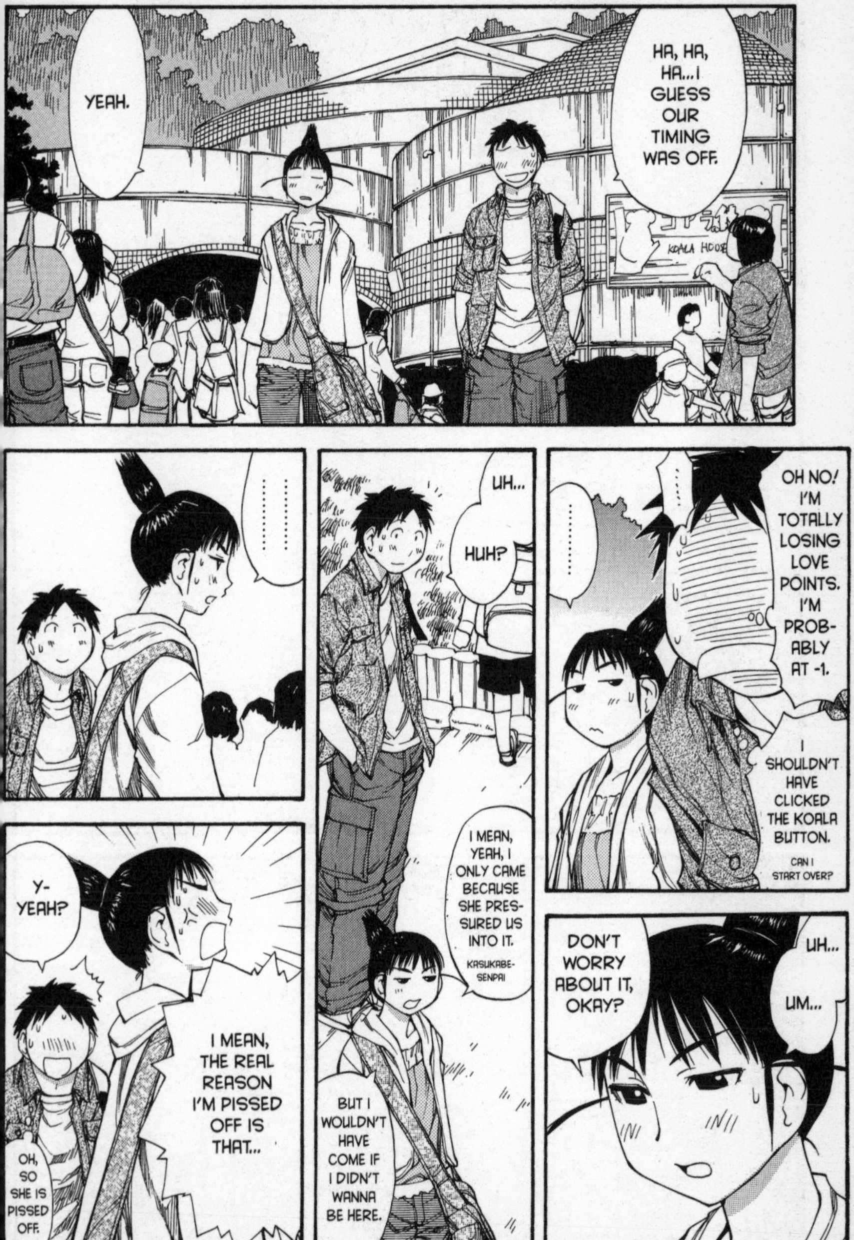

HA, HA, HA...I GUESS OUR TIMING WAS OFF.
YEAH.
......
....
OH NO! I'M TOTALLY LOSING LOVE POINTS. I'M PROB-ABLY AT -1.
I SHOULDN'T HAVE CLICKED THE KOALA BUTTON.
CAN I START OVER?
UH...
UM...
DON'T WORRY ABOUT IT, OKAY?
UH...
HUH?
I MEAN, YEAH, I ONLY CAME BECAUSE SHE PRES-SURED US INTO IT.
KASUKABE-SENPAI
BUT I WOULDN'T HAVE COME IF I DIDN'T WANNA BE HERE.
....
Y-YEAH?
I MEAN, THE REAL REASON I'M PISSED OFF IS THAT...
OH, SO SHE IS PISSED OFF.

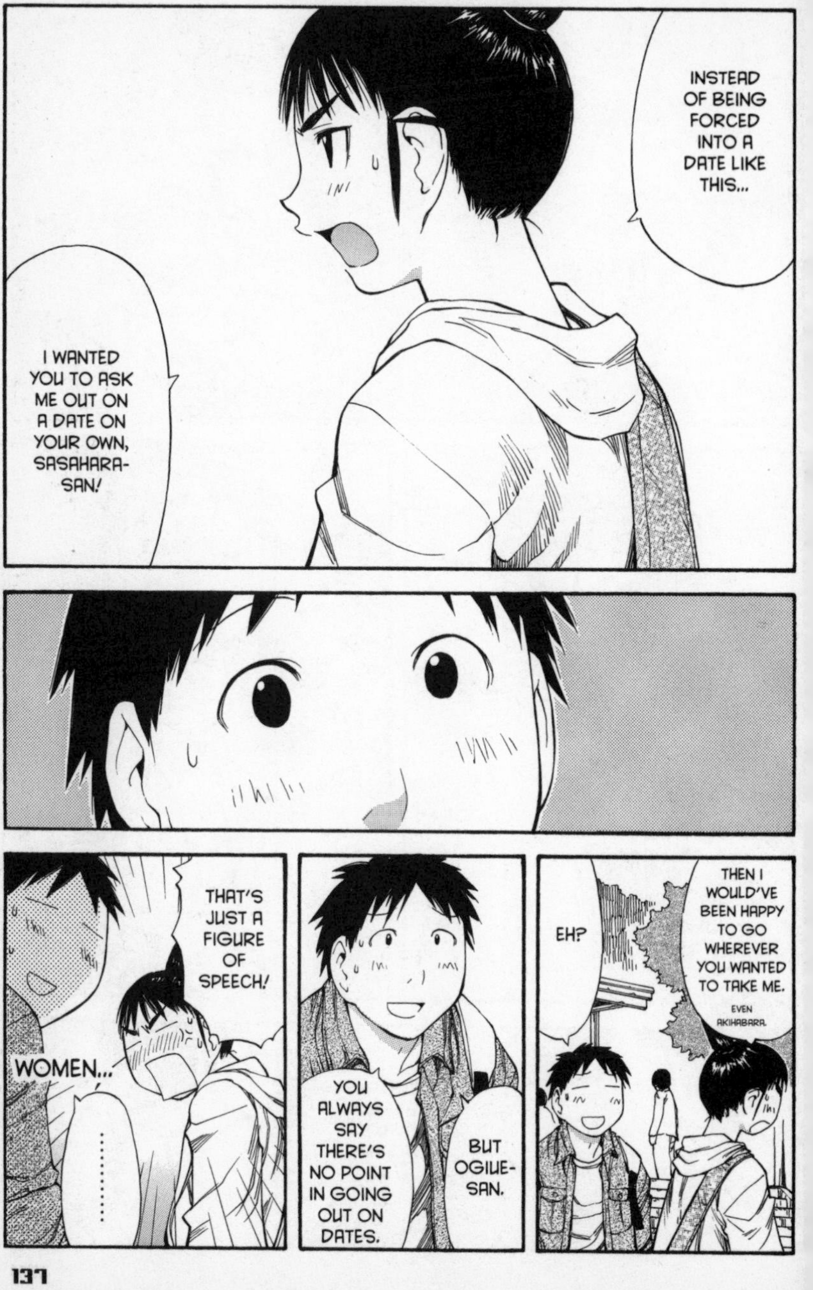
INSTEAD OF BEING FORCED INTO A DATE LIKE THIS...
I WANTED YOU TO ASK ME OUT ON A DATE ON YOUR OWN, SASAHARA-SAN!
THEN I WOULD'VE BEEN HAPPY TO GO WHEREVER YOU WANTED TO TAKE ME.
EVEN AKIHABARA.
EH?
BUT OGIUE-SAN.
YOU ALWAYS SAY THERE'S NO POINT IN GOING OUT ON DATES.
THAT'S JUST A FIGURE OF SPEECH!
WOMEN...
......

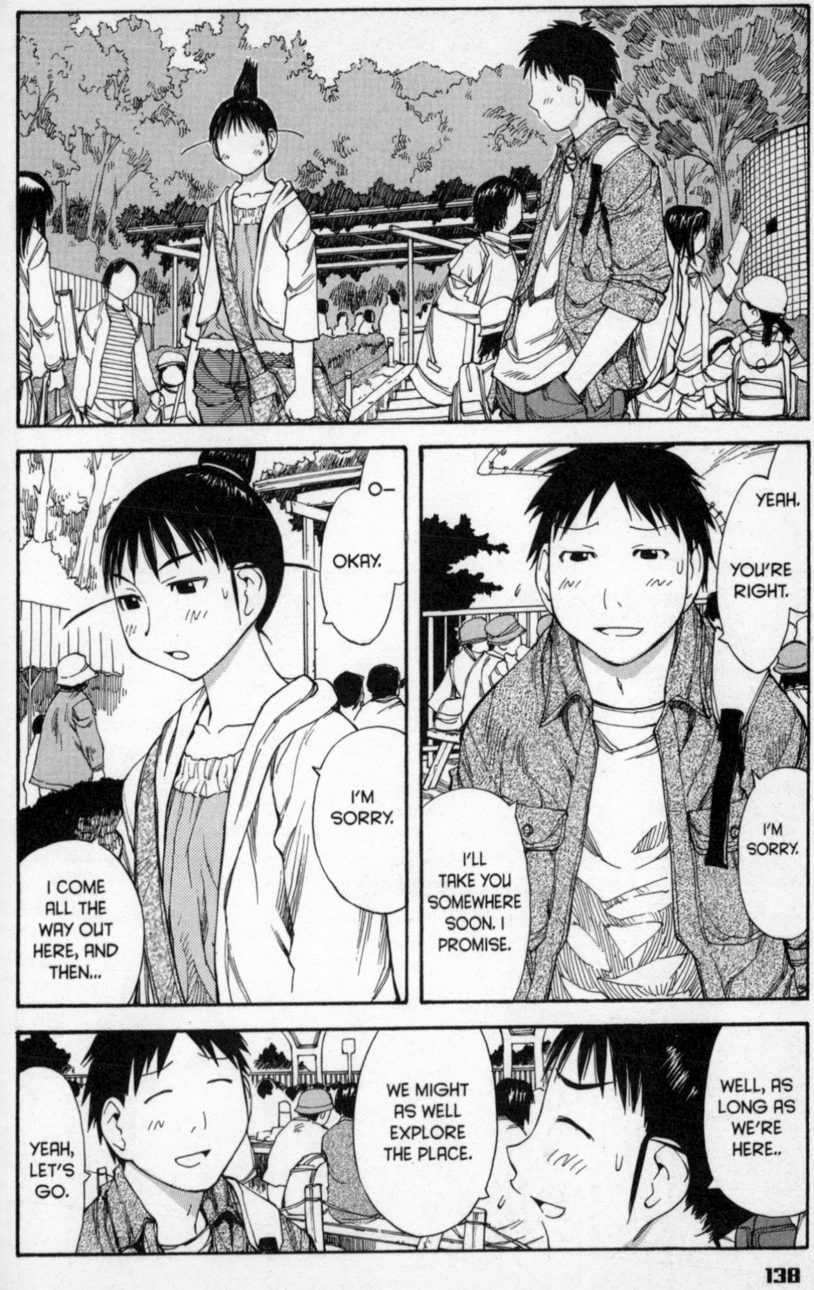
YEAH.
YOU'RE RIGHT.
I'M SORRY.
I'LL TAKE YOU SOMEWHERE SOON. I PROMISE.
O—
OKAY.
I'M SORRY.
I COME ALL THE WAY OUT HERE, AND THEN...
WELL, AS LONG AS WE'RE HERE..
WE MIGHT AS WELL EXPLORE THE PLACE.
YEAH, LET'S GO.

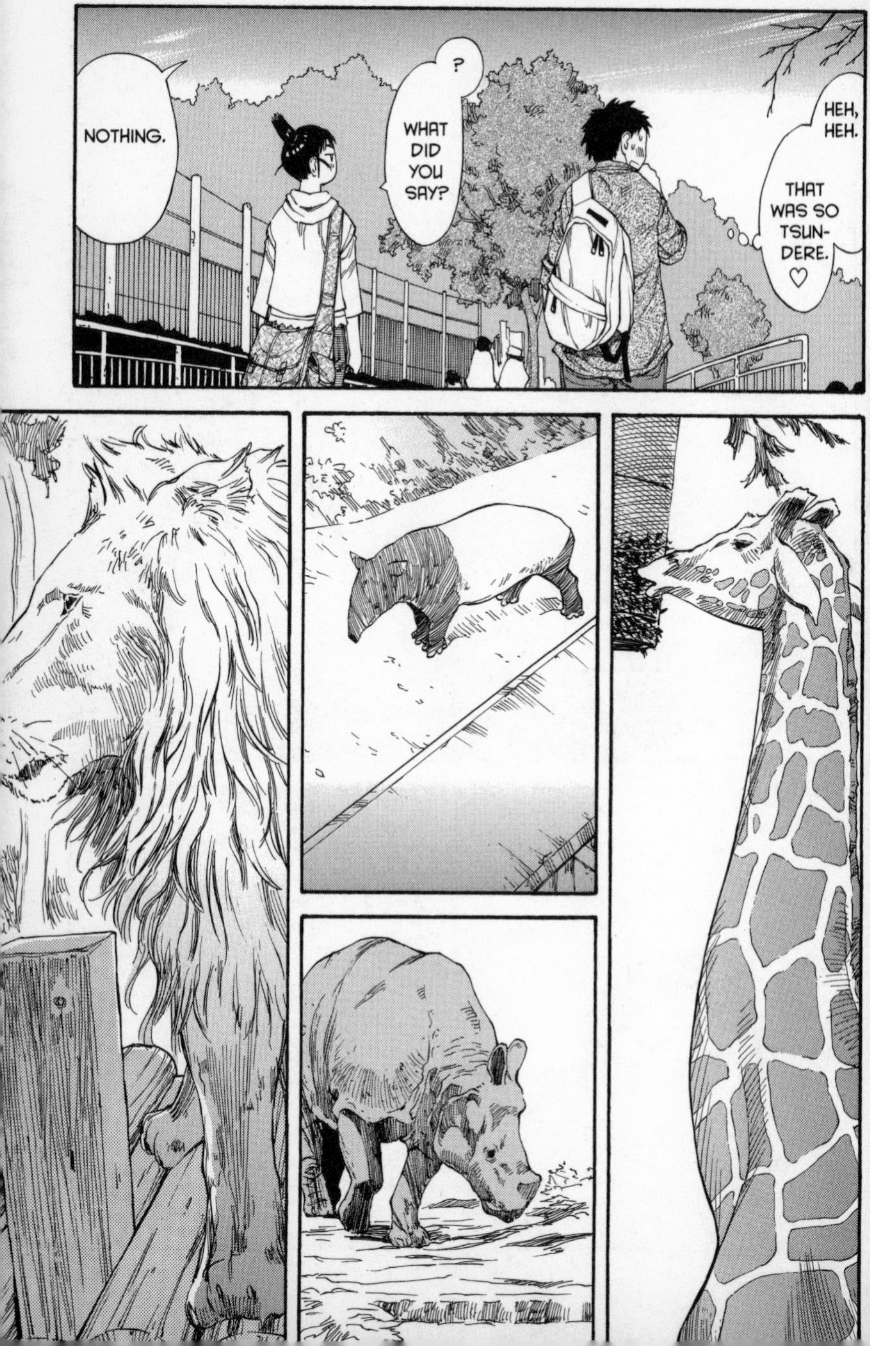
HEH, HEH.
THAT WAS SO TSUN-DERE. ♡
?
WHAT DID YOU SAY?
NOTHING.

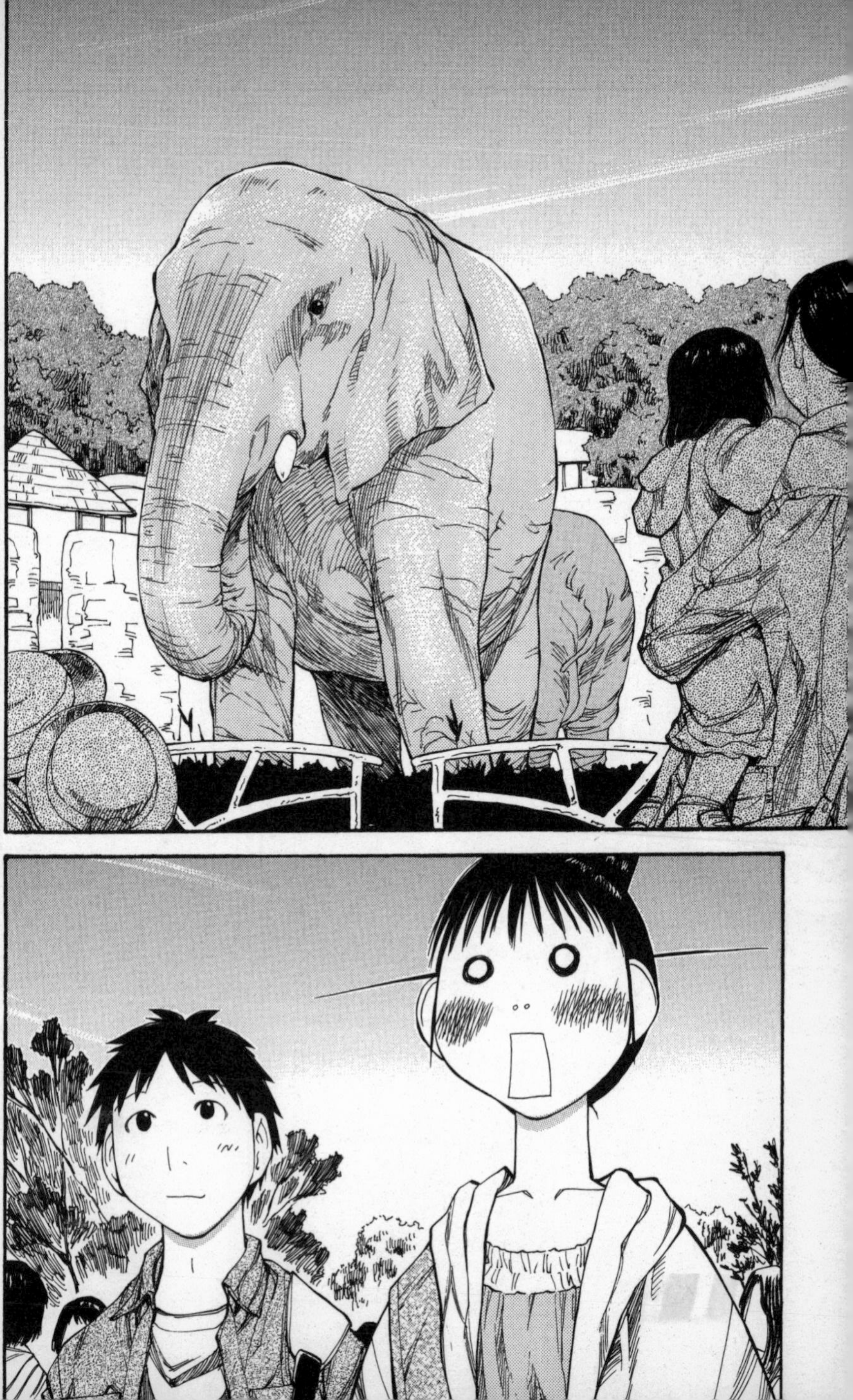

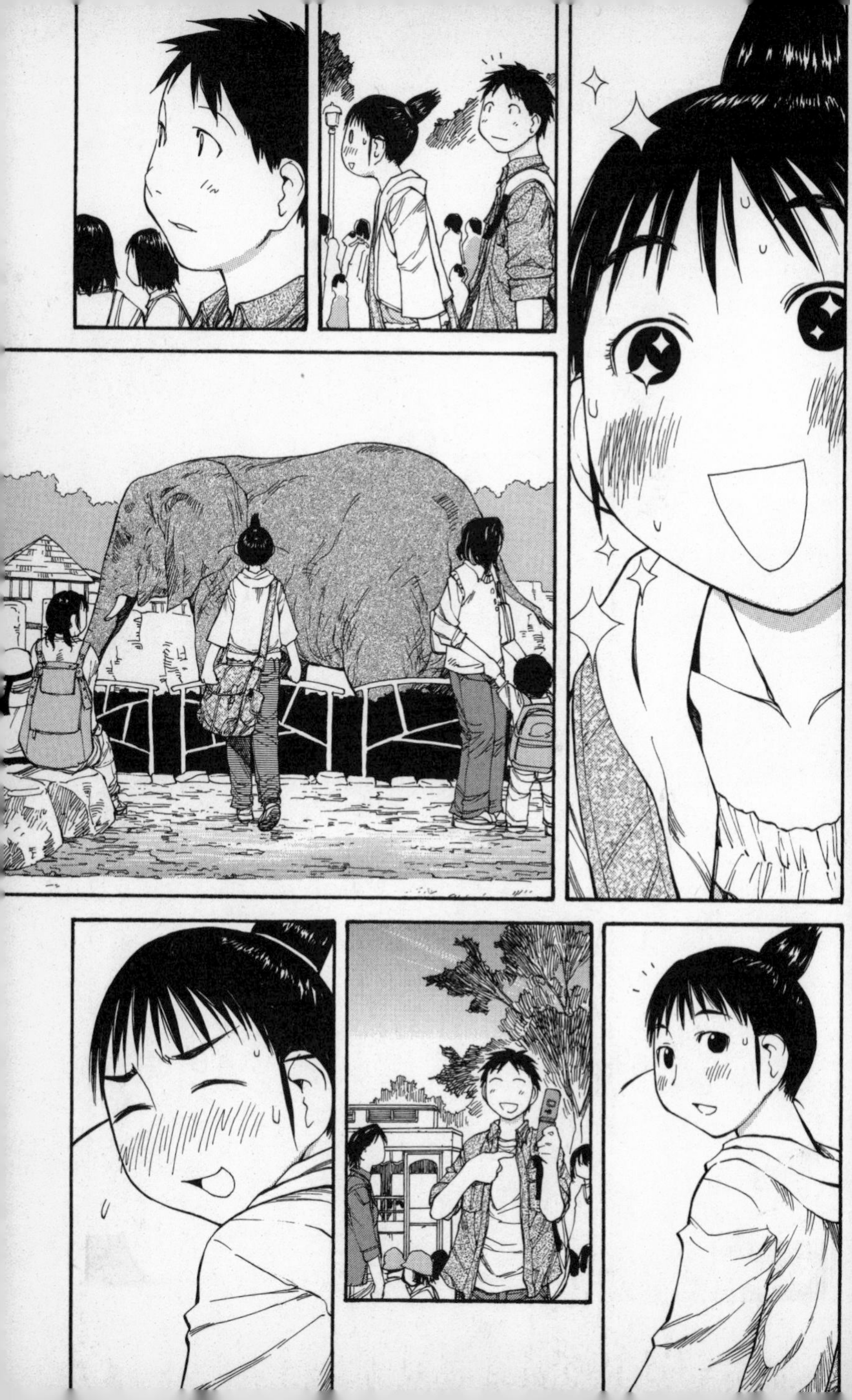

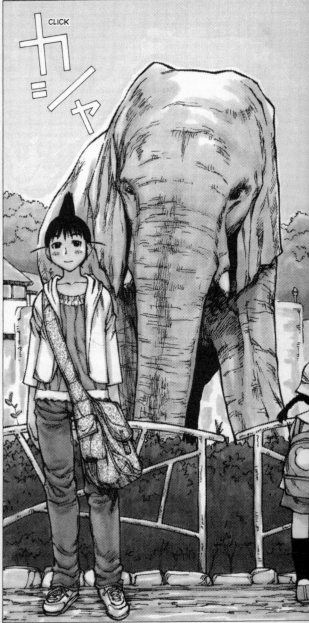

CLICK
カ＝シ／ャ

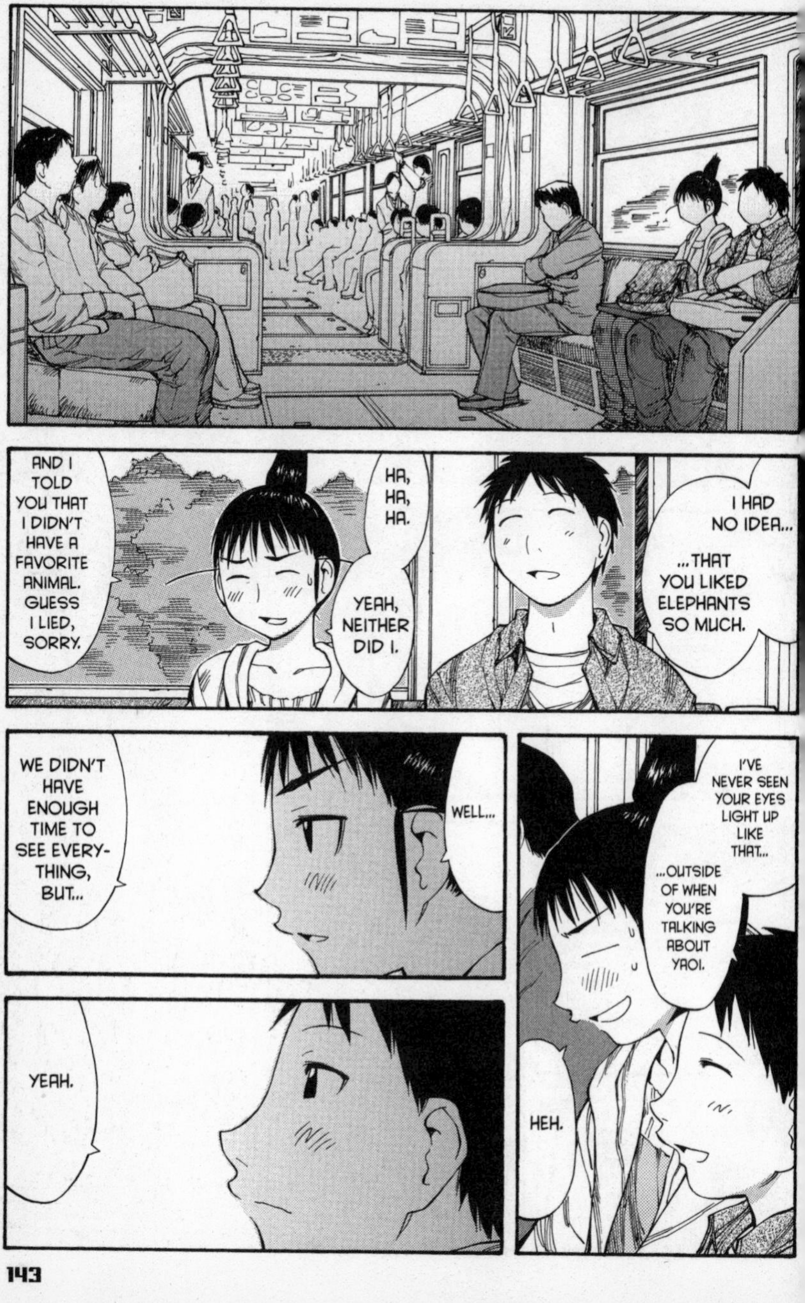
I HAD NO IDEA...
...THAT YOU LIKED ELEPHANTS SO MUCH.
HA, HA, HA.
YEAH, NEITHER DID I.
AND I TOLD YOU THAT I DIDN'T HAVE A FAVORITE ANIMAL. GUESS I LIED, SORRY.
I'VE NEVER SEEN YOUR EYES LIGHT UP LIKE THAT...
...OUTSIDE OF WHEN YOU'RE TALKING ABOUT YAOI.
HEH.
WELL...
WE DIDN'T HAVE ENOUGH TIME TO SEE EVERY-THING, BUT...
YEAH.

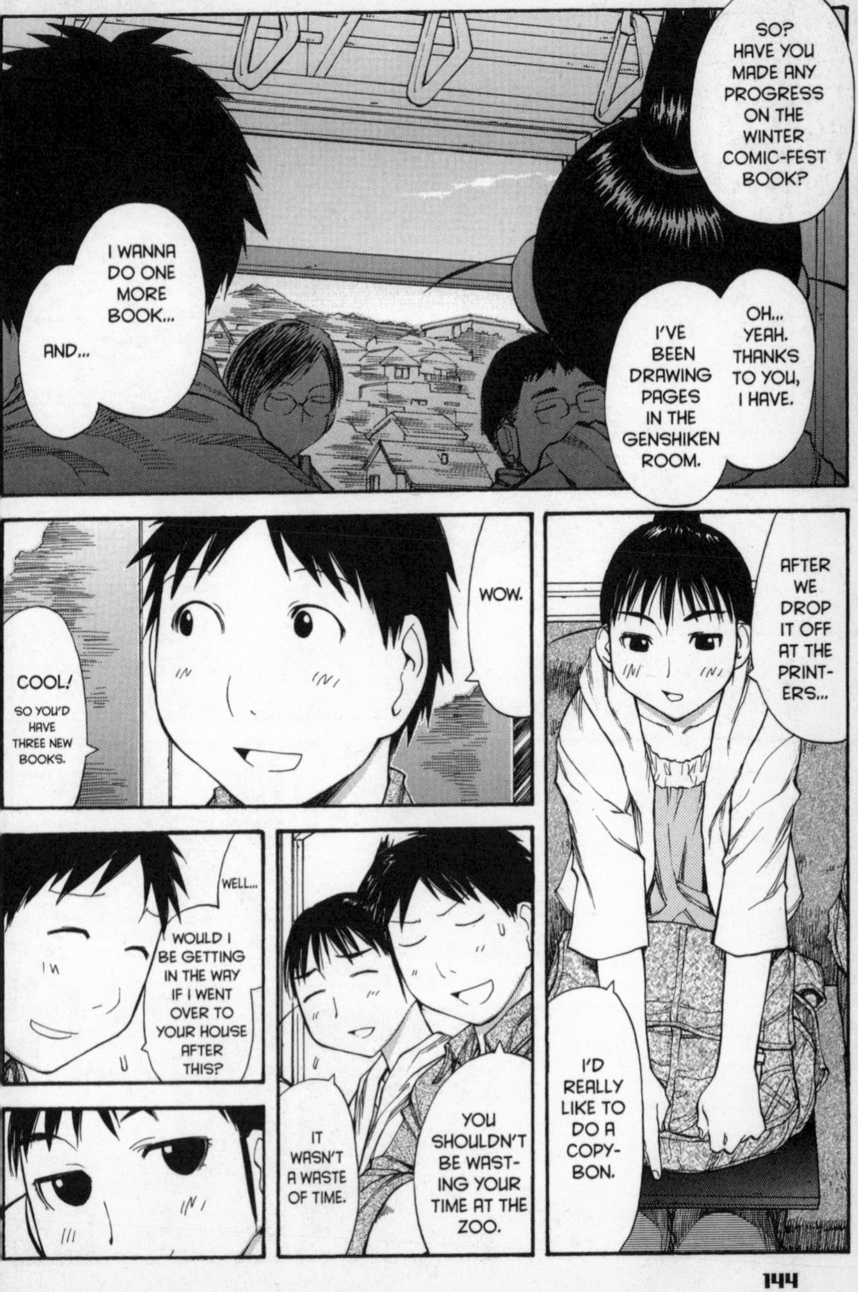
SO? HAVE YOU MADE ANY PROGRESS ON THE WINTER COMIC-FEST BOOK?
OH... YEAH. THANKS TO YOU, I HAVE.
I'VE BEEN DRAWING PAGES IN THE GENSHIKEN ROOM.
I WANNA DO ONE MORE BOOK...
AND...
AFTER WE DROP IT OFF AT THE PRINTERS...
I'D REALLY LIKE TO DO A COPY-BON.
WOW.
COOL!
SO YOU'D HAVE THREE NEW BOOKS.
YOU SHOULDN'T BE WASTING YOUR TIME AT THE ZOO.
IT WASN'T A WASTE OF TIME.
WELL...
WOULD I BE GETTING IN THE WAY IF I WENT OVER TO YOUR HOUSE AFTER THIS?

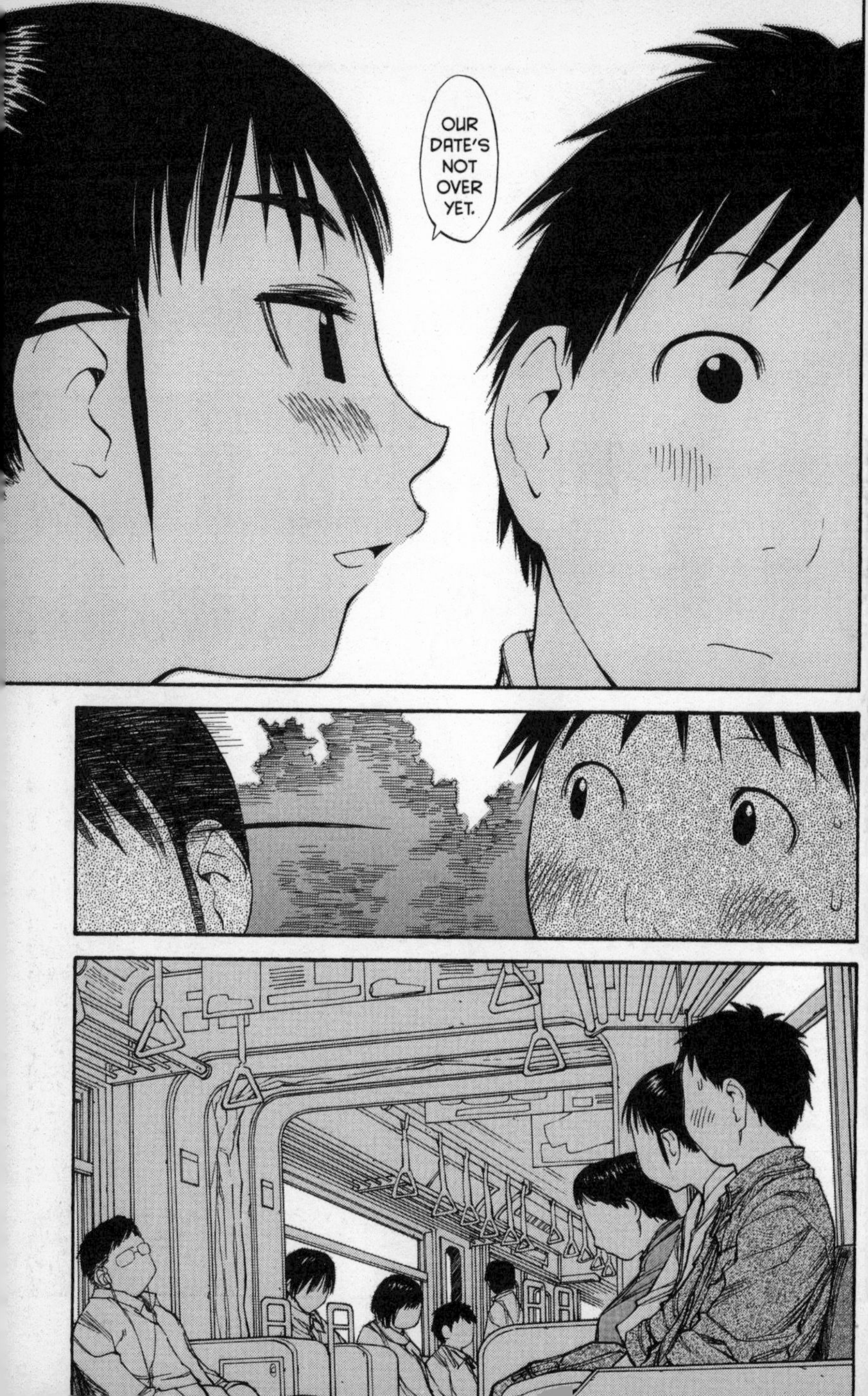
OUR DATE'S NOT OVER YET.

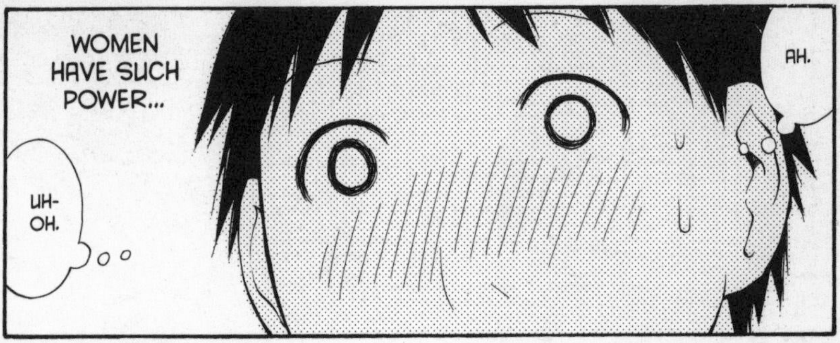
AH.
WOMEN HAVE SUCH POWER...
UH-OH.

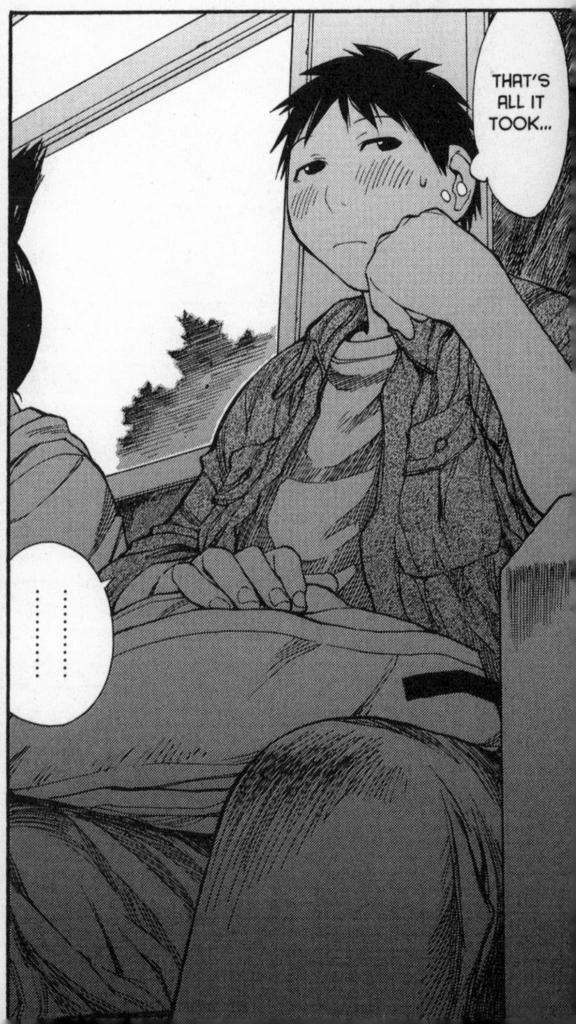
THAT'S ALL IT TOOK...
......

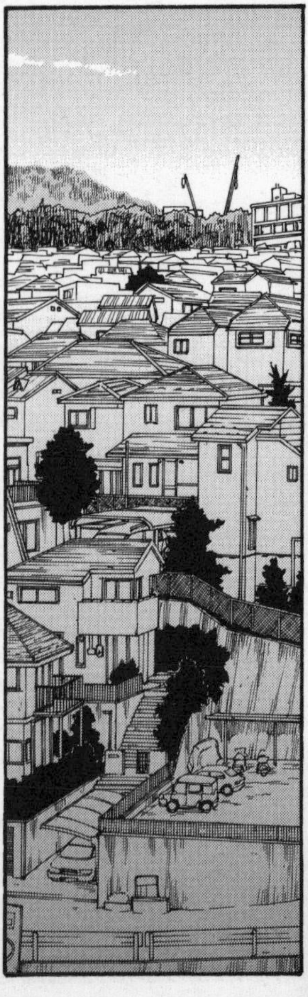

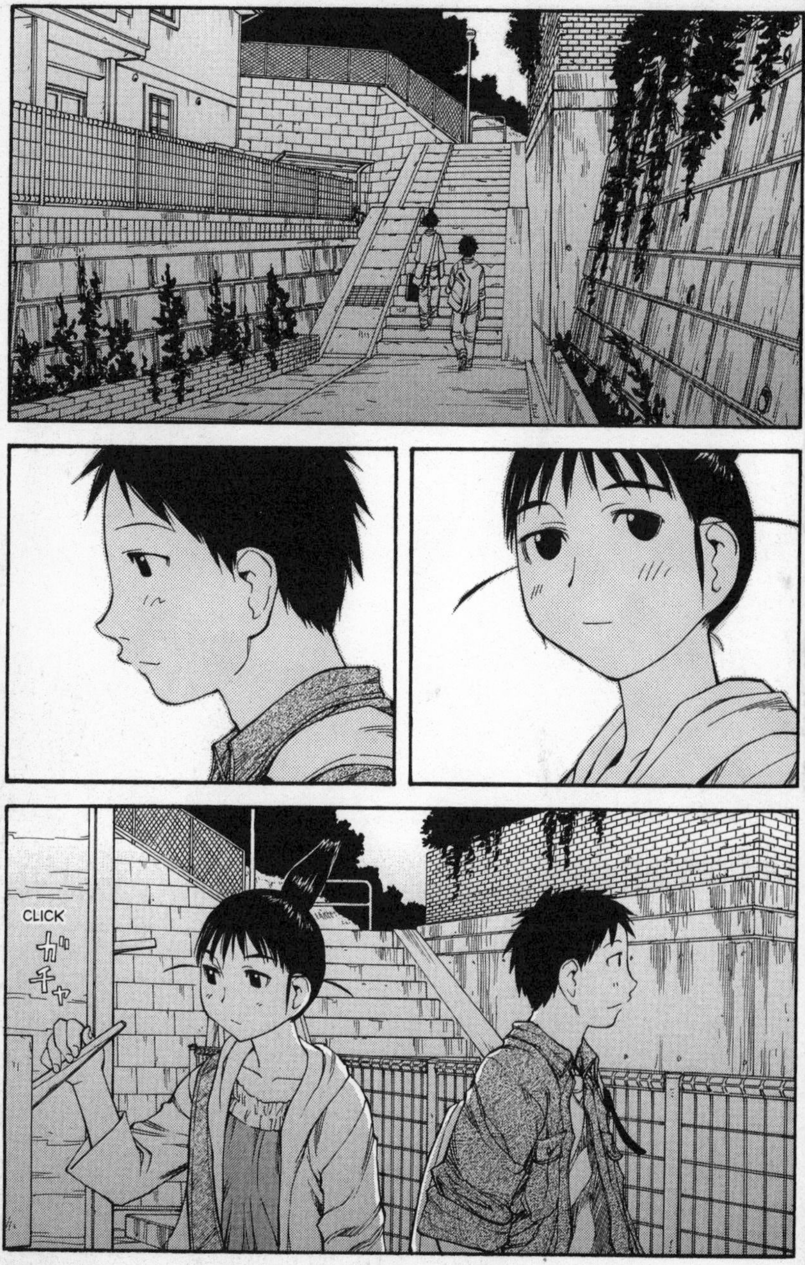
CLICK
ガチャ

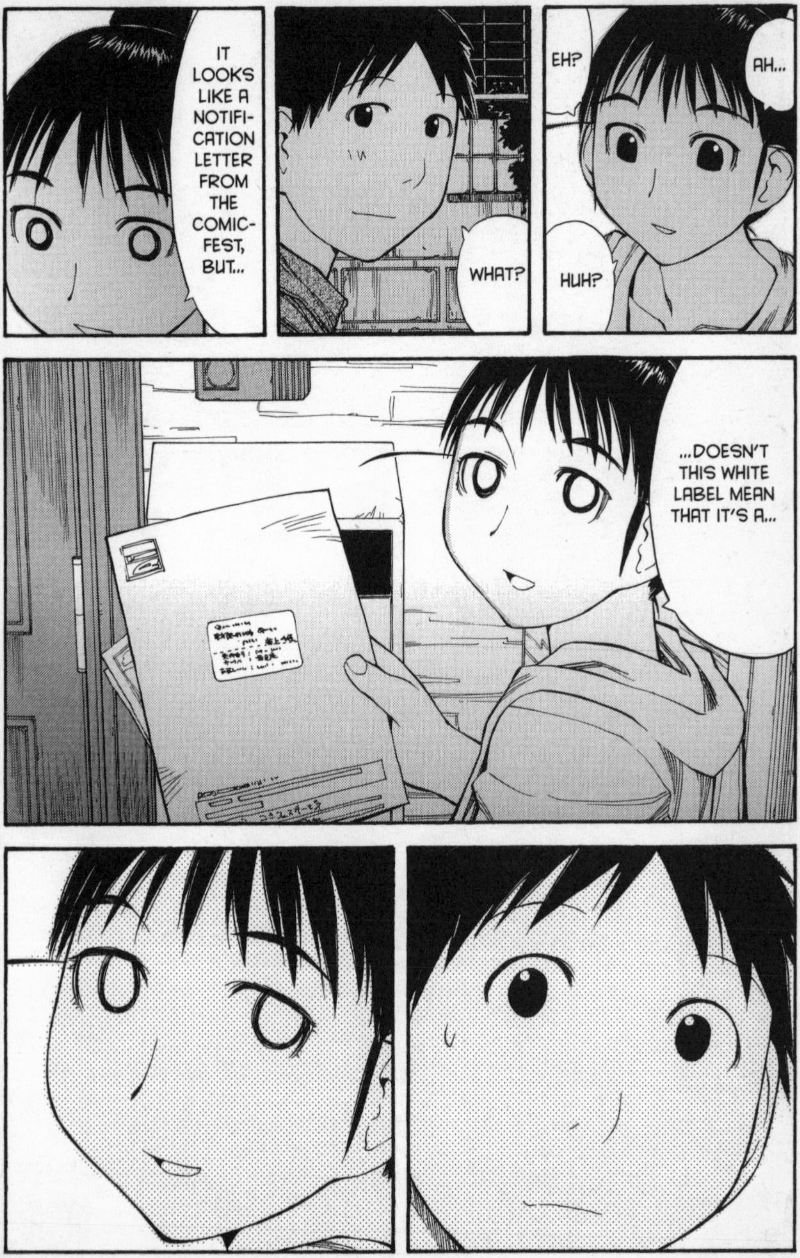
AH...
EH?
HUH?
WHAT?
IT LOOKS LIKE A NOTIFICATION LETTER FROM THE COMIC-FEST, BUT...
...DOESN'T THIS WHITE LABEL MEAN THAT IT'S A...

REFUSAL LETTER?

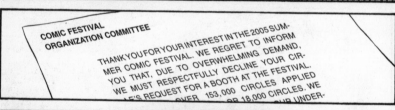

COMIC FESTIVAL ORGANIZATION COMMITTEE

THANK YOU FOR YOUR INTEREST IN THE 2005 SUMMER COMIC FESTIVAL. WE REGRET TO INFORM YOU THAT, DUE TO OVERWHELMING DEMAND, WE MUST RESPECTFULLY DECLINE YOUR CIRCLE'S REQUEST FOR A BOOTH AT THE FESTIVAL. OVER 153,000 CIRCLES APPLIED FOR 18,000 CIRCLES. WE UNDER-

...LOOKS LIKE IT.

YEAH...

IT...

149

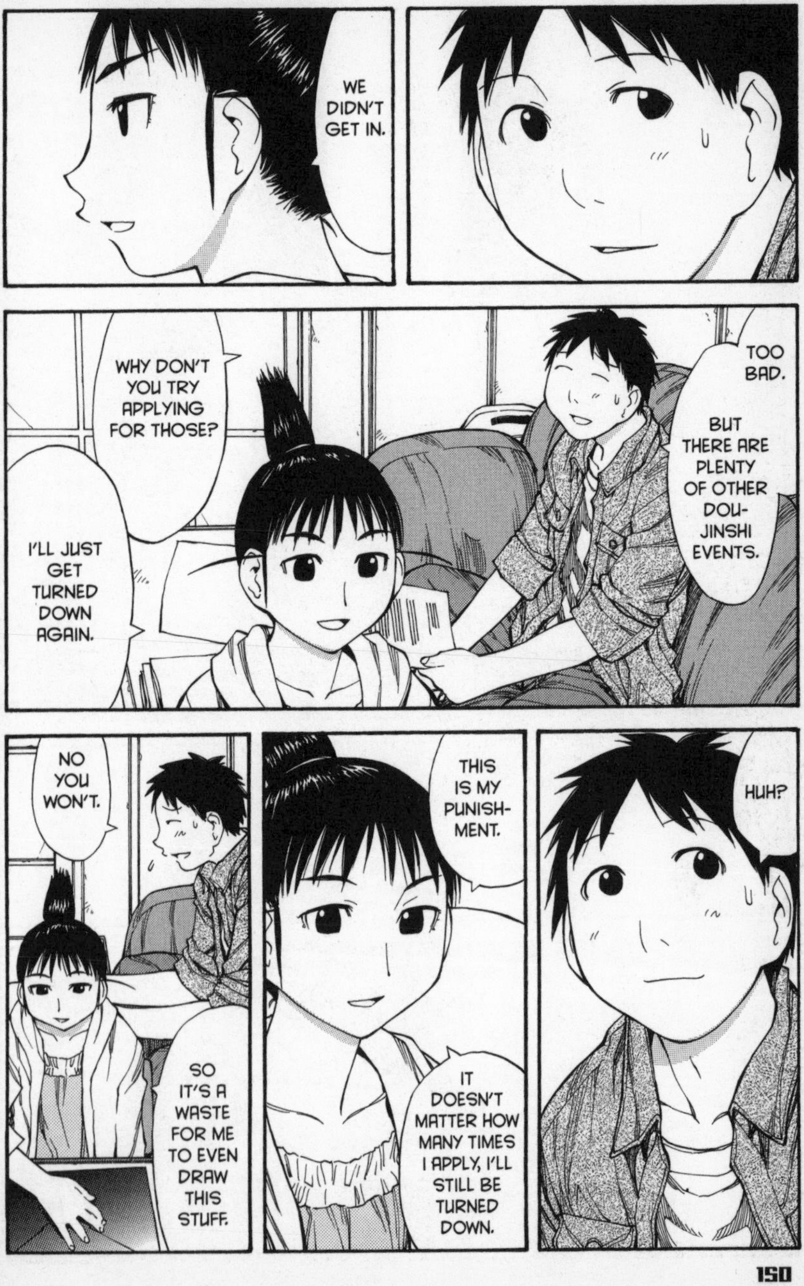
WE DIDN'T GET IN.
TOO BAD.
BUT THERE ARE PLENTY OF OTHER DOU-JINSHI EVENTS.
WHY DON'T YOU TRY APPLYING FOR THOSE?
I'LL JUST GET TURNED DOWN AGAIN.
HUH?
THIS IS MY PUNISH-MENT.
IT DOESN'T MATTER HOW MANY TIMES I APPLY, I'LL STILL BE TURNED DOWN.
NO YOU WON'T.
SO IT'S A WASTE FOR ME TO EVEN DRAW THIS STUFF.

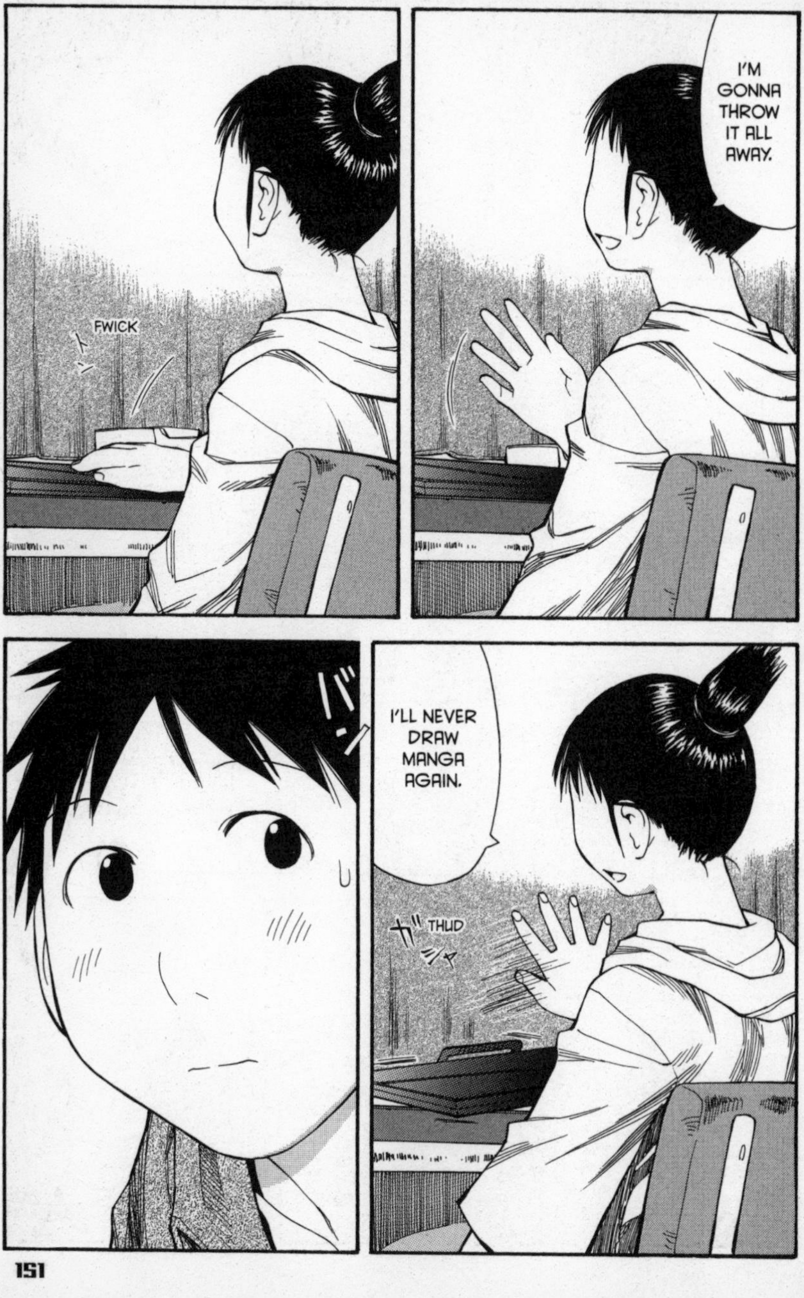

I'M GONNA THROW IT ALL AWAY.
FWICK
I'LL NEVER DRAW MANGA AGAIN.
THUD

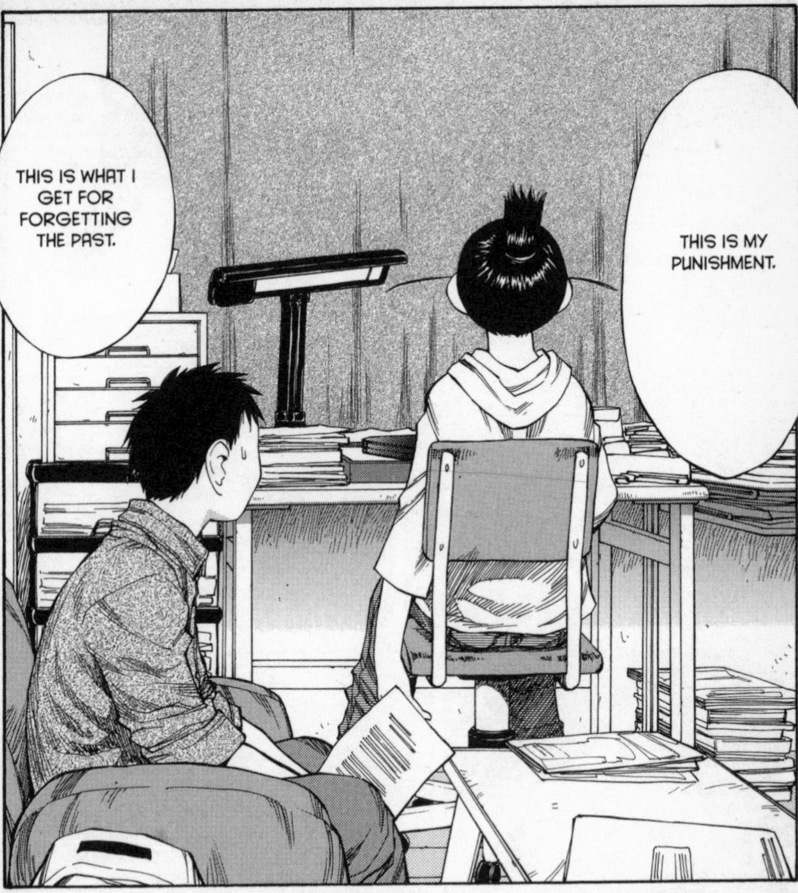
THIS IS MY PUNISHMENT.
THIS IS WHAT I GET FOR FORGETTING THE PAST.

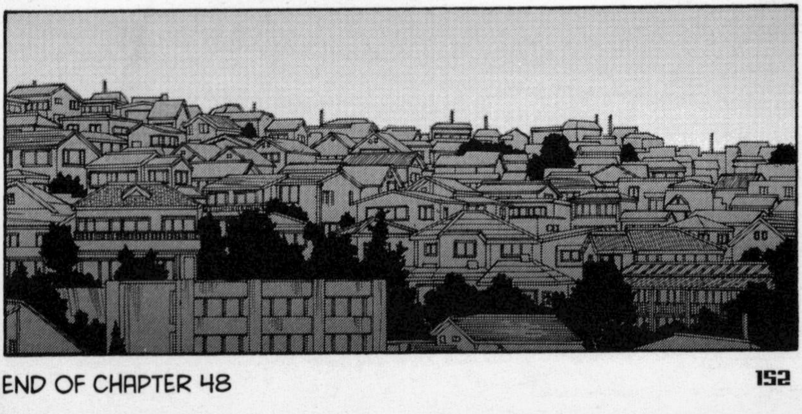

END OF CHAPTER 48

BEN- WELL, HERE WE HAVE THE VICE PRESIDENT.

PV- SHE SEEMS A LOT DIFFERENT FROM LAST SEASON.

BEN- BEFORE, SHE SEEMED LIKE A MUCH MORE SERI-OUS CHARACTER, ALTHOUGH SHE WAS KIND OF A GOOFOFF SOMETIMES.

PV- NOW SHE SPEAKS VERY FORMALLY, BUT SHE'S ALSO REALLY SARCASTIC. I GUESS SINCE THE PRESIDENT HAS BECOME SO MUCH MORE AGGRESSIVE, THEY'RE TRYING TO BALANCE IT OUT.

BEN- THAT MIGHT BE PART OF IT, BUT JUST LIKE THE PRESIDENT, IT SEEMS LIKE SHE'S GONE BACK TO HER PAST. IF YOU LOOK AT THE ORIGINAL MANGA, HER CHARACTER WAS VERY SIMILAR TO THIS.

PV- OH YEAH, I WONDER WHY SHE WASN'T LIKE THAT IN LAST SEASON'S ANIME.

BEN- I THINK IT'S BECAUSE OF THE RADIO DRAMA. BEFORE THE ANIME THEY DID THE RADIO SHOW, AND THEY WERE ON A VERY TIGHT SCHEDULE, SO I THINK THEY ENDED UP REALLY HAVING TO EXPLOIT EACH CHARACTER'S TRAITS AND ABILITIES. REMEMBER THE SCENES WHERE THE VICE PRESIDENT ROLLED OUT ALL THESE SECRET MECHANICAL INVENTIONS.

PV- OH YEAH, THAT...AYAKO KAWAZUMI DID A REALLY GREAT JOB OF PORTRAYING HER AS A WEIRD, QUIRKY CHARACTER. THERE'S THAT PART WHERE SHE REPEATS THE NAME OF THE MACHINE OVER AND OVER AGAIN. AND SHE SAYS, "THIS MIGHT COME IN HANDY."

BEN- I'D SAY SHE DID TOO GOOD A JOB, SO GOOD THAT THAT BECAME THE VICE PRESIDENT'S CHARACTER. OF COURSE, YOU CAN SAY THE SAME THING ABOUT THE PRESIDENT, BUT I THINK THE CREATORS RECOGNIZE THAT NOW. SO IN THIS SEASON, RATHER THAN EXPLOITING THOSE FAR-OUT CHARACTER TRAITS, THEY'RE GOING TO CONCENTRATE ON DEVELOPING THE CHAR-ACTERS MORE.

PV- WELL, THAT WAS SORT OF INTERESTING IN ITS OWN RIGHT.

BEN- IT WOULD BE FINE IF IT WAS THE OTHER WAY AROUND. IF THOSE KINDS OF STORIES WERE SUBPLOTS RATHER THAN BECOMING THE MAIN STORYLINE.

PV- YEAH...AND NOW THE VICE PRESIDENT HAS THESE SUPERNATURAL POWERS. SHE'S ONE OF THE TEN STRONGEST PEOPLE IN THE WORLD. I WONDER IF SHE COULD EVEN FIGHT AGAINST HER DAD.

BEN- YEAH, THIS IS PROBABLY ANOTHER AREA WHERE THEY DIDN'T WANNA REPEAT MISTAKES FROM LAST SEASON. APPARENTLY, THEY DID THAT SO SHE WOULDN'T HAVE TO KEEP DRAWING HER SWORD. YUU KUROGI SAID SOMETHING ABOUT HOW IT WOULD BE BETTER IF THE VICE PRESI-DENT WASN'T ALWAYS DRAWING HER SWORD.

PV- YEAH, IN A WAY, WHEN SHE'S SO QUICK TO DRAW HER SWORD, IT ALMOST MAKES HER LOOK WEAK.

BEN- NOW SHE'S THE STRONGEST CHARACTER.

PV- SO I WONDER IF HER FAMILY ISN'T GONNA BE PART OF THE YAKUZA ANYMORE.

BEN- WELL, THERE ARE DEFINITELY NO MOE CHARAC-TERS LIKE THAT. BUT, MAYBE IT WOULD'VE SEEMED MORE REALISTIC IF THEY'D KEPT IT THAT WAY.

PV- YEAH WELL, I DON'T THINK SHOWING A REALISTIC PORTRAYAL OF A YAKUZA FAMILY WOULD BE A GOOD THING.

WHAT IF THEY HAD HER FAMILY RUN A SHRINE? I COULD TOTALLY SEE HER HELPING OUT AROUND THE SHRINE.

BEN- THE ONE THING THAT WON'T CHANGE IS THAT SHE'S A VERY DIFFICULT CHARACTER TO DEAL WITH. THE SEVENTH EPISODE IS CENTERED AROUND THE VICE PRESIDENT, AND APPARENTLY YUU KUROKI ACTUALLY WROTE IT.

PV- HUH? REALLY? THE ANIME SCRIPT? EVEN KUROKI-SENSEI IS A MANGA ARTIST?

BEN- THAT'S RIGHT. APPARENTLY, IT'S A REALL DARK STORY, AND IT'S SUPPOSED TO P STICK OUT.

PV- YEAH, KUROKI-SENSEI LIKES STORIES LI

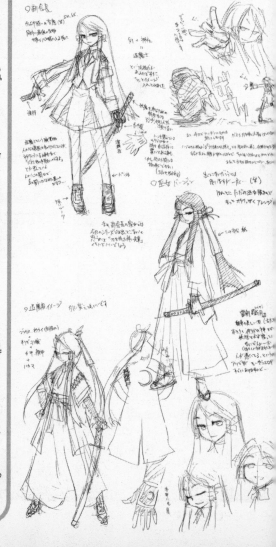

NOTHING BUT OTAKU TALK

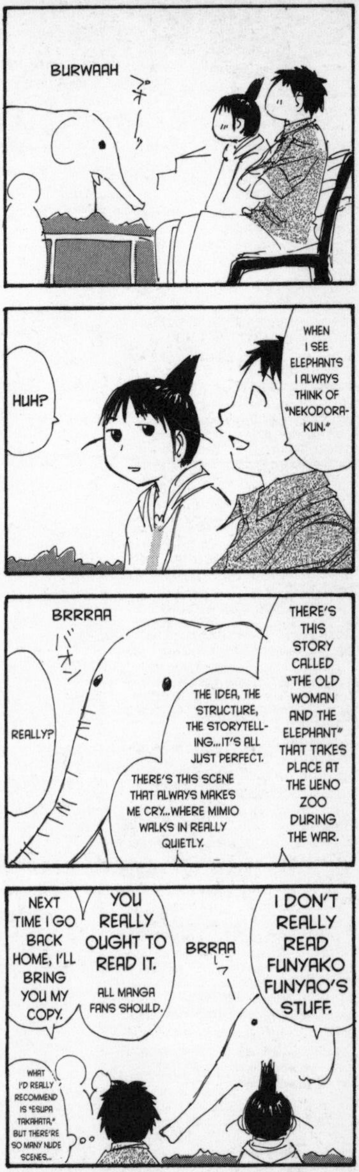
BURWAAH
WHEN I SEE ELEPHANTS I ALWAYS THINK OF "NEKODORA-KUN."
HUH?
THERE'S THIS STORY CALLED "THE OLD WOMAN AND THE ELEPHANT" THAT TAKES PLACE AT THE UENO ZOO DURING THE WAR.
THE IDEA, THE STRUCTURE, THE STORYTELLING...IT'S ALL JUST PERFECT.
THERE'S THIS SCENE THAT ALWAYS MAKES ME CRY...WHERE MIMIO WALKS IN REALLY QUIETLY.
BRRRAA
REALLY?
I DON'T REALLY READ FUNYAKO FUNYAO'S STUFF.
BRRAA
YOU REALLY OUGHT TO READ IT.
ALL MANGA FANS SHOULD.
NEXT TIME I GO BACK HOME, I'LL BRING YOU MY COPY.
WHAT I'D REALLY RECOMMEND IS "ESUPA TAKAHATA," BUT THERE'RE SO MANY NUDE SCENES...

AN EVEN BETTER DATE

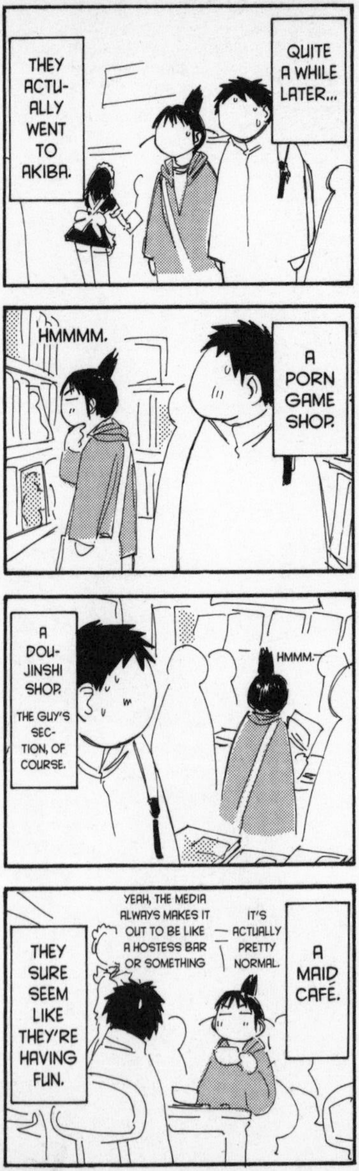
QUITE A WHILE LATER...
THEY ACTUALLY WENT TO AKIBA.
A PORN GAME SHOP.
HMMMM.
HMMM.
A DOUJINSHI SHOP.
THE GUY'S SECTION, OF COURSE.
A MAID CAFÉ.
IT'S ACTUALLY PRETTY NORMAL.
YEAH, THE MEDIA ALWAYS MAKES IT OUT TO BE LIKE A HOSTESS BAR OR SOMETHING
THEY SURE SEEM LIKE THEY'RE HAVING FUN.

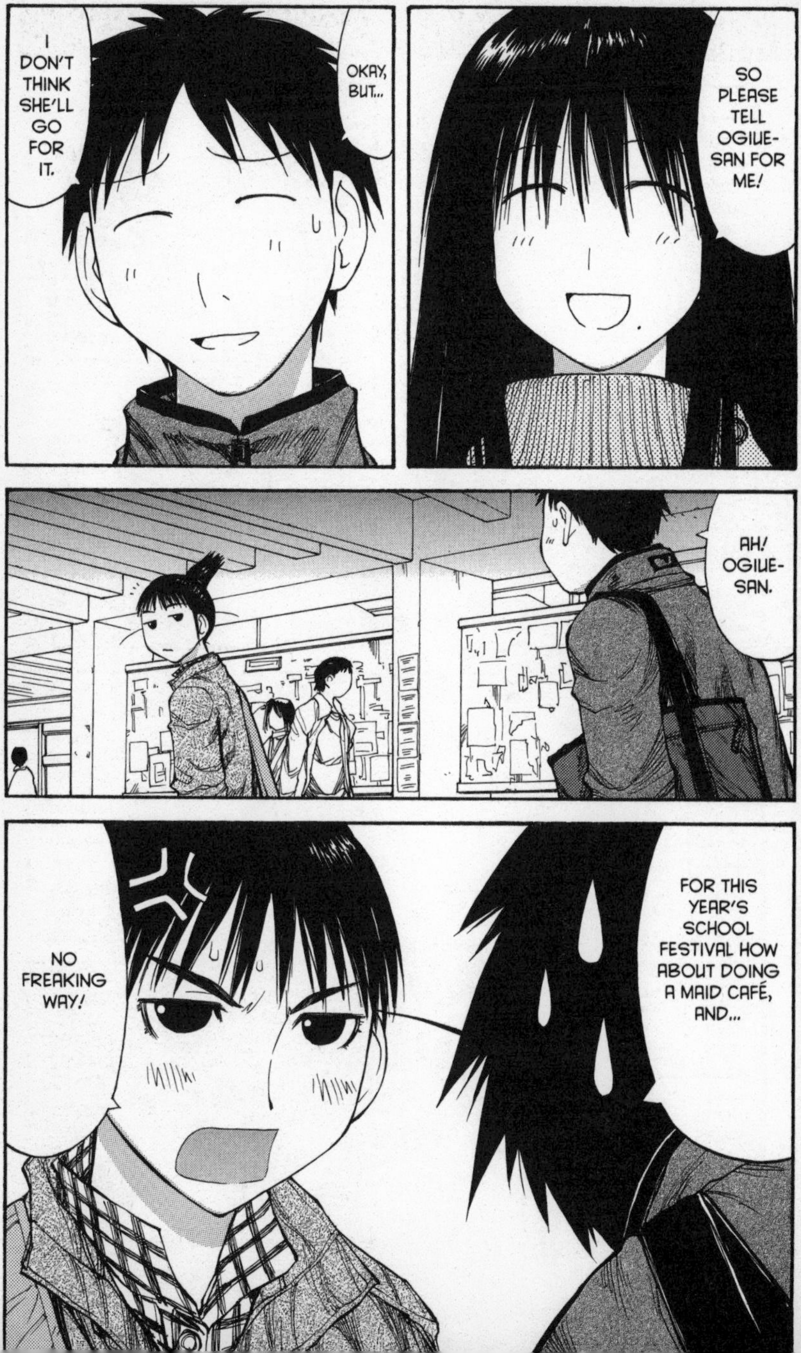
SO PLEASE TELL OGIUE-SAN FOR ME!
OKAY, BUT...
I DON'T THINK SHE'LL GO FOR IT.
AH! OGIUE-SAN.
FOR THIS YEAR'S SCHOOL FESTIVAL HOW ABOUT DOING A MAID CAFÉ, AND...
NO FREAKING WAY!

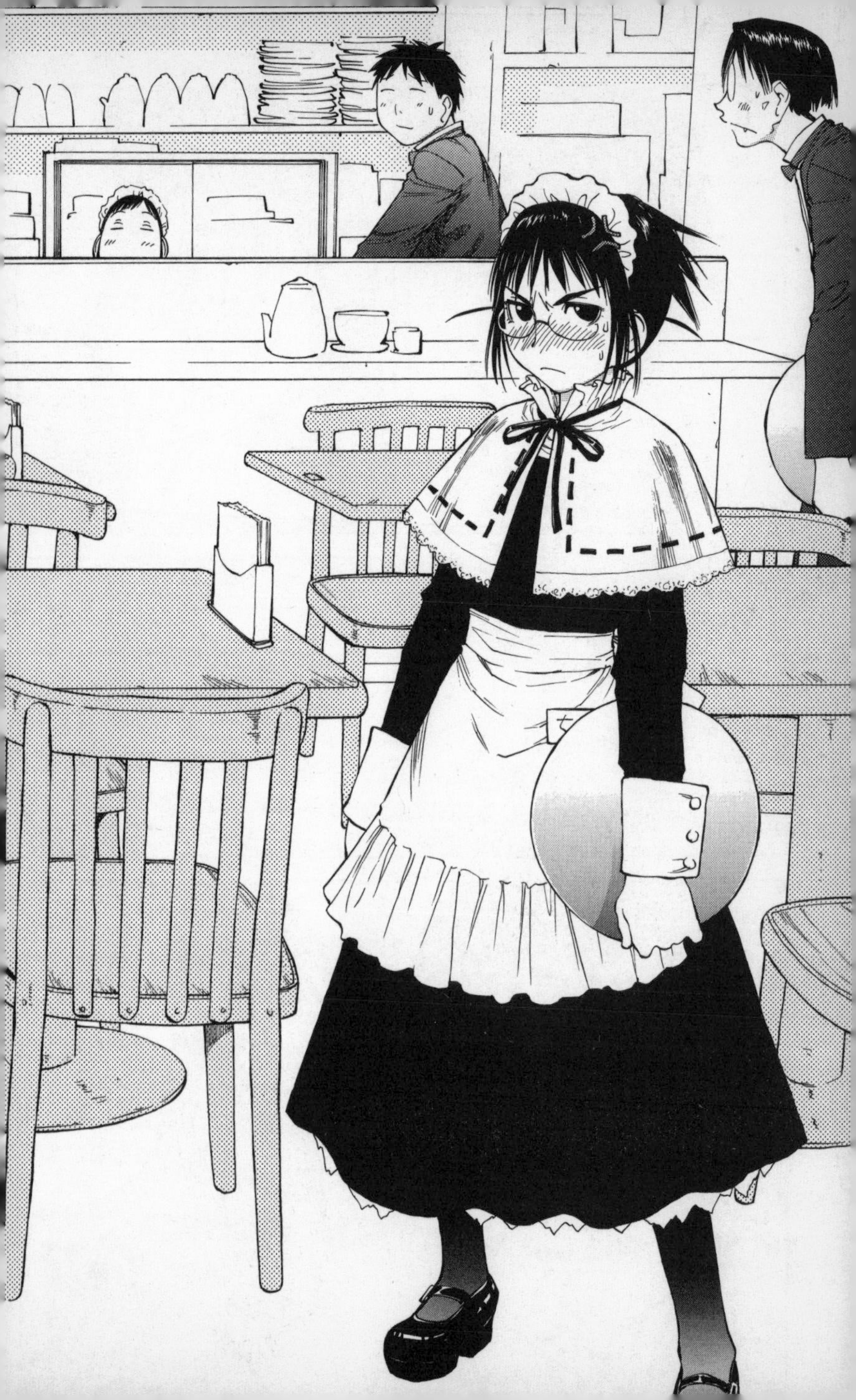

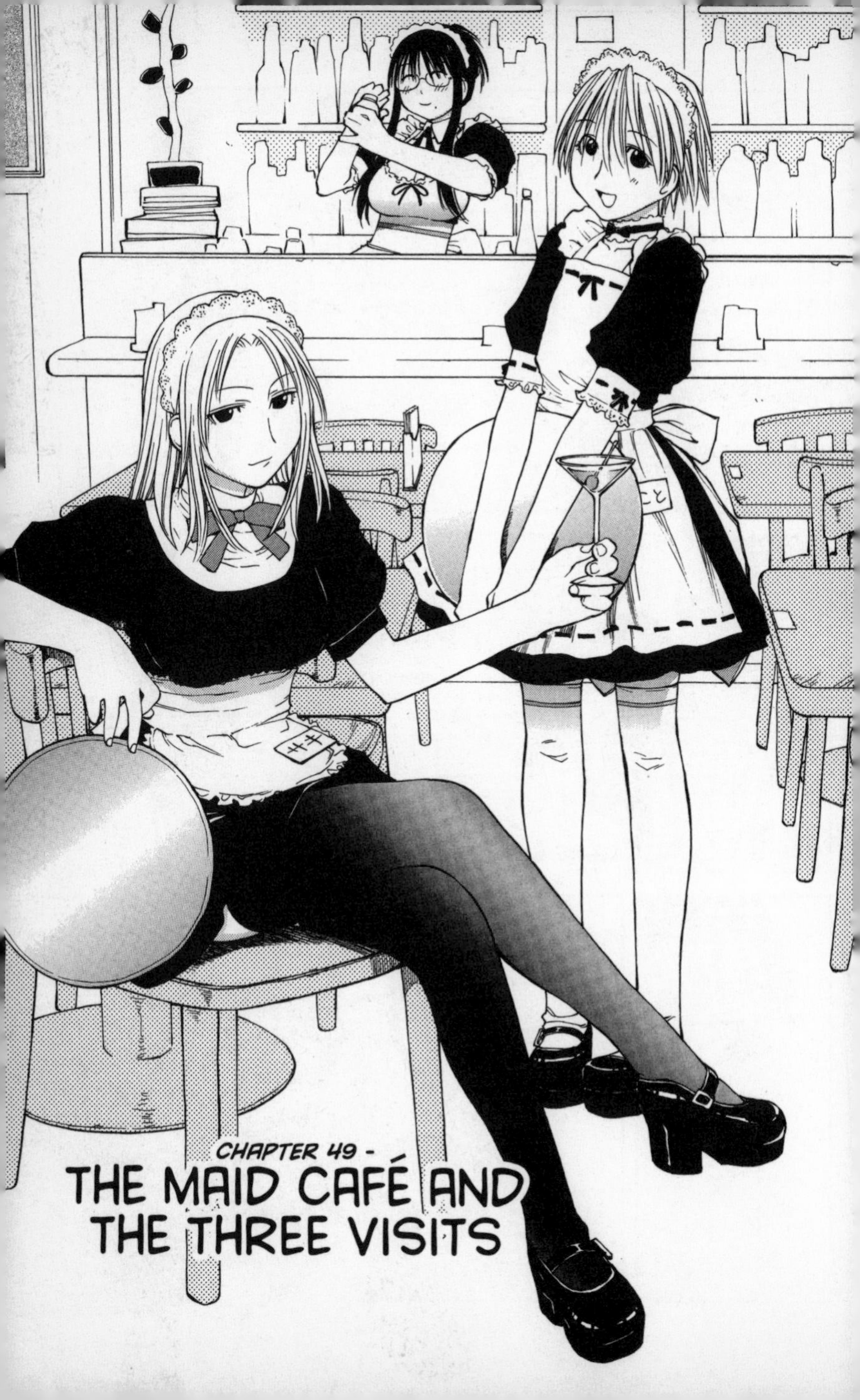
CHAPTER 49 -
THE MAID CAFÉ AND THE THREE VISITS

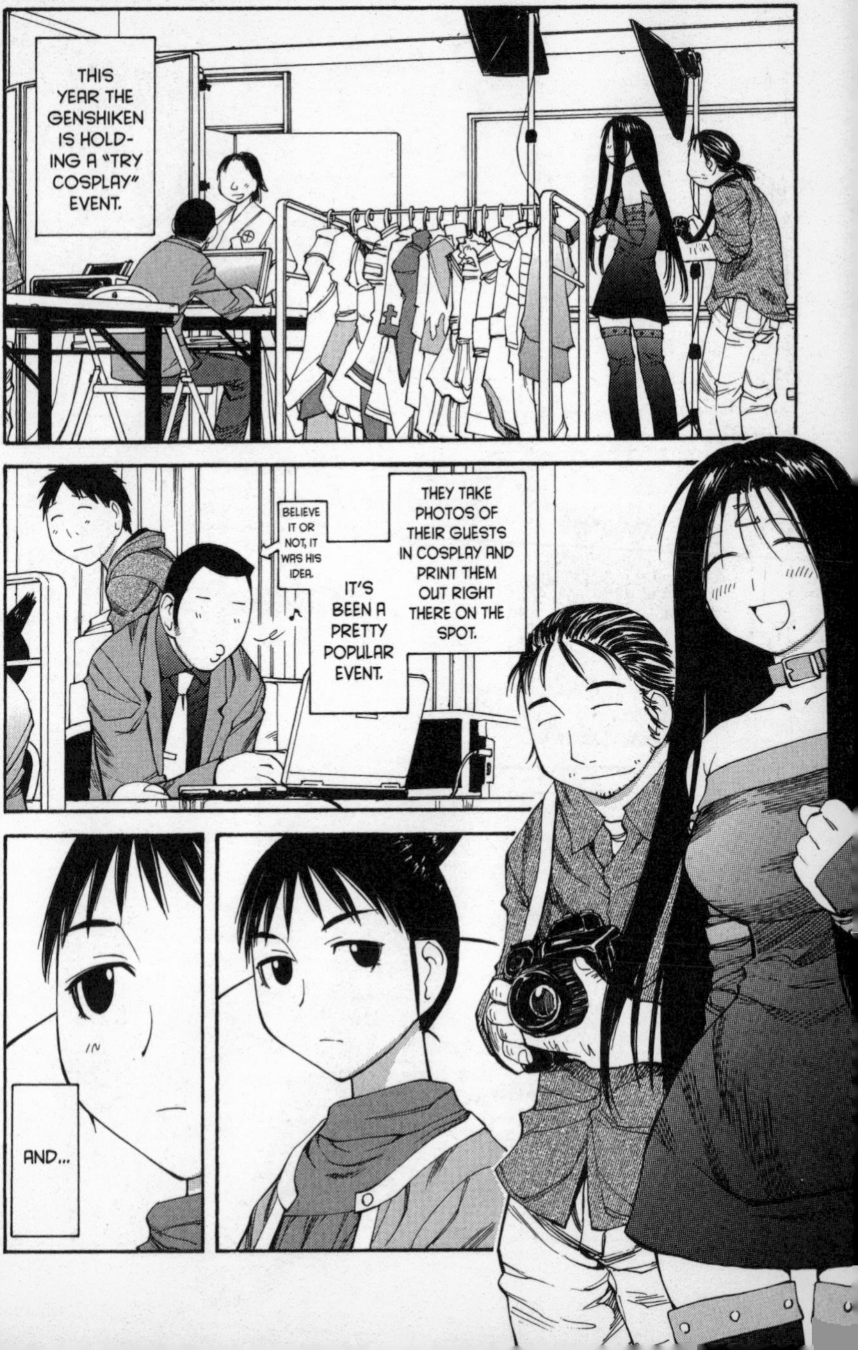
THIS YEAR THE GENSHIKEN IS HOLDING A "TRY COSPLAY" EVENT.
THEY TAKE PHOTOS OF THEIR GUESTS IN COSPLAY AND PRINT THEM OUT RIGHT THERE ON THE SPOT.
IT'S BEEN A PRETTY POPULAR EVENT.
BELIEVE IT OR NOT, IT WAS HIS IDEA.
AND...

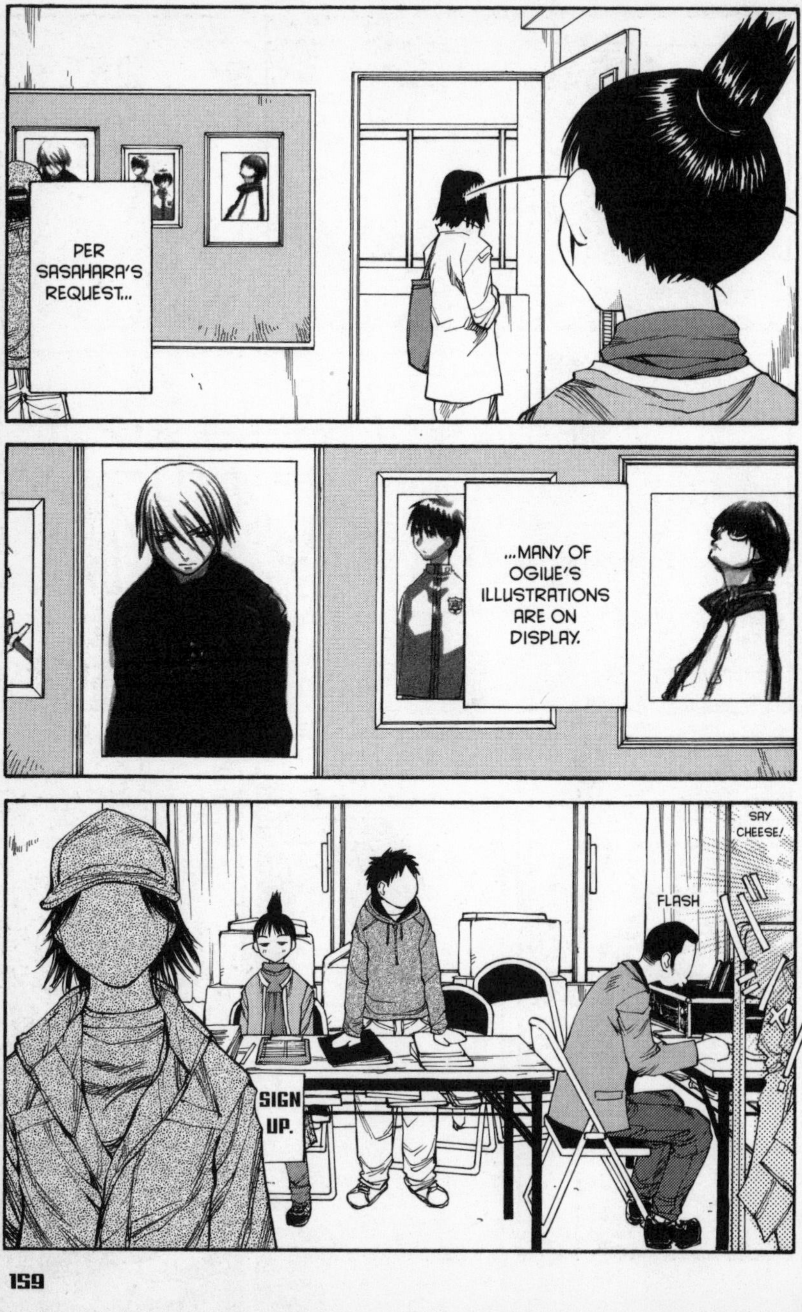
PER SASAHARA'S REQUEST...
...MANY OF OGIUE'S ILLUSTRATIONS ARE ON DISPLAY.
SAY CHEESE!
FLASH
SIGN UP.

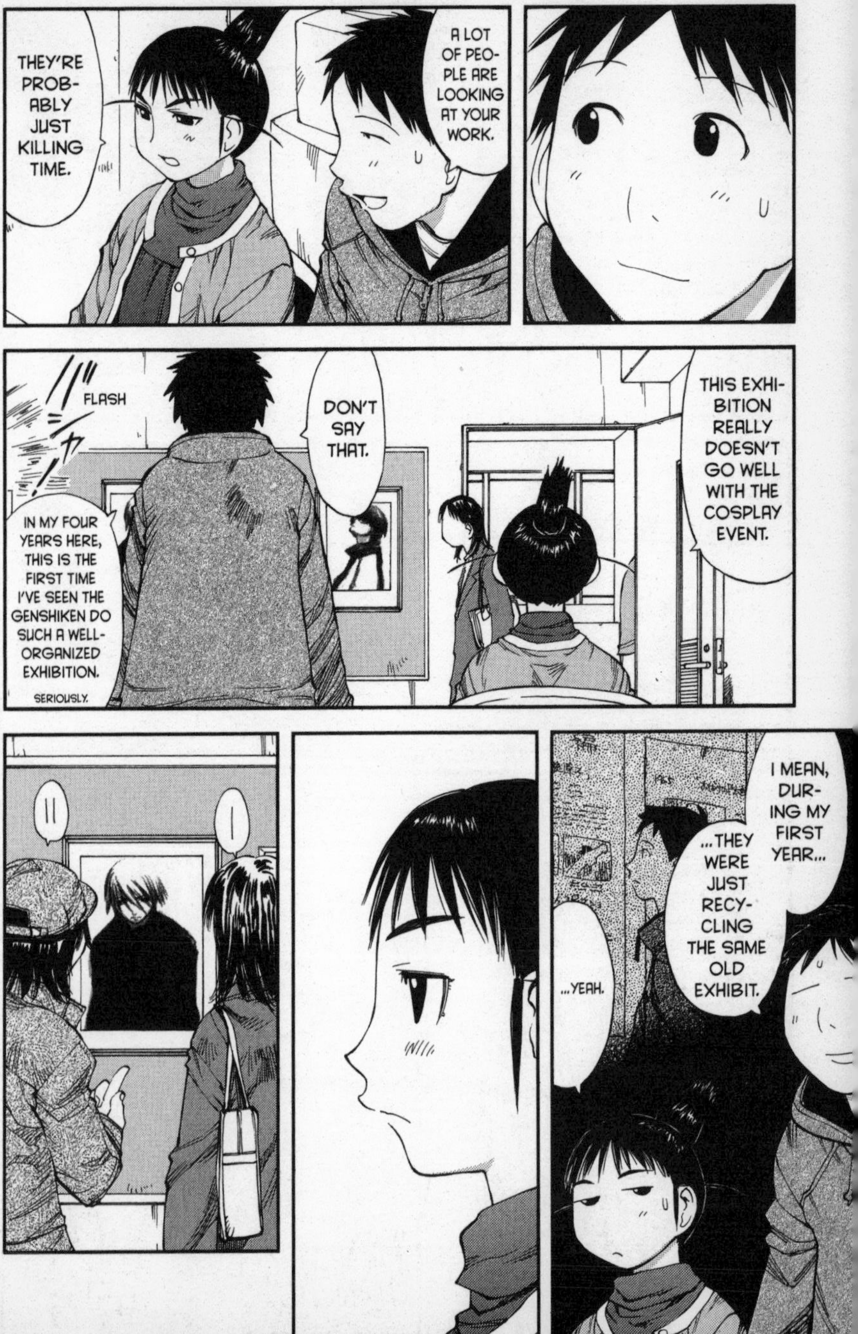
A LOT OF PEOPLE ARE LOOKING AT YOUR WORK.
THEY'RE PROBABLY JUST KILLING TIME.
THIS EXHIBITION REALLY DOESN'T GO WELL WITH THE COSPLAY EVENT.
DON'T SAY THAT.
FLASH
IN MY FOUR YEARS HERE, THIS IS THE FIRST TIME I'VE SEEN THE GENSHIKEN DO SUCH A WELL-ORGANIZED EXHIBITION.
SERIOUSLY.
I MEAN, DURING MY FIRST YEAR...
...THEY WERE JUST RECYCLING THE SAME OLD EXHIBIT.
...YEAH.

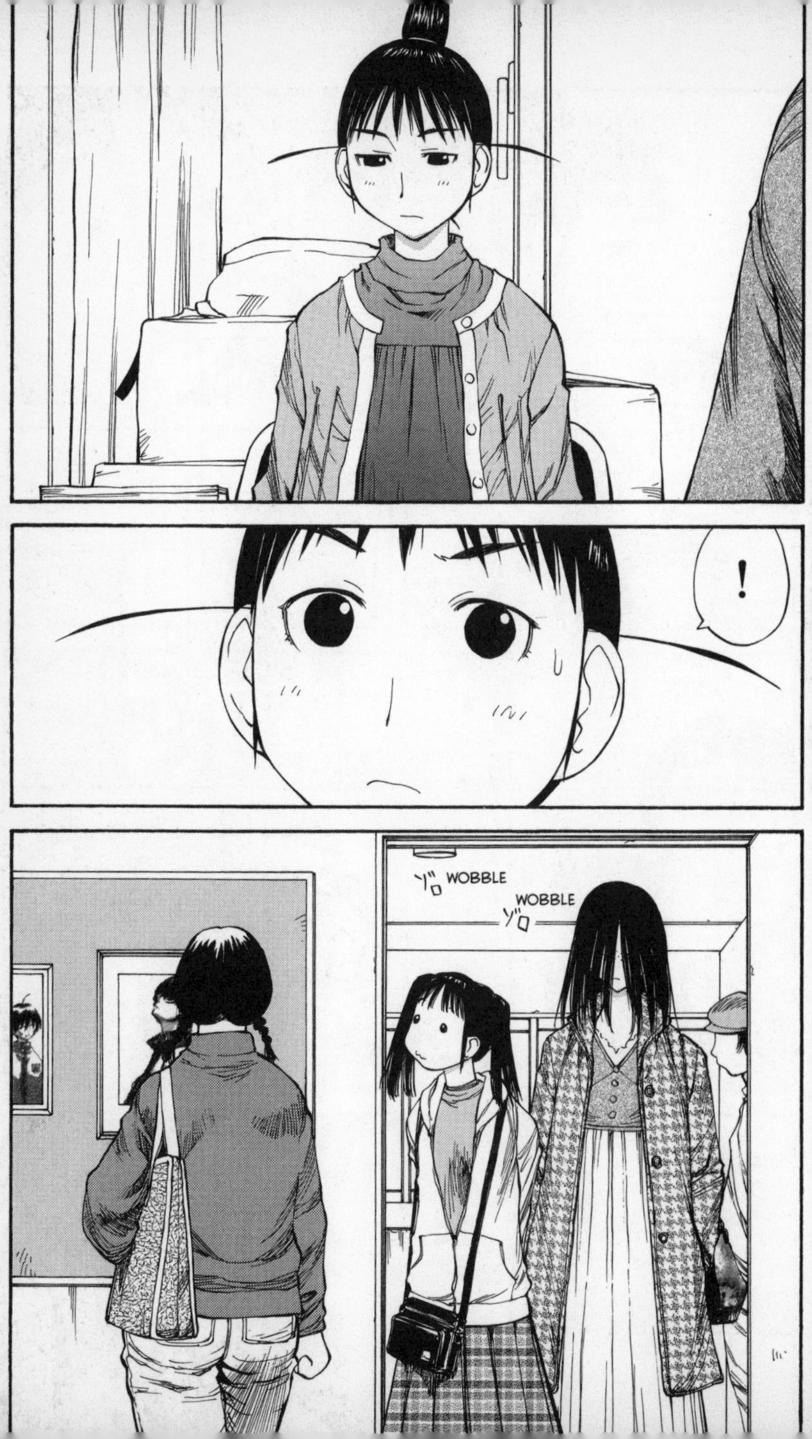
!
ゾロ WOBBLE
WOBBLE ゾロ

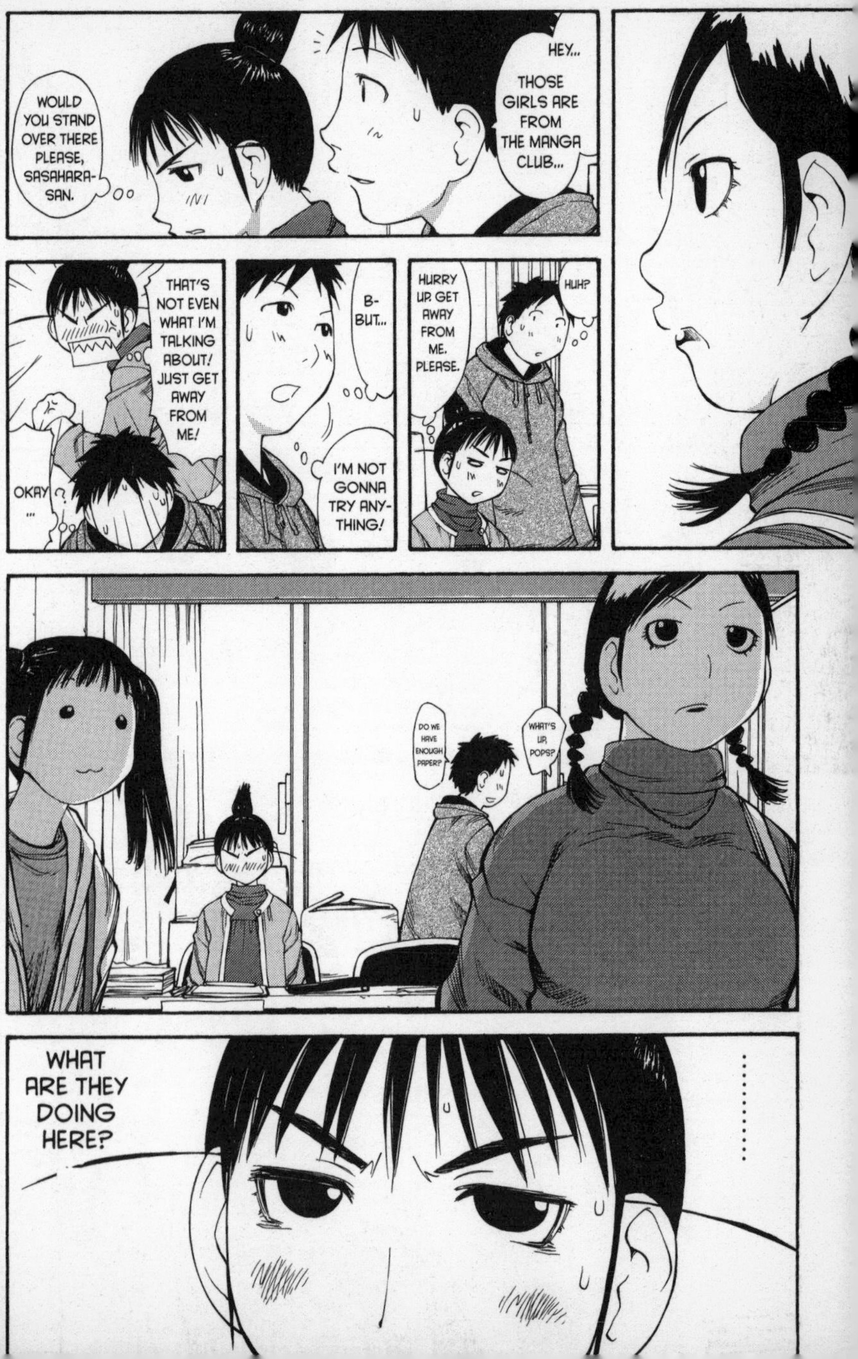
HEY...
THOSE GIRLS ARE FROM THE MANGA CLUB...
WOULD YOU STAND OVER THERE PLEASE, SASAHARA-SAN.
HUH?
HURRY UP. GET AWAY FROM ME. PLEASE.
B-BUT...
I'M NOT GONNA TRY ANY-THING!
THAT'S NOT EVEN WHAT I'M TALKING ABOUT! JUST GET AWAY FROM ME!
OKAY ...
WHAT'S UP, POPS?
DO WE HAVE ENOUGH PAPER?
....
WHAT ARE THEY DOING HERE?

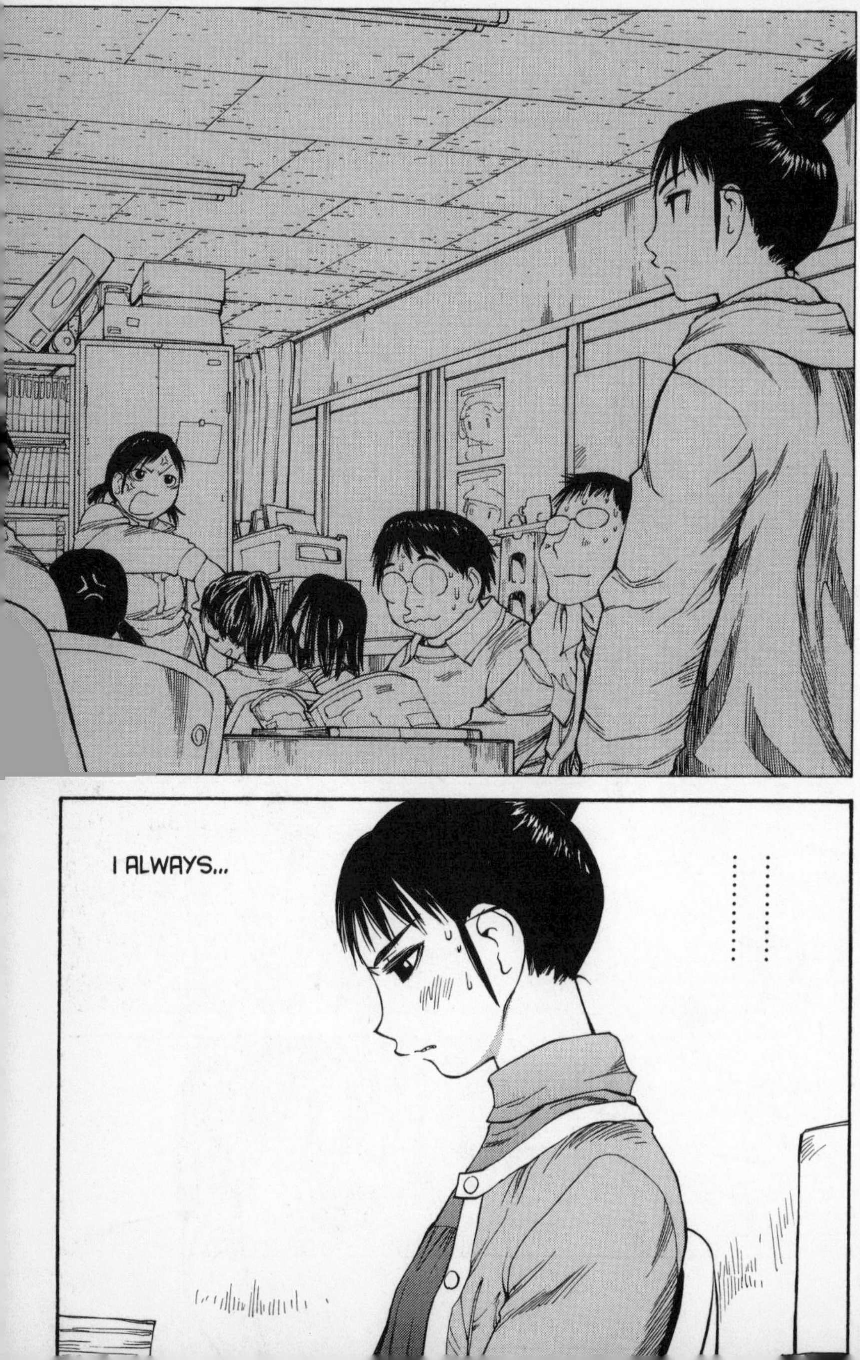
I ALWAYS...

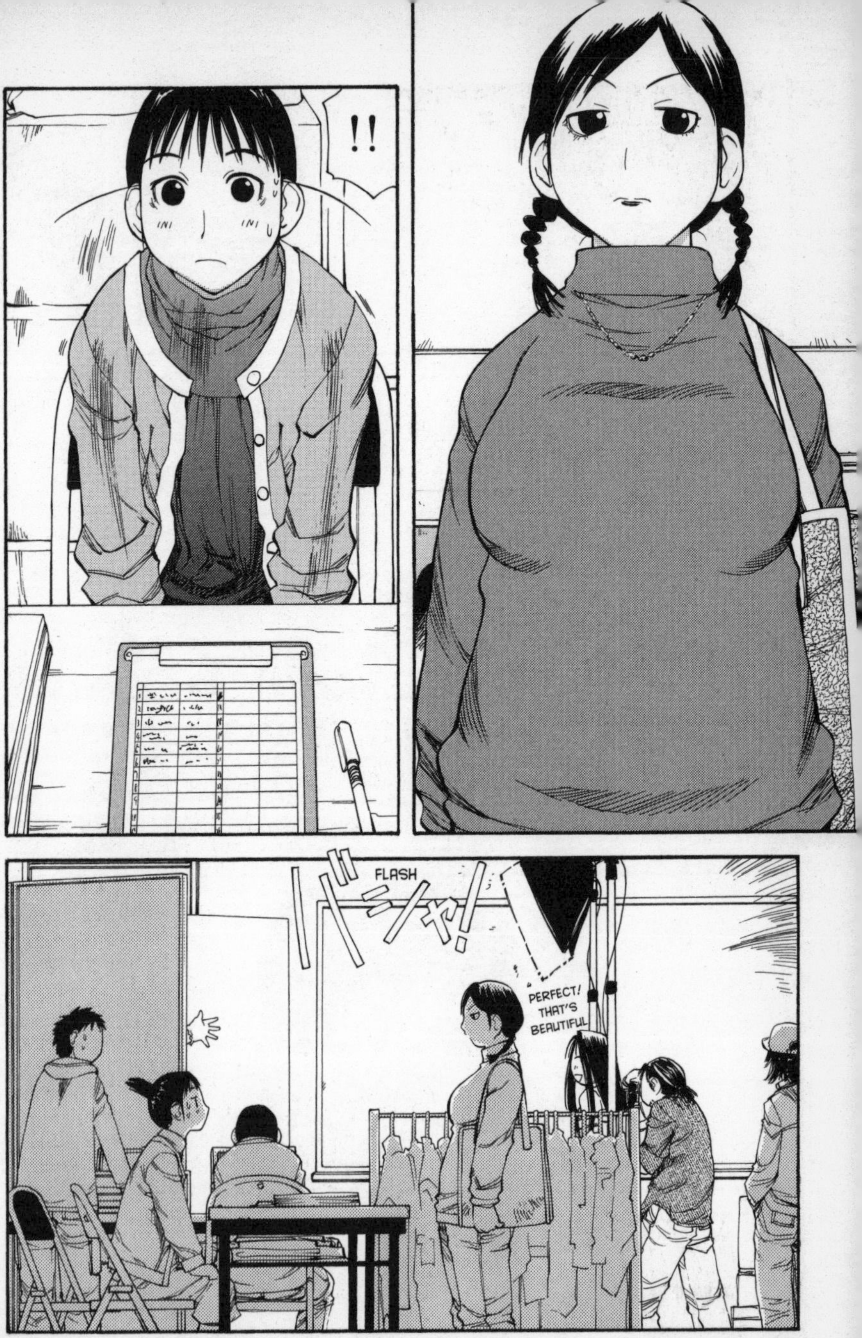
!!
バシャ!
FLASH
PERFECT! THAT'S BEAUTIFUL

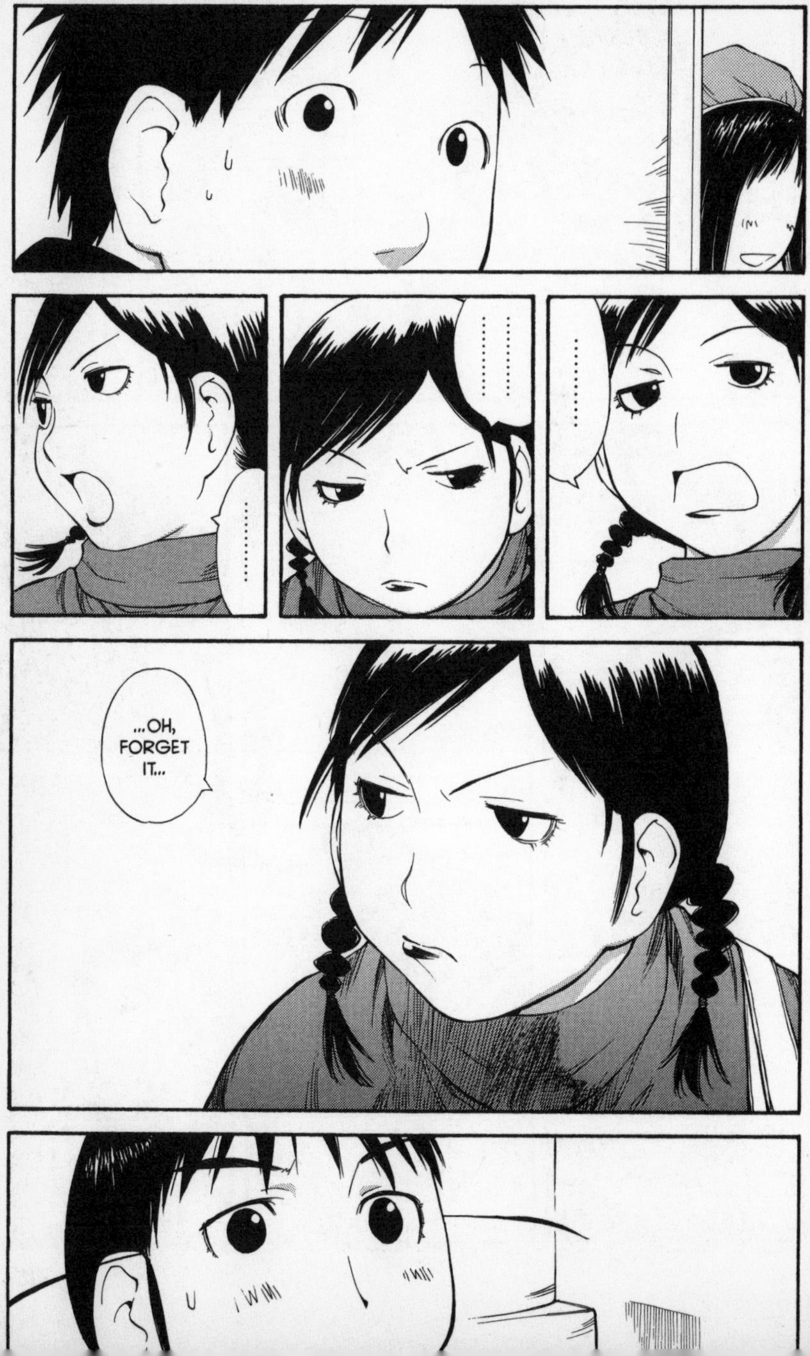
...OH, FORGET IT...

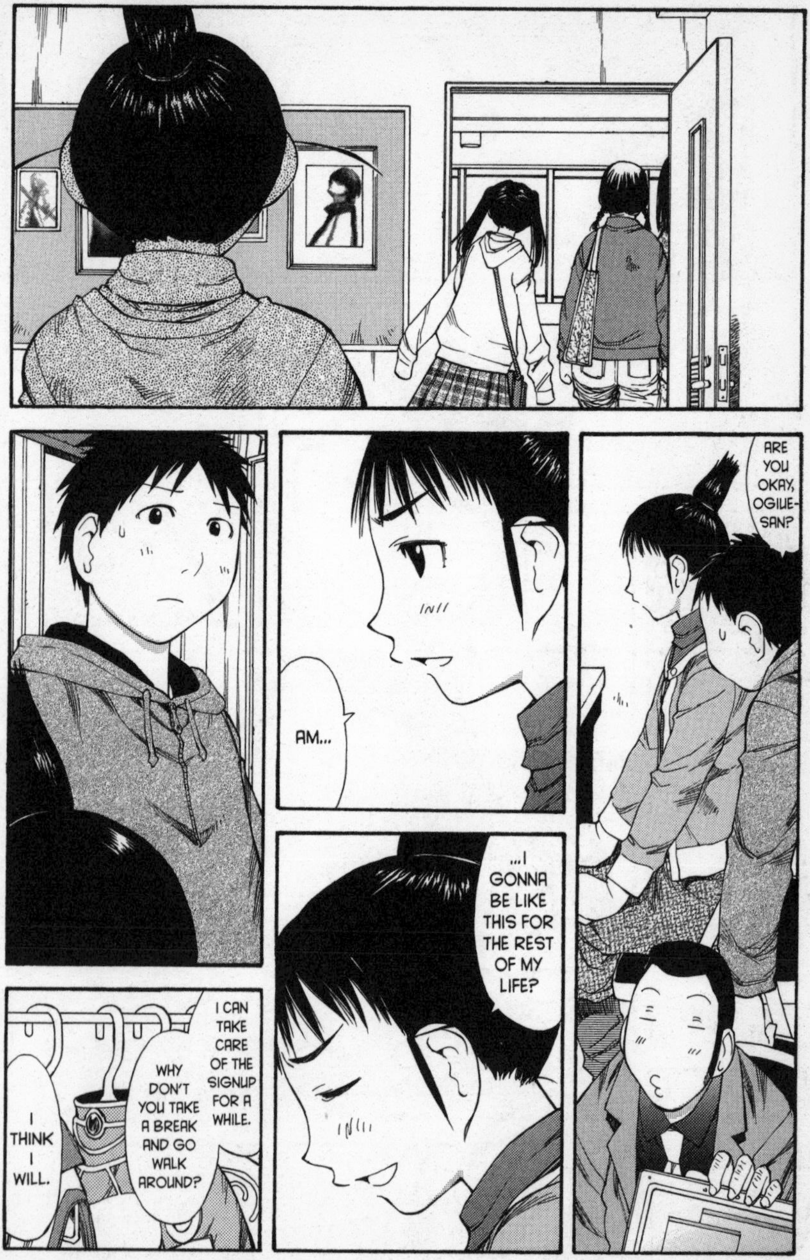
ARE YOU OKAY, OGIUE-SAN?
AM...
...I GONNA BE LIKE THIS FOR THE REST OF MY LIFE?
I CAN TAKE CARE OF THE SIGNUP FOR A WHILE.
WHY DON'T YOU TAKE A BREAK AND GO WALK AROUND?
I THINK I WILL.

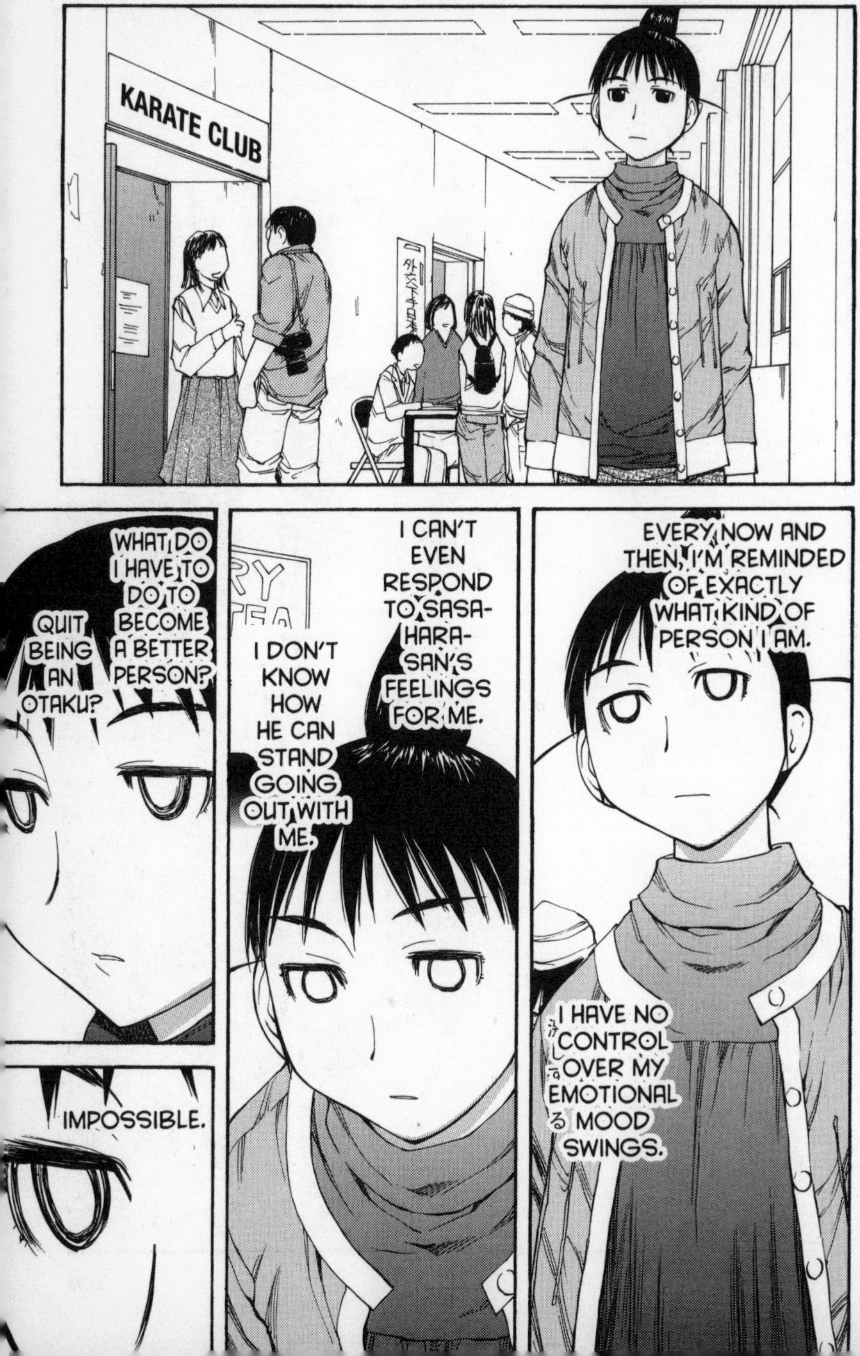
KARATE CLUB
EVERY NOW AND THEN, I'M REMINDED OF EXACTLY WHAT KIND OF PERSON I AM.
I HAVE NO CONTROL OVER MY EMOTIONAL MOOD SWINGS.
I CAN'T EVEN RESPOND TO SASA-HARA-SAN'S FEELINGS FOR ME.
I DON'T KNOW HOW HE CAN STAND GOING OUT WITH ME.
WHAT DO I HAVE TO DO TO BECOME A BETTER PERSON?
QUIT BEING AN OTAKU?
IMPOSSIBLE.

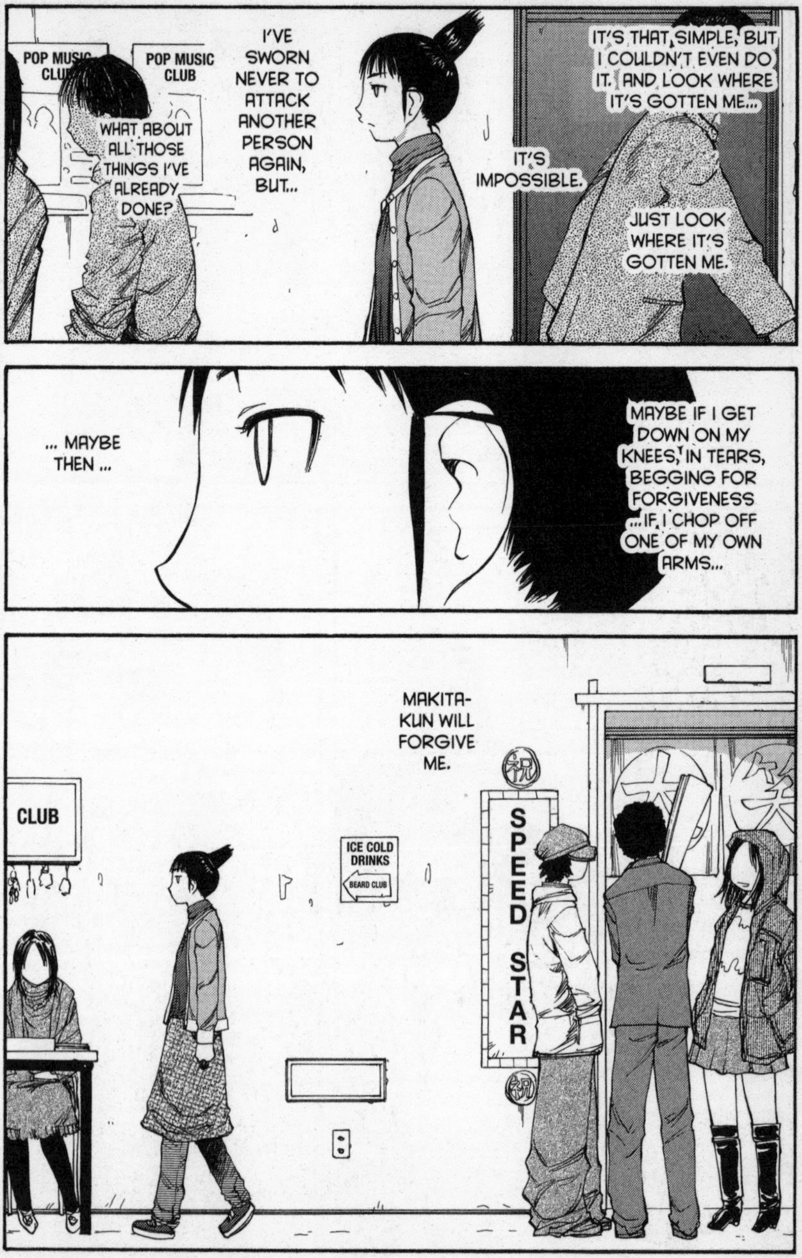
IT'S THAT SIMPLE, BUT I COULDN'T EVEN DO IT. AND LOOK WHERE IT'S GOTTEN ME...
JUST LOOK WHERE IT'S GOTTEN ME.
IT'S IMPOSSIBLE.
I'VE SWORN NEVER TO ATTACK ANOTHER PERSON AGAIN, BUT...
POP MUSIC CLUB
WHAT ABOUT ALL THOSE THINGS I'VE ALREADY DONE?
MAYBE IF I GET DOWN ON MY KNEES, IN TEARS, BEGGING FOR FORGIVENESS ...IF I CHOP OFF ONE OF MY OWN ARMS...
... MAYBE THEN ...
SPEED STAR
MAKITA-KUN WILL FORGIVE ME.
ICE COLD DRINKS
BEARD CLUB
CLUB

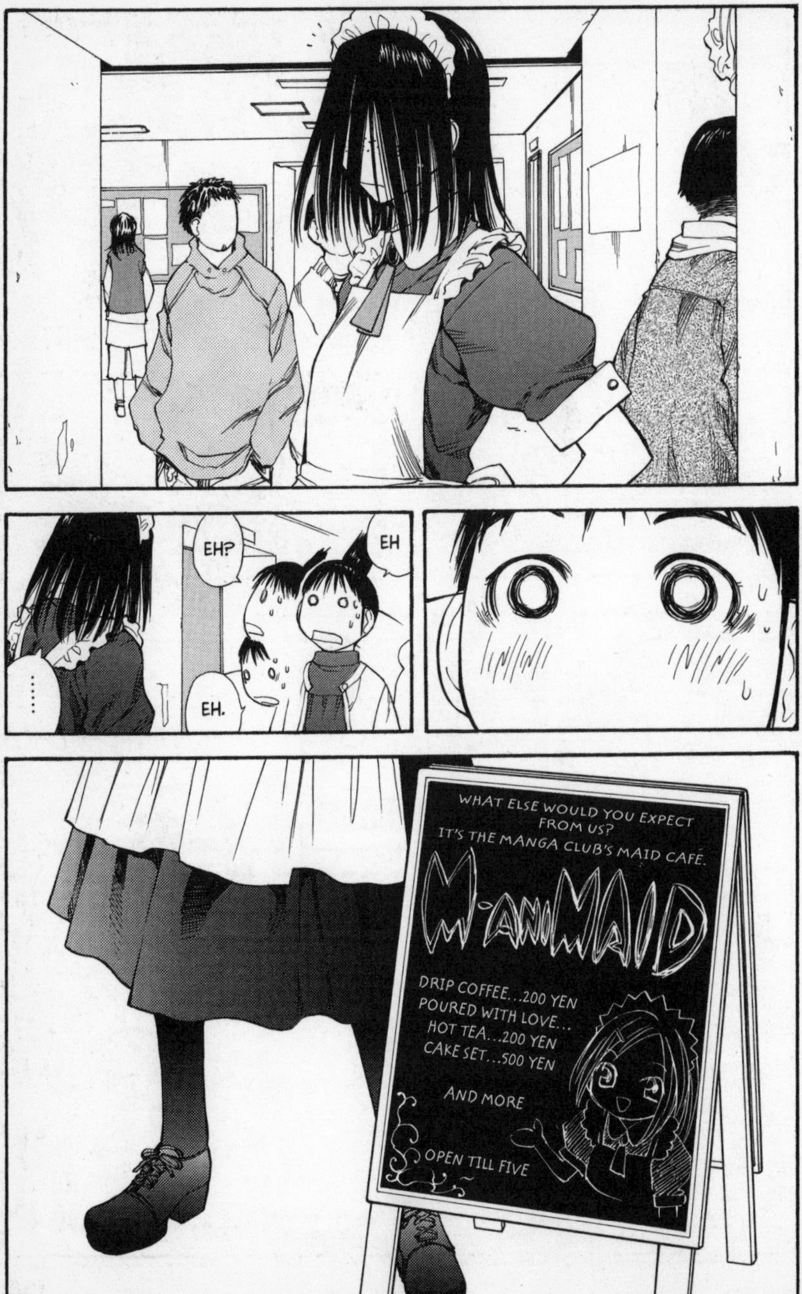
EH
EH?
EH.
......
WHAT ELSE WOULD YOU EXPECT FROM US?
IT'S THE MANGA CLUB'S MAID CAFE.
M-ANIMAID
DRIP COFFEE...200 YEN
POURED WITH LOVE...
HOT TEA...200 YEN
CAKE SET...500 YEN
AND MORE
OPEN TILL FIVE

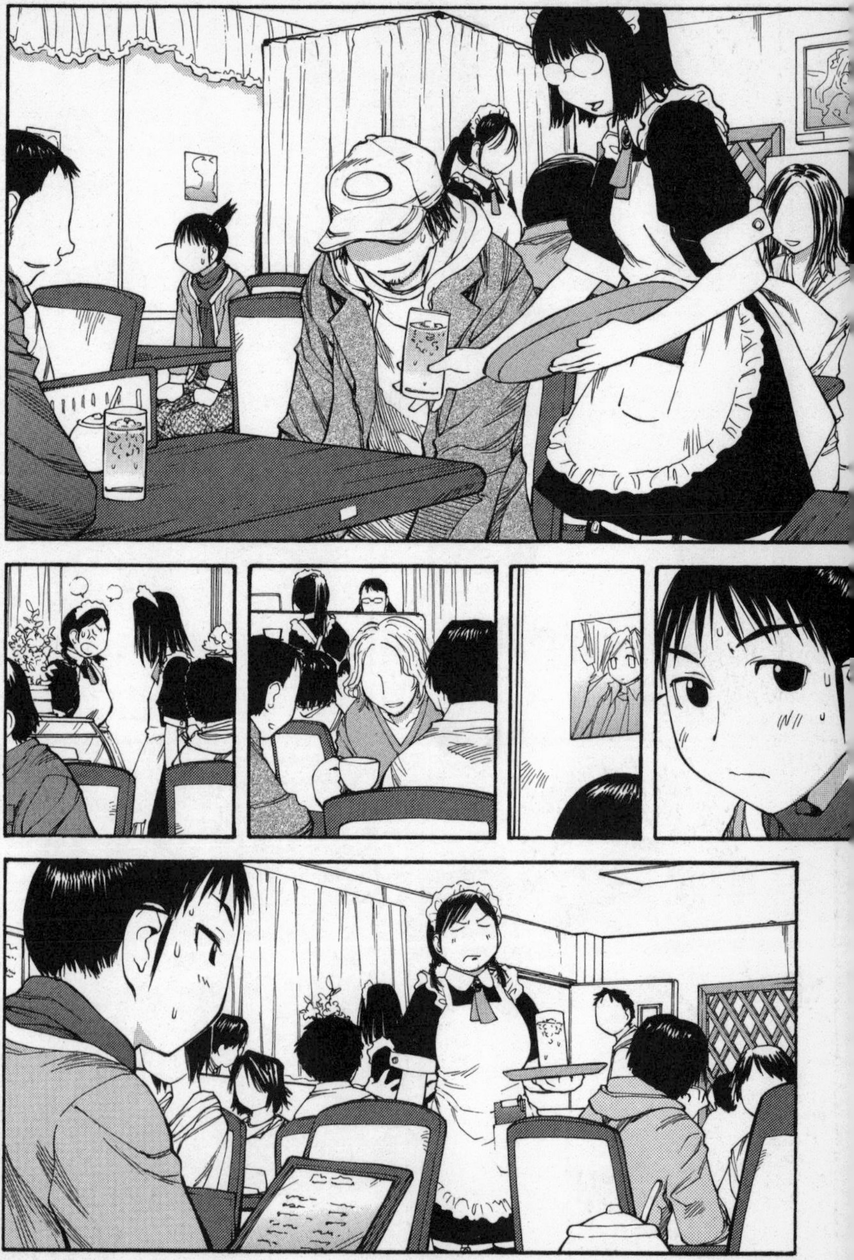

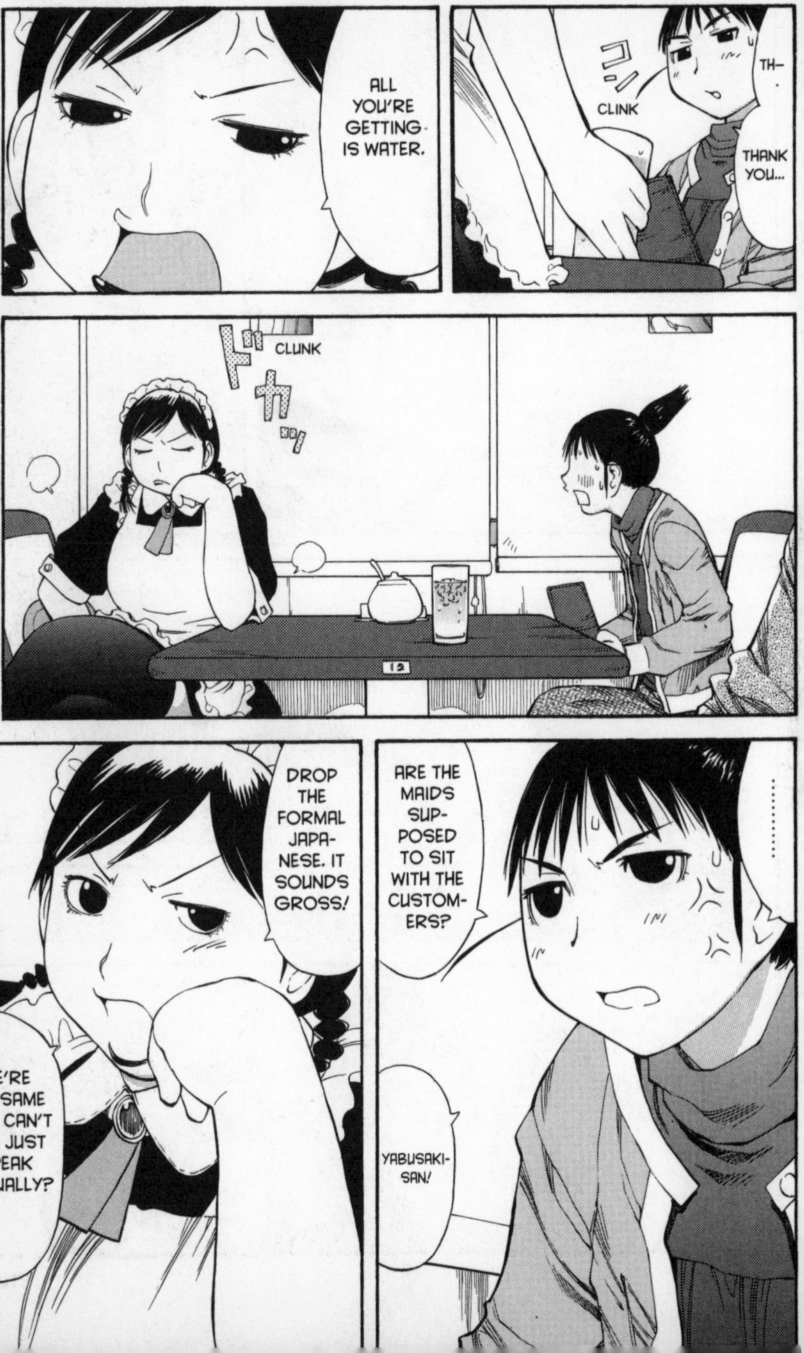
CLINK
TH-
THANK YOU...
ALL YOU'RE GETTING IS WATER.
CLINK
......
ARE THE MAIDS SUPPOSED TO SIT WITH THE CUSTOMERS?
YABUSAKI-SAN!
DROP THE FORMAL JAPANESE. IT SOUNDS GROSS!
WE'RE THE SAME AGE. CAN'T YOU JUST SPEAK CASUALLY?

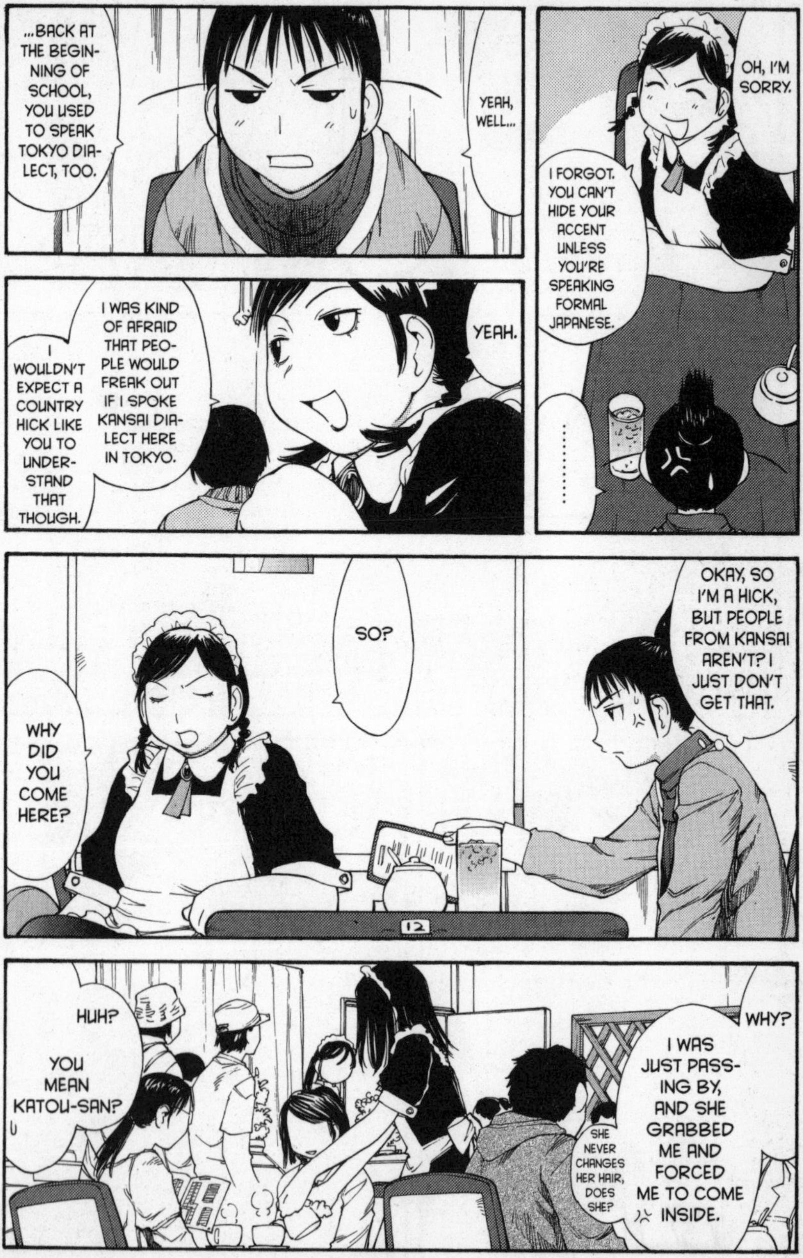
OH, I'M SORRY.
I FORGOT. YOU CAN'T HIDE YOUR ACCENT UNLESS YOU'RE SPEAKING FORMAL JAPANESE.
......
YEAH, WELL...
...BACK AT THE BEGIN-NING OF SCHOOL, YOU USED TO SPEAK TOKYO DIA-LECT, TOO.
YEAH.
I WAS KIND OF AFRAID THAT PEO-PLE WOULD FREAK OUT IF I SPOKE KANSAI DIA-LECT HERE IN TOKYO.
I WOULDN'T EXPECT A COUNTRY HICK LIKE YOU TO UNDER-STAND THAT THOUGH.
OKAY, SO I'M A HICK, BUT PEOPLE FROM KANSAI AREN'T? I JUST DON'T GET THAT.
SO?
WHY DID YOU COME HERE?
12
WHY?
I WAS JUST PASS-ING BY, AND SHE GRABBED ME AND FORCED ME TO COME INSIDE.
SHE NEVER CHANGES HER HAIR, DOES SHE?
HUH?
YOU MEAN KATOU-SAN?

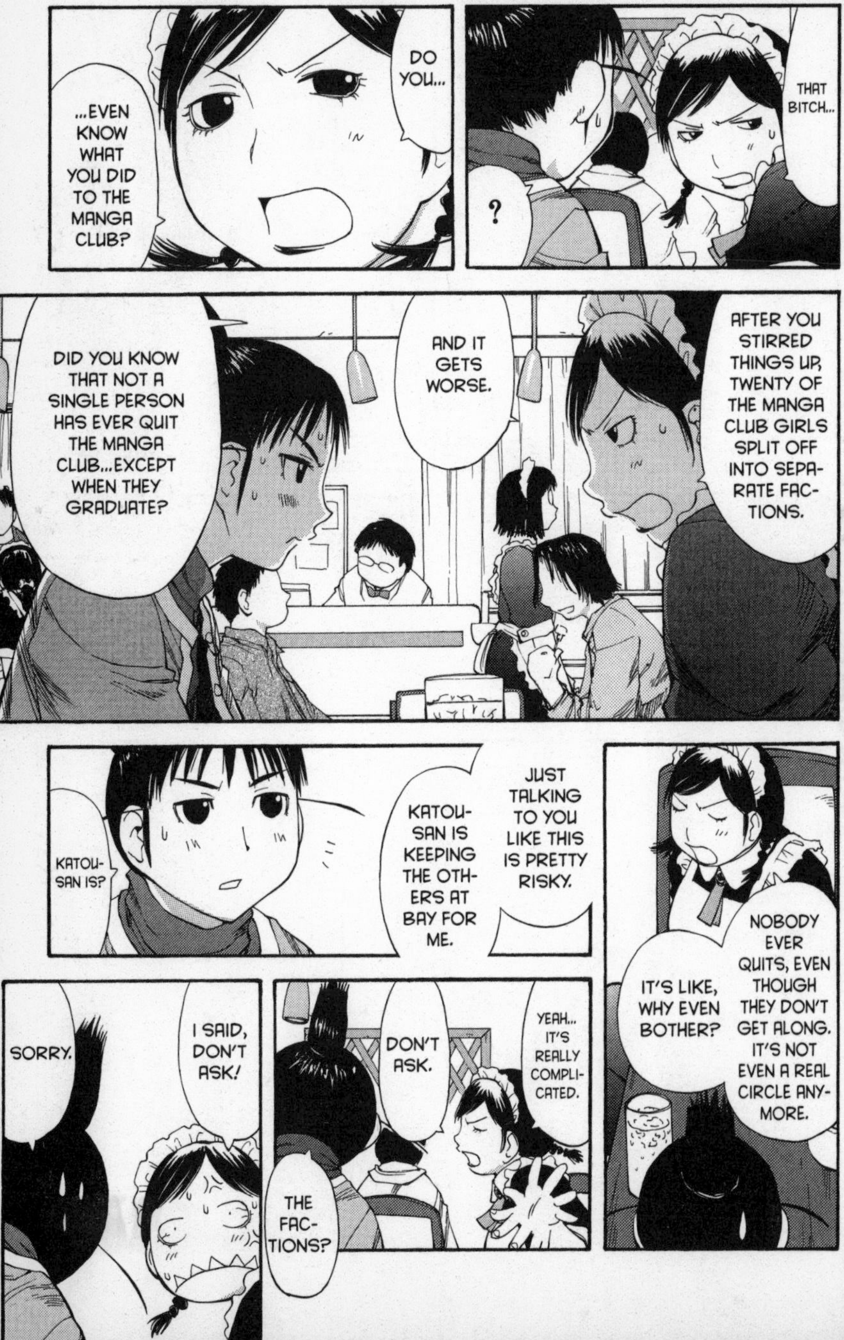
THAT BITCH...
?
DO YOU...
...EVEN KNOW WHAT YOU DID TO THE MANGA CLUB?
AFTER YOU STIRRED THINGS UP, TWENTY OF THE MANGA CLUB GIRLS SPLIT OFF INTO SEPARATE FACTIONS.
AND IT GETS WORSE.
DID YOU KNOW THAT NOT A SINGLE PERSON HAS EVER QUIT THE MANGA CLUB...EXCEPT WHEN THEY GRADUATE?
NOBODY EVER QUITS, EVEN THOUGH THEY DON'T GET ALONG. IT'S NOT EVEN A REAL CIRCLE ANYMORE.
IT'S LIKE, WHY EVEN BOTHER?
JUST TALKING TO YOU LIKE THIS IS PRETTY RISKY.
KATOU-SAN IS KEEPING THE OTHERS AT BAY FOR ME.
KATOU-SAN IS?
YEAH... IT'S REALLY COMPLICATED.
DON'T ASK.
THE FACTIONS?
I SAID, DON'T ASK!
SORRY.

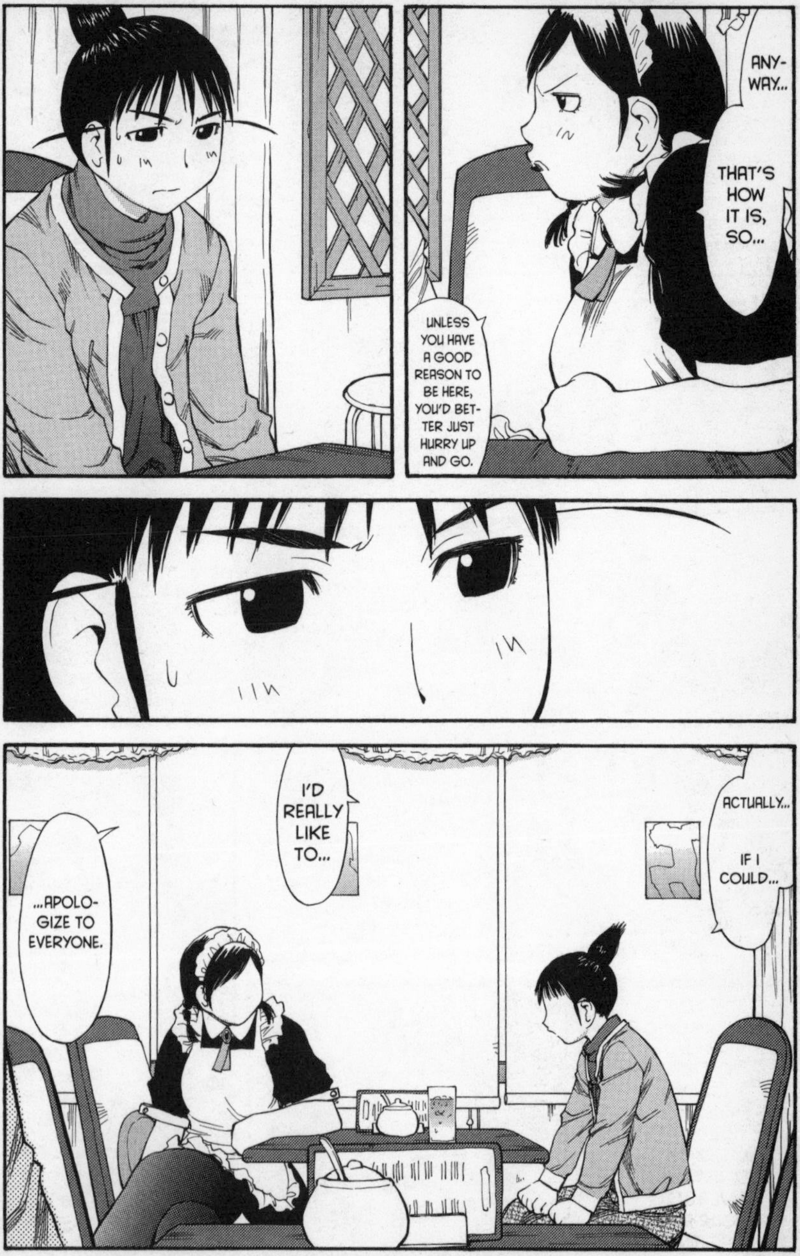
ANY-WAY...
THAT'S HOW IT IS, SO...
UNLESS YOU HAVE A GOOD REASON TO BE HERE, YOU'D BET-TER JUST HURRY UP AND GO.
ACTUALLY...
IF I COULD...
I'D REALLY LIKE TO...
...APOLO-GIZE TO EVERYONE.

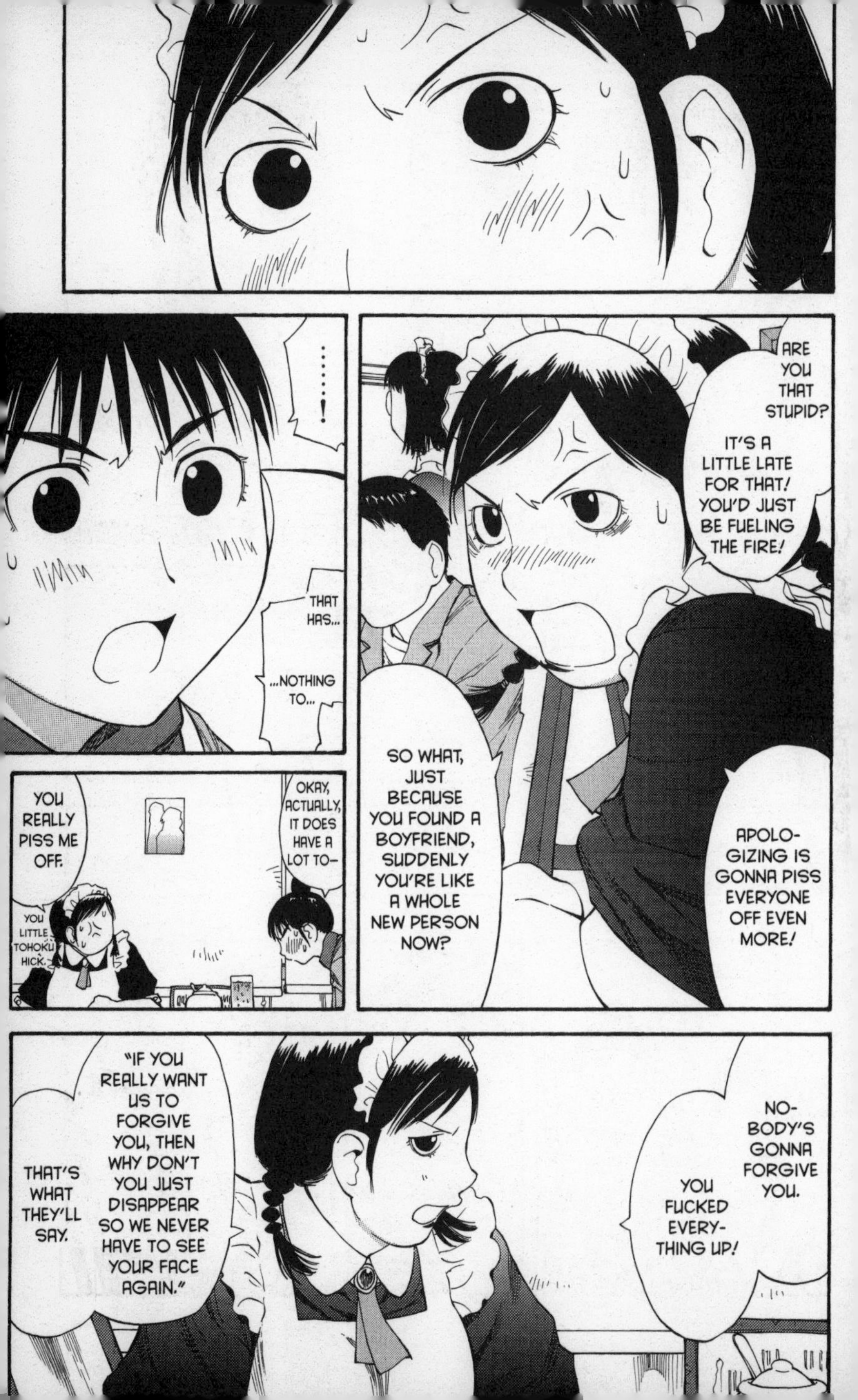

ARE YOU THAT STUPID?
IT'S A LITTLE LATE FOR THAT! YOU'D JUST BE FUELING THE FIRE!
APOLOGIZING IS GONNA PISS EVERYONE OFF EVEN MORE!
SO WHAT, JUST BECAUSE YOU FOUND A BOYFRIEND, SUDDENLY YOU'RE LIKE A WHOLE NEW PERSON NOW?
......!
THAT HAS...
...NOTHING TO...
OKAY, ACTUALLY, IT DOES HAVE A LOT TO—
YOU REALLY PISS ME OFF.
YOU LITTLE TOHOKU HICK.
NO-BODY'S GONNA FORGIVE YOU.
YOU FUCKED EVERY-THING UP!
"IF YOU REALLY WANT US TO FORGIVE YOU, THEN WHY DON'T YOU JUST DISAPPEAR SO WE NEVER HAVE TO SEE YOUR FACE AGAIN."
THAT'S WHAT THEY'LL SAY.

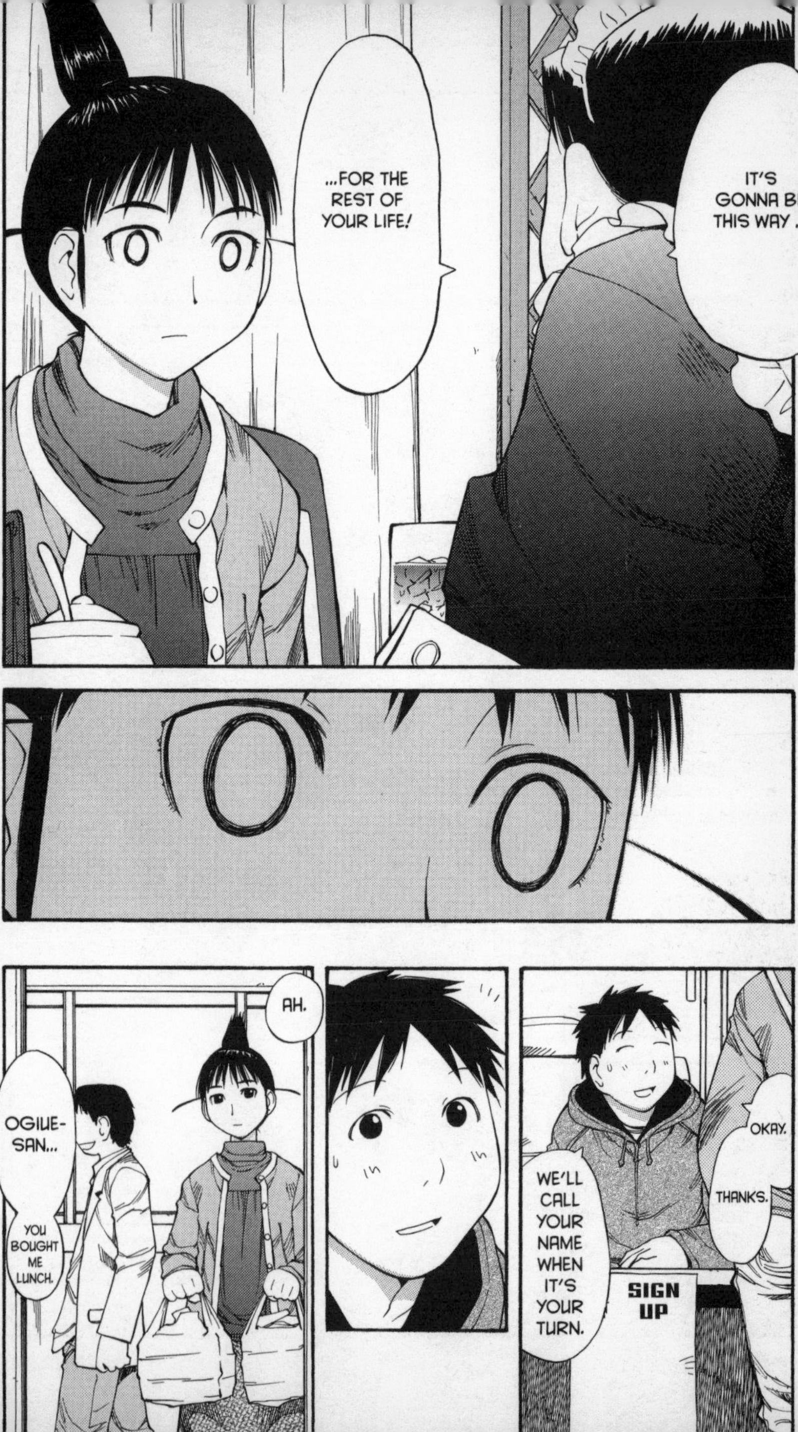
IT'S GONNA BE THIS WAY ...
...FOR THE REST OF YOUR LIFE!
OKAY.
THANKS.
WE'LL CALL YOUR NAME WHEN IT'S YOUR TURN.
SIGN UP
AH.
OGIUE-SAN...
YOU BOUGHT ME LUNCH.

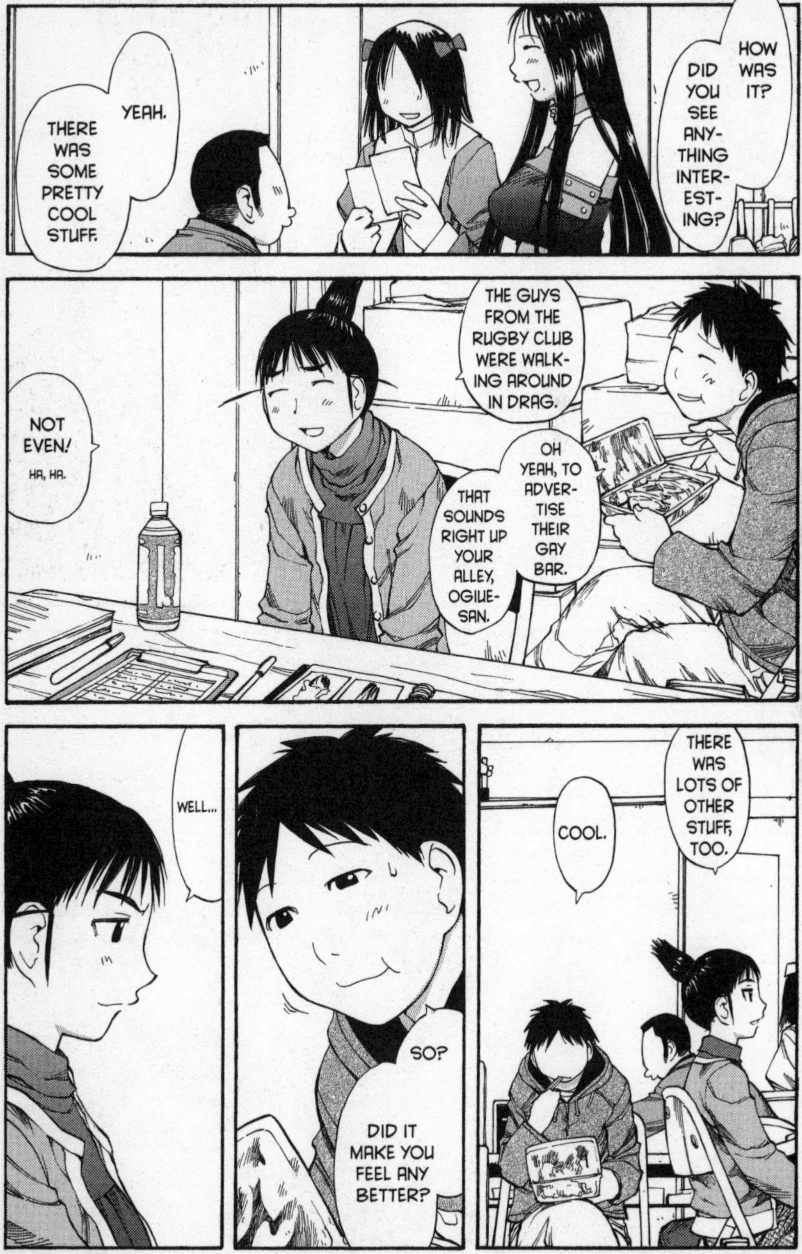
HOW WAS IT?
DID YOU SEE ANYTHING INTERESTING?
YEAH.
THERE WAS SOME PRETTY COOL STUFF.
THE GUYS FROM THE RUGBY CLUB WERE WALKING AROUND IN DRAG.
OH YEAH, TO ADVERTISE THEIR GAY BAR.
THAT SOUNDS RIGHT UP YOUR ALLEY, OGIUE-SAN.
NOT EVEN!
HA, HA.
THERE WAS LOTS OF OTHER STUFF, TOO.
COOL.
SO?
DID IT MAKE YOU FEEL ANY BETTER?
WELL...

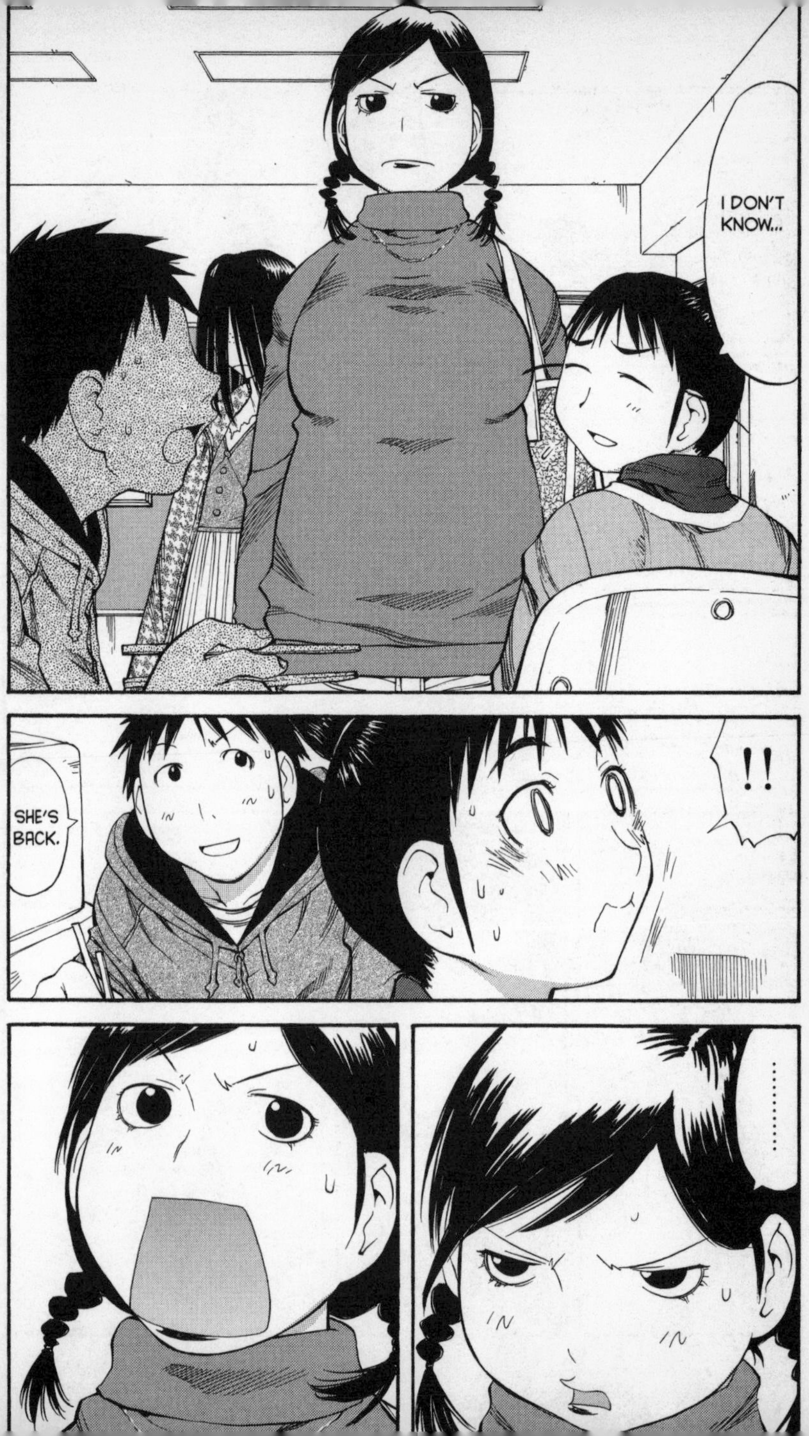
I DON'T KNOW...
...
!!
SHE'S BACK.
....

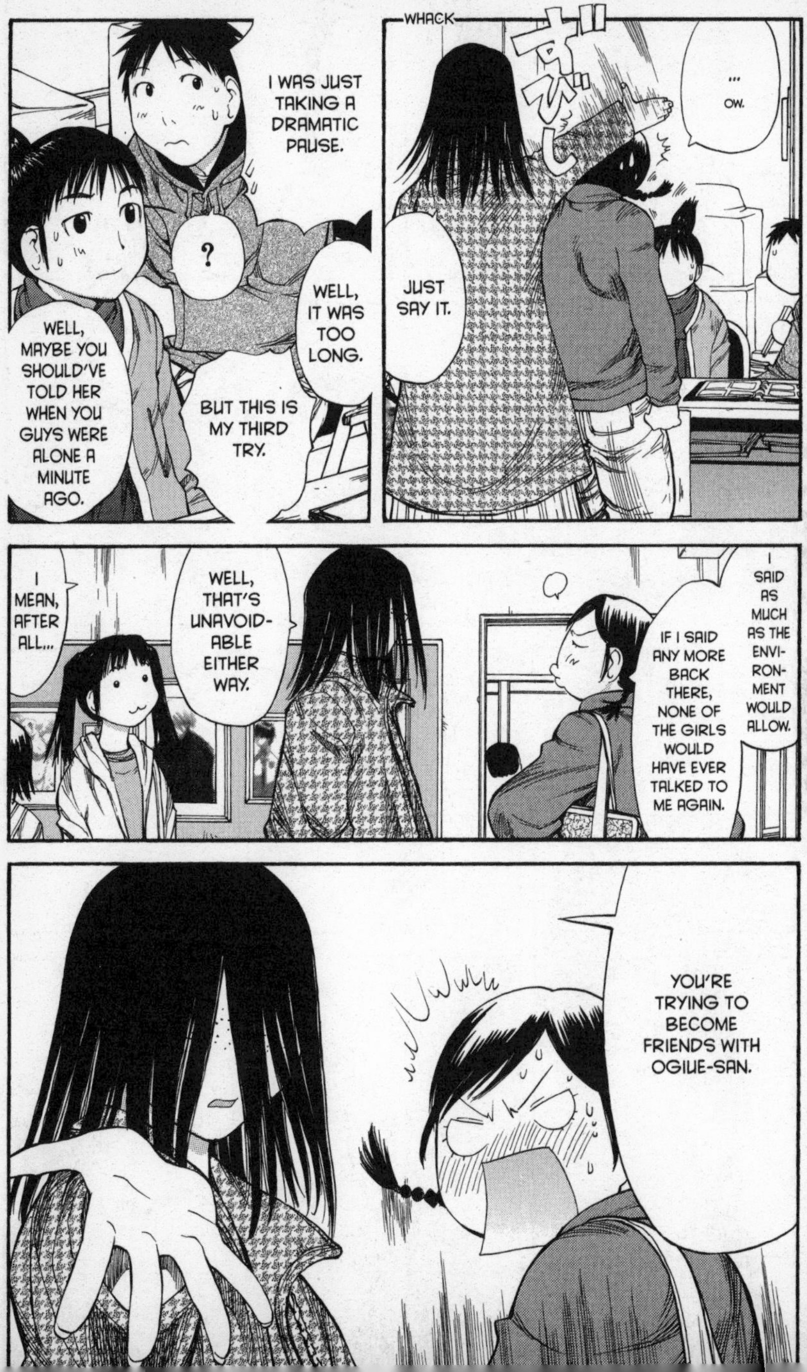
WHACK
ずびし
... OW.
JUST SAY IT.
I WAS JUST TAKING A DRAMATIC PAUSE.
?
WELL, IT WAS TOO LONG.
BUT THIS IS MY THIRD TRY.
WELL, MAYBE YOU SHOULD'VE TOLD HER WHEN YOU GUYS WERE ALONE A MINUTE AGO.
I SAID AS MUCH AS THE ENVIRONMENT WOULD ALLOW.
IF I SAID ANY MORE BACK THERE, NONE OF THE GIRLS WOULD HAVE EVER TALKED TO ME AGAIN.
WELL, THAT'S UNAVOIDABLE EITHER WAY.
I MEAN, AFTER ALL...
YOU'RE TRYING TO BECOME FRIENDS WITH OGIUE-SAN.

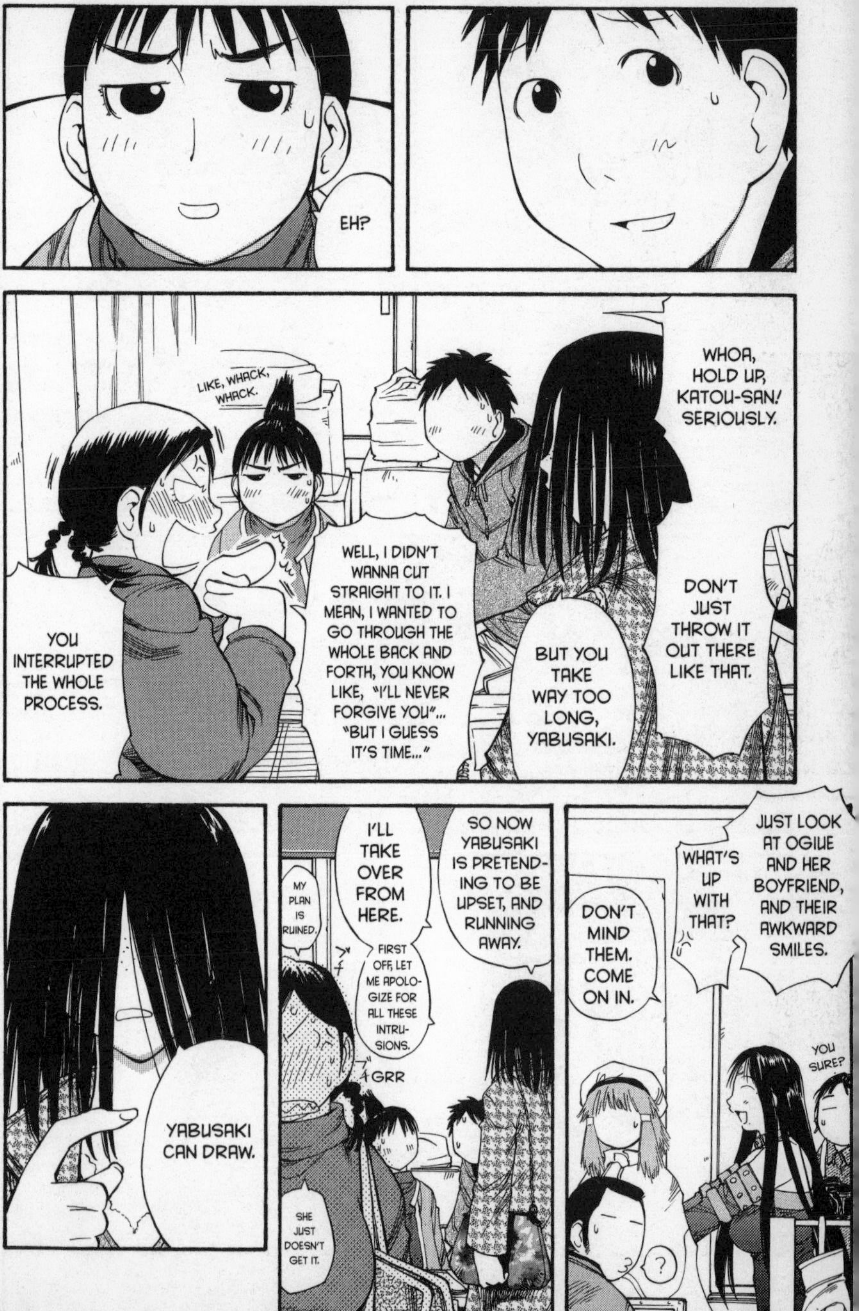
EH?
WHOA, HOLD UP, KATOU-SAN! SERIOUSLY.
DON'T JUST THROW IT OUT THERE LIKE THAT.
BUT YOU TAKE WAY TOO LONG, YABUSAKI.
LIKE, WHACK, WHACK.
WELL, I DIDN'T WANNA CUT STRAIGHT TO IT. I MEAN, I WANTED TO GO THROUGH THE WHOLE BACK AND FORTH, YOU KNOW LIKE, "I'LL NEVER FORGIVE YOU"... "BUT I GUESS IT'S TIME..."
YOU INTERRUPTED THE WHOLE PROCESS.
JUST LOOK AT OGIUE AND HER BOYFRIEND, AND THEIR AWKWARD SMILES.
WHAT'S UP WITH THAT?
DON'T MIND THEM. COME ON IN.
YOU SURE?
SO NOW YABUSAKI IS PRETENDING TO BE UPSET, AND RUNNING AWAY.
I'LL TAKE OVER FROM HERE.
MY PLAN IS RUINED.
FIRST OFF, LET ME APOLOGIZE FOR ALL THESE INTRUSIONS.
GRR
SHE JUST DOESN'T GET IT.
YABUSAKI CAN DRAW.

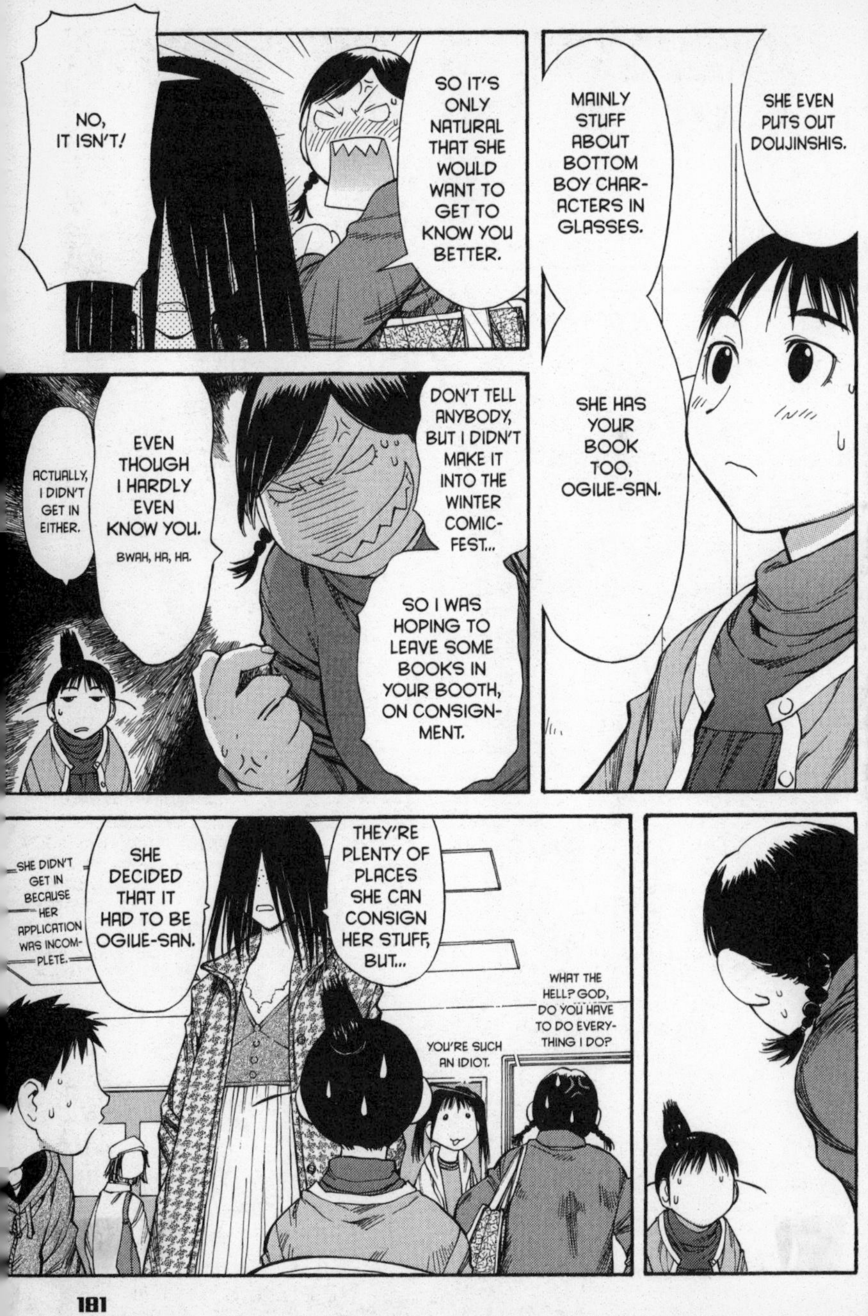
SHE EVEN PUTS OUT DOUJINSHIS.
MAINLY STUFF ABOUT BOTTOM BOY CHARACTERS IN GLASSES.
SHE HAS YOUR BOOK TOO, OGIUE-SAN.
SO IT'S ONLY NATURAL THAT SHE WOULD WANT TO GET TO KNOW YOU BETTER.
NO, IT ISN'T!
DON'T TELL ANYBODY, BUT I DIDN'T MAKE IT INTO THE WINTER COMIC-FEST...
SO I WAS HOPING TO LEAVE SOME BOOKS IN YOUR BOOTH, ON CONSIGNMENT.
EVEN THOUGH I HARDLY EVEN KNOW YOU.
BWAH, HA, HA.
ACTUALLY, I DIDN'T GET IN EITHER.
THEY'RE PLENTY OF PLACES SHE CAN CONSIGN HER STUFF, BUT...
SHE DECIDED THAT IT HAD TO BE OGIUE-SAN.
SHE DIDN'T GET IN BECAUSE HER APPLICATION WAS INCOMPLETE.
WHAT THE HELL? GOD, DO YOU HAVE TO DO EVERYTHING I DO?
YOU'RE SUCH AN IDIOT.

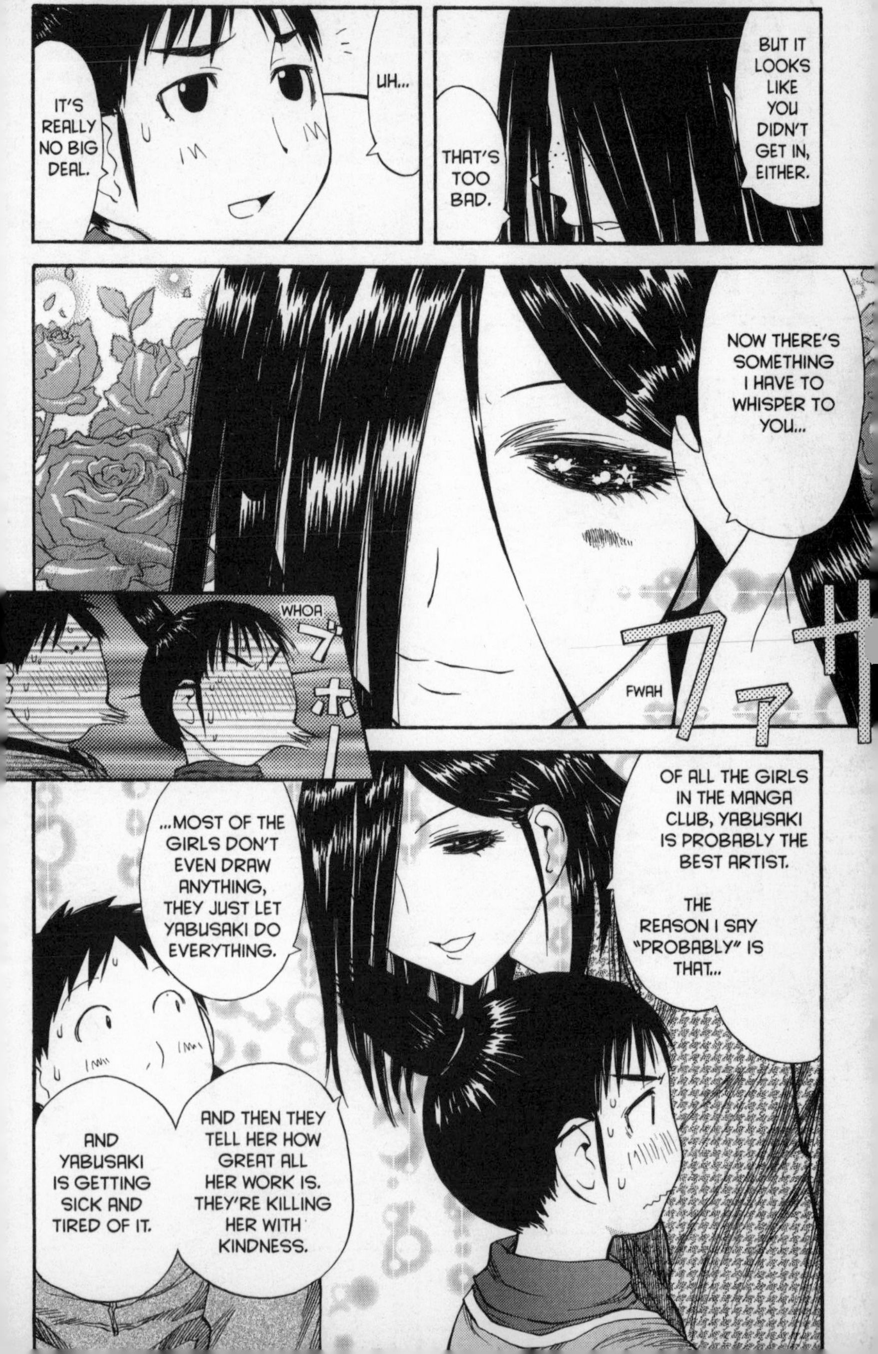
BUT IT LOOKS LIKE YOU DIDN'T GET IN, EITHER.
THAT'S TOO BAD.
UH...
IT'S REALLY NO BIG DEAL.
NOW THERE'S SOMETHING I HAVE TO WHISPER TO YOU...
FWAH
WHOA
OF ALL THE GIRLS IN THE MANGA CLUB, YABUSAKI IS PROBABLY THE BEST ARTIST.
THE REASON I SAY "PROBABLY" IS THAT...
...MOST OF THE GIRLS DON'T EVEN DRAW ANYTHING, THEY JUST LET YABUSAKI DO EVERYTHING.
AND THEN THEY TELL HER HOW GREAT ALL HER WORK IS. THEY'RE KILLING HER WITH KINDNESS.
AND YABUSAKI IS GETTING SICK AND TIRED OF IT.

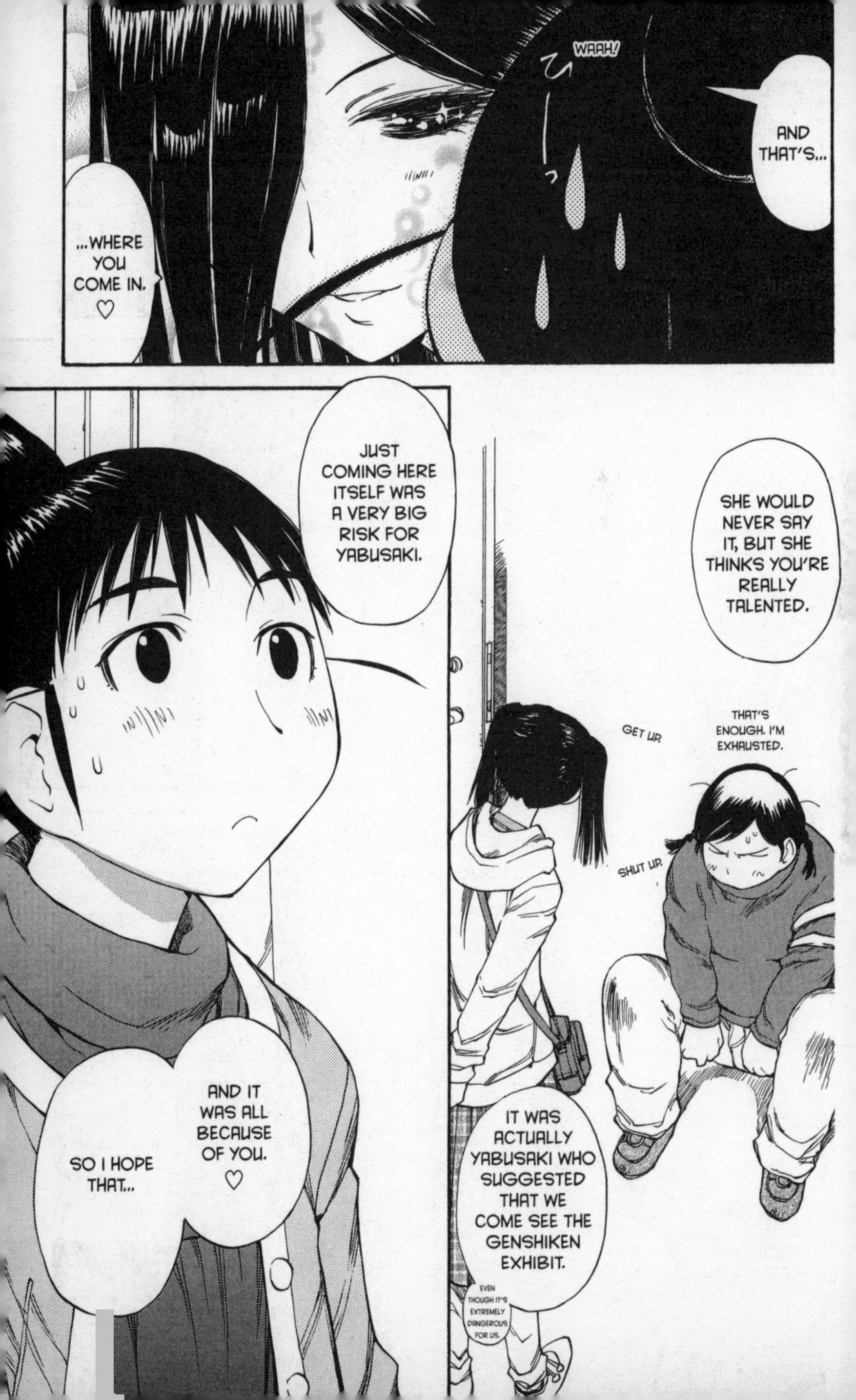
AND THAT'S...
WAAH!
...WHERE YOU COME IN. ♡
SHE WOULD NEVER SAY IT, BUT SHE THINKS YOU'RE REALLY TALENTED.
THAT'S ENOUGH. I'M EXHAUSTED.
GET UP.
SHUT UP.
IT WAS ACTUALLY YABUSAKI WHO SUGGESTED THAT WE COME SEE THE GENSHIKEN EXHIBIT.
EVEN THOUGH IT'S EXTREMELY DANGEROUS FOR US.
JUST COMING HERE ITSELF WAS A VERY BIG RISK FOR YABUSAKI.
AND IT WAS ALL BECAUSE OF YOU. ♡
SO I HOPE THAT...

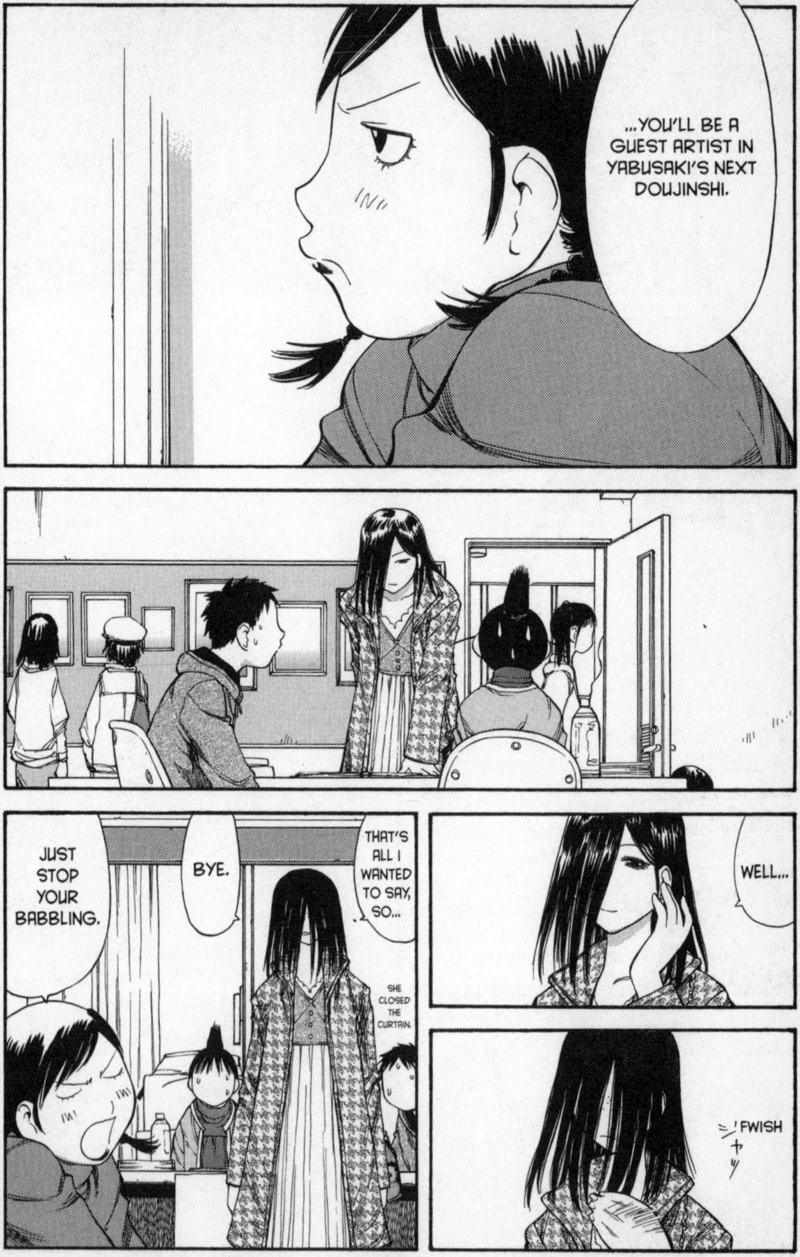
...YOU'LL BE A GUEST ARTIST IN YABUSAKI'S NEXT DOUJINSHI.
WELL...
シャッ FWISH
THAT'S ALL I WANTED TO SAY, SO...
SHE CLOSED THE CURTAIN.
BYE.
JUST STOP YOUR BABBLING.

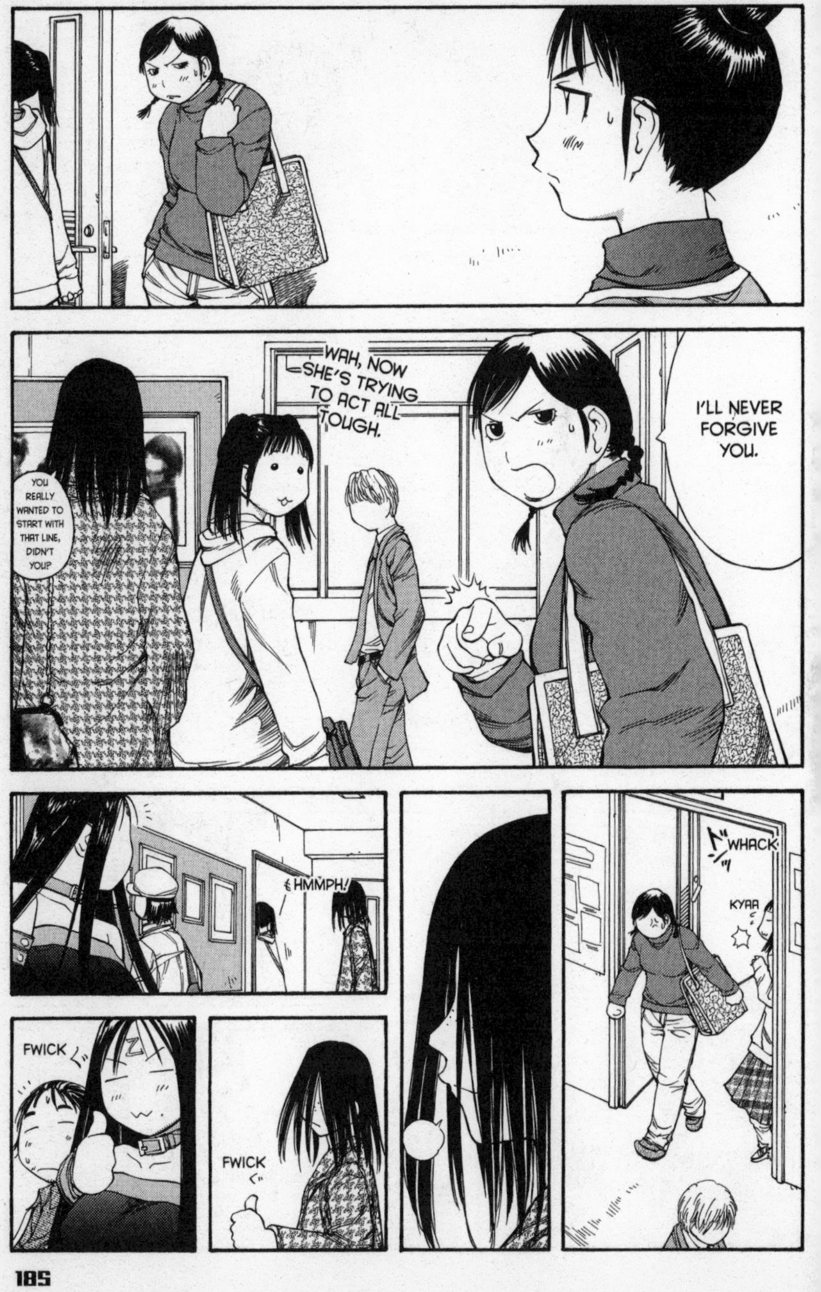
I'LL NEVER FORGIVE YOU.
WAH, NOW SHE'S TRYING TO ACT ALL TOUGH.
YOU REALLY WANTED TO START WITH THAT LINE, DIDN'T YOU?
WHACK
KYAA
HMMPH!
FWICK
FWICK

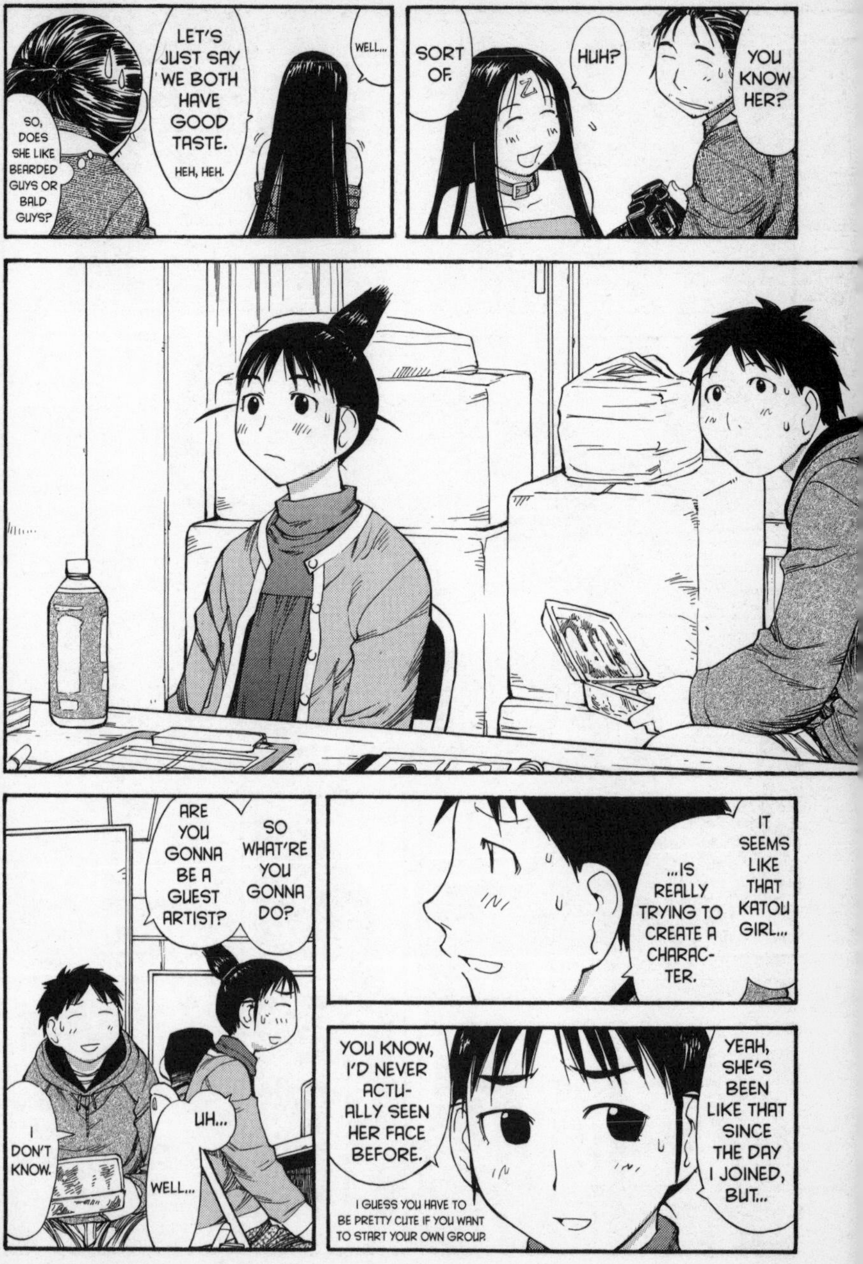
YOU KNOW HER?
HUH?
SORT OF.
WELL...
LET'S JUST SAY WE BOTH HAVE GOOD TASTE.
HEH, HEH.
SO, DOES SHE LIKE BEARDED GUYS OR BALD GUYS?
IT SEEMS LIKE THAT KATOU GIRL...
...IS REALLY TRYING TO CREATE A CHARAC-TER.
YEAH, SHE'S BEEN LIKE THAT SINCE THE DAY I JOINED, BUT...
YOU KNOW, I'D NEVER ACTU-ALLY SEEN HER FACE BEFORE.
I GUESS YOU HAVE TO BE PRETTY CUTE IF YOU WANT TO START YOUR OWN GROUP.
SO WHAT'RE YOU GONNA DO?
ARE YOU GONNA BE A GUEST ARTIST?
UH...
WELL...
I DON'T KNOW.

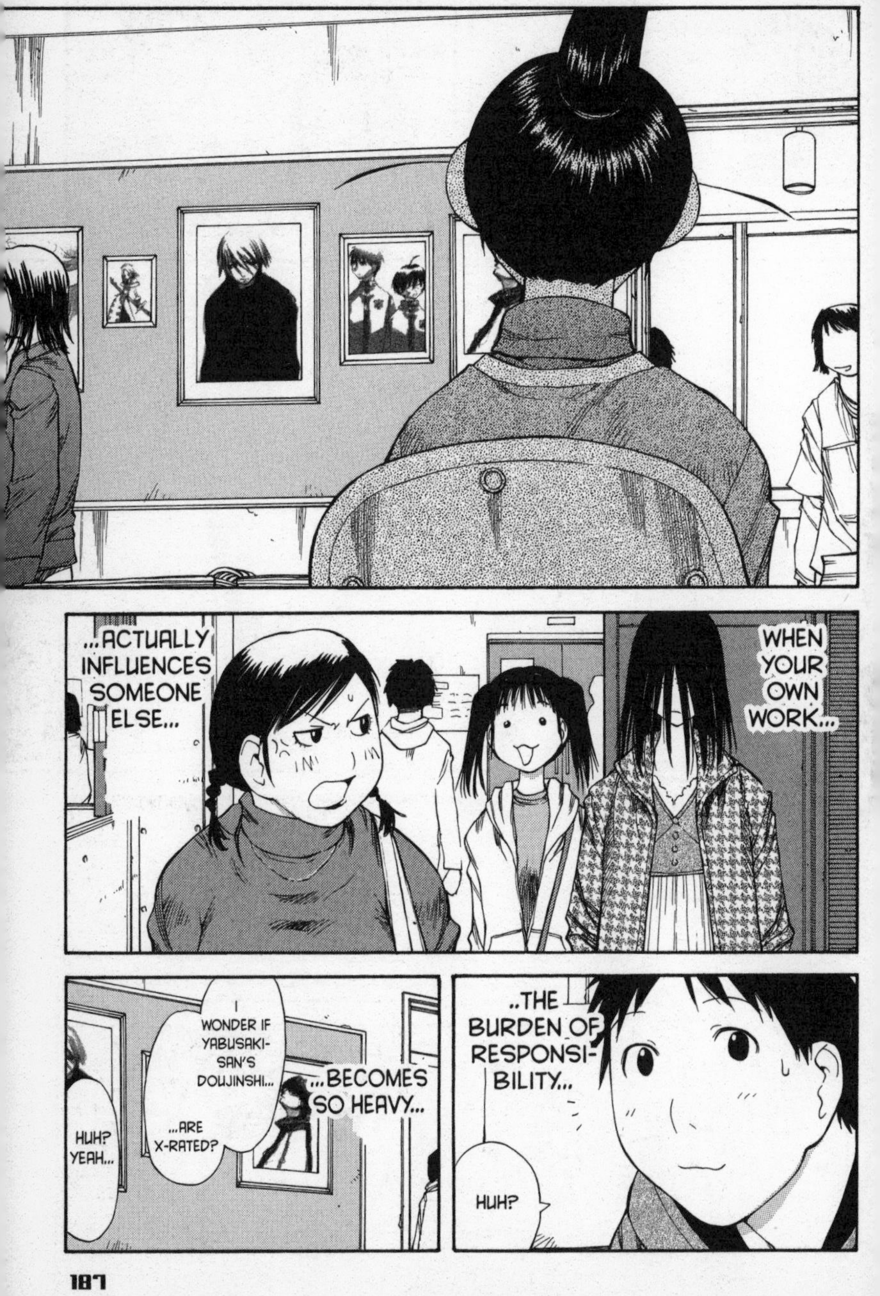
WHEN YOUR OWN WORK...
...ACTUALLY INFLUENCES SOMEONE ELSE...
..THE BURDEN OF RESPONSI-BILITY...
HUH?
...BECOMES SO HEAVY...
I WONDER IF YABUSAKI-SAN'S DOUJINSHI...
...ARE X-RATED?
HUH? YEAH...

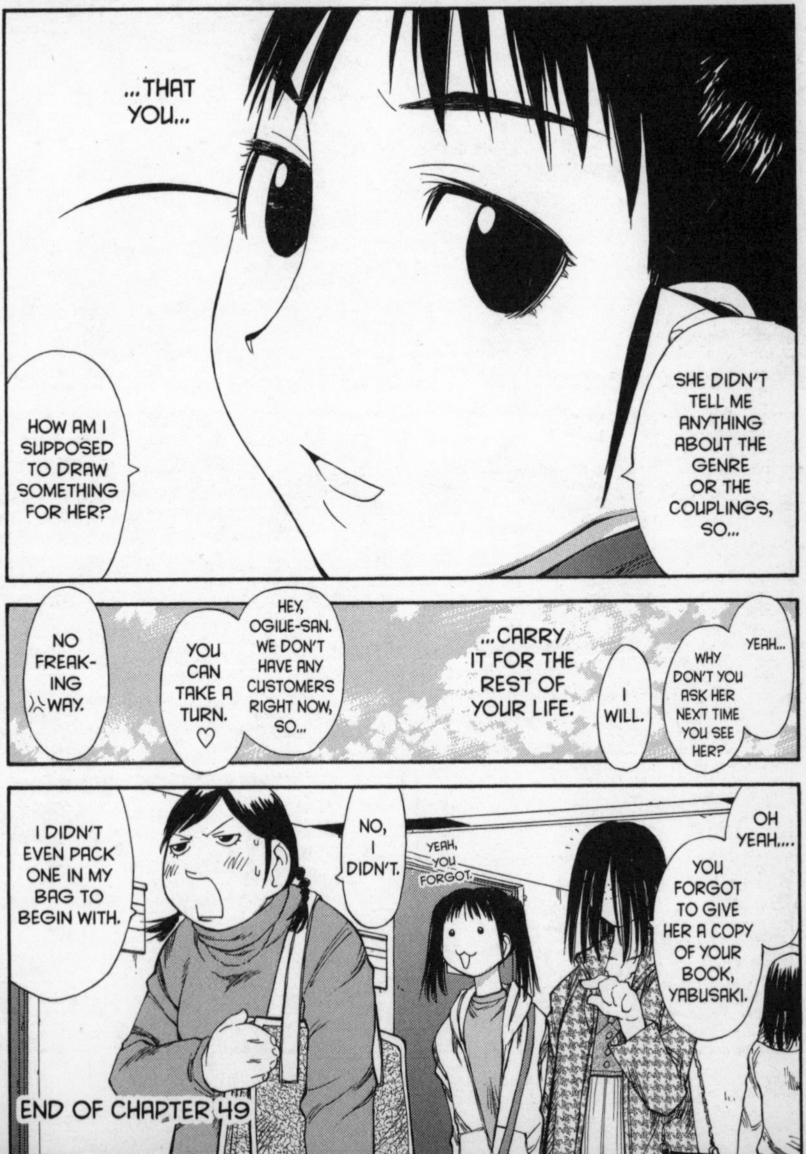
SHE DIDN'T TELL ME ANYTHING ABOUT THE GENRE OR THE COUPLINGS, SO...
HOW AM I SUPPOSED TO DRAW SOMETHING FOR HER?
...THAT YOU...
YEAH...
WHY DON'T YOU ASK HER NEXT TIME YOU SEE HER?
I WILL.
...CARRY IT FOR THE REST OF YOUR LIFE.
HEY, OGIUE-SAN. WE DON'T HAVE ANY CUSTOMERS RIGHT NOW, SO...
YOU CAN TAKE A TURN. ♡
NO FREAK-ING WAY.
OH YEAH....
YOU FORGOT TO GIVE HER A COPY OF YOUR BOOK, YABUSAKI.
YEAH, YOU FORGOT.
NO, I DIDN'T.
I DIDN'T EVEN PACK ONE IN MY BAG TO BEGIN WITH.
END OF CHAPTER 49

BEN- SO HERE WE'VE GOT TWO CHARACTERS WHO HAVE BEEN DEMOTED TO SUPPORTING ROLES, IZUMI AND KOMAKI.

PV- THAT'S A MEAN WAY TO PUT IT, BENJAMIN-KUN.

BEN- I MEAN, KOMAKI HAD HER OWN WEIRD FRINGE FAN CULTURE, BUT IZUMI...

PV- THEY HAD A FIGURE OF HER OUT. IT WAS REALLY WELL DONE.

BEN- DID ANYONE BUY IT?

PV- THAT I DON'T KNOW...SHIVER.

BEN- BUT EVEN THOUGH THEY'RE SUPPORTING CHARACTERS NOW, THEY STILL GET SPECIAL TREATMENT.

PV- YEAH, WELL, ONE OF THEM IS A NINJA AND ONE IS IN SPECIAL FORCES. THEY'RE BOTH SO POWERFUL.

BEN- YUU KUROKI SAID THAT NOW THE SCARF ACTUALLY HAS A MEANING.

PV- IT DIDN'T BEFORE?

BEN- AND NOW IZUMI'S GOGGLES ARE PART OF HER SPECIAL FORCES UNIFORM.

PV- THAT SEEMS A LITTLE FORCED.

BEN- WELL, AGAIN, THESE ROUGH SKETCHES ARE DIFFERENT FROM THE ACTUAL CHARACTER DESIGNS THEY'LL BE USING. IZUMI DOESN'T WORK UNDER THE VICE PRESIDENT. SHE'S NOW PART OF THE SPECIAL FORCES. THAT'S WHY SHE NO LONGER WEARS HER SHRINE UNIFORM.

PV- SO IF IT'S A "FORCE," DOES THAT MEAN THERE ARE OTHER MEMBERS TOO?

BEN- YES, AND THEY'RE ALL GIRLS.

PV- ARE THEY MOE?

BEN- IF A GUY JOINED, IT WOULD HAVE TO BE THE MAIN CHARACTER.

PV- WAH! SOUNDS LIKE A PORN GAME.

BEN- OKAY, ENOUGH OF THAT. ANYWAY, BOTH OF THESE CHARACTERS WILL BE APPEARING MIDWAY THROUGH THE SEASON.

PV- WHAT? ARE YOU SURE YOU SHOULD BE REVEALING THIS NEW KOMAKI NINJA VERSION THEN? ISN'T THAT A SPOILER?

BEN- WELL, SOON IT WON'T MATTER ANYMORE ANYWAY.

PV- ?

BEN- I WONDER HOW THEY'RE GONNA HAVE THESE TWO INTERACT WITH TOKINO. SUPPOSEDLY THEY'RE GONNA BE STRANGERS IN THE BEGINNING.

PV- IT'LL BE COOL IF THEY END UP GETTING ALONG AS WELL AS THEY DID LAST SEASON.

BEN- YEAH.

PV- AH, I JUST REALIZED SOMETHING VERY IMPORTANT.

BEN- WHAT?

PV- WE HAVEN'T EVEN TALKED ABOUT CHIHIRO, AND THIS IS THE LAST PAGE.

BEN- DOESN'T SOUND SO IMPORTANT TO ME.

PV- YEAH WELL, I GUESS HE'S JUST A GUY CHARACTER.

BEN- AND YUU KUROKI HASN'T EVEN DRAWN ANY SKETCHES OF CHIHIRO.

PV- HUH? NOT EVEN ONE?

BEN- NOT EVEN ONE.

PV- EVEN THOUGH HE'S THE MAIN CHARACTER?

BEN- EVEN THOUGH HE'S THE MAIN CHARACTER.

PV- WELL, ANYWAY, I HOPE THE ANIME IS A SUCCES

BEN- YOU CALL THAT A CONCLUSION?

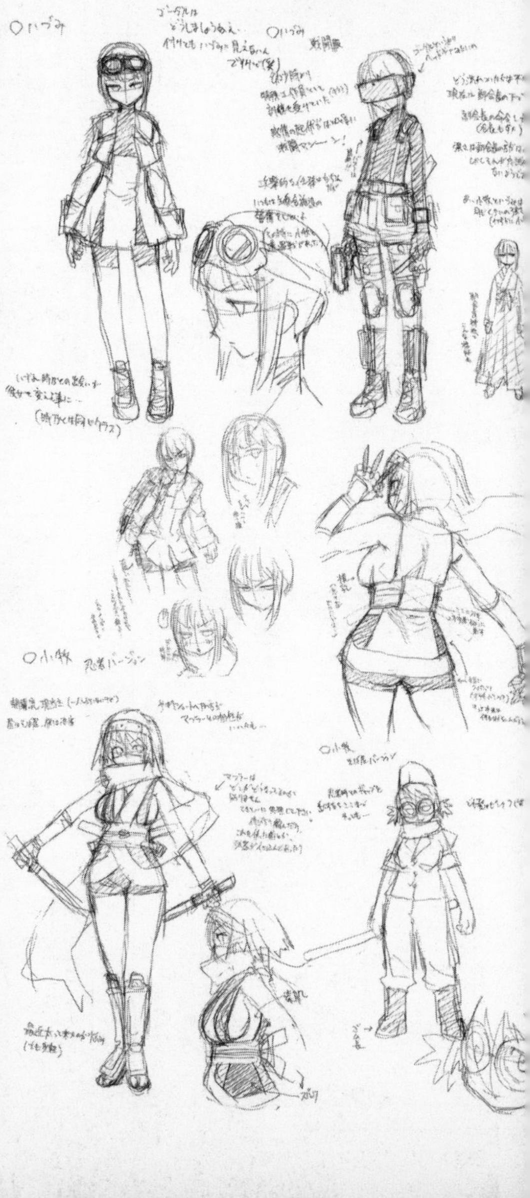

GOOD MORNING

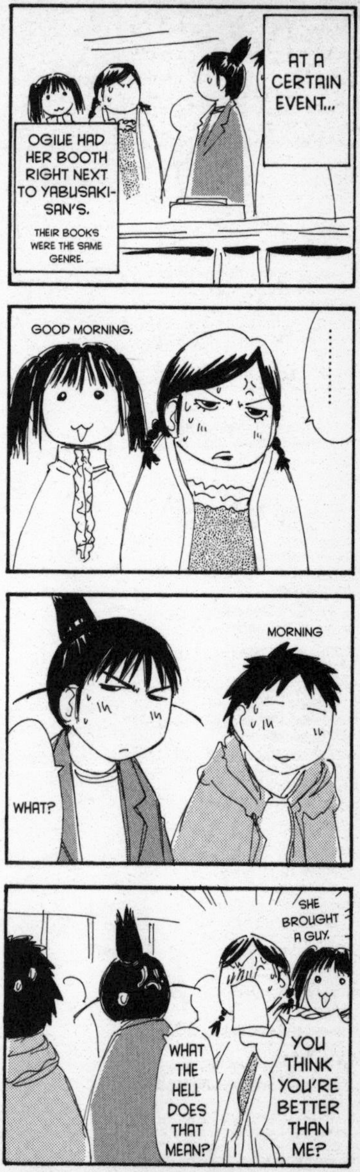
AT A CERTAIN EVENT...
OGIUE HAD HER BOOTH RIGHT NEXT TO YABUSAKI-SAN'S.
THEIR BOOKS WERE THE SAME GENRE.
......
GOOD MORNING.
MORNING
WHAT?
SHE BROUGHT A GUY.
YOU THINK YOU'RE BETTER THAN ME?
WHAT THE HELL DOES THAT MEAN?

THANKS

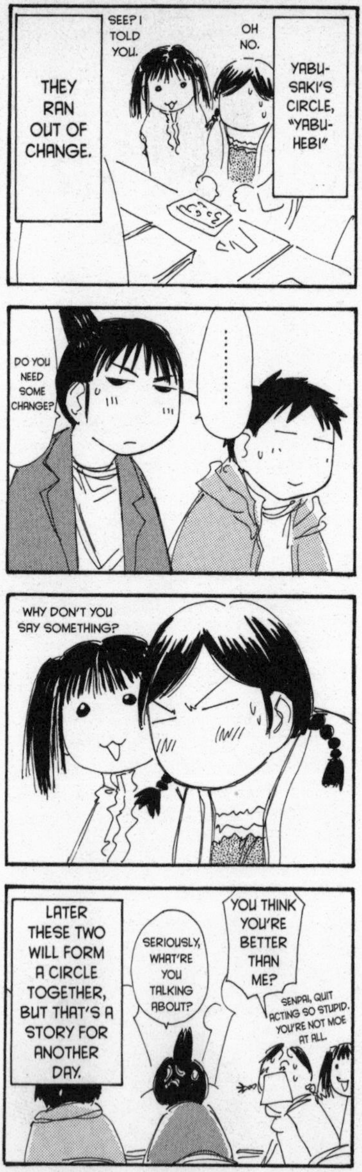
YABU-SAKI'S CIRCLE, "YABU-HEBI"
OH NO.
SEE? I TOLD YOU.
THEY RAN OUT OF CHANGE.
......
DO YOU NEED SOME CHANGE?
WHY DON'T YOU SAY SOMETHING?
YOU THINK YOU'RE BETTER THAN ME?
SENPAI, QUIT ACTING SO STUPID. YOU'RE NOT MOE AT ALL.
SERIOUSLY, WHAT'RE YOU TALKING ABOUT?
LATER THESE TWO WILL FORM A CIRCLE TOGETHER, BUT THAT'S A STORY FOR ANOTHER DAY.

END OF GENSHIKEN BOOK 8

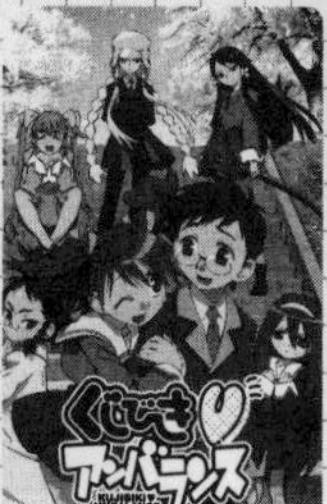

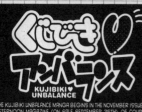

くじびき♥アンバランス
KUJIBIKI♥UNBALANCE

THE INSTITUTION ARTS OF CHARACTERS

THE KUJIBIKI UNBALANCE MANGA BEGINS IN THE NOVEMBER ISSUE OF KODANSHA'S AFTERNOON MAGAZINE (ON SALE SEPTEMBER 25TH). OF COURSE, A TANKOBAN BOOK WILL FOLLOW AND THE ANIME IS ALREADY ON THE AIR. IT BEGAN AS A MANGA WITHIN ANOTHER MANGA (GENSHIKEN), BUT IT'S NOW BEEN SPUN OFF INTO ITS OWN SERIES. NOT ONLY IS THERE AN ANIME AND A MANGA, THERE'S EVEN A VIDEO GAME. HERE WE HAVE SOME CHARACTER DESCRIPTIONS CREATED BY THE AUTHOR. EVEN IF YOU DON'T FEEL LIKE IT, PLEASE TAKE THE TIME TO LEARN ALL ABOUT KUJIBIKI UNBALANCE

ANIME DATA
STAFF
CREATOR....................KIO SHIMOKU
DIRECTOR....................TSUTOMU MIZUSHIMA
PRODUCER....................MICHIKO YOKOTE
ORIGINAL CHARACTER DESIGN....................KIO SHIMOKU, KENGO YAMOKU
CHARACTER DESIGNER....................YOSHIAKI YANAGIDA
ANIMATION DIRECTOR....................DO AJIA

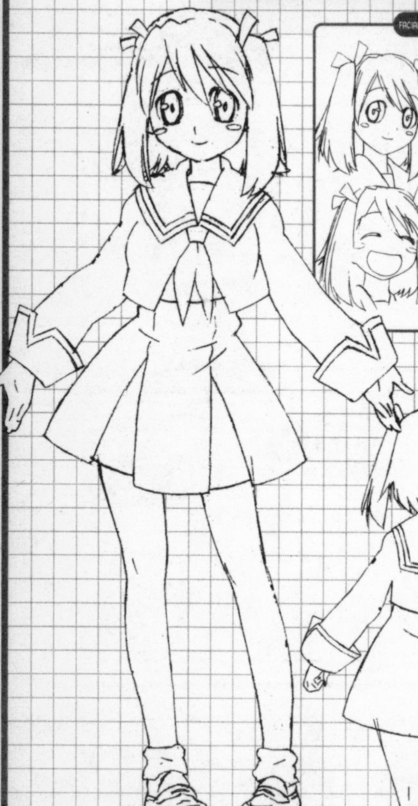

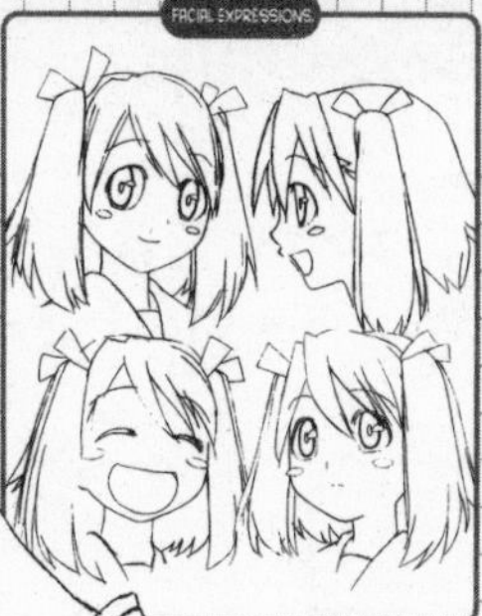
FACIAL EXPRESSIONS.

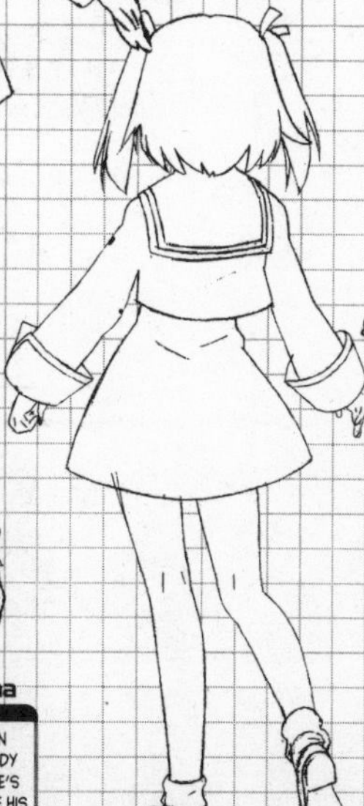

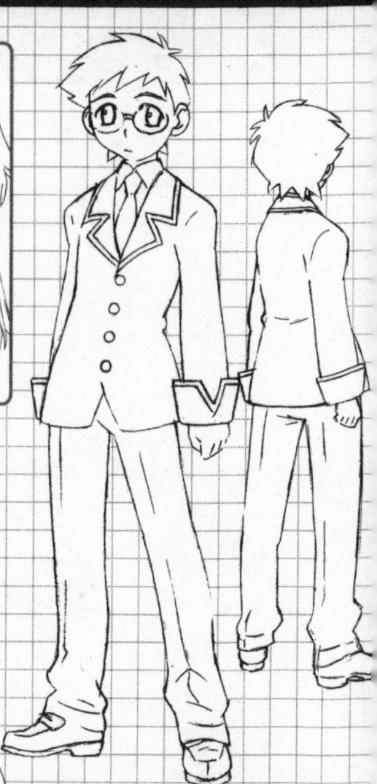

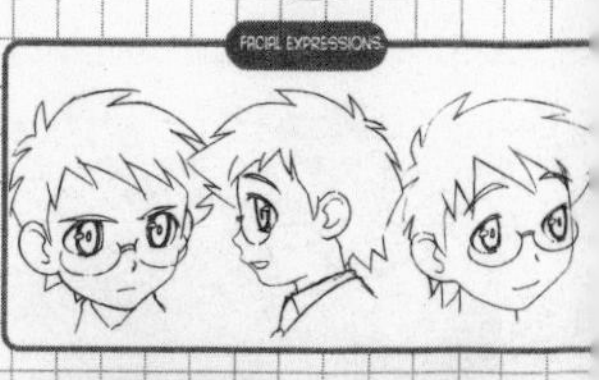
FACIAL EXPRESSIONS.

秋山 時乃 Tokino Akiyama

TOKINO, THE HEROINE, IS A FRESHMAN AT RITSUBASHI-IN HIGH. SHE WAS CHOSEN TO BE THE FUTURE STUDENT BODY VICE PRESIDENT AFTER WINNING A KUJIBIKI LOTTERY. SHE'S A CHILDHOOD FRIEND OF CHIHIRO'S. SHE'S ALMOST LIKE HIS LITTLE PUPPY. APPARENTLY SHE'S NOT PARTICULARLY FOND OF MUSHROOMS. (CV AI NONAKA)

榎本 千尋 Chihiro Enomoto

HIS NAME SOUNDS LIKE A GIRL'S BUT HE'S DEFINITELY A GUY. IN FACT, HE'S THE MAIN CHARACTER. HE'S A FRESHMAN AT RITSUBASHI-IN HIGH AND A CANDIDATE FOR PRESIDENT. ALONG WITH RENKO, TOKINO, AND KOYUKI, HE MUST GO THROUGH GREAT HARDSHIP IN ORDER TO BECOME THE NEXT LEADER OF THE STUDENT BODY. (CV FUJIKO TAKIMOTO)

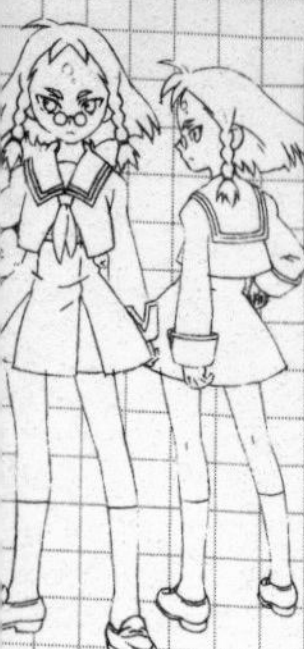

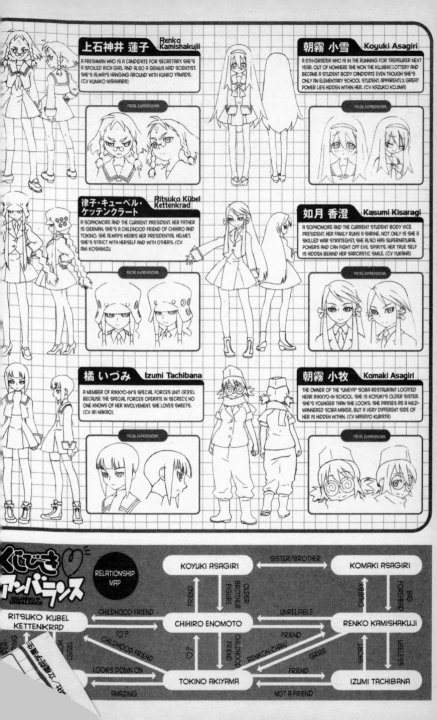

上石神井 蓮子 Renko Kamishakujii

A FRESHMAN WHO IS A CANDIDATE FOR SECRETARY. SHE'S A SPOILED RICH GIRL AND ALSO A GENIUS MAD SCIENTIST. SHE'S ALWAYS HANGING AROUND WITH KUNKO YAMADA. (CV KUMIKO NISHIHARA)

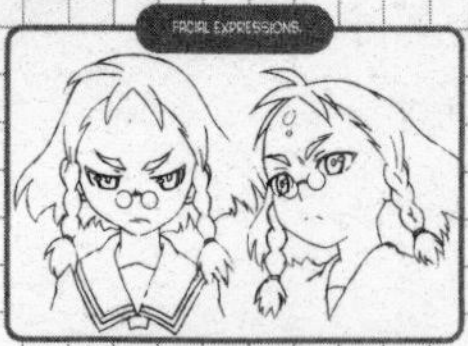
FACIAL EXPRESSIONS.

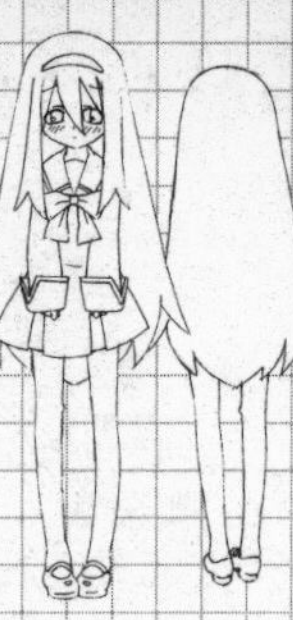

朝霧 小雪 Koyuki Asagiri

A 5TH-GRADER WHO IS IN THE RUNNING FOR TREASURER NEXT YEAR. OUT OF NOWHERE SHE WON THE KUJIBIKI LOTTERY AND BECAME A STUDENT BODY CANDIDATE EVEN THOUGH SHE'S ONLY AN ELEMENTARY SCHOOL STUDENT. APPARENTLY, GREAT POWER LIES HIDDEN WITHIN HER. (CV KAZUKO KOJIMA)

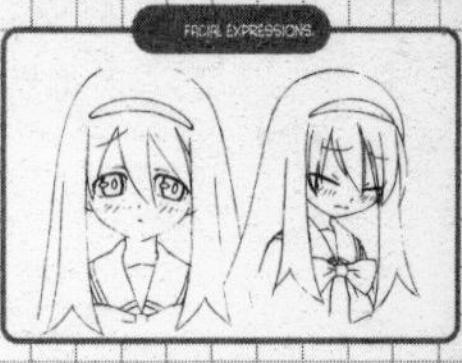
FACIAL EXPRESSIONS.

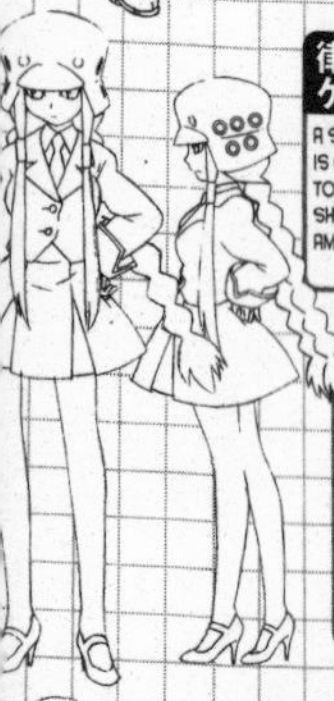

律子・キューベル・ケッテンクラート Ritsuko Kübel Kettenkrad

A SOPHOMORE AND THE CURRENT PRESIDENT. HER FATHER IS GERMAN. SHE'S A CHILDHOOD FRIEND OF CHIHIRO AND TOKINO. SHE ALWAYS WEARS HER PRESIDENTIAL HELMET. SHE'S STRICT WITH HERSELF AND WITH OTHERS. (CV AMI KOSHIMIZU

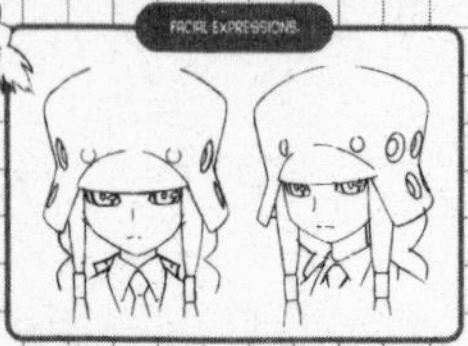
FACIAL EXPRESSIONS.

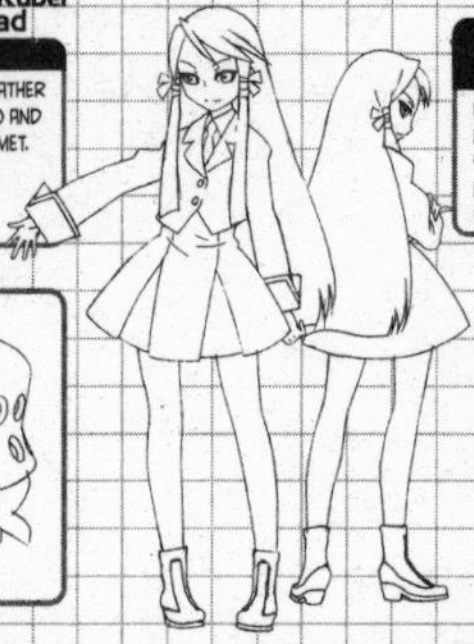

如月 香澄 Kasumi Kisaragi

A SOPHOMORE AND THE CURRENT STUDENT BODY VICE PRESIDENT. HER FAMILY RUNS A SHRINE. NOT ONLY IS SHE A SKILLED WAR STRATEGIST, SHE ALSO HAS SUPERNATURAL POWERS AND CAN FIGHT OFF EVIL SPIRITS. HER TRUE SELF IS HIDDEN BEHIND HER SARCASTIC SMILE. (CV YUKANA)

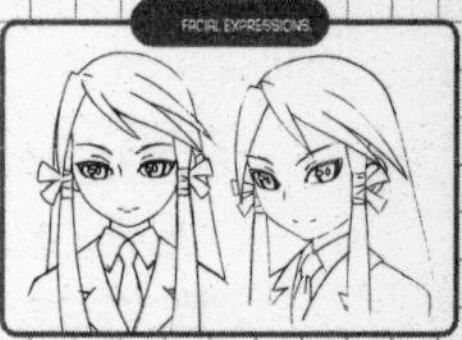
FACIAL EXPRESSIONS.

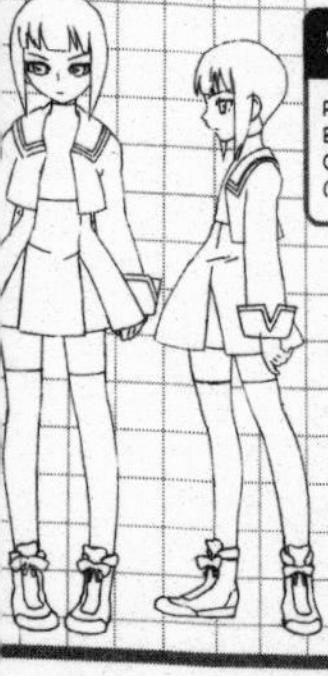

橘 いづみ Izumi Tachibana

A MEMBER OF RIKKYO-IN'S SPECIAL FORCES UNIT (R3S). BECAUSE THE SPECIAL FORCES OPERATE IN SECRECY, NO ONE KNOWS OF HER INVOLVEMENT. SHE LOVES SWEETS. (CV IRI NAKAO)

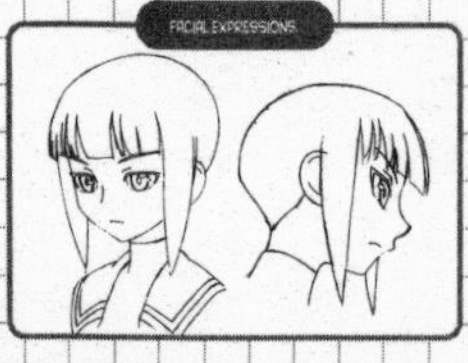
FACIAL EXPRESSIONS.

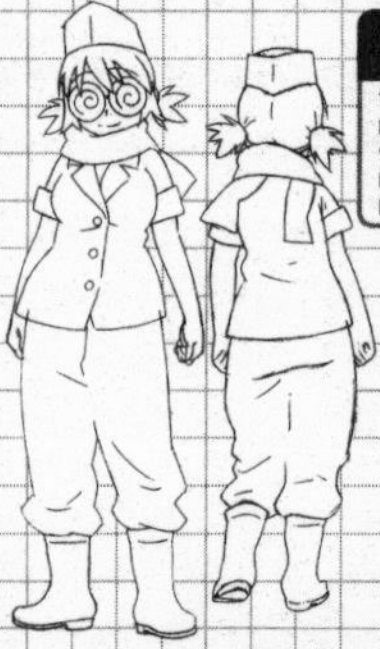

朝霧 小牧 Komaki Asagiri

THE OWNER OF THE "UMEYA" SOBA RESTAURANT LOCATED NEAR RIKKYO-IN SCHOOL. SHE IS KOYUKI'S OLDER SISTER. SHE'S YOUNGER THAN SHE LOOKS. SHE PASSES AS A MILD-MANNERED SOBA MAKER, BUT A VERY DIFFERENT SIDE OF HER IS HIDDEN WITHIN. (CV MASAYO KURATA)

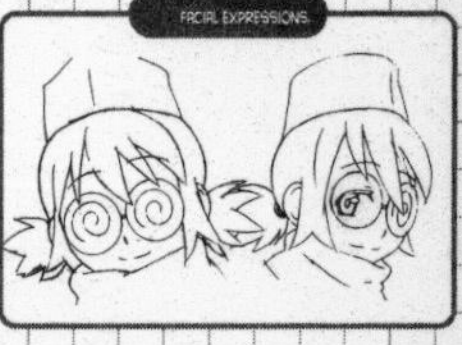
FACIAL EXPRESSIONS.

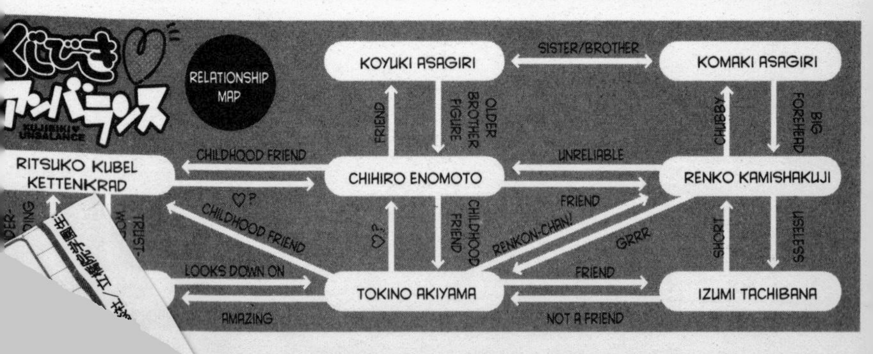
くじびきアンバランス
KUJIBIKI UNBALANCE
RELATIONSHIP MAP
KOYUKI ASAGIRI
SISTER/BROTHER
KOMAKI ASAGIRI
FRIEND
OLDER BROTHER FIGURE
CHUBBY
BIG FOREHEAD
RITSUKO KUBEL KETTENKRAD
CHILDHOOD FRIEND
CHIHIRO ENOMOTO
UNRELIABLE
RENKO KAMISHAKUJI
♡?
CHILDHOOD FRIEND
CHILDHOOD FRIEND
FRIEND
RENKON-CHAN!
GRRR
SHORT
USELESS
LOOKS DOWN ON
TOKINO AKIYAMA
FRIEND
IZUMI TACHIBANA
AMAZING
NOT A FRIEND

ABOUT THE AUTHOR

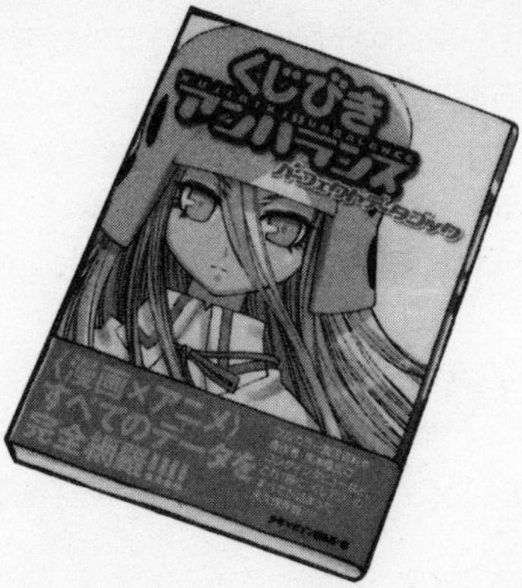
くじびき

KIO SHIMOKU WAS BORN IN 1974.
IN 1994 HIS DEBUT WORK, *TEN NO RYOIKI*, RECEIVED SECOND PLACE IN THE "AFTERNOON SHIKI PRIZE" CONTEST. OTHER PAST WORKS INCLUDE *KAGERIYBIKII*, *YONENSEI*, AND *GONENSEI*, ALL OF WHICH APPEARED IN *AFTERNOON* MAGAZINE.
HE HAS BEEN WORKING ON GENSHIKEN SINCE 2002.

Translation Notes

Japanese is a tricky language for most Westerners, and translation is often more art than science. For your edification and reading pleasure, here are notes on some of the places where we could have gone in a different direction in our translation of the work, or where a Japanese cultural reference is used.

Toppatsubon, *page 7*

This girl literally says, "We could just do a *toppatsubon.*" A *toppatsubon* is a simple type of doujinshi that's thrown together on short notice.

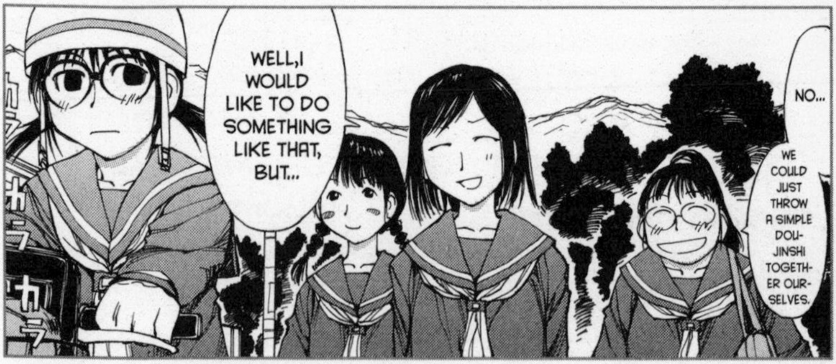
NO...
WE COULD JUST THROW A SIMPLE DOUJINSHI TOGETHER OURSELVES.
WELL, I WOULD LIKE TO DO SOMETHING LIKE THAT, BUT...

Illustration book, page 22

Ogiue is actually using the term *irasuto-bon,* which we translated as "illustration book."

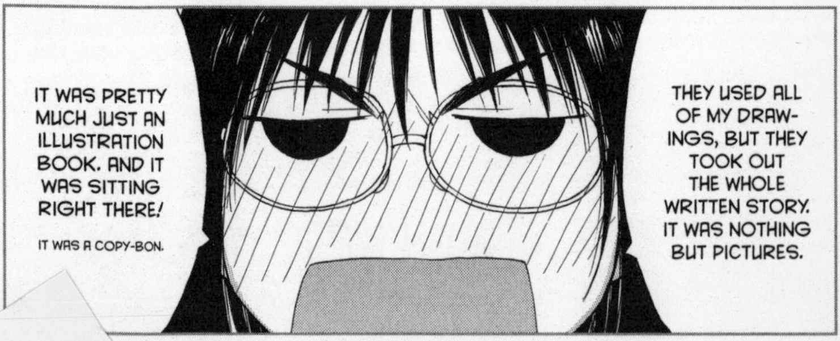
THEY USED ALL OF MY DRAWINGS, BUT THEY TOOK OUT THE WHOLE WRITTEN STORY. IT WAS NOTHING BUT PICTURES.
IT WAS PRETTY MUCH JUST AN ILLUSTRATION BOOK. AND IT WAS SITTING RIGHT THERE!
IT WAS A COPY-BON.

Copy-bon, *page 22*

A *copy-bon* is a doujinshi that is created by a copy-duplication process, as opposed to those that are professionally printed.

Homoue, page 23

"Homoue" is a play on Chika's last name, Ogiue. Apparently she earned it by creating hard-core homo-erotic illustrations.

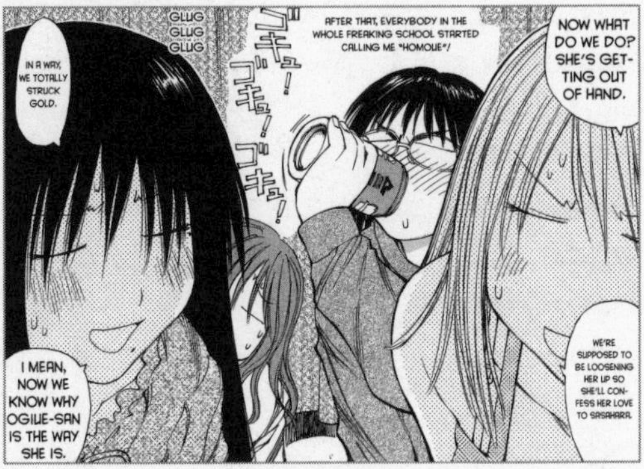
NOW WHAT DO WE DO? SHE'S GETTING OUT OF HAND.
AFTER THAT, EVERYBODY IN THE WHOLE FREAKING SCHOOL STARTED CALLING ME "HOMOUE"!
GLUG GLUG GLUG
IN A WAY, WE TOTALLY STRUCK GOLD.
WE'RE SUPPOSED TO BE LOOSENING HER UP SO SHE'LL CONFESS HER LOVE TO SASAHARA.
I MEAN, NOW WE KNOW WHY OGIUE-SAN IS THE WAY SHE IS.

Sou-uke, *page 29*

Sou-uke is a yaoi term. The *uke* is the "bottom" of a homosexual *yaoi* couple. *Sou-uke* is an emphatic term and means something like "total bottom."

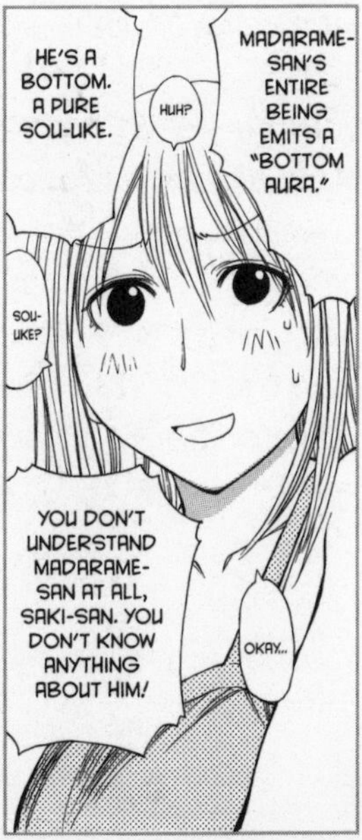
MADARAME-SAN'S ENTIRE BEING EMITS A "BOTTOM AURA."
HUH?
HE'S A BOTTOM. A PURE SOU-UKE.
SOU-UKE?
OKAY...
YOU DON'T UNDERSTAND MADARAME-SAN AT ALL, SAKI-SAN. YOU DON'T KNOW ANYTHING ABOUT HIM!

Sneezing, page 30

In Japan they say that when someone talks about you behind your back, it causes you to sneeze.

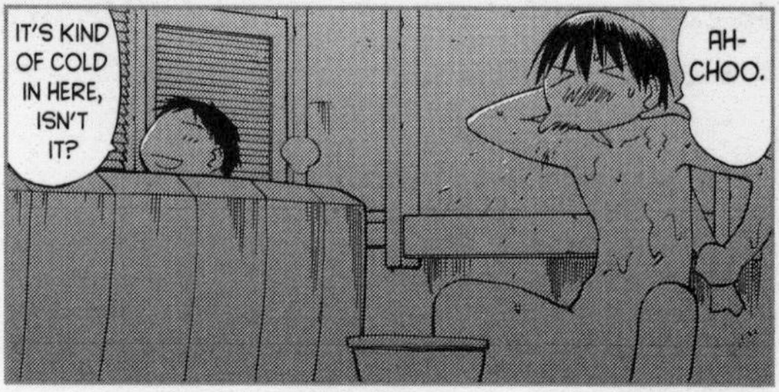
AH-CHOO.
IT'S KIND OF COLD IN HERE, ISN'T IT?

Weak top, page 30

Ogiue uses the term *Hetare-seme*, which refers to a "top" who is not particularly aggressive or dominant.

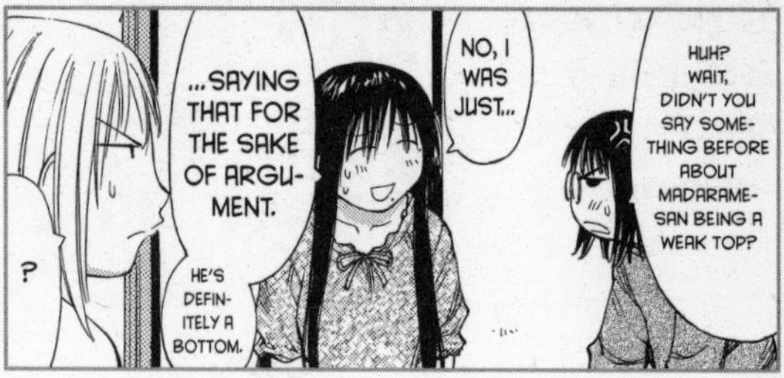
HUH? WAIT, DIDN'T YOU SAY SOME-THING BEFORE ABOUT MADARAME-SAN BEING A WEAK TOP?
NO, I WAS JUST...
...SAYING THAT FOR THE SAKE OF ARGU-MENT.
HE'S DEFIN-ITELY A BOTTOM.
?

The guys at work, page 83

Madarame is picking out *omiyage*, or souvenirs, for his co-workers. In Japan *omiyage* is a social requirement. Anyone going on a trip is expected to bring *omiyage* back for their friends and co-workers. Snacks and candies are a popular choice.

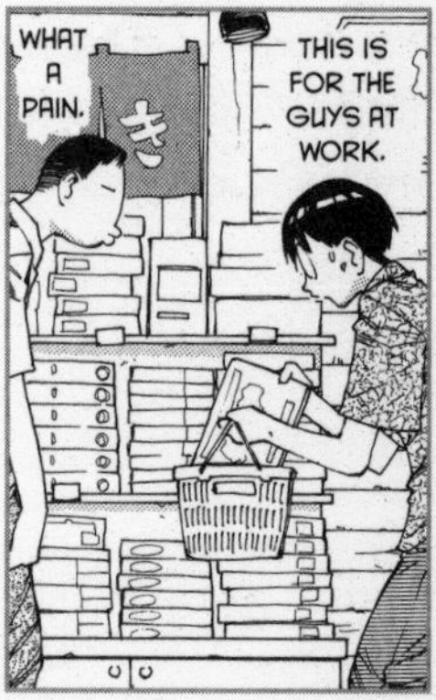
THIS IS FOR THE GUYS AT WORK.
WHAT A PAIN.

Sergeant Kuryuryu, page 87

Probably a reference to the character First Sergeant Kururu from the anime Keroro Gunso.

Iyabon rule, page 123

The "*iyabon* rule" refers to a common manga/anime cliche. When a hero character is in a desperate fight against his foe and yells *Iya!*, meaning "no," the foe will finally fall with a *bon*, or thud.

Tohoku hick, page 175

Tohoku is the region Ogiue is from.

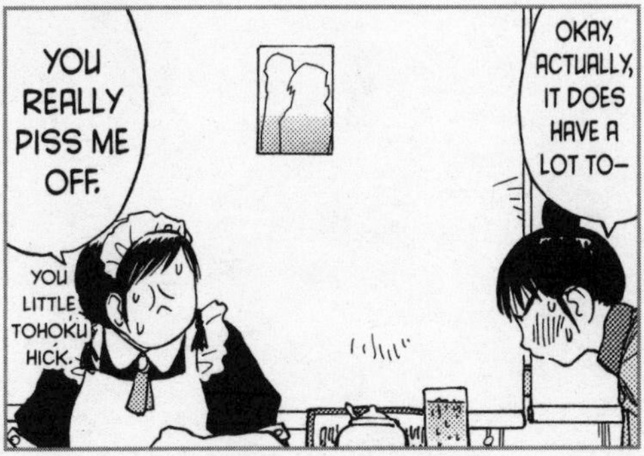
OKAY, ACTUALLY, IT DOES HAVE A LOT TO–
YOU REALLY PISS ME OFF.
YOU LITTLE TOHOKU HICK.

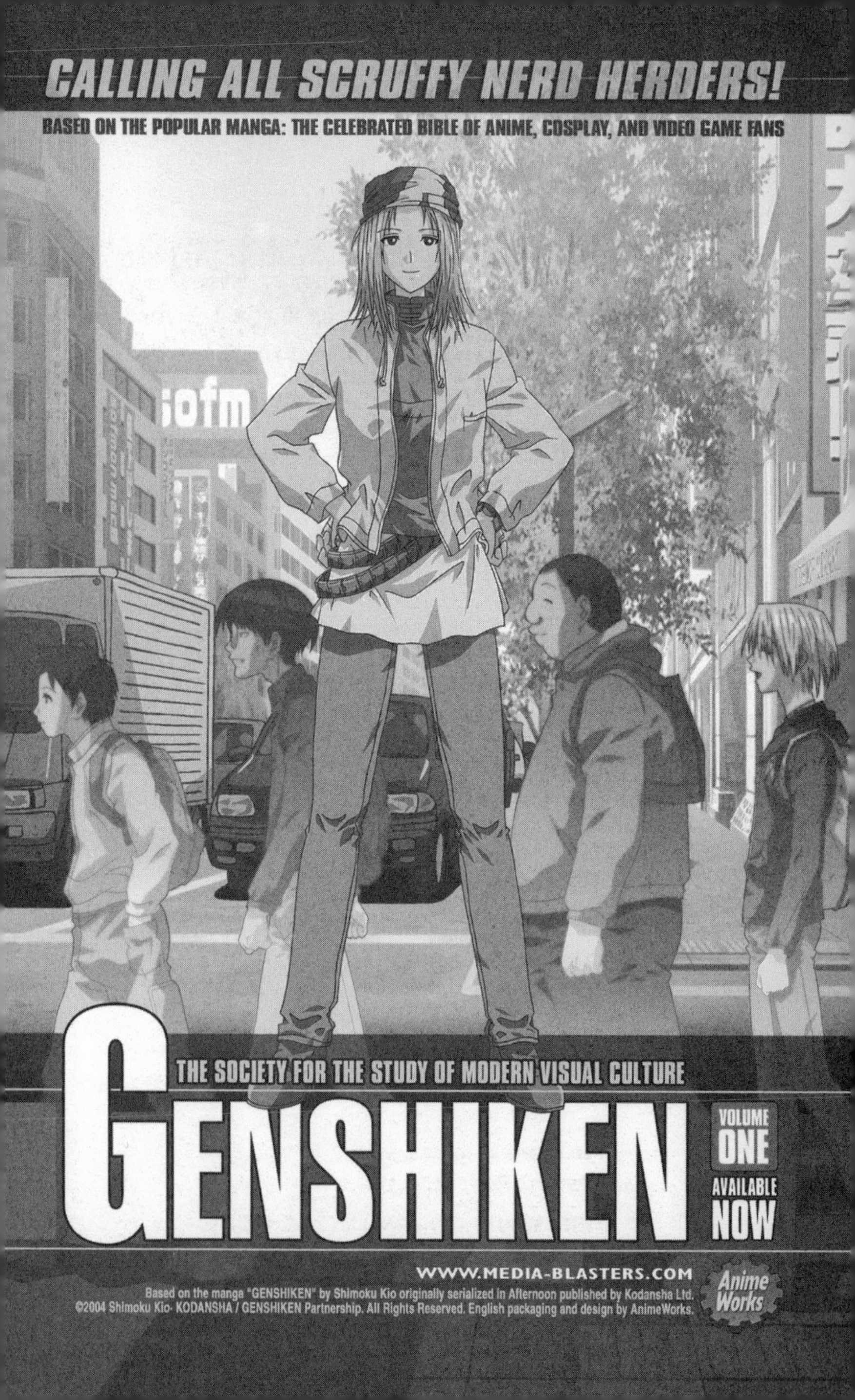
CALLING ALL SCRUFFY NERD HERDERS!
BASED ON THE POPULAR MANGA: THE CELEBRATED BIBLE OF ANIME, COSPLAY, AND VIDEO GAME FANS
iofm
THE SOCIETY FOR THE STUDY OF MODERN VISUAL CULTURE
GENSHIKEN
VOLUME ONE
AVAILABLE NOW
WWW.MEDIA-BLASTERS.COM
Based on the manga "GENSHIKEN" by Shimoku Kio originally serialized in Afternoon published by Kodansha Ltd.
©2004 Shimoku Kio· KODANSHA / GENSHIKEN Partnership. All Rights Reserved. English packaging and design by AnimeWorks.
Anime Works

xxxHOLiC™

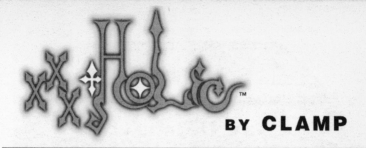

BY CLAMP

Watanuki Kimihiro is haunted by visions. When he finds himself irresistibly drawn into a shop owned by Yûko, a mysterious witch, he is offered the chance to rid himself of the spirits that plague him. He accepts, but soon realizes that he's just been tricked into working for the shop to pay off the cost of Yûko's services! But this isn't any ordinary kind of shop . . . In this shop, Yûko grants wishes to those in need. But they must have the strength of will not only to truly understand their need, but to give up something incredibly precious in return.

CLAMP
CREATORS OF CHOBITS!
1
xxxHOLiC

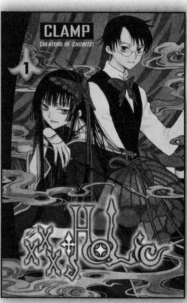

Ages: 13+

Special extras in each volume! Read them all!

DEL REY

VISIT WWW.DELREYMANGA.COM TO:

- View release date calendars for upcoming volumes
- Sign up for Del Rey's free manga e-newsletter
- Find out the latest about new Del Rey Manga series

BY OH!GREAT

Itsuki Minami needs no introduction—everybody's heard of the "Babyface" of the Eastside. He's the strongest kid at Higashi Junior High School, easy on the eyes but dangerously tough when he needs to be. Plus, Itsuki lives with the mysterious and sexy Noyamano sisters. Life's never dull, but it becomes downright dangerous when Itsuki leads his school to victory over vindictive Westside punks with gangster connections. Now he stands to lose his school, his friends, and everything he cares about. But in his darkest hour, the Noyamano girls give him an amazing gift, one that just might help him save his school: a pair of Air Trecks. These high-tech skates are more than just supercool. They'll enable Itsuki to execute the wildest, most aggressive moves ever seen—and introduce him to a thrilling and terrifying new world.

Ages: 16 +

Special extras in each volume! Read them all!

VISIT WWW.DELREYMANGA.COM TO:
- Read sample pages
- View release date calendars for upcoming volumes
- Sign up for Del Rey's free manga e-newsletter
- Find out the latest about new Del Rey Manga series

School Rumble

BY JIN KOBAYASHI

SUBTLETY IS FOR WIMPS!

She . . . is a second-year high school student with a single all-consuming question: Will the boy she likes ever really notice her?

He . . . is the school's most notorious juvenile delinquent, and he's suddenly come to a shocking realization: He's got a huge crush, and now he must tell her how he feels.

Life-changing obsessions, colossal foul-ups, grand schemes, deep-seated anxieties, and raging hormones—School Rumble portrays high school as it really is: over-the-top comedy!

Ages: 16+

Special extras in each volume! Read them all!

VISIT WWW.DELREYMANGA.COM TO:
- Read sample pages
- View release date calendars for upcoming volumes
- Sign up for Del Rey's free manga e-newsletter
- Find out the latest about new Del Rey Manga series